W9-BBT-593

VERA S. KOSTROVITSKAYA

100 Lessons in Classical Ballet

TRANSLATED BY OLEG BRIANSKY

Limelight Editions New York

Eighth Limelight Edition   June 2004

Translation Copyright © 1981 Oleg Briansky
Published by arrangement with Doubleday & Company, Inc.

All rights reserved under international and Pan-American
Copyright Conventions. Published in the United States by
Proscenium Publishers Inc., New York

Cover Photograph by Alex Gotfryd
Photos on pages 13–19 by Beverley Gallegos

Library of Congress Cataloging-in-Publication Data

Kostrovitskaia, V. S. (Vera Sergeevna)
100 lessons in classical ballet.

1. Ballet dancing—Study and teaching.   I. Title.
II. Title: One hundred lessons in classical ballet.
GV1788.5.K668   1987   792.8'2'07   86-27743
ISBN 0-87910-068-0

Contents

FOURTH YEAR

FIFTH YEAR

SIXTH YEAR

SEVENTH YEAR

EIGHTH YEAR

Preface

THE PURPOSE of this book is to present a working textbook for teachers in choreographic institutes, ballet schools, colleges, and universities. It is dedicated to the systematic development of a teaching technique for the ballet lesson.

The lessons offered as examples are composed in accordance with the eight-year study program approved by the U.S.S.R. Ministry of Culture for ballet students. The book does not analyze the execution of each step inasmuch as this has already been covered in A. Vaganova's *Basic Principles of the Classical Ballet* and in *The School of Classical Ballet,* by the teachers of the Leningrad Choreographic Institute, V. Kostrovitskaya and A. Pisarev and other contributing faculty members of the school.

It is in the elementary and intermediate classes that the teacher lays the foundation of ballet principles through the assimilation of a large number of steps. Accordingly, the largest number of lessons in this book is directed toward these levels.

The book contains nine sample lessons* for the first year, eight lessons for the second through the fifth years and four lessons for the sixth through the eighth years. In addition, the book contains forty-seven exercises on pointes. Naturally, these examples are not intended to do away with all the other possibilities of conducting a ballet lesson, but they can serve as models for teachers in their independent composition of lessons. All basic steps are covered in the two semesters of the first year and in the first semester of the second year. These steps are broken down according to the musical beats. Any change in the musical tempo indicates the degree of the technical accomplishment of the movement.

---

* TRANSLATOR'S NOTE: All the classes in this book will be referred to as lessons and the eight classes according to the U.S.S.R. Ministry of Culture's eight-year full program of study will be indicated as years.

7

During the second semester of the second year, separate steps are put together, first in simple combinations, then in complicated ones. In the first semester of the following years, the combinations of the previous year's study become more complex and new steps are mastered separately. These new steps are included in the combinations during the second semester.

In the intermediate years, fourth and fifth, and in the advanced years, sixth, seventh, and eighth, the analysis of steps in musical terms is rare; as a rule, we teachers limit ourselves only to the indication of the number of musical bars (especially in adagio and allegro).

In these lessons, the successive study of steps is taken into account. It is indicated also in class that a certain number of practiced steps and combinations must be repeated. The reader should keep in mind that all the exercises are done on the right and the left leg alternately, starting and ending in fifth position. If the preparatory position is not in fifth, this will be specially indicated. The starting position for battements frappés, battements doubles frappés, ronds de jambe en l'air, and petits battements sur le cou-de-pied is indicated in the first lessons, but not in the later ones. Each class ends with the port de bras and bending of the body, indicated in the footnote of the first lesson of each year. All steps except those on pointes can be executed by men and women alike. When certain steps or combinations are carried out by women only, it is particularly stated in the footnote, indicating the required step or combination recommended by us. In the book, exercises on pointes are given at the end of each lesson. However, the lessons should be constructed in such a way that the exercises on pointes should not be given on the same day as the jumps.

One of the fundamental requirements of classical ballet method is a sharply defined musical education. At the Leningrad Choreographic Institute, the musical accompaniment of a class is based on improvisation. The exercises at the barre and in the center are almost entirely accompanied by musical improvisation. In adagio, allegro, and steps on pointes, improvisation alternates with written music.

An improvisation can be inspired by a personal musical thought, or the pianist may subjectively interpret any written musical composition. The music must strictly adhere to the dancing pattern proposed by the teacher and contain a definite rhythm corresponding to the character of the steps.

If, for example, battements fondus are executed in one combination with battements frappés, then the rhythm of the musical phrase must reflect different characters emphasizing a flowing melodiousness in the execution of battements fondus, and then changing to sharp staccato during the battements frappés. By providing a definite tempo, meter, and rhythm, the music exposes and accentuates the characteristics of the steps and thereby helps in their execution. Simultaneously it trains the students to discern the correspondence between the elements of the music and the steps by bringing them into relief. The observance of the rhythm together with the creative fantasy of the pianist (good, varied improvisation) enriches the quality of the class. A definite meter, tempo, and rhythmical pattern expose and accentuate the precision of the steps; the melody, presented in varied harmonies, creates an emotional coloring of the movement, subordinating the step to the music and providing a musical ambience for the lesson. We disapprove of the notated music conventionally used in the exercises at the barre and in the center, because the creative coordination of steps with a rigidly followed accompaniment either inhibits the teacher in the construction of the combination or may conflict with the musical composition. Notated music is only helpful in providing tempo and meter. In allegro and pointes exercises notated music—fragments of musical compositions and ballet music—must be selected by the pianist according to the character of the steps and combination.

If in ballet performance the ballet master submits completely to the music, translating its form and content into choreographic imagery, then just the reverse takes place in the classroom—here the music must submit in its form to the movement. All the combinations of a lesson must be constructed with due regard to the musical phrases (regular beats), starting and ending in conjunction with them. The musical phrases can be short or long: eight, sixteen, thirty-two measures, etc. It is also possible to construct combinations and adagio exercises on one and a half musical phrases such as: twelve, twenty-four measures, etc. The pianist participates creatively in the course of the daily lesson and in the musical education of the students. He skillfully selects ballet music in those instances when the teacher's exercise requires notated music.

A diagram of a ballet studio is shown, with lines that determine the placement of the poses and the direction of the steps, whether in a straight line or a diagonal, or in a circle during the exercises in the center. The aim of the book is to assist the inquiring teacher in the independent composition of classes and in the planning of each year's course of study.

We hope also that the experience of the teachers of the Leningrad Choreographic Institute, which provides the basis for this textbook, will help in the preparation of the task at hand.

Vera Kostrovitskaya with Oleg Briansky in Leningrad.

Introduction

by OLEG BRIANSKY

I WAS fifteen when I choreographed my first full evening of ballet. After its performance at the Palais des Beaux-Arts in Brussels, a Russian delegate of the Belgian-Soviet mission approached me and offered me the possibility of a ballet career in the Soviet Union. I would have had to leave Belgium for the intensive course of study that is the Russian system of ballet education, and I ultimately decided that the offer carried with it too many unacceptable conditions. And yet for the boy that I was then, son of Russian émigrés who had left their homeland as part of the same wave that brought Diaghilev, Nijinsky, Fokine, and Anna Pavlova to the West, Russia loomed for me, inevitably, as a sort of fountainhead of the dancer's art. As it was, most of my ballet training in the

West was with such Russian teachers as Loubov Egorova, Victor Gsovsky, Olga Preobrajenskaya, and Igor Schwezoff and with Soviet teachers Vladimir Bourmeister, Leonide Gontcharov, Valentina Pereyslavec, and Olga Lepeshinskaya. After establishing my career as a principal dancer with several companies in the West, I was again offered an opportunity to dance in the Soviet Union, this time, in the form of an invitation to partner Olga Lepeshinskaya of the Bolshoi Ballet. Unfortunately, I was prevented by an injury which in fact forced my early retirement from the stage.

As a Russian, I never lost the desire to see for myself the country my parents left so long ago and which they never saw again. As a dancer, and even more as a teacher of dance, my curiosity grew to see the Soviet ballet at home, and especially to see more of how the world-famous Soviet ballet technique is taught.

Finally, as one so often must, I made my own opportunity. I organized a group of ballet students and balletomanes as eager as I to see the Soviet Union, and arranged a tour through Intourist. The trip was deeply satisfying to me and, apparently to my companions. It became the first of many visits on which I have escorted groups to Leningrad, Moscow and other cities, and arranged for them to meet directors, choreographers, and teachers at the famous schools of ballet in the Soviet Union, and to observe classes and rehearsals there.

In 1976, our tour bore unexpected fruit. One of our group members, Earle Mack, decided to produce and finance a documentary film that would preserve for all time the inner workings of the Vaganova Choreographic Institute in Leningrad, once the Imperial Ballet School of Russia and certainly one of the greatest sources of genius in ballet in the world. The time I spent at the school acting as artistic director of this film, *The Children of Theatre Street,* gave me an even deeper understanding and respect for the unique fabric of the school, specifically the relentless cooperative striving of the students and teachers for achievement and artistry on the highest level. In fact the sensitive but total dedication of those who give the training and those who receive it, became one of the most important subjects of our film.

Which brings us to the project at hand. One day, Galina Stupnikova, a teacher at the Vaganova Institute gave me, as a present, a copy of *One Hundred Lessons in Classical Ballet* by Vera Sergeevna Kostrovitskaya, a textbook held in very high esteem among Kostrovitskaya's colleagues in the Soviet Union, as well as among the dancers and teachers in the West who were able to read it in Russian. I soon realized the unusual significance of this text; here I had, in book form, the source of ballet study developed by Agrippina Vaganova, a teacher so remarkable that the Choreographic Institute of Leningrad has been renamed to honor her. With high anticipation, I arranged to visit Kostrovitskaya at her apartment in the suburbs of Leningrad. I approached her with respect, and after a lively discussion of technique and terminology in the teaching of that international language, we developed a mutual regard and I left with her agreement that I should translate her book into English.

Since my earlier translation of *Classes in Classical Ballet* by the Bolshoi ballet master Asaf Messerer, had met with unprecedented success, I was confident that my publisher would accept this new project. My enthusiasm for it was twofold. First, there is to my knowledge simply nothing like it in the literature of ballet. It is a vast compilation of lessons effectively detailed to inspire and assist the teacher, and to augment the teacher's function, so that it is actually invaluable for teacher and student alike. Second, the book makes available in the West the entire eight-year curriculum taught at the Vaganova Choreographic Institute. Vaganova's teaching has been famous for decades within the ballet world, but in the last few years interest in it has become worldwide, as the method that produced the Russian luminaries Rudolf Nureyev, Natalia Makarova, and Mikhail Baryshnikov.

Kostrovitskaya was a student and a protégé of Vaganova and this book details the lessons she herself taught at the Vaganova school, following the precepts of her famous mentor. She presents a progressive approach to the combination of lessons taught from the first year to the eighth, creating a system that results in complete technical mastery by the student of exercises at the barre, in the center of the studio, of the allegro, and the work on pointes. I know of no such complete training anywhere else in book form for students starting at the age of eight or ten, all the way to the advanced lessons of the graduate year.

But any teacher or dancer on any level can draw great benefit from studying this book. When I have tested the lessons in my own teaching, I have been struck by the clarity with which the planned combinations of steps unfold for the student. Interestingly, I also ran across certain details of technique that were beyond the capabilities of students not trained in the Soviet ballet method, and these I delete in my classes. Understanding this textbook will provide new insight into the scope and range of the teacher in ballet, and I believe without any doubt that this book will raise the standards of teaching wherever it is used. I do not mean, of course, to proselytize the Vaganova method as the one correct system of teaching ballet. I mean only to affirm the very positive influence that the Russian Soviet school of ballet has had on dance the world over in this century. We have been inspired and moved by its artists; we can only benefit from a study of the methods that produced them.

In a way, the publication of *One Hundred Lessons in Classical Ballet* is like the return of a gift. In past centuries, the emerging dance tradition of Russia accepted avidly all it could learn from the great ballet masters of the West, helping it to create a magnificent classical ballet of its own. As a result, the influence of its world-renowned émigrés has enriched our ballet heritage immeasurably. Today the West, especially the United States, has again emerged as the standard bearer for innovation and explosive popularity in dance, while Russia returns to us a challenge in upholding the highest classical standards in ballet education. The process of influences has come full circle.

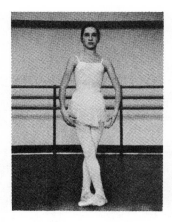

Preparatory arm position.

First arm position.

Second arm position.

Third arm position.

*Pose croisée front, pointe
tendue (big pose).*

*Pose croisée front
(big pose).*

*Pose effacée front, pointe
tendue (small pose).*

*Pose effacée front, pointe
tendue (big pose).*

*Pose effacée front
(big pose).*

Pose ecartée front, pointe tendue.

Pose ecartée back, pointe tendue.

Pose ecartée back.

Arabesque allongée.

Attitude effacée.

Jeté à terre on pointes (piqué).

Sissonne soubresaut.

Pose first arabesque, pointe tendue.

Pose first arabesque.

Pose second arabesque, pointe tendue.

Pose second arabesque.

Pose third arabesque, pointe tendue.

Pose third arabesque.

Pose fourth arabesque, pointe tendue.

Pose fourth arabesque.

About Using this Book

ANY TEXTBOOK, however valuable, can become confining if used in a dogmatic way. It is my hope that teachers will learn from the progression of exercises in this book, without losing sight of the real capabilities of individual students. The book should be used creatively to help the teacher devise the most constructive combinations for the students' technical development. It should not be a substitute for the teacher's own creativity, but rather a source of inspiration in planning lessons. If it is used in this way, both experienced and inexperienced teachers will find the book an invaluable source of material, and yet their teaching will remain flexible and alive.

Certain terms used by the author of this book will be unfamiliar to those not versed in Soviet ballet terminology. I have no desire to become embroiled in a discussion of "correct" terminology; the important thing here is to understand the author's intentions. For a better understanding of Russian usage, I urge the serious reader to study *Fundamentals of the Classic Dance* by Agrippina Vaganova. I have included below a discussion of some important terms that may seem ambiguous to the reader of this text.

ALLONGÉ applies to the position of the hand or hands, extended from the wrist through the fingers as in the arm position of an arabesque.

JETÉ ON POINTES used as piqué on pointes, traveling in any direction.

A SMALL POSE refers to the position of arms held, one in second (arm) position, the other in first (arm) position.

A BIG POSE refers to the position of arms held, one in second (arm) position, the other in third (arm) position.

RELEVÉ LENT TO 90° breaks down in the following manner: from fifth position, brush the working foot on the floor as in battement tendu and without interruption in the slow motion, raise the leg to 90°, in any direction. Thereafter lower the leg down in the starting position.

TOUR designates a turn of the body on one leg. It has been retained in the translation, instead of the more common use of the western term PIROUETTE.

TOUR LENT denotes a slow turn on the supporting leg and corresponds with the western term TOUR DE PROMENADE.

TOUR TIRE-BOUCHON used here for the pirouette, where the placement of the working foot is under the knee of the supporting leg, also identified as retiré.

SISSONNE SOUBRESAUT is a combined jump composed of a soubresaut and a grande sissonne ouverte, which is executed in a flight to the front, to the back, in big poses, in attitude croisée, attitude effacée and in pose croisée and pose effacée front.

GRANDE SISSONNE À LA SECONDE DE VOLÉE EN TOURNANT EN DEDANS is a combined step executed facing the mirror and in diagonal starting with step-coupé, or a small sissonne tombé in fourth position croisée, as well as from pas chassé. It ends with pas de bourrée dessus en tournant or with soutenu en tournant en dedans. The breakdown of the step is the following: after the small sissonne tombée croisée to the front, execute a pas chassé, the right arm in first, the left arm in second position, then shifting the weight of the body onto the right leg in demi-plié (fourth position croisée) execute a big jump taking off from the heel of the supporting foot (right foot) and by the way of a grand battement of the left leg à la seconde at 90°, execute a full turn in the air en dedans, to the right side, the left leg at 90°, raising the arms in third position. End the jump in demi-plié facing front (side 1) and follow with pas de bourrée dessus en tournant.

BIG SCENIC SISSONNE as it is called in Russian, is executed with a big jump, while the arms move through first position and open respectively one in second, the other in third position. The hands stretched out through the fingers, as if in an arabesque hand position (allongé).

JETÉ ENTRELACÉ refers to the western term GRAND JETÉ EN TOURNANT

And now, dancers, take your places, let's begin the lesson.

First Year

Introducing the elementary exercises for mastering the placement of the body, the legs, the arms, and the head, developing elementary skills in the coordination of steps.

First, the students execute the exercises while standing, facing the barre, and holding it with both hands. Later, they will hold it with one hand facing one direction, then the other, while executing the exercises on the left leg, then on the right leg. The opening of the arms from the preparatory position to the first and second arm positions—preparation at the barre and in the center—is executed to the beat of four introductory chords. The closing of the arms back into the preparatory position is done to two concluding chords.

At the end of the first year of study, the preparation for the arm positions is executed on two introductory chords.

Demi-plié in first position, facing the barre.

First Semester
First Lesson

EXERCISES AT THE BARRE[1]

1. DEMI-PLIÉ. Measure 4/4.
Two demi-pliés in first, second, third, and fifth positions. Each demi-plié is done in 2 measures, and the change of positions on 4 chords.

2. BATTEMENTS TENDUS IN FIRST POSITION. 32 measures in 4/4.
Four battements tendus to the front, to the side, to the back, and to the side. Each battement is done in 2 measures.

[1] All exercises are done facing the barre.

3. BATTEMENTS TENDUS IN FIRST POSITION WITH DEMI-PLIÉ. 16 measures in 4/4.

In the first measure: battement tendu front. In the second measure: demi-plié back to first position. Repeat, then execute the same movement twice to the side, twice to the back, and again twice to the side.

4. PASSÉ À TERRE IN FIRST POSITION. 16 measures in 4/4.

In the first measure, battement tendu to the front, without stopping in first position, battement tendu to the back. In the second measure, again passé through first position and battement tendu front, etc. The exercise is repeated 8 times.

5. DEMI-ROND DE JAMBE À TERRE (a quarter circle). Measure 4/4.

Starting in first position. En dehors: a) On 2 beats slide the foot of the extended working leg to the front, on 2 beats slide the foot to the side, on 2 beats bring the foot to first position, on 2 beats hold still in this position. Repeat the exercise 4 times.

b) On 2 beats slide the foot to the side, on 2 beats slide it to the back, on 2 beats bring the foot in first position and on 2 beats hold still in this position. Repeat the exercise 4 times.

En dedans: Repeat the same movements to the reverse side; slide the foot to the back, then to the side; thereafter, to the side, then to the front.

6. EXERCISE FOR THE ARMS. Measure 3/4 (Slow Waltz).

Stand sideways to the barre either in first or in fifth position, holding the barre with one hand and with the other arm in the preparatory position.

a) In 2 measures: from the preparatory position, the arm rises in the front to first arm position. In 2 measures: Hold this position. In 2 measures: The arm comes down to the preparatory position. In 2 measures: The arm remains in the preparatory position.

b) In 2 measures: from the preparatory position, the arm rises in front to first arm position, then lifts to third arm position. In 2 measures: the arm comes down to first position. In 2 measures: the arm closes in the preparatory position.

c) In 2 measures: the arm rises from the preparatory position to first position. In 2 measures: open the arm to second position. In 2 measures: hold the position. In 2 measures: the arm comes down to the preparatory position.

d) In 2 measures: the arm rises to first arm position. In 2 measures: lift the arm to third arm position. In 2 measures: the arm opens to the side to second arm position. In 2 measures: the arm comes down to the preparatory position. Each of the movements enumerated above is repeated 4 times.

7. BATTEMENTS TENDUS IN FIFTH POSITION. 32 measures in 4/4.

Four battements tendus to the front (each battement tendu in 2 measures), to the side, to the back and to the side.

8. PREPARATORY EXERCISE TO THE BATTEMENTS TENDUS JETÉS IN FIRST POSITION. Measure 4/4.

On the first and second beats of the measure: the working foot brushes forward on the floor. On the third beat: the leg is raised to 45°. On the fourth beat: the leg comes down, pointe tendue, on the floor. On the first two beats of the following measure: the foot closes in first position. On the last two beats: the leg is held in first position (preparatory position). The exercise is repeated 4 times, then it is executed to the side and to the back.

9. PREPARATORY EXERCISE FOR BATTEMENTS FRAPPÉS. Measure 2/4.

On 2 introductory chords: the foot brushes, pointe tendue, to the side from the first or fifth position (préparation). In the first measure: bending the knee, the foot is placed sur le cou-de-pied front. In the second measure: the position is maintained. In the third measure: the leg extends with pointe tendue to the side on the floor. In the fourth measure: the position is maintained. The exercise is repeated 4 times, consequently it is executed sur le cou-de-pied back.

10. RELEVÉ IN FIRST POSITION. 32 measures in 4/4.

a) First measure: rise slowly on half-toe. Second measure: stand on half-toe. Third measure: come down slowly. Fourth measure: stand still in first position.

b) First and second beats: rise on half-toe. Third and fourth beats: stand still. First and second beats: come down in first position. Third and fourth beats: stand still. Each exercise is repeated 4 times.

EXERCISES IN THE CENTER

1. EXERCISE FOR THE ARMS. Measure 3/4. (Slow Waltz)

The exercise (as indicated in exercises at the barre no. 6) is executed simultaneously with the two arms. The legs are in first position (halfway turned out).

2. Measure 2/4. March.

Hands on the hips. The exercise starts with the right foot; the tempo of the movement changes; proceed with slow marching steps and progress first to fast ones, then to a fast run, etc. The exercise is done in a circle or on the diagonal from corner to corner: 6 to 2, from 2 to 6, from 4 to 8, from 8 to 4 (See diagram).

THE FIXED POINTS OF THE STUDIO

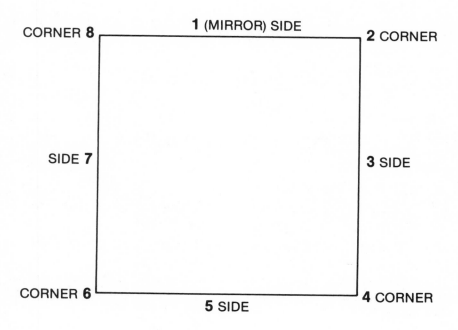

CORNER 8   1 (MIRROR) SIDE   2 CORNER

SIDE 7   3 SIDE

CORNER 6   5 SIDE   4 CORNER

Fifth position, facing the barre.

Second Lesson

EXERCISES AT THE BARRE

1. DEMI-PLIÉ. Measure 4/4.
Two demi-pliés in first, second, third, fifth, and fourth positions—2 measures for each plié. This is executed facing the barre.

2. BATTEMENTS TENDUS IN FIFTH POSITION. 16 measures in 4/4.
Four battements tendus to the front, to the side, to the back, and to the side again. Each movement is executed to a full measure of 4 beats, facing the barre.

3. ONE HAND HOLDING THE BARRE, repeat the previous exercise only with 2 battements tendus in each direction.

4. BATTEMENTS TENDUS JETÉS IN FIFTH POSITION. Measure 4/4.

On the first beat: brush the working foot front, pointe tendue, on the floor. On the second beat: throw the leg to 45°. On the third beat: bring the leg down, pointe tendue, on the floor. On the fourth beat: close the foot in fifth position. Repeat 4 times in each direction, to the front, to the side, to the back and to the side. This is executed facing the barre.

5. ONE HAND HOLDING THE BARRE, repeat the previous exercise only with 2 battements jetés in each direction.

6. RONDS DE JAMBE À TERRE. 16 measures in 4/4.

Starting in first position. En dehors: On the first and second beats: slide the working foot to the front, pointe tendue on the floor. On the third and fourth beats: slide the foot to the side, pointe tendue on the floor. On 2 beats of the following measure: slide the foot to the back, pointe tendue on the floor. On the third and fourth beats: bring the foot back in first position. Repeat the exercise 4 times en dehors and 4 times en dedans, facing the barre.

7. ONE HAND HOLDING THE BARRE, repeat the previous exercise 4 times en dehors and 4 times en dedans. Concluding the exercise, execute a simple port de bras: from the preparatory position, the arm rises to the first arm position, then to the third arm position, opens in the second position, and comes down in the preparatory position.

8. BATTEMENTS FRAPPÉS. 8 measures in 4/4.

Preparatory position: the working leg extended to the side, pointe tendue, on the floor. On the first beat: bend the knee of the working leg, striking the supporting leg sur le cou-de-pied front. On the second beat: extend the leg to the side, pointe tendue, on the floor. On the third and fourth beats: maintain this position. Subsequently, the stroke is done sur le cou-de-pied back, etc. The exercise is done facing the barre and repeated 8 times.

9. PETITS BATTEMENTS SUR LE COU-DE-PIED. 32 measures in 2/4.

Preparatory position: the working foot sur le cou-de-pied front. In the first measure: the foot slightly opens to the side in second position. In the second measure: bring the working foot sur le cou-de-pied back. In the third measure: the foot slightly opens to the side in second position. In the fourth measure: bring the foot sur le cou-de-pied front. The exercise is executed facing the barre and repeated 8 times.

10. BATTEMENTS RELEVÉS LENTS TO 45°. Measure 4/4.

In the first measure: raise the working leg slowly forward to 45°, from the first or the fifth position. In the second measure: maintain the position. In the third measure: the leg comes down slowly into the preparatory position. In the fourth measure: maintain the position in first or in fifth position. The exercise is executed twice to the front, to the side, to the back, facing the barre.

11. RELEVÉ ON HALF-TOE IN FIRST, SECOND, AND FIFTH POSITIONS. Measure 2/4.

a) In the first measure: rise on half-toe. In the second measure: come down to the starting position. Execute the exercise 4 times in each position.

b) On the first beat: demi-plié. On the second beat: rise on half-toe. On the 2 beats of the following measure: come down slowly. Execute the exercise 4 times in each position, facing the barre.

12. BENDING THE BODY IN FIRST POSITION, FACING THE BARRE. Measure 3/4 (Waltz).

In 4 measures: lean the body forward, straighten back into the starting position. In 4 measures: bend the body backward, straighten back into the starting position. In 4 measures: bend the body to the right side. In 4 measures: bend the body to the left side. Execute the exercise 4 times.

EXERCISES IN THE CENTER

1. DEMI-PLIÉ. Measure 4/4.

Two demi-pliés in first, second, third, and fifth positions,[1] 2 measures for each plié.

2. BATTEMENTS TENDUS IN FIRST POSITION. 16 measures in 4/4.

Four battements tendus to the front, to the side, to the back and to the side, 1 measure for each battement.

---

[1] Demi-plié in third and fifth positions are done en face with the right foot or the left foot front.

3. BATTEMENTS TENDUS IN FIFTH POSITION. 8 measures in 4/4.

Two battements tendus to the front, to the side, to the back and to the side, 1 measure for each battement.

4. BATTEMENTS TENDUS IN FIFTH POSITION WITH DEMI-PLIÉ. 16 measures in 4/4.

In 1 measure: battement tendu. In 1 measure: demi-plié. Execute twice to the front, to the side, to the back, and to the side.

5. EXERCISE FOR THE ARMS. Measure 2/4 or 3/4.

Raising and lowering the arms slowly in all (arm) positions: first, second, first, third, second, then the following combination of arm positions: right arm in first position, left arm in second position; left arm in first position, right arm in second position; right arm in first position, left arm in third position; left arm in first position, right arm in third position, etc.[2]

[2] First position of the feet.

Pointe tendue on the floor, facing the barre.

Third Lesson

EXERCISES AT THE BARRE[1]

1. DEMI-PLIÉ. Measure 4/4.
Two demi-pliés in first, second, third, fourth, and fifth positions—2 measures for each plié.

2. BATTEMENTS TENDUS IN FIFTH POSITION. 16 measures in 2/4.
Four battements tendus to the front, to the side, to the back, and to the side again. Each movement is executed to a full measure of 2 beats.

[1] The exercises 1 through 10 are executed holding the barre with one hand.

3. BATTEMENTS TENDUS DOUBLES IN FIFTH POSITION (lowering the heel in second position). 8 measures in 4/4.

On the first beat: extend the working leg to the side, pointe tendue on the floor. On the second beat: lower the heel to second position. On the third beat: raise the heel, pointe tendue on the floor. On the fourth beat: bring the foot in fifth position. Repeat the movement 8 times.

4. BATTEMENTS TENDUS JETÉS IN FIFTH POSITION. 16 measures in 2/4.

Execute without stopping: On the first beat: throw the leg to 45°. On the second beat: bring the leg down to fifth position. Four battements tendus jetés to the front, to the side, to the back, each battement on 2 beats, and thereafter in 4 measures: relevé lent to the side in second position at 45°.

5. RONDS DE JAMBE À TERRE. Measure 4/4.

En dehors. On the first beat, starting in first position, slide the working foot front, and hold in fixed position. On the second beat: slide the foot to the side, hold in fixed position. On the third beat: slide the foot to the back, hold in fixed position. On the fourth beat: slide the foot to first position. Repeat the exercise 4 times. Subsequently on the identical musical measure of 4/4, execute the movement flowingly, without any stop to the front, to the side and to the back. Repeat the same exercise en dedans. Concluding the exercise, execute a simple port de bras on 2 measures of 4/4.

6. BATTEMENTS SOUTENUS IN FIFTH POSITION. 8 measures in 4/4.

Execute twice in each direction. On the first and second beats: extend the working leg to the requested direction (pointe tendue) according to the principle of battement tendu; simultaneously come down in demi-plié on the supporting leg. On the third and fourth beats: bring the working leg back in fifth position, stretching the supporting leg.

7. BATTEMENTS FRAPPÉS IN ALL DIRECTIONS. Measure 4/4.

Starting position: the working leg extended to the side, pointe tendue. On the first beat: bend the knee, the foot striking the supporting leg sur le cou-de-pied front. On the second beat: extend the leg to the front (pointe tendue). On the third and fourth beats: maintain this position. Subsequently execute the same movement to the side, to the back, and to the side. This combination is repeated 8 to 16 times.

8. BATTEMENTS DOUBLES FRAPPÉS. 8 measures in 4/4.

Starting position: the working leg extended to the side, pointe tendue on the floor. On the first beat, bend the knee, the foot striking the supporting leg sur le cou-de-pied front. On the second beat, open the foot slightly to the side and bring it sur le cou-de-pied back. On the third beat, extend the leg to the side, pointe tendue on the floor. On the fourth beat: maintain the position. Execute the following double frappés striking sur le cou-de-pied back and bringing the working foot sur le cou-de-pied front. Repeat 8 times.

9. PETITS BATTEMENTS SUR LE COU-DE-PIED. 16 measures in 2/4.

Extend the working leg to the side, pointe tendue, on 2 introductory chords; simultaneously raise the arm from the preparatory position to first arm position. On the following 2 chords, bend the knee and place the foot sur le cou-de-pied front; the arm opens simultaneously to second arm position. First measure: the foot opens slightly to the side in second position and returns sur le cou-de-pied back. In the second measure: the foot opens slightly to the side in second position and returns sur le cou-de-pied front. Repeat 8 times.

10. GRAND PLIÉ IN FIRST, SECOND, THIRD, AND FIFTH POSITIONS. Measure 4/4.

Execute 2 grands pliés in all the enumerated positions; each grand plié is done in 2 measures.

11. PRÉPARATION FOR RONDS DE JAMBE EN L'AIR. Measure 4/4.

Facing the barre, starting position: raise the working leg to the side to 45°. First measure: bend the knee, bringing the foot (pointe tendue) to the middle of the calf of the supporting leg. Second measure: extend the leg to the side to 45°. Repeat the movement 4 to 8 times. After a short time this exercise is carried out to the accompaniment of 1 measure of 4/4.

12. BATTEMENTS RELEVÉS LENTS TO 90° TO THE SIDE IN SECOND POSITION. 8 measures in 4/4.

Facing the barre. First measure: raise the working leg to the side to 90°, from the first or the fifth position. Second measure: maintain the position. Third measure: bring the leg down to the starting position (first or fifth). Fourth measure: hold this position. Repeat twice.

13. RELEVÉ ON HALF-TOE IN FIRST, SECOND, FIFTH POSITIONS. Measure 4/4.

Facing the barre. First measure: on the first beat, demi-plié; on the second beat: rise on half-toe; on the third and fourth beats: maintain the position. Second measure: on the first and second beats, come down in demi-plié; on the third and fourth beats, stretch the knees. Repeat the exercise 4 times in each position.

EXERCISES IN THE CENTER

1. DEMI-PLIÉ. Measure 4/4.

Two demi-pliés in first, second, third, fourth, and fifth positions, 2 measures for each demi-plié.

2. BATTEMENTS TENDUS IN FIFTH POSITION. 16 measures in 4/4.

Four battements tendus to the front, to the side, to the back, and to the side again. Each battement to 1 measure of 4 beats.

3. BATTEMENTS TENDUS JETÉS IN FIRST POSITION TO THE SIDE. Measure 2/4.

Eight battements tendus jetés, each battement on 2 beats.

4. DEMI-ROND DE JAMBE À TERRE. 16 measures in 4/4.

En dehors. First measure: on the first beat, slide the working foot to the front. On the second beat, slide the foot to the side. On the third beat, close the foot in first position. On the fourth beat, maintain the position. Second measure: execute the second half of the rond de jambe à terre en dehors. Repeat the exercise 4 times, following with en dedans.

5. STUDYING ÉPAULEMENT CROISÉ AND EFFACÉ IN FIFTH POSITION.

6. CROISÉ AND EFFACÉ POSITIONS FRONT AND BACK. Measure 3/4 (Waltz).

Position croisée front, fifth position, épaulement croisé, right foot front. First and second measures: lift the arms to first arm position. Third and fourth measures: raise the left arm to third arm position, open the right arm to second position, turning the head to the right. Fifth and sixth measures: slide the right foot to the front, croisé, pointe tendue. Seventh and eighth measures: maintain the position. Hold this position during the 4 subsequent measures. Thirteenth and fourteenth measures: open the left arm to second position. Fifteenth and sixteenth measures: bring the arms down to the preparatory position, closing simultaneously the right foot in fifth position. Carry out, likewise, the study of croisé position to the back, effacé position to the front, and to the back.

7. FIRST PORT DE BRAS. Measure 4/4.

Starting position: fifth position, épaulement croisé, right foot front, arms in preparatory position. First measure: on the first and second beats, raise the arms to the first arm position. On the third and fourth beats, raise the arms to the third arm position. Second measure: on the first and second beats, open the arms in second position. On the third and fourth beats, lower the arms in the preparatory position.

8. SECOND PORT DE BRAS. Measure 4/4.

Starting position: fifth position, épaulement croisé, right foot front, left arm in third arm position, right arm in second position.[2] First measure: on the first and second beats, open the left arm to second position. On the third and fourth beats, lower the left arm to the preparatory position, raising the right arm to the third arm position. Second measure: on the first and second beats, the arms meet in first arm position. On the third and fourth beats, open the arms to the starting position. Repeat the exercise 4 times.

You must note that in the further examples of combinations the subdivision of big and small poses does not indicate at great length the position of the arms, though variants of arm and head positions in the poses exist. They are put into practice according to the task given by the instructor only after the study of fundamental positions. In all big poses, the arms can be: one in third position, the other in second, one in first position, the other in third, or both arms in third position.

In the small poses, the position of arms varies between the first and second.

In arabesque poses at 90° or 45°, so-called half arabesques, different arm positions can be chosen, but in all the poses the version of the arm position must depend on the change of the body placement, whether leaning or slightly bending.

The differentiation of small and big poses pertains to the execution of small steps at 45° or to big steps at 90°. This allows for a diversity in the artistic line of the dancer.

[2] Carry out the starting position on 4 introductory chords.

Fifth position.

Fourth Lesson

EXERCISES AT THE BARRE

The student holds the barre with one hand.

1. DEMI-PLIÉ AND GRAND-PLIÉ IN FIRST, SECOND, FOURTH, AND FIFTH POSITIONS. Measure 4/4.

In first position: one demi-plié in 2 measures; two demi-pliés in 1 measure, each; two grand-pliés in 2 measures, each. Execute the same in second, fourth, and fifth positions.

2. BATTEMENTS TENDUS IN FIFTH POSITION. 16 measures in 2/4.

Four battements tendus to the front, each on 2 beats. Two double battements tendus to the side, each in 2 measures. Four battements tendus to the back, each on 2 beats, and 2 doubles battements to the side, each in 2 measures.

3. BATTEMENTS TENDUS JETÉS PIQUÉS IN FIFTH POSITION. Measure 4/4.

On the first and second half beats, a controlled throw of the working leg to the front to 45°. On the third half beat, a short battement piqué. On the fourth half beat, hold the leg off the floor at 45°. On the fifth half beat, a short battement piqué. On the sixth half beat, hold the leg off the floor at 45°. On the seventh and eighth half beats, bring the leg down, closing in fifth position. Repeat the exercise, then execute the same twice to the side, to the back and to the side. At the conclusion of this exercise, take a pose croisée front (pointe tendue, on the floor) on 4 measures of 4/4.

4. RONDS DE JAMBE À TERRE. Measure 4/4.

En dehors: On the first beat: starting in first position, the working foot slides to the front and, without pause, on the second beat, slides to the side in second position. On the third beat: without pause, the foot slides to the back. On the fourth beat: place the foot in first position flowingly, without pause; continue the circular movement. Execute 4 times, then repeat the same en dedans. At the conclusion, execute the third port de bras with a bending of the body on 2 measures of 4/4.

5. BATTEMENTS FONDUS.[1] 8 measures in 4/4.

Starting position: the working leg is pointed to the side. On the first and second beats: bend the knee of the working leg, and place the foot sur le cou-de-pied front;[2] simultaneously, come down in demi-plié on the supporting leg. On the third and fourth beats: extend the working leg, placing it pointe tendue, on the floor; simultaneously, stretch the supporting leg. The exercise is executed twice to the front, to the side, to the back and to the side.

6. BATTEMENTS FRAPPÉS IN ALL DIRECTIONS. Musical measure 4/4.

It is executed in the similar manner as described in the third lesson.

---

[1] Battements fondus are executed facing the barre during the third and fourth lessons.
[2] Sur le cou-de-pied front is practiced conditionally.

At the conclusion, end with a pose croisée to the back, pointe tendue, and hold the position for 4 measures.

7. BATTEMENTS DOUBLES FRAPPÉS IN ALL DIRECTIONS. Measure 4/4.

Starting position: the working leg extends to the side, pointe tendue on the floor. On the first beat: bend the knee, the foot striking the supporting leg sur le cou-de-pied back. On the second beat: slightly open the leg and bring it sur le cou-de-pied front. On the third beat: extend the leg, pointe tendue, on the floor. On the fourth beat, maintain the position. Execute the same movement to the side, to the front, to the side, and repeat once again.

8. RONDS DE JAMBE EN L'AIR EN DEHORS AND EN DEDANS. Measure 4/4.

Facing the barre. Starting position: raise the working leg to the side to 45°. En dehors. On the first and second beats, bend the knee and while executing the first half of the conventional circle, bring the foot, pointe tendue, to the middle of the calf of the supporting leg. On the third and fourth beats: concluding the second half of the circle, stretch the leg into the starting position. Repeat the movement 4 times, lower the leg into fifth position and subsequently raise again to the side to 45° to continue the exercise en dedans.

9. PETITS BATTEMENTS SUR LE COU-DE-PIED.

Similar execution as described in the third lesson. At the conclusion of the exercise, rise on half-toe in fifth position, holding the barre with one hand for 2 measures of 4/4.

10. BATTEMENTS RELEVÉS LENTS TO 90° TO THE SIDE AND TO THE BACK. Measure 4/4.

Facing the barre. First measure: starting in fifth position, raise the leg to 90°. Second measure: on the first and second beats, maintain the position. On the third and fourth beats, lower the leg to the starting position. The movement is executed 2 times to the side and 2 times to the back.

11. BATTEMENTS RELEVÉS LENTS TO 90°, FRONT.

As described in the previous exercise (10), but the student holds the barre with one hand.

12. GRANDS BATTEMENTS JETÉS. Measure 4/4.

Facing the barre, the student executes grands battements jetés to the side and to the back; thereafter holding the barre with one hand, he continues to the front.[3] On the first beat: the working leg extends from the first or fifth position in the given direction, pointe tendue on the floor. On the second beat: throw the leg to 90°. On the third beat: lower the leg on the floor, pointe tendue. On the fourth beat: bring the leg in first or fifth position. Repeat 4 times to the side and then separately 4 times to the back.

13. RELEVÉ ON HALF-TOE IN FIRST, SECOND, AND FIFTH POSITION. Measure 4/4.

Facing the barre. On the first beat: demi-plié. On the second beat: come up on half-toe. On the third beat: come down in demi-plié. On the fourth beat: stretch the knees. Repeat the exercise 4 times in each position.

EXERCISES IN THE CENTER

1. DEMI-PLIÉ. 16 measures in 4/4.

One demi-plié in 2 measures, 2 demi-pliés each in 1 measure in first, second, fourth, and fifth positions. In the fourth and fifth positions, the exercise is done with épaulement croisé.

2. BATTEMENTS TENDUS IN FIFTH POSITION.[4] 16 measures in 2/4.

Four battements tendus to the front, to the side, to the back and side. Each battement on 2 beats.

3. BATTEMENTS TENDUS JETÉS IN FIFTH POSITION. 24 measures in 2/4.

Four battements tendus jetés to the front, to the side, to the back, and to the side. Each battement on 2 beats. Subsequently, in 4 measures, execute the pose croisée front with the left leg. First measure: extend the working leg to the front (pointe tendue on the floor); simultaneously raise the arms to first (arm) position. Second measure: open the arms, the right arm to the third (arm) position and the left to the second (arm) position. Third measure: lower the right arm to the second (arm)

---

[3] After several lessons, the student must execute 4 grands battements jetés in all directions, holding the barre with one hand.

[4] Standing in fifth position, épaulement croisé, is recommended at the beginning of the exercises in the center, when starting this lesson. When opening the arms in first and second (arm) positions, turn the body en face. Concluding the exercise in fifth position, the placement is in épaulement croisé.

position. Fourth measure: the leg closes in fifth position; simultaneously the arms come down to the preparatory position. Follow with the similar execution in the pose croisée back with the right leg.

4. RONDS DE JAMBE À TERRE. Measure 4/4.

En dehors. On the first beat: the working leg extends to the front, and holds the fixed point. On the second beat: slide to the side; hold the fixed point. On the third beat: slide to the back; again hold the fixed point. On the fourth beat: bring the leg in first position. Execute the movement 4 times, subsequently follow with en dedans.

5. POSES IN CROISÉ AND EFFACÉ. Flowing execution. Measure 3/4 (Waltz).

Pose croisée front. Fifth position épaulement croisé, right foot front. First and second measures: raise the arms to first (arm) position; simultaneously extend the right leg to croisé front (pointe tendue) on the floor. Third and fourth measures: raise the left arm to third (arm) position, while the right arm opens to second (arm) position. The head turns to the right. Fifth and sixth measures: the left arm opens to second (arm) position. Seventh and eighth measures: the arms lower to the preparatory position; simultaneously, the right leg closes in fifth position. Repeat the poses from 2 to 4 times, front and back, thereafter follow with the execution of poses in effacé.

6. THE STUDY OF THE POSES IN ÉCARTÉ BACK AND FRONT. Measure 3/4 (Waltz).

Pose écartée back. Fifth position, épaulement effacé, right foot front. First and second measures: raise the arms to first (arm) position; simultaneously extend the right leg to the side, pointe tendue on the floor, toward the directional corner 4. Third and fourth measures: raise the right arm to third (arm) position, while the left arm opens to second (arm) position. The head turns to the left. Fifth and sixth measures: the left arm open to second (arm) position. Seventh and eighth measures: the arms lower to the preparatory position; simultaneously, the right leg closes in fifth position. Repeat the poses from 2 to 4 times, and approach the study of poses in écartée front in a similar manner.

7. FIRST AND SECOND ARABESQUES (elementary study). Measure 3/4 (Waltz).

Stand facing direction 3, in a not fully turned out first or fifth position. First and second measures: raise the arms to first (arm) position. Third and fourth measures: move the arms, the right to the front, the left to the side, while getting into the proper arabesque position. (In the elementary study of poses in arabesque, the working foot remains pointe tendue on the floor.) Fifth and sixth measures: extend the left foot to the back, pointe tendue on the floor. Seventh, eighth, ninth, tenth, eleventh, and twelfth measures: hold the position. Thirteenth, fourteenth, fifteenth, and sixteenth measures: lower the arms to the preparatory position; simultaneously, close the left foot to first or fifth position. Repeat the pose 2 to 4 times. Subsequently follow with the study of second arabesque.

8. SECOND PORT DE BRAS.

Execution similar to that described in the third lesson.

9. TEMPS LEVÉ (JUMPS) IN FIRST AND SECOND POSITIONS. Measure 4/4.

Facing the barre.

a) On the first and second beats: demi-plié, then jump between the second and third beats, ending in demi-plié on the third beat. On the fourth beat, stretch the knees. Repeat the exercise 4 times in first and second positions.

b) On the first beat: demi-plié, jump between the first and second beats, ending on the second beat in demi-plié. On the third and fourth beats, stretch the knees.[5]

10. PORT DE BRAS LEANING THE BODY TO THE FRONT, BENDING BACK AND TO THE SIDE, IN A NOT FULLY TURNED OUT FIRST POSITION.[6]

---

[5] Within a few lessons, temps levé is executed in fifth position. After the execution in first and second positions facing the barre, repeat the same movement in the center.

[6] It is recommended that all subsequent lessons be concluded with the port de bras and bending the body.

Leg raised in front, at the barre.

Fifth Lesson

EXERCISES AT THE BARRE

1. DEMI-PLIÉ AND GRAND-PLIÉ IN FIRST, SECOND, FOURTH, AND FIFTH POSITIONS. Musical measure 4/4.

Two demi-pliés, each on 4 beats, in first position, 1 grand plié in 2 measures. Same execution in second, fourth and fifth positions.

2. BATTEMENTS TENDUS IN FIFTH POSITION. 16 measures in 2/4.

Four battements tendus front, each on 2 beats, 2 battements tendus in demi-plié to the side, each in 2 measures. Distribute the movement in the following manner: on the first beat, extend the working leg to the side, on the second beat, close in fifth position in demi-plié. On the first beat of the subsequent measure, the demi-plié is deeper; on the second beat, stretch the knees. Four battements tendus to the back, each on 2 beats and 2 battements tendus in demi-plié to the side, each in 2 measures.

3. BATTEMENTS TENDUS JETÉS IN FIFTH POSITION. 16 measures in 2/4.

Four battements tendus jetés front, side, back and side, each on 2 beats. At the conclusion, take a pose écartée to the back in 4 measures and follow with a pose écartée front in 4 measures.

4. PRÉPARATION FOR RONDS DE JAMBE À TERRE. 16 measures in 4/4.

En dehors. First measure: on the first beat, demi-plié in first position; on the second beat, the working leg slides to the front (pointe tendue); simultaneously raise the arm to first (arm) position. On the third and fourth beats, bring the leg to the side, the arm opens simultaneously to the second (arm) position while the knee of the supporting leg is straightened. Second measure: on the first and second beats, maintain the position; on the third and fourth beats, bring the leg in first position, while the arm lowers simultaneously to the preparatory position. Repeat the movement 4 times and subsequently follow with en dedans.

5. RONDS DE JAMBE À TERRE.

Similar execution, as described in the fourth lesson. At the conclusion, trace a half circle in plié (rond de jambe à terre) in 2 measures of 4/4.

En dehors. First measure: on the first beat, demi-plié in first position; on the second beat, extend the working leg to the front (pointe tendue); simultaneously raise the arm in first (arm) position; on the third and fourth beats, bring the leg simultaneously with the arm to second position.

Second measure: on the first and second beats, bring the leg to the back; on the third and fourth beats, place the leg in first position, while stretching the knee of the supporting leg and lowering the arm to the preparatory position. Subsequently, trace a half circle in plié en dedans in a similar manner.

6. BATTEMENTS FONDUS.

Similar execution, as described in the fourth lesson. At the conclusion of the exercise, move into the second arabesque pose (pointe tendue on the floor), holding for 2 measures of 4/4.

7. BATTEMENTS FRAPPÉS.

8. BATTEMENTS DOUBLES FRAPPÉS.

9. RONDS DE JAMBE EN L'AIR.

10. PETITS BATTEMENTS SUR LE COU-DE-PIED.
Execution similar to that described in the fourth lesson.

11. BATTEMENTS RELEVÉS LENTS TO 90° IN FIFTH POSITION.
16 measures in 4/4.

Two relevés front to 90°, to the side, to the back, and to the side, each in 2 measures. Execute the exercise, holding the barre with one hand.

12. GRANDS BATTEMENTS JETÉS IN FIFTH POSITION. 16 measures in 4/4.

Execute 2 grands battements jetés front, to the side, to the back, and to the side, each on 4 beats. The breakdown of the movement is the following: on the first beat, throw the working leg to 90°; on the second beat, lower the leg in fifth position; on the third and fourth beats, hold still in fifth position.

13. RELEVÉ ON HALF-TOE IN FIRST, SECOND, AND FIFTH POSITIONS.
Execution similar to that described in the fourth lesson.

14. PAS DE BOURRÉE WITH CHANGING FEET EN DEHORS AND EN DEDANS. Musical measure 4/4.

Facing the barre in fifth position, right foot front. En dehors. On the upbeat, demi-plié on the right leg, lift the left foot sur le cou-de-pied back. On the first beat, step on the left foot, half toe, and bring the right foot sur le cou-de-pied front; on the second beat, step to the side on the right foot, half toe, the left foot sur le cou-de-pied front; on the third beat, demi-plié on the left leg, the right foot sur le cou-de-pied back; on the fourth beat, maintain the position. Repeat the movement subsequently to the right and to the left side from 4 to 8 times. Execute likewise the pas de bourrée en dedans.[1]

---

[1] After several lessons, this pas de bourrée can be taught to the modified musical measure of 3/4 or 2/4.

EXERCISES IN THE CENTER

1. DEMI-PLIÉ AND GRAND PLIÉ IN FIRST, SECOND, FOURTH, AND FIFTH POSITIONS. Musical measure 4/4.

In first position: 2 demi-pliés, each on 4 beats; 1 grand plié in 2 measures. Execute likewise the movement in second position, and continue in fourth and fifth positions with 2 demi-pliés, each on 4 beats.[2]

2. BATTEMENTS TENDUS IN FIFTH POSITION. 32 measures in 2/4.

Eight battements tendus front, side and back, each on 2 beats. At the conclusion, move into a pose écartée back with the left leg, and in 4 measures, take a pose écartée front, with the right leg.

3. BATTEMENTS TENDUS JETÉS IN FIFTH POSITION. 24 measures in 2/4.

Four battements tendus jetés front, to the side, to the back and to the side, each on 2 beats. At the conclusion move into first arabesque position with the left leg in 4 measures, and thereafter in 4 additional measures to second arabesque position.

4. RONDS DE JAMBE À TERRE. 12 measures in 4/4.

Four ronds de jambe à terre en dehors and 4 en dedans, each on 4 beats. Execute flowingly, without any stop. End in fifth position, épaulement croisé, and continue with the second port de bras twice, in 2 measures of 4/4 each.

5. BATTEMENTS SOUTENUS IN FIFTH POSITION. Musical measure 4/4.

Similar execution, as described in the third lesson (exercises at the barre, paragraph 6).

6. THIRD ARABESQUE. Musical measure 3/4. Waltz.

Learn in succession, as indicated in the fourth lesson, paragraph 7 (First and second arabesques).[3]

---

[2] Execute the demi-plié in fourth position with épaulement croisé.

[3] According to the degree of mastery, open the arms through the first, second, and third arabesque positions, while simultaneously stretching the leg, pointe tendue on the floor.

7. THIRD PORT DE BRAS. Musical measure 4/4.[4]

First measure: on the first and second beats, bend the body forward; on the third and fourth beats, straighten the body. Second measure: on the first and second beats, bend the body backward; on the third and fourth beats, straighten the body.

8. TEMPS LEVÉ IN FIRST, SECOND, AND FIFTH POSITIONS. Musical measure 4/4.

Similar execution, as described in the fourth lesson.

9. CHANGEMENTS DE PIEDS. Musical measure 4/4.

The execution is done facing the barre or in the center, according to the level of mastery.

a) On the first and second beats, demi-plié; jump between the second and third beats, ending in demi-plié on the third beat; stretch the knees on the fourth beat.

b) On the first beat, demi-plié; jump between the first and second beats, ending in demi-plié on the second beat; stretch the knees on the third and fourth beats. Repeat the movement 8 times.

[4] Port de bras can be executed as well in 3/4 (waltz). In this instance, each beat of a measure in 4/4 or in 2/4 corresponds to a single measure of the waltz.

Battement soutenu.

Second Semester
Sixth Lesson

EXERCISES AT THE BARRE

1. DEMI-PLIÉ, GRAND PLIÉ, AND RELEVÉ ON HALF-TOE IN FIRST, SECOND, FOURTH, AND FIFTH POSITIONS. Musical measure 4/4.

In first position: 2 demi-pliés, each on 4 beats; 2 grands pliés, each in 2 measures; 2 relevés on half-toe, each on 4 beats. Same execution in second, fourth, and fifth positions.

2. BATTEMENTS TENDUS IN FIFTH POSITION. 8 measures in 4/4.

Two battements tendus front, to the side, to the back and to the side, each on 2 beats. Repeat in the reverse direction and in 2 measures, move with a slow half turn (on the flat foot) toward the barre.

3. BATTEMENTS TENDUS JETÉS IN FIFTH POSITION. 16 measures in 2/4.

Four battements tendus jetés front, to the side, to the back and to the side, each on 2 beats. At the conclusion, move with a half turn away from the barre (on the flat foot) to the count of 4 measures.

4. RONDS DE JAMBE À TERRE. Musical measure 2/4.

En dehors. On 4 introductory chords, préparation en dehors; subsequently 8 ronds de jambe à terre, each on 2 beats.[1] Execute préparation en dedans, on 4 chords, thereafter 8 ronds de jambe à terre en dedans, each on 2 beats. In 4 measures, make a circular movement in plié en dehors and in 4 measures again, another circular movement in plié en dedans. At the end, conclude with the third port de bras with the bending of the body, twice, each time in 4 measures.

5. BATTEMENTS SOUTENUS RISING ON HALF-TOE IN FIFTH POSITION. 8 measures in 4/4.

Two battements soutenus to the front, to the side, to the back, and to the side twice in each direction. On the first and second beats, brush the working leg, pointe tendue on the floor and come down simultaneously in demi-plié on the supporting leg; on the third and fourth beats, bring the working leg to the supporting leg, while stretching it, in fifth position half-toe.

6. BATTEMENTS FRAPPÉS TO THE SIDE AT 45°. 8 measures in 2/4.

Starting position: extend the working leg to the side at 45°. On the upbeat, the working foot strikes the supporting leg sur le cou-de-pied front; on the first beat, extend quickly to the side at 45°; on the second beat, maintain the position. Repeat the movement 8 times.[2]

7. BATTEMENTS DOUBLES FRAPPÉS TO THE SIDE. 8 measures in 2/4.

Starting position: extend the working leg to the side, pointe tendue on the floor. On the first beat, the working foot strikes the supporting leg sur le cou-de-pied front; on the second half beat, pass the foot sur

---

[1] In the execution of the rond de jambe à terre in 2/4, the passé through the first position is done on the second beat. Subsequently, when the execution is in 1/4, the passé through the first position (ending each rond de jambe) is done on one beat.

[2] It is helpful to combine the battements frappés on the floor, pointe tendue, with the battements frappés off the floor at 45°, with the execution of the first half of the exercise with pointe tendue on the floor, and the second half off the floor at 45°.

le cou-de-pied back; on the second beat, extend the leg quickly to the side, on the fourth half beat, maintain the position. Repeat the exercise 4 times with pointe tendue on the floor and 4 times with battements at 45°.

8. RONDS DE JAMBE EN L'AIR. 8 measures in 4/4.

Starting position: the working leg is open to the side at 45°. Execute rond de jambe on the first and second beats; maintain the starting position on the third and fourth beats. Execute the exercise 4 times en dehors and 4 times en dedans.

9. PETITS BATTEMENTS SUR LE COU-DE-PIED. Measure 2/4.

Extend slightly the working leg from the cou-de-pied front position to the side, then on the first beat, return the foot sur le cou-de-pied back; on the second half beat, extend slightly to the side; and on the second beat, return the foot sur le cou-de-pied front. Repeat the exercise 8 to 16 times.

10. BATTEMENTS DÉVELOPPÉS FROM THE FIFTH POSITION TO THE SIDE AND TO THE BACK. Measure 4/4.

Facing the barre.[3] First measure: on the first and second beats, bring the working foot sur le cou-de-pied and maintain this position.[4] On the third and fourth beats, raise the foot to the knee of the supporting leg (front or back) and maintain this position as well. Second measure: extend the leg at 90° in the given direction. Third measure: maintain the position. Fourth measure: lower the leg into fifth position. Repeat the exercise 2 to 4 times.

11. GRANDS BATTEMENTS JETÉS POINTÉS. 16 measures in 4/4.

On the first beat: a sharp throw of the working leg to 90°. On the second beat: lower the leg, pointe tendue. On the third and fourth beats: maintain the position. Repeat the exercise 4 to 8 times in all directions.

12. RELEVÉ ON HALF-TOE IN FIRST, SECOND, AND FIFTH POSITIONS.

Execute as in the previous lessons.

---

[3] According to the degree of mastery, execute the developpés to the front, to the side and to the back holding the barre with one hand.

[4] The cou-de-pied position is conventionally applied to the front and to the back depending on the position of the foot in the exercise.

EXERCISES IN THE CENTER

1. DEMI-PLIÉ, GRAND PLIÉ, AND RELEVÉ ON HALF-TOE IN FIRST, SECOND, FOURTH, AND FIFTH POSITIONS.
Similar execution as in the exercise at the barre.[5]

2. BATTEMENTS TENDUS IN FIFTH POSITION. 32 measures in 2/4.
Eight battements tendus to the front, to the side and to the back, each on 2 beats. At the conclusion, execute a pose croisée to the front, with the left leg, to the count of 4 measures; then with the right leg a pose in third arabesque, pointe tendue on the floor.

[5] Execute the demi-plié and grand plié in fourth position with épaulement effacé or croisé.

3. BATTEMENTS TENDUS JETÉS IN FIFTH POSITION. 16 measures in 2/4.

Four battements tendus jetés to the front, to the side, to the back and to the side, each on 2 beats.

4. RONDS DE JAMBE À TERRE. Measure 2/4.

En dehors. Execute the préparation on 4 introductory chords and follow with 8 ronds de jambe à terre, each on 2 beats. In 4 measures, execute a half circle, in plié, en dehors, ending in fifth position; then in 4 measures the third position port de bras. Repeat the combination on the other leg and then the same exercise en dedans.

5. BATTEMENTS FONDUS, POINTE TENDUE ON THE FLOOR. 8 measures in 4/4.

Two battements fondus to the front, to the side, to the back, and to the side, each on 4 beats.

6. BATTEMENTS FRAPPÉS TO THE SIDE.

Execution similar to that in the exercise at the barre, but with pointe tendue on the floor.[6]

7. PAS DE BOURRÉE EN DEHORS AND EN DEDANS (CHANGING FEET)

Follow the execution as in the fifth lesson of the exercise at the barre.

8. PAS DE BOURRÉE SUIVI EN TOURNANT.

Turn on half-toe in fifth position (on the spot).

ALLEGRO

1. TEMPS LEVÉ IN FIRST, SECOND, AND FIFTH POSITIONS. Measure 4/4.

Execute 4 times in all positions, each on 4 beats.

---

[6] It is recommended that in the previous lessons, a close study be made of the proper position sur le cou-de-pied, in the center.

2. CHANGEMENTS DE PIEDS. 8 measures in 4/4.

Execute 8 times, each on 4 beats.

3. PAS ÉCHAPPÉ. Measure 4/4.

Execute facing the barre; according to the degree of mastery, follow with the execution in the center.

a) First measure: on the first beat, demi-plié in fifth position, jump between the first and second beats ending in second position demi-plié on the second beat; stretch the knees on the third and fourth beats. Second measure: demi-plié in second position on the first beat, jump between the first and second beats ending in fifth position demi-plié on the second beat; stretch the knees on the third and fourth beats.

b) On the first beat, demi-plié and jump between the first and second beats, ending in second position demi-plié on the second beat; jump between the second and third beats, ending in fifth position demi-plié on the third beat; stretch the knees on the fourth beat. Repeat the exercise 4 to 8 times.

4. PAS ASSEMBLÉ. Measure 4/4.

Facing the barre; according to the degree of mastery, follow with the execution in the center. On the first beat, demi-plié, jump between the first and second beats, ending in demi-plié on the second beat; stretch the knees on the third and fourth beats. Repeat the exercise 4 to 8 times.

EXERCISE ON POINTES

1. RELEVÉ IN FIRST, SECOND, AND FIFTH POSITIONS. Measure 4/4.

Execute facing the barre; thereafter, according to the degree of mastery (6 to 8 lessons), follow with execution in the center. On the first beat, demi-plié; come up on pointes on the second beat; come down in demi-plié on the third beat, and stretch the knees on the fourth beat. Repeat the exercise in each position 8 times.

Leg raised in front at 45°, at the barre.

Seventh Lesson

EXERCISES AT THE BARRE

1. DEMI-PLIÉ, GRAND PLIÉ, AND RELEVÉ ON HALF-TOE IN FIRST, SECOND, FOURTH, AND FIFTH POSITIONS. Measure 4/4.

Execution similar to that in the sixth lesson.

2. BATTEMENTS TENDUS IN FIFTH POSITION. 16 measures in 2/4.

Eight battements tendus to the front, to the side, to the back, and to the side, on 2 beats. At the conclusion, execute a half turn toward the barre to the count of 2 measures and follow with a relevé on half-toe in fifth position to the count of 2 measures.

3. BATTEMENTS TENDUS JETÉS IN FIFTH AND FIRST POSITIONS. 32 measures in 2/4.

From fifth position, 8 battements tendus jetés to the front, to the side, and to the back, on 2 beats each. Four battements tendus jetés to the side in first position, each on 2 beats, and 4 piqués to the side, on 2 beats each.

4. RONDS DE JAMBE À TERRE.

Similar execution as in the sixth lesson.

5. BATTEMENTS FONDUS AT 45°. 8 measures in 4/4.

Starting position: the working leg is opened to the side at 45°. Two battements fondus to the front, to the side, to the back, and to the side, each on 4 beats.

6. BATTEMENTS FRAPPÉS AT 45°. 16 measures in 2/4.

Starting position: the working leg is opened to the side at 45°. Four battements frappés to the front, to the side, to the back, and to the side, each on 2 beats.

7. BATTEMENTS DOUBLES FRAPPÉS AT 45°. 16 measures in 2/4.

Starting position: the working leg is opened to the side at 45°. Execute battements doubles frappés to the front, to the side, to the back, and to the side, each on 2 beats. Repeat the exercise 4 times.

8. RONDS DE JAMBE EN L'AIR. 16 measures in 2/4.

En dehors. Three ronds de jambe en l'air, each on 2 beats; on the subsequent 2 beats, hold the working leg at 45°. Two ronds de jambe en l'air, each on 2 beats; lower the leg, pointe tendue on the floor on 2 beats, and raise again to 45°, on 2 beats. From this position, resume the exercise en dedans.

9. PETITS BATTEMENTS SUR LE COU-DE-PIED.

Execution similar to that in the sixth lesson.

10. BATTEMENTS DÉVELOPPÉS. 16 measures in 4/4.

First measure: on the first beat, bring the working foot sur le cou-de-pied, maintaining this position; on the second beat, raise the working foot to the knee of the supporting leg and hold in this fixed position; on the third and fourth beats, extend the leg at 90° in the given direction. Second measure: on the first and second beats, hold the position; on the third and fourth beats, lower the leg in fifth position. Repeat each exercise twice, to the front, to the side, to the back and to the side.

11. GRANDS BATTEMENTS JETÉS. 16 measures in 2/4.

On the upbeat, a controlled throw of the working leg to 90°; on the first beat, the leg lowers to fifth position; on the second beat, hold the position. Execute the exercise 4 times in all directions.

12. RELEVÉ ON HALF-TOE IN FIRST, SECOND, AND FIFTH POSITION.

Execution similar to that in the previous lessons.

EXERCISES IN THE CENTER

1. DEMI-PLIÉ, GRAND PLIÉ, AND RELEVÉ ON HALF-TOE IN FIRST, SECOND, FOURTH, AND FIFTH POSITIONS.

Execution similar to that in the exercise at the barre.

2. BATTEMENTS TENDUS IN FIFTH POSITION. 16 measures in 2/4.

Four battements tendus to the front, to the side, to the back and to the side, each on 2 beats.

3. BATTEMENTS TENDUS JETÉS IN FIFTH POSITION. 16 measures in 2/4.

Four battements tendus jetés to the front, to the side, to the back, and to the side, each on 2 beats.

4. BATTEMENTS FONDUS, POINTE TENDUE ON THE FLOOR AND OFF THE FLOOR AT 45°. 8 measures in 4/4.

Two battements fondus on the floor, on 4 beats; 2 battements fondus on the floor to the side, on 4 beats. Repeat with 2 battements fondus to the front and to the side opening the leg to 45°. After a pause, repeat the exercise in the reverse direction.[1]

5. BATTEMENTS FRAPPÉS TO THE SIDE, POINTE TENDUE ON THE FLOOR, AND AT 45°. 16 measures in 2/4.

Two battements frappés to the front, to the side, to the back, and to the side, pointe tendue on the floor, each on 2 beats, and 2 battements frappés at 45° in the same directions each on 2 beats.

[1] In this lesson, the ronds de jambe à terre are eliminated as new, complicated steps are studied.

6. BATTEMENTS DOUBLES FRAPPÉS ON THE FLOOR AND AT 45°. 16 measures in 2/4.

Eight battements doubles frappés to the side, pointe tendue on the floor, each on 2 beats, and 8 at 45°, each on 2 beats.

7. PETITS BATTEMENTS SUR LE COU-DE-PIED.

Similar execution as in the exercise at the barre.

8. BATTEMENTS RELEVÉS LENTS TO THE SIDE (90°). Musical measure 4/4.

First measure: raise the working leg to 90°. Second measure: maintain the position on the first and second beats; lower the leg into fifth position on the third and fourth beats.[2] Repeat the exercise 4 times.

9. TEMPS LIÉ À TERRE TO THE FRONT AND TO THE BACK. Musical measure 4/4.

Execute each temps lié in 2 measures, 4 times to the front and 4 times to the back.[3]

ALLEGRO

1. TEMPS LEVÉ IN FIRST, SECOND, AND FIFTH POSITIONS. Musical measure 4/4.

In first position: on the first beat, demi-plié; jump between the first and second beats, ending in demi-plié on the second beat; stretch the knees on the third and fourth beats. Repeat 1 more time; thereafter jump a third time, stretching the knees on the third beat; demi-plié on the fourth beat followed by three consecutive jumps, each on 1 beat (3 beats of a measure) and on the fourth beat stretch the knees. The whole exercise consists of 4 measures. Follow with the same execution in second and fifth positions.

2. CHANGEMENTS DE PIEDS.

Execution similar to that in temps levé.

---

[2] After several lessons, the battements relevés lents is executed to the front, to the side and to the back.

[3] An accurate descriptive breakdown of the temps lié in musical beats is referred to in my booklet "The Method of Stylish Movements" (Edition "Soviet Russia" Moscow 1961).

3. PAS ASSEMBLÉ.

Execution similar to that in the sixth lesson, 8 moving forward and 8 moving backward, each on 4 beats.

4. PAS ÉCHAPPÉ. Musical measure 4/4.

On the first beat, demi-plié; jump between the first and second beats, ending in second position demi-plié on the second beat; jump between the second and third beats, ending in fifth position demi-plié on the third beat; stretch the knees on the fourth beat.[4]

5. PAS BALANCÉ. Musical measure 3/4.

Execute 8 to 16 times.

6. PAS DE BASQUE (SCENIC FORM). Musical measure 3/4. (Waltz)

Execute 8 to 16 times.

[4] Execute changements de pieds, assemblé, and échappé without épaulement. According to the mastery of the steps during the last semester of the school year, the jumps are executed in fifth position with épaulement.

Second position on pointes.

FIRST EXAMPLE OF EXERCISES ON POINTES

1. RELEVÉS IN FIRST, SECOND, AND FIFTH POSITIONS.
Execution similar to that in the sixth lesson.

2. PAS ÉCHAPPÉ IN SECOND POSITION. 8 measures in 4/4.
First facing the barre and then, according to the degree of mastery, in the center of the studio. On the first beat, demi-plié; come up on pointes in second position on the second beat; come down in fifth position demi-plié on the third beat; stretch the knees on the fourth beat. Execute the exercise 8 times.[5]

3. PAS DE BOURRÉE SUIVI IN FIFTH POSITION. Musical measure 2/4.
First facing the barre and then, according to the degree of mastery of the movement, in the center of the studio. Demi-plié; on 2 preparatory chords, come up on pointes in fifth position. On each beat, each foot, in turn, comes off the floor and back on pointes in fifth position. Repeat the movement 16 to 32 times. Later, the tempo is accelerated and each movement is executed in 1 half beat. At the end of the school year, pas de bourrée suivi is done with a slight moving forward in a straight line or on the diagonal.

[5] Pas échappé is worked out en face; at the end of the year, épaulement is introduced in fifth position.

Leg raised in front, at the barre.

Eighth Lesson

EXERCISES AT THE BARRE

1. DEMI-PLIÉ, GRAND PLIÉ, RELEVÉ ON HALF-TOE, BATTE-MENTS TENDUS, BATTEMENTS TENDUS JETÉS, RONDS DE JAMBE À TERRE, BATTEMENTS FONDUS TO 45°, AND BATTE-MENTS FRAPPÉS.

Execution similar to that in the seventh lesson.

2. RONDS DE JAMBE EN L'AIR. 32 measures in 2/4.

En dehors. Seven ronds de jambe en l'air, each on 2 beats. Lower the working leg to fifth position on 2 beats. Take a pose effacée front in 4 measures and then a pose écartée back in another 4 measures; follow with ronds de jambe en l'air en dedans and then in 4 measures take a pose effacée back, and a pose écartée front in 4 measures.

3. PETITS BATTEMENTS SUR LE COU-DE-PIED. 8 measures in 2/4.

On the upbeat, open slightly the working foot and bring it sur le cou-de-pied back, again open slightly and bring the foot sur le cou-de-pied front. In this manner, each petit battement is executed and ended on 1 beat. Repeat the exercise 16 times.

4. BATTEMENTS DÉVELOPPÉS AND BATTEMENTS RELEVÉS LENTS TO 90°. 16 measures in 4/4.

One relevé lent to the front in 2 measures, 1 développé front on 2 beats. Continue in a similar fashion to the side, to the back and to the side.

5. GRANDS BATTEMENTS JETÉS.

Execution similar to that in the seventh lesson.

EXERCISES IN THE CENTER

1. TEMPS LIÉ À TERRE TO THE FRONT AND TO THE BACK.

2. BATTEMENTS TENDUS, BATTEMENTS TENDUS JETÉS, RONDS DE JAMBE À TERRE.

Execution similar to that in the seventh lesson.

3. BATTEMENTS FONDUS AT 45°. 8 measures in 4/4.

Two battements fondus to the front, to the side, to the back and to the side, each on 4 beats.

4. BATTEMENTS FRAPPÉS AND DOUBLES FRAPPÉS TO THE SIDE. 16 measures in 2/4.

Eight battements frappés at 45°, each on 2 beats. Four doubles frappés at 45°, each on 2 beats. In the last 4 measures, lower the working leg to fifth position and take a pose in third arabesque, pointe tendue on the floor.

5. PETITS BATTEMENTS SUR LE COU-DE-PIED. 24 measures in 2/4.

Sixteen petits battements, each on 1 beat. At the conclusion, take a pose in first and second arabesques, pointe tendue on the floor, in 8 measures.

6. BATTEMENTS DÉVELOPPÉS. 16 measures in 4/4.

Two développés to the front, to the side, to the back and to the side, each in 2 measures.

7. GRANDS BATTEMENTS JETÉS.

Execution similar to that in the exercise at the barre.

ALLEGRO

1. TEMPS LEVÉ IN FIRST, SECOND, AND FIFTH POSITIONS.

Execution similar to that in the seventh lesson.

2. PAS ASSEMBLÉ. Musical measure 4/4.

Three assemblés, each on 4 beats, in turn with the right and the left leg. Stretch the knees after the third assemblé, on the third beat; demi-plié on the fourth beat; and on 2 beats of the following measure, 2 consecutive assemblés, each on 1 beat. Stretch the knees on the third and fourth beats. Repeat the exercise once more and then in the reverse direction (backward).

3. PAS ÉCHAPPÉ. Musical measure 4/4.

On the upbeat, demi-plié and jump, ending on the first beat in second position demi-plié; jump between the first and second beats, ending in fifth position demi-plié on the second beat; stretch the knees on the third beat; on the fourth beat, demi-plié preparing for the following jump, etc. Repeat the exercise 4 to 8 times.

4. PAS JETÉ. Musical measure 4/4.

Facing the barre, then according to the mastery of the steps, in the center of the studio. Demi-plié, on the first beat; jump between the first and second beats, landing in demi-plié on 1 foot on the second beat, while the other foot is placed sur le cou-de-pied; bring the bent leg into fifth position demi-plié on the third beat and stretch the knees on the fourth beat. Repeat the exercise 4 to 8 times, moving forward and then moving backward.[1]

---

[1] Pas jeté is executed without épaulement in the first year.

5. CHANGEMENTS DE PIEDS. Musical measure 4/4.

On the upbeat, demi-plié and jump, ending in demi-plié on the first beat. Immediately from this demi-plié, make a second jump, ending on the second beat; stretch the knees on the third beat; on the fourth beat, demi-plié to execute the subsequent jumps, etc. In this manner, each changement de pied is executed on 1 beat.

SECOND EXAMPLE OF EXERCISES ON POINTES

1. RELEVÉS IN FIRST, SECOND, AND FIFTH POSITIONS.
Execution similar to that in the previous lessons.

2. PAS ÉCHAPPÉ.
Execution similar to that in the seventh lesson.

3. ASSEMBLÉ SOUTENU. Musical measure 4/4.
On the first beat, demi-plié and simultaneously extend the working leg to the side, pointe tendue on the floor; on the second beat, bring the legs together on pointes in fifth position; on the third beat, demi-plié; on the fourth beat, stretch the knees. Repeat the exercise 4 to 8 times, moving forward and then backward.

4. PAS DE BOURRÉE SUIVI IN FIFTH POSITION.
Execution similar to that in the seventh lesson.

5. PAS COURU IN FIRST POSITION TO THE FRONT AND TO THE BACK. Musical measure 2/4.
Each small step moving forward or backward is done on 1 beat, then on 1 half beat, and at the end of the school year, on 1 quarter beat.

Battement fondu at the barre.

Ninth Lesson

EXERCISES AT THE BARRE

1. GRANDS PLIÉS IN FIRST, SECOND, FOURTH, AND FIFTH POSITIONS. Musical measure 4/4.

Two grands pliés in every position, each on 4 beats.[1]

[1] In the first year, up to the end of the school year, the grand plié is executed in 1 slow measure of 4/4.

2. BATTEMENTS TENDUS IN FIFTH POSITION. 8 measures in 4/4.

Eight battements tendus front, side, and back, each on 1 beat.[2] Four battements tendus to the side, each on 1 beat. Make a half turn toward the barre, on 4 beats.

3. BATTEMENTS TENDUS JETÉS IN FIFTH POSITION. 8 measures in 4/4.

Six battements tendus jetés front, each on 1 beat; end the seventh battement in demi-plié on 2 beats. Repeat the same to the side and to the back. Four battements tendus jetés to the side, each on 1 beat, then make a half turn away from the barre on 4 beats.

4. RONDS DE JAMBE À TERRE. Musical measure 2/4.

En dehors: on 4 introductory chords, execute the preparation and follow with 8 ronds de jambe à terre, each on 1 beat. Repeat the same en dedans. In 4 measures, trace a half circle in plié en dedans and in 4 more measures, a half circle in plié en dehors, ending in fifth position. In the subsequent 8 measures, execute twice the third port de bras.

5. BATTEMENTS FONDUS AND FRAPPÉS AT 45°. 12 measures in 4/4.

Two battements fondus front, to the side, to the back and to the side, each on 4 beats. Three battements frappés to the side, each on 1 beat, and pause on the fourth beat. Repeat 2 more times and in the last measure, bring the working leg down in fifth position and rise on half-toe.[3]

6. BATTEMENTS DOUBLES FRAPPÉS. 8 measures in 2/4.

Eight doubles frappés to the front, to the side, to the back, to the side, etc., pointe tendue on the floor, each on 1 beat, and 8 doubles frappés to the side at 45°, each on 1 beat.

7. RONDS DE JAMBE EN L'AIR. 16 measures in 2/4.

Eight ronds de jambe en l'air en dehors and 8 en dedans, each on 2 beats.

---

[2] In the execution of battements tendus and battements tendus jetés on 1 beat, the strong brush of the working foot is done before the beat on the half beat, the closing of the foot in fifth or first position, on the beat.

[3] In the execution of battements frappés on 1 beat, a stroke sur le cou-de-pied is done before the beat on the half beat, stretching the working leg on the beat.

8. PETITS BATTEMENTS SUR LE COU-DE-PIED.

Execution similar to that in the eighth lesson.

9. BATTEMENTS DÉVELOPPÉS AND RELEVÉS LENTS TO 90°. 16 measures in 4/4.

One relevé lent to the front, to the side, to the back, and to the side, in 2 measures each. One developpé front, side, back, and side, in 2 measures each.

10. GRANDS BATTEMENTS JETÉS POINTÉS. 16 measures in 2/4.

Four grands battements jetés front, side, back, and side, each on 2 beats.

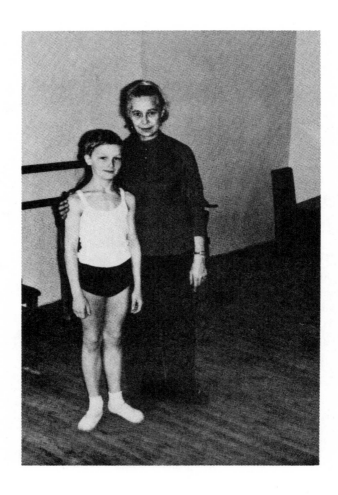

EXERCISES IN THE CENTER

1. GRAND PLIÉ, DEMI-PLIÉ, AND RELEVÉ ON HALF-TOE IN FIRST, SECOND, FOURTH, AND FIFTH POSITIONS. Musical measure 4/4.

In first position: 2 grands pliés, each on 4 beats. One demi-plié on 4 beats, and relevé on half-toe on 4 beats. Repeat the same in second, fourth, and fifth positions.

2. BATTEMENTS TENDUS AND TENDUS JETÉS IN FIFTH POSITION. 16 measures in 2/4.

Four battements tendus front, side, back, and side, each on 1 beat, and 4 battements tendus jetés front, side, back, and side, each on 1 beat.

3. RONDS DE JAMBE À TERRE.

Execution similar to that in the exercise at the barre.

4. BATTEMENTS FONDUS AND FRAPPÉS AT 45°. 8 measures in 4/4.

Two battements fondus to the front, 2 to the side, each on 4 beats; 8 battements frappés to the side, each on 1 beat. Lower the working leg in fifth position in 2 measures and take a pose croisée front with the left leg. Repeat the exercise separately in the opposite direction ending in a pose croisée back. Battements frappés are done as doubles.

5. RONDS DE JAMBE EN L'AIR. 16 measures in 2/4.

Four ronds de jambe en l'air en dehors and 4 en dedans, each on 2 beats. At the conclusion, execute a pose in first and second arabesques, pointe tendue on the floor, in 8 measures.

6. PETITS BATTEMENTS SUR LE COU-DE-PIED. 8 measures in 2/4.

Sixteen petits battements, each on 1 beat.

7. BATTEMENTS DÉVELOPPÉS AND RELEVÉS LENTS TO 90°.

Execution similar to that in the exercise at the barre.

8. GRANDS BATTEMENTS JETÉS. 8 measures in 2/4.

Two grands battements jetés front, side, back, and side, each on 2 beats.

ALLEGRO

1. TEMPS LEVÉ IN FIRST AND SECOND POSITION. Musical measure 4/4.

On the upbeat, demi-plié and jump, ending in demi-plié on the first beat; immediately execute a second jump, ending on the second beat; stretch the knees on the third beat; demi-plié to repeat the subsequent 2 jumps, etc., on the fourth beat. Repeat the exercise 4 times in first and second positions.

2. PAS ÉCHAPPÉ.

Execution similar to that in the eighth lesson.

3. PAS ASSEMBLÉ. 8 measures in 4/4.

On the upbeat, demi-plié and jump, ending on the first beat; immediately execute a second jump, ending on the second beat; stretch the knees on the third beat; repeat the subsequent 2 jumps, starting with demi-plié on the fourth beat. Repeat 4 times, starting in turn with the right foot in front or the left foot in front, then execute the whole combination in the opposite direction (backward).

4. PAS JETÉ.

Execution similar to that in the eighth lesson.

5. SISSONNE SIMPLE. Musical measure 4/4.

Facing the barre, or, according to the mastery of the step, in the center. On the first beat, demi-plié, jump between the first and second beats, ending in demi-plié on 1 leg on the second beat, the other foot is sur le cou-de-pied front or back; on the third beat, bring the foot sur le cou-de-pied in fifth position demi-plié and stretch the knees on the fourth beat. Repeat the exercise 4 times with sur le cou-de-pied front and back.

6. CHANGEMENTS DE PIEDS. 8 measures in 2/4.

Six changements de pieds on 1 beat each; stretch the knees on 1 beat, and on another beat, demi-plié; repeat the exercise once more.

THIRD EXAMPLE OF EXERCISES ON POINTES

1. RELEVÉ IN FIRST AND SECOND POSITIONS. 16 measures in 4/4.

On the upbeat, demi-plié, come up on toe; on the first beat, come down in demi-plié; on the second beat, come up on toe; on the third beat and on the fourth beat, demi-plié, etc. Repeat the exercise 8 times in first position and 8 times in second position.

2. PAS ÉCHAPPÉ. 8 measures in 2/4.

On the upbeat, demi-plié; come up on toe in second position, on the first beat; come down in fifth position demi-plié, on the second beat. Repeat échappé 2 more times; subsequently stretch the knees and come down in demi-plié, repeating once more 3 échappés, each on 2 beats.

3. ASSEMBLÉ SOUTENU. Musical measure 2/4.

On the first beat, demi-plié, simultaneously extend the working leg to the side, pointe tendue on the floor; on the second beat, join the legs together in fifth position on pointes, then, from this position, resume the following assemblé soutenu. Repeat 4 to 8 times moving forward and then moving back.

4. PAS DE BOURRÉE, CHANGING FEET EN DEHORS AND EN DE-DANS. Musical measure 2/4 or 3/4.

Execution similar to that in the same exercise on half-toe.

5. PAS DE BOURRÉE SUIVI IN FIFTH POSITION WITH A SLIGHT MOVE TO THE SIDE.

6. PAS COURU IN FIRST POSITION FRONT AND BACK ON AN ACCELERATED TEMPO.

Second Year

During this period of study, one repeats the former exercises in an increased number, stressing the development of strength in the legs and feet through exercises on half-toe and on pointes, and the coordination between the movements. Starting in the second year, the preparation of the arms opening in second position is done on two introductory chords in the exercises at the barre and in the center. The arms come down simultaneously at the end of the exercise into the preparatory position. The arms open into the second position in battements fondus, battements soutenus, and battements développés as well as in any given pose simultaneously from the beginning of the exercise.

Position à la seconde en l'air (45°).

First Semester
First Lesson

The execution of all exercises at the barre and in the center is done on the right and on the left leg.

EXERCISES AT THE BARRE

1. DEMI-PLIÉ AND GRAND PLIÉ. Musical measure 4/4.
Two demi-pliés and 2 grand pliés in first, second, fourth, and fifth positions, each on 4 beats.

2. BATTEMENTS TENDUS AND BATTEMENTS TENDUS JETÉS. 32 measures in 2/4.

Eight battements tendus front, side, back, and side, each on 1 beat, and 8 battements tendus jetés in the same directions, each on 1 beat.

3. RONDS DE JAMBE À TERRE AND RONDS DE JAMBE EN L'AIR. 12 measures in 4/4.

On 2 introductory chords, préparation en dehors. Eight ronds de jambe à terre and 8 ronds de jambe en l'air en dehors, each on 1 beat. Repeat the same en dedans. In 2 measures, make a half circle in plié en dedans and en dehors, and in 2 measures a third port de bras in deep plié, bending the body forward and back.

4. BATTEMENTS FONDUS, BATTEMENTS FRAPPÉS, AND DOUBLE FRAPPÉS AT 45°.[1] 16 measures in 2/4.

Two battements fondus front, side, back, and side, each on 2 beats; 7 battements frappés to the side, each on 1 beat and on the last beat, maintain the position (pause); 7 doubles frappés to the side, each on 1 beat, maintain the position (pause).

5. PETITS BATTEMENTS SUR LE COU-DE-PIED. 16 measures in 2/4.

Eight petits battements with accent to the front (stop) and 8 with the accent to the back, each on 1 beat. Repeat once more.

6. BATTEMENTS RELEVÉS LENTS TO 90°. 16 measures in 4/4.

Two relevés lents in effacé position front, 2 to the side, 2 in effacé position back, 2 to the side, each in 2 measures.

7. GRANDS BATTEMENTS JETÉS. 8 measures in 2/4.

Four battements jetés to the front, to the side, to the back and to the side, each on 1 beat.

8. STUDY OF SMALL POSES IN CROISÉ, EFFACÉ AND ÉCARTÉ FRONT AND BACK, POINTE TENDUE ON THE FLOOR, ON A STRETCHED SUPPORTING LEG AND ALSO IN PLIÉ.

---

[1] In the second year, battements fondus start directly from fifth position.

EXERCISES IN THE CENTER

1. DEMI-PLIÉS AND GRANDS PLIÉS.

Execution similar to that in the exercise at the barre.

2. BATTEMENTS TENDUS AND BATTEMENTS TENDUS JETÉS. 16 measures in 2/4.

Eight battements tendus in a small pose croisée front (right foot); 8 battements tendus in a small pose croisée back (left foot); 8 to the side (right foot), each on 1 beat, and again 8 battements tendus to the side, each on 1 beat.

3. RONDS DE JAMBE À TERRE. 8 measures in 4/4.

On 2 introductory chords, préparation en dehors. Eight ronds de jambe à terre en dehors and 8 en dedans, each on 1 beat; follow with a half circle in plié and port de bras as described in the exercise at the barre.

4. BATTEMENTS FONDUS AND BATTEMENTS FRAPPÉS AT 45°. 16 measures in 2/4.

Two battements fondus front, side, back, and side, each on 2 beats. Eight frappés to the side, each on 1 beat; in 4 measures, a small pose in croisée front plié, pointe tendue on the floor.

5. BATTEMENTS DOUBLES FRAPPÉS. 8 measures in 2/4.

Twelve doubles frappés on the floor, each on 1 beat, to the front, to the side, to the back and end in a small pose croisée back, pointe tendue on the floor in plié.

6. BATTEMENTS RELEVÉS LENTS AND DÉVELOPPÉS TO 90°. 16 measures in 4/4.

Two relevés lents in the pose effacée front (right leg), 2 in the pose effacée back (left leg), each in 2 measures. Four battements développés to the side (right leg), each in 2 measures.

In the second year, the battement développé is broken down in musical parts in the following manner: First measure: on the first beat, raise the working leg pointe tendue to the knee; on the second beat, extend the leg in the given direction; on the third and fourth beats, maintain the position. Second measure: on the first and second beats, maintain the position; on the third and fourth beats, lower the leg to the starting position.

7. GRANDS BATTEMENTS JETÉS.
Execution similar to that in the exercise at the barre.[2]

ALLEGRO

1. PAS ASSEMBLÉ. 8 measures in 4/4.
Two assemblés front to the side (changing feet), each on 2 beats; on the second beat, stay still in plié; 2 assemblés, each on 1 beat; stretch the legs on 1 beat, and on 1 beat, demi-plié. Repeat once more and follow in the reverse direction.

2. PETITS ÉCHAPPÉS IN SECOND AND FOURTH POSITIONS. 8 measures in 2/4.
On 2 beats, échappé in fourth position croisée; on 2 beats, échappé in second position, changing feet. Repeat 4 times.

3. PAS JETÉ. 16 measures in 4/4.
On the upbeat, demi-plié and jump, brushing the foot and throwing the leg out to the side, landing on one leg, the other sur le cou-de-pied; on the first beat, come down in demi-plié; on the second beat, bring the foot down to fifth position from sur le cou-de-pied, in demi-plié; on the third beat, stretch the knees; on the fourth beat demi-plié for the subsequent jump. Repeat the exercise 8 times, first with sur le cou-de-pied back and 8 times with sur le cou-de-pied front, with the right leg and the left leg in turn.

4. TEMPS LEVÉS IN FIRST AND SECOND POSITIONS. 4 measures in 4/4.
Eight temps levés in first position and 8 in second position, each on 1 beat.[3]

[2] In the second year, during the exercises in the center, it is sometimes permissible to omit exercises such as petits battements sur le cou-de-pied, ronds de jambe en l'air, and grands battements jetés. One may omit only one such exercise, but it must be included in the following lesson without fail.

[3] It is recommended that all lessons be concluded with the port de bras from first position, bending the body, or with the fourth and fifth port de bras.

FIRST EXAMPLE OF EXERCISES ON POINTES[4]

1. RELEVÉ IN FIRST, SECOND, AND FOURTH POSITIONS. Musical measure 2/4.

Sixteen relevés in first and second positions. Eight relevés in fourth position croisée (first with the right foot front, then with the left foot front) each on 2 beats.

2. PAS ÉCHAPPÉ IN SECOND AND FOURTH POSITIONS. 16 measures in 2/4.

Three échappés in fourth position croisée, 1 in second position, changing feet, each on 2 beats. Repeat 4 times.

3. DOUBLE ÉCHAPPÉ. 8 measures in 4/4.

Eight doubles échappés, coming down on the heel in second position, each on 4 beats.

4. ASSEMBLÉ SOUTENU ENDING IN A SMALL POSE CROISÉE. 16 measures in 2/4.

Eight to the front and 8 to the back, each on 2 beats.

5. PAS DE BOURRÉE SUIVI TRAVELING ON THE DIAGONAL. 16 measures in 2/4.

Execute on half a beat.

6. PAS COURU ON THE DIAGONAL TO THE FRONT AND TO THE BACK. Musical measure 2/4.

Execute on 1 quarter beat.

[4] In the second year, just as in the senior classes, exercise on pointes twice a week is recommended in place of the allegro.

Position croisée front, pointe tendue on the floor.

Second Lesson

EXERCISES AT THE BARRE

1. GRANDS PLIÉS. Musical measure 4/4.
Two grands pliés and 2 demi-pliés with relevé on half-toe, in all positions, each on 4 beats.

2. BATTEMENTS TENDUS AND BATTEMENTS TENDUS JETÉS. 16 measures in 4/4.
Eight battements tendus in a big pose effacée front, 8 in a big pose écartée back, 8 in a big pose effacée back and 8 in a big pose écartée

front, each on 1 beat. Eight battements tendus jetés front, side, back and 4 to the side, each on 1 beat, and on 4 beats, half a turn toward the barre, in fifth position on half-toe.*

3. RONDS DE JAMBE À TERRE. 12 measures in 4/4.

On 2 introductory chords, préparation en dehors. Eight ronds de jambe à terre, each on 1 beat; on the eighth rond de jambe, stay still, the foot in front, pointe tendue. In 2 measures, relevé front to 45° and demi rond de jambe en dehors, ending to the side, pointe tendue on the floor. From this position, continue with ronds de jambe à terre en dedans, relevé back to 45° with demi rond de jambe en dedans. In 4 measures, trace a half circle back in plié and follow with the port de bras. Execute in a manner similar to that described in the first lesson.

4. BATTEMENTS FONDUS AT 45°. 16 measures in 2/4.

On 2 beats, fondu front; on 2 beats, plié-relevé. Repeat once more and continue the same to the side, to the back and to the side. At the conclusion, make a half turn away from the barre in fifth position half toe, in 2 measures.

5. BATTEMENTS FRAPPÉS AT 45° ON HALF-TOE. 16 measures in 2/4.

Starting position: the working leg is open to the side at 45°. Six battements frappés, each on 1 beat; come up on half-toe on 2 beats. Six battements frappés, each on 1 beat on half-toe; come down on the flat foot on 2 beats. Repeat the exercise.

6. BATTEMENTS DOUBLES FRAPPÉS AT 45° ON HALF-TOE.

Execution similar to that in the ordinary frappés.

7. RONDS DE JAMBE EN L'AIR. Musical measure 4/4.

On 4 introductory chords, préparation temps relevé en dehors at 45°, on the flat foot. Eight ronds de jambe en l'air, each on 1 beat, and in 2 measures, a small pose écartée to the back in plié, pointe tendue on the floor. Repeat en dedans.

8. PETITS BATTEMENTS SUR LE COU-DE-PIED. 8 measures in 4/4.

Eight petits battements, each on 1 beat, and in 2 measures, a small pose in effacé front plié, pointe tendue on the floor. Repeat the petits battements and end in effacé back plié.

---

* TRANSLATOR'S NOTE: As indicated in lesson three of the first year (exercise 8 in the center), the arm position in a big pose is one arm in third arm position with the other in first or second arm position.

9. BATTEMENTS DÉVELOPPÉS. 16 measures in 4/4.

Two développés in a big pose effacée front, 2 to the side, 2 in a big pose effacée back, and 2 to the side, each in 2 measures.

10. GRANDS BATTEMENTS JETÉS POINTÉS. 8 measures in 2/4.

Three grands battements jetés pointés and 1 in fifth position front; continue same to the side, to the back and to the side, each on 1 beat.

11. TOMBÉ AND COUPÉ ON HALF-TOE. Musical measure 4/4.

Préparation: open the right leg to the side at 45°. On the first beat, tombé on the right foot in demi-plié fifth position, bring the left foot sur le cou-de-pied back or front; on the second beat, come up on half toe of the left foot (coupé), simultaneously open the right leg to the side at 45°; on the third and fourth beats, maintain the position.

EXERCISES IN THE CENTER

1. GRAND PLIÉ AND DEMI-PLIÉ WITH RELEVÉ ON HALF-TOE.

Execution similar to that in the exercise at the barre.

2. BATTEMENTS TENDUS AND BATTEMENTS TENDUS JETÉS. 16 measures in 2/4.

Four battements tendus in the small pose effacée front, 4 to the side, 4 battements tendus in the small pose effacée back, and 4 to the side, each on 1 beat. Execute in a similar manner the battements tendus jetés.

3. BATTEMENTS FONDUS AT 45° AND PORT DE BRAS. 16 measures in 2/4.

On 2 beats, battement fondu front; on 2 beats, plié-relevé. Continue the same to the side, to the back and to the side. At the conclusion, step forward to fifth position half-toe, raising the arms to third position (arm position), to the count of 2 measures. Repeat another step forward and come down in straight fifth position and in 2 measures, execute a third port de bras.

4. RONDS DE JAMBE EN L'AIR. 4 measures in 4/4.

Eight ronds de jambe en l'air en dehors, each on 1 beat, and in 2 measures, plié in the small pose effacée front, pointe tendue on the floor. Execute separately en dedans with a small pose in effacée back.

5. PETITS BATTEMENTS SUR LE COU-DE-PIED. 16 measures in 2/4.

Fourteen petits battements, each on 1 beat; on 2 beats, lower the supporting leg in plié with épaulement croisé while bringing the left foot sur le cou-de-pied back; continue with 8 pas de bourrée en dehors (changing feet), each on 2 beats. Repeat the petits battements on the other leg; subsequently repeat once more on the right leg with pas de bourrée en dedans.

6. PAS DE BOURRÉE WITHOUT CHANGING FEET FROM SIDE TO SIDE.[1]

Study first in 4/4, then in 3/4 and 2/4, each pas de bourrée.

7. BATTEMENTS DÉVELOPPÉS.

Execution similar to that in the exercise at the barre.

8. TEMPS LIÉ WITH BENDING OF THE BODY.

Execute 4 times front and 4 times back, in 4 measures, of 4/4 each.

ALLEGRO

1. PAS ASSEMBLÉ. 8 measures in 4/4.

Two assemblés to the side, moving forward and changing feet, each on 1 beat; on 1 beat, stretch the knees; on 1 beat, demi-plié for the subsequent jump. Repeat 4 times and follow same in the reverse direction.

2. PAS ASSEMBLÉ FORWARD AND BACKWARD.

Study the same way as in assemblé to the side.

3. PETIT ÉCHAPPÉ IN SECOND AND FOURTH POSITIONS. 8 measures in 4/4.

On 2 beats, échappé in fourth position effacée, changing feet; 2 échappés in second position, changing feet, each on 2 beats. On the subsequent 2 beats, stretch the knees and continue with demi-plié for the following échappés, starting on the other leg. Repeat 4 times.

---

[1] Each pas de bourrée ends pointe tendue on the floor; at the end of the first six months, at 45°.

4. PAS JETÉ ENDING IN A SMALL POSE CROISÉE. 16 measures in 2/4.

First measure: on the upbeat, demi-plié and jump, ending in a small pose croisée (sur le cou-de-pied back) on the first beat; on the second beat, maintain the position. Second measure: repeat the jeté on the other leg. Third measure: from the position, sur le cou-de-pied, bring the foot in fifth position demi-plié. Fourth measure: stretch the knees. Repeat 4 times and then in the reverse direction.

5. PETITS CHANGEMENTS DE PIEDS. 8 measures in 4/4.

On the first and second beats, 2 changements de pieds; on the third beat, stretch the knees; on the fourth beat, demi-plié preparing for the following jumps. Repeat 8 times.

6. TEMPS LEVÉ IN FIRST AND SECOND POSITIONS. 4 measures in 4/4.

Eight temps levé in first position and 8 in second position, each on 1 beat.

SECOND EXAMPLE OF EXERCISES ON POINTES

1. RELEVÉ IN FIRST, SECOND, AND FOURTH POSITIONS. Musical measure 2/4.

Eight relevés in first and second positions. Eight relevés in fourth position effacée (on the right and left leg), each on 2 beats.

2. RELEVÉ AND ÉCHAPPÉ. 16 measures in 2/4.

Three relevés in fifth position, each on 2 beats; on 2 beats, échappé in second position, changing feet. Repeat 4 times.

3. ÉCHAPPÉ IN SECOND AND FOURTH POSITIONS. 16 measures in 2/4.

One échappé in fourth position croisée, 1 in fourth position effacée and 2 échappés in second position, changing feet, each on 2 beats. Repeat 4 times.

4. PAS DE BOURRÉE EN DEHORS AND EN DEDANS, CHANGING FEET AND ENDING IN A SMALL POSE CROISÉE.

Execute each pas de bourrée in 3/4 or 2/4.

5. PAS DE BOURRÉE FROM SIDE TO SIDE WITHOUT CHANGING FEET AND ENDING POINTE TENDUE ON THE FLOOR.

Execute each pas de bourrée in 3/4 or 2/4.

6. GLISSADE TO THE SIDE. Musical measure 4/4.

Fifth position, right foot front. On the first beat, demi-plié, simultaneously brush the right foot to the side, pointe tendue on the floor. On the second beat, step on the right foot (sur les pointes); simultaneously slide the left foot to fifth position. On the third beat, demi-plié; on the fourth beat, stretch the knees.[2] Execute the exercise changing feet and without changing feet.

7. PAS DE BOURRÉE SUIVI AND PAS COURU TRAVELING ON THE DIAGONAL.

Execution similar to that in the first example of exercises on pointes in the first lesson.

[2] According to the mastery of the exercise, glissade is worked out forward as well as backward.

Position à la seconde (120°).

Third Lesson

EXERCISES AT THE BARRE

1. GRAND PLIÉ AND RELEVÉ ON HALF-TOE. Musical measure 4/4.

Two grands pliés and 2 relevés on half-toe in first, second, fourth, and fifth positions, each on 4 beats.

2. BATTEMENTS TENDUS. 8 measures in 4/4.

Four battements tendus front, each on 1 beat; 2 battements tendus doubles to the side, each on 2 beats. Execute in the reverse direction and repeat once more.

3. BATTEMENTS TENDUS JETÉS. 16 measures in 2/4.

Two battements tendus jetés front, each on 1 beat, 3 on half a beat each; on the fourth half beat, stand still. Repeat once more and continue the same to the side, to the back, and to the side.

4. RONDS DE JAMBE À TERRE. 12 measures in 4/4.

On 2 introductory chords, préparation en dehors. Eight ronds de jambe à terre, each on 1 beat. In 2 measures, relevé lent to the front to 90°. Repeat ronds de jambe à terre en dedans and relevé lent to the back to 90°. In 2 measures, trace a half circle in plié en dedans and en dehors; in 2 measures, port de bras in deep plié, bending the body forward and backward.

5. BATTEMENTS FONDUS AT 45° AND BATTEMENTS FRAPPÉS AT 45° ON HALF-TOE. 16 measures in 2/4.

One battement fondu front, side, back, and side on the flat foot, each on 2 beats. Repeat the same on half-toe. Remaining on half-toe, execute 8 frappés to the side, each on 1 beat, and in 4 measures, take a small pose in effacée front, pointe tendue on the floor, in plié.

6. RONDS DE JAMBE EN L'AIR ON HALF-TOE. 16 measures in 2/4.

On 2 introductory chords, préparation temps relevé en dehors on the flat foot to 45°. Six ronds de jambe en l'air, each on 1 beat; on 2 beats, come up on half-toe. Six ronds de jambe en l'air on half-toe, each on 1 beat; on 2 beats, come down on the flat foot. Repeat all en dedans.

7. PETITS BATTEMENTS SUR LE COU-DE-PIED ON HALF-TOE. 16 measures in 2/4.

Twelve petits battements, each on 1 beat; come up on half-toe to the count of 2 measures; 8 petits battements on half-toe and take a small pose in effacé back plié, pointe tendue on the floor to the count of 4 measures.

8. BATTEMENTS DÉVELOPPÉS PASSÉ. 16 measures in 4/4.

First measure: développé front. Second measure: passé at 90°. Third measure: développé front. Fourth measure: bring the working leg down in fifth position. Repeat the same to the side, to the back, and to the side.

9. ATTITUDE EFFACÉE, ATTITUDE CROISÉE, AND SECOND ARABESQUE. Musical measure 4/4.

The attitudes and arabesque poses are studied in the beginning by means of relevés to 90°; and later on through développés to the count of 2 measures for each pose.

10. GRANDS BATTEMENTS JETÉS. 8 measures in 2/4.

Two grands battements jetés front, side, back, and side, each on 1 beat. Repeat once more.

EXERCISES IN THE CENTER

1. TEMPS LIÉ WITH BENDING OF THE BODY. 32 measures in 4/4.

Four times front, 4 times back, to the count of 4 measures each.

2. BATTEMENTS TENDUS AND BATTEMENTS TENDUS JETÉS. 16 measures in 2/4.

Right foot front, 4 battements tendus and 4 battements tendus jetés in a big pose croisée front, each on 1 beat. Left foot back, 4 battements tendus and 4 battements tendus jetés in a big pose croisée back, each on 1 beat. Eight battements tendus and 8 battements tendus jetés to the side (right foot), each on 1 beat.

3. RONDS DE JAMBE À TERRE AND RONDS DE JAMBE EN L'AIR. 12 measures in 4/4.

On 2 introductory chords, préparation en dehors. Eight ronds de jambe à terre, 8 ronds de jambe en l'air en dehors, each on 1 beat; 8 ronds de jambe à terre and 8 ronds de jambe en l'air en dedans, each on 1 beat. In 2 measures, trace a half circle in plié en dedans and en dehors; in 2 measures, port de bras in deep plié, bending the body in épaulement croisé.

4. BATTEMENTS FONDUS AND BATTEMENTS FRAPPÉS AT 45°. 8 measures in 4/4.

On 2 beats, battement fondu front; on 2 beats, plié relevé; repeat the same to the side, to the back and to the side. Eight frappés to the side, each on 1 beat; 4 doubles frappés, each on 1 beat; on 4 beats, bring the working leg down to fifth position back in plié and from fifth position plié, make a full turn changing feet (détourné) (right foot front) and raising the arms in third (arm) position at the end of the exercise.

5. PETITS BATTEMENTS SUR LE COU-DE-PIED. 16 measures in 2/4.

Fourteen petits battements, each on 1 beat; on 2 beats, tombé in fifth position onto the working right leg; simultaneously open the left leg to the side, pointe tendue on the floor (dégagé) and continue with 8 pas de bourrée without changing feet from side to side, each on 2 beats.

6. GRANDS BATTEMENTS JETÉS POINTÉS. 8 measures in 2/4.

Three grands battements jetés pointés and 1 closing in fifth position front; continue the same to the side, to the back, and to the side, each on 1 beat.

7. RELEVÉ TO 90° IN FIRST, SECOND, AND THIRD ARABESQUE. 24 measures in 4/4.

Two relevés in each arabesque position, in 4 measures each. First measure: releve to 90°. Second measure: maintain the position. Third measure: lower the leg gently. Fourth measure: maintain the position in first or fifth.

8. FIFTH PORT DE BRAS. Musical measure 4/4 or 3/4 (Waltz).

Study to the count of 2 measures of 4/4 each or to 8 measures of a waltz.

9. PAS DE BOURRÉE BALLOTTÉ IN EFFACÉ AND CROISÉ, POINTE TENDUE ON THE FLOOR.

Study to the count of 4/4 or 2/4.

ALLEGRO

1. PAS ASSEMBLÉ. 4 measures in 2/4.

Eight assemblés to the side, moving forward (changing feet), then separately 8 assemblés back (changing feet) each on 1 beat.

2. DOUBLE ASSEMBLÉ. 8 measures in 4/4.

On the first and second beats, double assemblé; on the third beat, stretch the knees; on the fourth beat, demi-plié, in order to repeat the subsequent double assemblé. Repeat 4 times; execute also in the reverse direction.

3. PAS JETÉ. 16 measures in 2/4.

Two jetés (with a hold) sur le cou-de-pied back, each on 1 beat; on the subsequent 2 beats, bring the foot in fifth position demi-plié, down from sur le cou-de-pied position, stretch the knees, and again demi-plié for the subsequent jetés. Repeat 4 times; execute also in the reverse direction.

4. SISSONNE OUVERTE TO THE SIDE, POINTE TENDUE ON THE FLOOR. Musical measure 4/4.

a) On the first beat, demi-plié; jump between the first and second beats, ending in demi-plié on the second beat; on the third and fourth beats, the leg opens to the side, pointe tendue on the floor, closes in fifth position demi-plié, subsequently stretching the knees.

b) On the first beat, demi-plié; jump between the first and second beats, ending in demi-plié on the second beat; between the second and third beats, assemblé, ending on the third beat; on the fourth beat, stretch the knees.[1] Repeat 4 times, opening the foot through sur le cou-de-pied front and 4 times opening the foot through sur le cou-de-pied back.

5. GRANDS CHANGEMENTS DE PIEDS. Musical measure 4/4.

On the first beat, demi-plié; jump between the first and second beats, ending on the second beat; on the third and fourth beats, stretch the knees.[2] Repeat the exercise 4 to 8 times.

6. TEMPS LEVÉ IN FIRST AND SECOND POSITIONS. 4 measures in 4/4.

Eight temps levé in first and 8 temps levé in second position, each on 1 beat. Starting with this lesson, executing the temps levé with a big jump is recommended.

7. PETITS CHANGEMENTS DE PIEDS. 8 measures in 2/4.

Six changements de pieds, each on 1 beat; on 2 beats, stretch the knees, demi-plié and repeat the jumps once more.

8. SISSONNES IN FIRST AND SECOND ARABESQUES (SCENIC FORM). Musical measure 3/4 (Waltz).

Execute on the diagonal from corner 6 to corner 2 and from corner 4 to corner 8.

---

[1] After two or three lessons, one learns the sissonne ouverte to the front and to the back as well.

[2] At the beginning, one learns en face, then with épaulement.

THIRD EXAMPLE OF EXERCISES ON POINTES

1. RELEVÉ IN FIRST, SECOND, AND FOURTH POSITIONS.
Execution similar to that in the second lesson.

2. PAS ÉCHAPPÉ. 16 measures in 2/4.
Four échappés in second position, changing feet, each on 2 beats; 2 doubles échappés, each in 2 measures. Repeat once more.

3. SUS-SOUS FRONT AND BACK. Musical measure 4/4.
On the first beat, demi-plié; on the second beat, spring onto pointes in fifth position, traveling forward; on the third beat, come down in demi-plié; on the fourth beat, stretch the knees. Repeat the exercise 8 times forward and 8 times backward in small croisé poses.[3]

4. GLISSADES IN ALL DIRECTIONS AND IN SMALL CROISÉ AND EFFACÉ POSES FRONT AND BACK. Musical measure 4/4 or 2/4.
a) On the first beat, demi-plié in fifth position; on the second beat, glissade to the given direction; on the third beat, come down in demi-plié; on the fourth beat, stretch the knees.

b) On the upbeat, demi-plié; on the first beat, glissade; on the second beat, demi-plié, etc.

5. TURNING IN FIFTH POSITION ON ONE SPOT (PAS DE BOUR-RÉE SUIVI EN TOURNANT)

6. PAS DE BOURRÉE SUIVI AND PAS COURU TRAVELING IN A STRAIGHT LINE, TO THE SIDE AND ON THE DIAGONAL.

---

[3] Toward the end of the first six-month course, sus-sous is done on 2 beats: on the upbeat, demi-plié; on the first beat, fifth position sur les pointes; on the second beat, demi-plié, etc.

Fifth position on pointes—sus-sous.

Fourth Lesson

Beginning with this lesson, execute the battements fondus, frappés, doubles frappés, ronds de jambe en l'air, and petits battements sur le cou-de-pied on half-toe at the barre. Execute the battements frappés and double frappés from the starting position on half-toe, with the working leg opened to the side at 45°, while the supporting leg simultaneously comes up on half-toe.

EXERCISES AT THE BARRE

1. GRAND PLIÉ AND RELEVÉ ON HALF-TOE. Musical measure 4/4.
One grand plié, 1 relevé on half-toe, each on 1 beat, twice in all positions.

2. BATTEMENTS TENDUS AND BATTEMENTS TENDUS JETÉS. 24 measures in 4/4.

Six battements tendus to the front, each on 1 beat, demi-plié on the sixth battement tendu, and on 2 beats, from fifth position, make a half turn on demi-pointes toward the barre, ending in demi-plié. Six battements tendus to the back, each on 1 beat, demi-plié on the sixth battement tendu, and on 2 beats, from fifth position, make a half turn on half-toe toward the barre, ending in demi-plié. Eight battements tendus doubles to the side, each on 2 beats. Repeat the whole exercise in the reverse direction with half turns on half-toe away from the barre; continue with tendus jetés: 4 on 1 beat each, 3 and another 3 on half a beat each (on the fourth half beat, hold the position) to the front, to the side, to the back, and to the side.

3. RONDS DE JAMBE À TERRE. 12 measures in 4/4.

On 2 introductory chords, préparation en dehors. Six ronds de jambe à terre, each on 1 beat and follow with préparation en dehors on 2 beats. Repeat once more; subsequently, execute the same en dedans, ending the last rond de jambe in fifth position front. In 4 measures, execute the third port de bras twice.

4. BATTEMENTS FONDUS AND BATTEMENTS FRAPPÉS AT 45°. 32 measures in 2/4.

Three battements fondus to the front, each on 2 beats; plié-relevé with demi-rond en dehors, on 2 beats. Two fondus to the side on 2 beats each and in 2 measures, tombé-coupé. Repeat the same in the reverse direction (back) and continue with 4 frappés to the front, to the side, to the back, and to the side, each on 1 beat. Then in 8 measures: a half turn toward the barre in fifth position, half-toe, ending in épaulement effacé and bring the arm up in third arm position. Follow further by lowering the arm in the preparatory arm position while making a small pose in effacée, plié, pointe tendue on the floor.

5. RONDS DE JAMBE EN L'AIR. 8 measures in 4/4.

On 2 introductory chords, préparation temps relevé en dehors on half-toe. Eight ronds de jambe en l'air, on 1 beat each; on 2 beats, carry the working leg front at 45°; on 2 beats to the side; on 2 beats to the back and on 2 beats to the side. Repeat the same en dedans.

6. PETITS BATTEMENTS SUR LE COU-DE-PIED. 16 measures in 2/4.

Eight petits battements with accent and stop to the front, 8 with accent and stop to the back, each on 1 beat. In 4 measures, second arabesque plié, pointe tendue on the floor; in 4 measures, relevé to 90° in second arabesque.

7. BATTEMENTS DÉVELOPPÉS. 16 measures in 4/4.

First measure: développé front. Second measure: demi-rond de jambe en dehors to the side. Third measure: passé at 90° to the pose attitude effacée. Fourth measure: maintain the position for 2 beats and lower the leg in fifth position on 2 beats. Repeat the same in the reverse direction: développé to the back, demi-rond de jambe en dedans to the side, passé at 90° to the pose attitude effacée front. Repeat the whole combination once more.

8. GRANDS BATTEMENTS JETÉS. 8 measures in 4/4.

Eight grands battements in effacé front, 8 to the side, 8 in effacé back and 8 to the side, each on 1 beat.

EXERCISES IN THE CENTER

1. GRANDS PLIÉS AND RELEVÉS LENTS TO 90°. 20 measures in 4/4.

Two grands pliés in first position, each on 4 beats; in 2 measures, relevé lent to 90° front. Repeat 2 grands pliés in first position and relevé lent to 90° back. Two grands pliés in second position and 2 relevés on half toe, each on 4 beats. Two grands pliés in fourth position croisée and 2 relevés on half-toe, each on 4 beats. Two grands pliés in fifth position on 4 beats each, and in 2 measures, relevé lent to 90° to the side.

2. BATTEMENTS TENDUS AND BATTEMENTS TENDUS JETÉS. 16 measures in 2/4.

Four battements tendus and 4 battements tendus jetés in a big pose effacée front, each on 1 beat. Repeat the same in écarté back, effacé back, and écarté front.

3. BATTEMENTS FONDUS AND BATTEMENTS FRAPPÉS AT 45°. 16 measures in 2/4.

Two battements fondus in a small pose croisée front, 2 to the side, 2 in a small pose croisée back and 2 to the side, each on 2 beats. Frappés: 2 to the front, to the side, to the back and to the side, each on 1 beat;

4 doubles frappés to the side, on 1 beat each and in 2 measures, bring the working leg to fifth position back in demi-plié and follow with relevé on half-toe with épaulement croisé; raise the left arm to the third arm position and the right arm to first arm position.

4. RONDS DE JAMBE EN L'AIR. 8 measures in 2/4.

On 2 introductory chords, préparation temps relevé en dehors. Eight ronds de jambe en l'air, each on 1 beat and in 4 measures, développé in attitude croisée. Execute separately the ronds de jambe en dedans, and développé in attitude effacée.

5. PETITS BATTEMENTS SUR LE COU-DE-PIED. 16 measures in 2/4.

Fifteen petits battements, each on 1 beat; on 1 beat, tombé on the working leg in fifth position demi-plié, and bend the other leg sur le cou-de-pied back. In 8 measures execute 4 pas de bourrée ballotté in effacé pointe tendue on the floor.

6. GRANDS BATTEMENTS JETÉS. 4 measures in 4/4.

Four grands battements jetés in effacé front, 4 to the side, 4 in effacé back and 4 to the side, each on 1 beat.

Instructor correcting the leg raised in croisé front (90°).

7. BATTEMENTS DÉVELOPPÉS. 8 measures in 4/4.

In 2 measures, développé croisé front; in 2 measures, développé effacé front; in 2 measures, développé to the side and in 2 measures, développé into third arabesque.

8. FOURTH PORT DE BRAS. Musical measure 4/4 or 3/4 (Waltz).

Study this exercise in 2 measures of 4/4 each or in 8 measures of a waltz.

ALLEGRO

1. PAS ASSEMBLÉ AND DOUBLE ASSEMBLÉ. 8 measures in 2/4.

Four assemblés to the side moving front, changing feet, each on 1 beat; 2 doubles assemblés, each on 2 beats. Repeat once more and execute in the reverse direction.

2. PAS JETÉ. 8 measures in 2/4.

On 1 beat, jeté to the side, ending in a small pose croisée; on 1 beat, assemblé croisé back. Repeat 8 times and execute in the reverse direction.

3. SISSONNE OUVERTE, POINTE TENDUE ON THE FLOOR. 8 measures in 4/4.

On the upbeat, demi-plié and sissonne ouverte in the small pose croisée front, ending on the first beat; assemblé between the first and second beats, ending on the second beat; on the third beat, stretch the knees; on the fourth beat, demi-plié for the subsequent sissonne ouverte. In this manner, execute 3 sissonnes ouvertes in croisé front and 1 to the side, changing feet. Repeat the same on the other leg and execute the whole exercise in the reverse direction.

4. GLISSADE TO THE SIDE. Musical measure 4/4.

a) Fifth position, right foot front. On the first beat, demi-plié; simultaneously extend the right leg to the side, pointe tendue on the floor; jump between the first and second beats, ending in demi-plié on the second beat, right foot front; on the third and fourth beats, stretch the knees.

b) On the first beat, demi-plié in fifth position; jump between the first and second beats, ending on the second beat; on the third and fourth beats, stretch the knees.[1]

5. PAS ÉCHAPPÉ IN SECOND POSITION LANDING ON ONE LEG. Musical measure 4/4.

a) Fifth position, right foot front. On the first beat, demi-plié; jump between the first and second beats, ending in second position demi-plié on the second beat; jump on the second and third beats, landing on the left leg demi-plié on the third beat, the right foot sur le cou-de-pied back; on the fourth beat, bring the right foot in fifth position and stretch the knees. Study also landing on one leg with the other foot sur le cou-de-pied front.

b) On the upbeat, demi-plié and jump, ending in second position on the first beat; on the second beat, jump, landing on one leg; on the third beat, assemblé; stretch the knees between the third and fourth beats and on the fourth beat, demi-plié for the subsequent jump.

6. GRAND ÉCHAPPÉ IN SECOND POSITION. Musical measure 4/4.

On the first beat, demi-plié; jump between the first and second beats, ending in second position demi-plié on the second beat; jump between the second and third beats, ending in fifth position demi-plié on the third beat; on the fourth beat, stretch the knees. Repeat the exercise 4 to 8 times.

7. GRANDS CHANGEMENTS DE PIEDS.

Execution similar to that in the third lesson.

8. PETITS CHANGEMENTS DE PIEDS. 8 measures in 2/4.

Sixteen changements de pieds, each on 1 beat.

9. BALANCÉ EN TOURNANT IN A QUARTER TURN. Musical measure 3/4 (waltz).

Four balancés en face, facing front, 4 en tournant, each on a quarter turn. Repeat once more and execute on the other leg.

---

[1] Study the glissade to the side with and without the change of feet. After a few lessons, begin studying the glissade to the front and to the back; thereafter in the small pose croisée and effacée. At the end of the six-month course, begin the glissade on the upbeat and execute each on 1 beat.

FOURTH EXAMPLE OF EXERCISES ON POINTES

1. RELEVÉ IN FIRST AND SECOND POSITIONS. 16 measures in 2/4.

Eight relevés in first and 8 relevés in second position, each on 2 beats.

2. DOUBLE ÉCHAPPÉ. 16 measures in 4/4.

Three doubles échappés in fourth position croisée, 1 double échappé in second position, changing feet, each on 4 beats. Execute the same on the other leg, and repeat the whole exercise once more.

3. TEMPS LIÉ. Musical measure 2/4 or 3/4 (Waltz).

Four temps liés to the front and 4 to the back, each in 2 measures of 2/4 or 4 measures of a waltz.[2]

4. PAS ÉCHAPPÉ IN SECOND POSITION, ENDING ON ONE LEG.[3] Musical measure 4/4.

Fifth position, right foot front. On the upbeat, demi-plié and échappé in second position on the first beat; on the second beat, demi-plié in second position; on the third beat, come up on pointe (left foot) with the right foot sur le cou-de-pied back; on the fourth beat, demi-plié in fifth position. Study the exercise in the same way on one foot, with the other sur le cou-de-pied front.

5. PAS DE BOURRÉE BALLOTTÉ IN CROISÉ AND EFFACÉ, POINTE TENDUE ON THE FLOOR.

Execute each step in 2/4.

6. PAS DE BOURRÉE SUIVI IN A STRAIGHT LINE AND ON THE DIAGONAL.

Execute the step on the half beat.

[2] Temps lié is composed of 2 glissades, each executed in 2/4.
[3] Study, facing the barre, then, after a few lessons, in the center, ending on one leg in small poses croisées back and front.

Pose écartée back, pointe tendue on the floor.

Second Semester
Fifth Lesson

EXERCISES AT THE BARRE

1. TWO DEMI-PLIÉS AND TWO GRANDS PLIÉS IN FIRST, SECOND, FOURTH, AND FIFTH POSITIONS. 8 measures in 4/4.

Each on 4 beats.

2. BATTEMENTS TENDUS AND BATTEMENTS TENDUS JETÉS. 16 measures in 2/4.

Two battements tendus front, each on 1 beat; 3 battements tendus jetés front, each on half a beat. Repeat once more. Execute also to the side, back, and side.

3. RONDS DE JAMBE À TERRE. 12 measures in 4/4.

On 2 introductory chords, préparation en dehors. Eight ronds de jambe à terre, each on 1 beat, ending pointe tendue front. Two piqués, each on half a beat; on 1 beat, raise the foot slightly off the floor, carry it to the side and lower on the floor, pointe tendue. Following the same musical breakdown, piqué in second position; carry the foot to the back, piqué to the back and bring the foot in second position pointe tendue, then piqué and end carrying the foot to the front, pointe tendue. Repeat the same en dedans. In 2 measures: trace a half circle in plié, en dehors, then en dedans, and remaining in demi-plié (the working leg is pointed front) execute port de bras, bending the body in 2 measures.

4. BATTEMENTS SOUTENUS, POINTE TENDUE ON THE FLOOR AND FRAPPÉS. 16 measures in 2/4.

Two battements soutenus in a small pose effacée front, each on 2 beats. Two battements soutenus in écarté back, each on 2 beats. Execute also in effacé back and écarté front. Two battements soutenus to the side, each on 2 beats. Do not end the second soutenu and from the demi-plié position on the supporting leg, with the working leg pointed on the floor, come up on half toe, while raising the working leg to 45° to prepare for the frappé. Frappé: 4 to the side, each on 1 beat; 6 doubles frappés, each on 1 beat; on 2 beats, demi-plié in fifth position and make a half turn on half-toe away from the barre.

5. RONDS DE JAMBE EN L'AIR. 32 measures in 2/4.

On 2 beats, préparation temps relevé en dehors; 10 ronds de jambe en l'air en dehors, each on 1 beat; on 2 beats, bring the working leg down to fifth position back; on 2 beats, move into épaulement effacé. In 8 measures, execute twice, développé in attitude effacée. Repeat the whole exercise en dedans with développé in effacé front at 90°.

6. PETITS BATTEMENTS SUR LE COU-DE-PIED. 16 measures in 2/4.

Six petits battements front, each on 1 beat; on the sixth battement, the arm in second (arm) position lowers to the preparatory (arm) position. On 2 beats, tombé front on the working foot, then coupé, opening the working leg to the side at 45° and the arm to second (arm) position. Repeat the exercise once more and execute petits battements and tombé-coupé in the reverse direction. During the tombé-coupé to the back, the arm remains in second position. In tombé, the body leans slightly to the back, and straightens back on coupé.

7. BATTEMENTS DÉVELOPPÉS. 16 measures in 4/4.

First measure: développé front. Second measure: passé at 90° and développé front. Third measure: passé at 90° and développé to the side. Fourth measure: maintain the position for 2 beats and on the other 2 beats, bring the working leg down in fifth position. Fifth and sixth measures: développé in écarté back. Seventh and eighth measures: repeat développé and execute a small pose in écarté back, in plié, pointe tendue on the floor. Repeat the same in the reverse direction, concluding with a pose in écarté front.

8. GRANDS BATTEMENTS JETÉS. 8 measures in 4/4.

Eight grands battements front, 8 in écarté back, 8 to the back and 8 in écarté front, each on 1 beat.

EXERCISES IN THE CENTER

1. 16 measures in 4/4.

Two grands pliés in first position, each on 4 beats. In 2 measures, développé right leg front and a demi-rond en dehors to the side; on the last beat, bring the working leg down in second position. Two grands pliés in second position, each on 4 beats. In 2 measures, développé right leg to the back and demi-rond en dedans to the side; on the last beat, bring the working leg down in fifth position front. In 2 measures, raise the left arm in third (arm) position, the right arm in second position and execute the first half of the fourth port de bras; in 2 measures, extend the left leg in croisé back, pointe tendue on the floor. In this manner, begin the study of the fourth arabesque. Maintain the arabesque pose, pointe tendue on the floor for the subsequent 4 measures.

2. BATTEMENTS TENDUS AND BATTEMENTS TENDUS JETÉS. 16 measures in 2/4.

Right foot: 4 battements tendus front, each on 1 beat; 2 battements tendus jetés, each on 1 beat, 3 on half a beat each. Continue the same with the left foot to the back. Right foot: 8 battements tendus to the side, each on 1 beat; 2 battements tendus jetés, each on 1 beat and 3 on half a beat each; end the last battement in fifth position plié and in 2 measures, step forward on half-toe in fifth position, the right arm raised in third (arm) position, the left arm in first (arm) position. The head position is given according to the teacher's indication.

3. RONDS DE JAMBE À TERRE. 12 measures in 4/4.

On 2 introductory chords, préparation en dehors. Eight ronds de jambe à terre and 8 ronds de jambe en l'air en dehors, each on 1 beat. From this position, when the leg is opened to the side at 45°, continue with ronds de jambe à terre and ronds de jambe en l'air en dedans. In 2 measures, trace a half circle in plié en dehors, starting in croisé front and ending in croisé back. At the conclusion, stretch the knee of the supporting leg and in 2 measures move into port de bras in deep plié, bending the body.

4. BATTEMENTS SOUTENUS, FONDUS, AND FRAPPÉS. 16 measures in 2/4.

Starting with the right leg, 2 battements soutenus, pointe tendue on the floor in effacé front; with the left leg, 2 battements soutenus effacés back, each on 2 beats. With the right leg, 4 fondus to the side, each on 2 beats. Eight frappés to the side, on 1 beat each, ending the eighth frappé in plié and in 4 measures execute pas de bourrée from side to side, without changing feet. End each pas de bourrée with the leg raised at 45°.[1]

5. DOUBLES FRAPPÉS POINTE TENDUE ON THE FLOOR. 16 measures in 2/4.

To the front, to the side, to the back and to the side, each on 1 beat. Repeat once more. Four doubles frappés to the side, each on 1 beat; close the working leg in fifth position back on 2 beats, and move on the diagonal in the small pose effacée back plié; on 2 beats, execute pas de bourrée en dehors, changing feet and end in fifth position, with the arms slightly open in first (arm) position. In 2 measures, left leg in third arabesque pointe tendue on the floor; to 2 measures, move the arms and the body in position for the fourth arabesque; to 4 measures, maintain the fourth arabesque.

6. ADAGIO. 16 measures in 4/4.

First measure: grand plié in fifth position (right foot front) ending by opening the left arm in third (arm) position and the right arm in second (arm) position. Second measure: relevé on half-toe. Third and fourth measures: fourth port de bras. Fifth and sixth measures: right leg, développé to the side and demi-rond en dedans to the front. Seventh and eighth measures: right leg, développé to the side and demi-rond

---

[1] During the second semester, study the pas de bourrée without changing feet and the pas de bourrée ballotté in croisé and effacé, with the leg raised at 45°.

en dehors to the back. Ninth and tenth measures: left leg, développé in croisé front. Eleventh and twelfth measures: right leg, développé in attitude croisée. Thirteenth and fourteenth measures: left leg, relevé lent to 90° in first arabesque. Fifteenth and sixteenth measures: right leg, fourth arabesque, pointe tendue on the floor.

ALLEGRO

1. 8 measures in 4/4.

Two assemblés to the side, with the right and left leg, on 1 beat each; on 2 beats, échappé in second position, changing feet. Repeat 4 times, thereafter in the reverse direction.

2. 8 measures in 2/4.

Three jetés, starting on the right leg, each on 1 beat; on 1 beat, assemblé croisé to the back. Repeat 4 times and execute separately in the reverse direction.

3. 8 measures in 2/4.

Fifth position, left foot front. On 1 beat, glissade to the side, starting on the right foot, without changing feet; on 1 beat, assemblé to the side, with the right leg, ending in fifth position, right foot front; on 2 beats, échappé in fourth-position croisée. Continue on the other leg, repeating the whole combination 4 times. Execute the same in the reverse direction. (Starting glissade in fifth position to the side on the front foot).

4. SISSONNE OUVERTE AT 45°. Musical measure 4/4.

On the first beat, demi-plié; jump between the first and second beats, ending on the supporting leg in demi-plié on the second beat, the other leg open to the side at 45°. Assemblé, between the second and third beats, ending on the third beat; on the fourth beat, stretch the knees. Study in the same manner, sissonnes ouvertes in all other poses.[2]

---

[2] After two weeks, based on the teacher's decision, sissonnes ouvertes may begin on the upbeat and are executed on 1 beat, ending with assemblé on the next beat.

5. 16 measures in 3/4.

Échappé in second position, landing on one leg, and ending with assemblé with the right and the left leg, each on 3 beats. Two échappés in second position, changing feet with a temps levé from second position, each on 3 beats. Repeat 4 times and execute separately the same in the reverse direction.

6. GRANDS CHANGEMENTS DE PIEDS AND GRANDS ÉCHAPPÉS.

Execution similar to that in the previous lessons.

7. PAS DE BASQUE. Musical measure 3/4.

Pas de basque front; on the first and second beats of the first measure, demi-plié on the supporting leg and demi-rond de jambe à terre en dehors to second position; on the third beat, maintain the position. In the following measure, execute the pas de basque. Study in this manner, the pas de basque to the back.[3]

8. 8 measures in 2/4.

Eight temps levés in first and 8 temps levés in second position, each on 1 beat.

9. 8 measures in 2/4.

Sixteen petits changements de pieds, each on 1 beat.

FIFTH EXAMPLE OF EXERCISES ON POINTES

1. RELEVÉS. Musical measure 2/4.

Sixteen relevés in first and 16 relevés in second position, each on 2 beats.

2. 8 measures in 4/4.

Three échappés in fourth-position croisée (right foot front) raising the right arm to third (arm) position and the left arm to second (arm) position; 1 échappé in fourth-position effacée, changing feet and the left arm to first (arm) position and the right arm to second (arm) position, each on 2 beats. Repeat the same on the other leg. Two doubles échappés

---

[3] According to the mastery, the pas de basque is studied to one measure in 3/4 or 2/4. Whether in one or the other measure, the demi-rond de jambe à terre is done on the upbeat.

in second position, each on 4 beats. One échappé in fourth position croisée, 1 in fourth position effacée, on the right and left leg in turn, each on 2 beats.

3. 16 measures in 2/4.

Three sus-sous traveling front in croisé, each on 2 beats; on 2 beats, échappé in second position, changing feet. Repeat the combination 4 times, and in the reverse direction, traveling backward.

4. 8 measures in 4/4.

Three pas de bourrée en dehors, changing feet, each on 2 beats, ending in fifth position; on 2 beats, relevé in fifth position, the arms in a small pose croisée. Two échappés in second position, ending with one foot sur le cou-de-pied back, each on 4 beats. Repeat the combination on the other leg. Execute in the reverse direction with pas de bourrée en dedans; end échappé on one leg, the other sur le cou-de-pied front.

5. PAS DE BOURRÉE SUIVI. 32 measures in 3/4 (Slow Waltz).

8 measures. Starting on the right foot, pas de bourrée suivi front in croisé, gradually lift the arms to third (arm) position; in the subsequent 8 measures, continue pas de bourrée suivi, gradually opening the arms to the second (arm) position. Come down on demi-plié, in the last measure and close the arms in the preparatory (arm) position.

16 measures. Starting on the right foot, pas de bourrée suivi in a straight line (from side 7 to side 3), lift the right arm to third (arm) position and the left arm to second (arm) position. Come down in demi-plié in the last measure, transferring the left foot to fifth position front, open the arms to second (arm) position and finally lower them to the preparatory (arm) position.

6. SISSONNES SIMPLES.[4] Musical measure 4/4.

a) On the first beat, demi-plié; on the second beat, spring onto pointes on one foot, bending the other leg sur le cou-de-pied front. On the third beat, come down in fifth position demi-plié; on the fourth beat, stretch the knees.

b) On the upbeat, demi-plié; on the first beat, spring onto pointes; on the second beat, come down in demi-plié; on the third beat, stretch the knees; on the fourth beat, demi-plié for the subsequent sissonne.

---

[4] First, the students execute the sissonnes simples facing the barre, then en face, facing the mirror in the center of the studio, later with épaulement.

Demi-plié in second position.

Sixth Lesson

EXERCISES AT THE BARRE

1. 16 measures in 4/4.

Two grands pliés and 2 relevés on half-toe in first, second, fourth, and fifth positions, each on 4 beats.

2. BATTEMENTS TENDUS AND BATTEMENTS TENDUS JETÉS. 12 measures in 4/4.

Four battements tendus front, right foot, each on 1 beat. Four battements tendus back, left foot, each on 1 beat; 2 battements tendus to the side, right foot, each on 1 beat and on 2 beats, 1 battement tendu in demi-plié. Repeat 2 battements tendus to the side and 1 in demi-plié. Repeat the whole combination in the reverse direction, starting with the right foot back. Three battements tendus jetés front, each on half a beat (stand still on the fourth half beat). Repeat once more and continue the same to the side, to the back and to the side.

3. RONDS DE JAMBE À TERRE. 24 measures in 2/4.

On 2 introductory chords, préparation en dehors. Eight ronds de jambe à terre, each on 1 beat, end the last at 45° front; on 2 beats, carry the working leg to the side; on 2 beats, to the back; on 2 beats, to the side; and on 2 beats to the front (rond de jambe en dehors—en dedans). Repeat the same en dedans, and in 4 measures trace a half circle in plié en dedans—en dehors; in 4 measures, port de bras in deep plié, bending the body.

4. BATTEMENTS FONDUS AT 45° AND BATTEMENTS FRAPPÉS. 12 measures in 4/4.

On 2 beats, fondu front; on 2 beats, plié-relevé, with demi-rond en dehors to second position; on 2 beats, fondu to the side; on 2 beats, plié-relevé, with demi-rond en dehors to the back. Continue the same in the reverse direction with demi-rond en dedans. Frappés: 4 front, 4 side, 4 back, and 4 front, each on 1 beat. Doubles frappés: front, side, back, side and again 4 to the side, each on 1 beat. On 2 beats, bring the working leg down to fifth position back in demi-plié and make a half turn on half-toe away from the barre; on 2 beats, pose effacée back (left leg) pointe tendue on the floor in plié; on 2 beats, soutenu in fifth position, half-toe and on 2 beats, pose écartée to the front in plié, pointe tendue on the floor.

5. RONDS DE JAMBE EN L'AIR. 8 measures in 2/4.

On 2 introductory chords, préparation temps relevé en dehors. Six ronds de jambe en l'air, each on 1 beat; on 2 beats, bring the working leg in fifth position front. In 4 measures, développé in écarté back. Execute the same en dedans, ending in écarté front.

6. PETITS BATTEMENTS SUR LE COU-DE-PIED. 16 measures in 2/4.

Seven petits battements front, each on 1 beat; on the seventh, demi-plié on the supporting leg; on 1 beat, stand still. Seven petits battements back, each on 1 beat; on the seventh, demi-plié; on 1 beat, stand still. Six petits battements front, each on 1 beat; on 2 beats, demi-plié in fifth position and make a half turn on half-toe toward the barre; on 2 beats, pose effacée front (left leg) pointe tendue on the floor in plié; on 2 beats, soutenu on half-toe in fifth position and on 2 beats, pose écartée back, pointe tendue on the floor in plié.

7. GRANDS RONDS DE JAMBE DÉVELOPPÉS. 16 measures in 4/4.

En dehors. First measure: développé front. Second measure: carry the working leg to the side. Third measure: carry the leg to the back. Fourth measure: on the first and second beats, bring the leg down in fifth position; on the third and fourth beats, battement tendu to the side, ending in fifth position front, to repeat the next grand rond de jambe développé en dehors. Execute the same en dedans.

8. GRANDS BATTEMENTS JETÉS. 8 measures in 2/4.

Four grands battements in effacé front, 4 in écarté back, 4 in effacé back and 4 in écarté front, each on 1 beat.

EXERCISES IN THE CENTER

1. 16 measures in 4/4.

First measure: grand plié in first position. Second measure: demi-plié and relevé on half-toe, raising the right arm to third (arm) position and the left to second (arm) position. Third and fourth measures: execute the same in second position. Fifth and sixth measures: développé croisé front (right leg) holding in the beginning the right arm in third (arm) position and the left arm in second (arm) position; thereafter opening the right arm to second (arm) position and the left to third (arm) position. Seventh and eighth measures: développé attitude croisée (left leg). Ninth and tenth measures: développé to the side (right leg). Eleventh and twelfth measures: développé écarté back (left leg). Thirteenth and fourteenth measures: pose in fourth arabesque pointe tendue on the floor and relevé to 90° (left leg). Fifteenth and sixteenth measures: bring the leg down in fifth position and step forward on the right foot in fifth position, half-toe; open the left arm front and the right arm in second (arm) position.

2. BATTEMENTS TENDUS AND BATTEMENTS TENDUS JETÉS. 32 measures in 2/4.

Four battements tendus croisés front (right foot), each on 1 beat, gradually lifting the arms, the right to the third (arm) position and the left to second (arm) position; 4 battements tendus, on 1 beat each, opening the right arm to second (arm) position, the left raised to third (arm) position. Eight battements tendus croisés back (left foot), each on 1 beat (of which 4 with arms maintained in the previous position and 4 opening the left arm to second (arm) position and raising the right arm to third (arm) position). Eight battements tendus to the side (right foot), each on 1 beat; 4 battements tendus jetés to the side, each on 1 beat; 3 on half a beat each (stay still on the fourth half beat); and repeat 3 jetés once more. Continue the whole combination on the other leg.

3. BATTEMENTS FONDUS AT 45° AND BATTEMENTS FRAPPÉS. 24 measures in 2/4.

On 2 beats, fondu front; on 2 beats, plié-relevé. Continue the same to the side, to the back and to the side. Frappés: 8 to the side, each on 1 beat. Doubles frappés: 6 each on 1 beat; on 2 beats, bring the working leg down in fifth position front. Two measures: développé in third arabesque (left leg) the arms meet in first (arm) position and move to fourth arabesque. Maintain the position for 4 measures; on the last 2 beats, bring the working leg down in fifth position.

Attitude effacée.

4. RONDS DE JAMBE EN L'AIR.

Repeat the combination of ronds de jambe en l'air from the exercise at the barre.

5. PETITS BATTEMENTS SUR LE COU-DE-PIED. 16 measures in 2/4.

Fifteen petits battements, each on 1 beat; on 1 beat, tombé on the working right foot in fifth position front, the left foot sur le cou-de-pied back; 6 pas de bourrée ballottés in effacé at 45°, each on 2 beats; on 2 beats, pas de bourrée en dehors, changing feet, ending in fifth position; on 2 beats, relevé in fifth position half-toe, raising the arms to third (arm) position.

6. GRANDS BATTEMENTS JETÉS. 8 measures in 2/4.

Four grands battements front, 4 in écarté back; 4 back and 4 in écarté front, each on 1 beat.

7. ADAGIO. 16 measures in 4/4.

First and second measures: fifth port de bras (right foot front). Third and fourth measures: fourth port de bras. Fifth, sixth, seventh, and eighth measures: grand rond de jambe développé en dehors. Ninth and tenth measures: développé effacé front (left leg) ending in fifth position back. Eleventh and twelfth measures: développé attitude effacée (left leg), ending in fifth position front. Thirteenth, fourteenth, fifteenth, and sixteenth measures: grand rond de jambe développé en dedans (right leg).

ALLEGRO

1. 8 measures in 4/4.

Three assemblés to the side, changing feet with the right, the left, and the right leg, each on 1 beat; on 1 beat, sauté in fifth position. Repeat 4 times and execute in the reverse direction.

2. 8 measures in 2/4.

Fifth position, left foot front. On 1 beat, glissade to the side, without changing feet (right foot); on 1 beat, jeté on the right leg; on 1 beat, assemblé croisé back; on half a beat, stretch the knees and on half a beat demi-plié for the continuation of the combination on the other leg. Repeat 4 times and subsequently the whole combination in the reverse direction.

3. 8 measures in 2/4.

Right foot front. Two échappés in second position, changing feet, each on 2 beats; sissonne ouverte to the side at 45° with the right and left leg, ending each sissonne with assemblé, each on 2 beats. Two échappés in second position, changing feet, each on 2 beats; sissonne ouverte in effacé front with the right and left leg, ending with assemblé, each on 2 beats. Execute the same in the reverse direction.

4. SISSONNE FERMÉE. Musical measure 4/4.

a) On the first and second beats, demi-plié; jump in the given direction, between the second and third beats, ending in demi-plié on the third beat; on the fourth beat, stretch the knees.

b) On the upbeat, demi-plié and jump in the given direction; on the first beat, end the jump in demi-plié; on the second and third beats, stretch the knees; on the fourth beat, demi-plié for the next jump. Repeat the exercise 4 to 8 times.[1]

5. PAS DE BASQUE. 8 measures in 3/4.

On 3 beats, pas de basque front; on 3 beats, stretch the knees; on the last beat of the second measure, come down in demi-plié for the execution of the following pas de basque. Repeat 4 times, and then the same with pas de basque back.

6. GRAND ÉCHAPPÉ IN SECOND AND FOURTH POSITIONS. 8 measures in 4/4.

On the upbeat, demi-plié and grand échappé in fourth position croisée, ending in demi-plié on the first beat. Next, jump between the first and second beats, ending in fifth-position demi-plié on the second beat; on the third beat, stretch the knees; on the fourth beat, demi-plié for the next échappé. Execute 3 times and then 1 grand échappé in second position, changing feet. Repeat the same on the other leg.

7. GRANDS CHANGEMENTS DE PIEDS. 8 measures in 2/4.

On the upbeat, demi-plié and 2 grands changements de pieds, each on 1 beat; on 1 beat, stretch the knees and on 1 beat, demi-plié for the preparation of the following 2 jumps. Repeat 4 times.

8. 8 measures in 2/4.

Sixteen petits changements de pieds, each on 1 beat.

---

[1] In the beginning, study the sissonne fermée to the side with and without changing feet and then, after a few lessons, sissonne fermée to the front and to the back.

SIXTH EXAMPLE OF EXERCISES ON POINTES

1. 32 measures in 2/4.

Seven relevés in fifth position, each on 2 beats; on 2 beats, échappé in second position, changing feet. Repeat 4 times.

2. 16 measures in 4/4.

Three doubles échappés in fourth-position croisée, each on 4 beats; on 4 beats, 1 double échappé in fourth position effacée, changing feet. Repeat 4 times.

3. 16 measures in 2/4.

Three sus-sous traveling forward (right foot front) in croisé, each on 2 beats. End the third sus-sous on the right foot demi-plié, the left sur le cou-de-pied back. Three pas de bourrée en dehors, changing feet, each on 2 beats, ending in fifth position. Two glissades croisé front, each on 2 beats. Repeat on the other leg, and execute the combination in the reverse direction.

4. SISSONNE SIMPLE. 16 measures in 2/4.

On the upbeat, demi-plié. Three sissonnes simples, changing feet, with the right, the left and the right foot, each on 2 beats; on 2 beats, stretch the knees and demi-plié for the following sissonnes. Repeat 4 times, and execute the combination in the reverse direction.

5. 16 measures in 3/4 (Slow Waltz).

8 measures: from corner 6 to corner 2, on the diagonal, pas de bourrée suivi; demi-plié in fifth position in the last measure. Six balancés (moving slightly backward) each in 1 measure. One measure: demi-plié in fifth position. One measure: fifth position on pointes, the arms raised in third (arm) position.

Bending the body to the side.

Seventh Lesson

EXERCISES AT THE BARRE

1. 16 measures in 4/4.

Two demi-pliés and 2 grands pliés in first, second, fourth, and fifth positions, each on 4 beats.

2. BATTEMENTS TENDUS AND BATTEMENTS TENDUS JETÉS. 32 measures in 2/4.

Two battements tendus front, each on 1 beat; on 2 beats, 1 battement tendu in demi-plié. Repeat 4 times, and continue the same to the side, the back and the side. Battements tendus jetés: 2 to the front, each on half a beat, in 2 half beats, 1 in demi-plié. Repeat 4 times and continue the same to the side, to the back and to the side. Battements tendus jetés to the side, in first position; 7, each on half a beat (on 1 half beat, pause), repeat once more. In 4 measures, port de bras, bending the body to the side, toward the barre, and, while bending, raise the arm from second (arm) position to third (arm) position. When the body returns to the straightened position, so does the arm to second (arm) position.

3. RONDS DE JAMBE À TERRE. 24 measures in 2/4.

On 2 introductory chords, préparation en dehors. Eight ronds de jambe à terre, each on 1 beat, ending the last one front, pointe tendue on the floor. A quick passé through first position back to 45° (tendu jeté) and a quick passé through first position front to 45° (tendu jeté), each on 1 beat. Execute 8 times. Repeat the same en dedans. Four measures: trace a half circle in plié en dedans and en dehors; 4 measures: port de bras in deep plié, bending the body.

4. BATTEMENTS FONDUS AT 45° AND FRAPPÉS. 16 measures in 4/4.

Two fondus front (right leg), each on 2 beats; 2 fondus back (left leg), each on 2 beats; 4 fondus to the side (right leg), each on 2 beats. Starting with the right foot back, repeat the fondus in the reverse direction.

Frappés: 4 to the side, each on 1 beat; on 2 beats, close the working leg in fifth position front, demi-plié; on 2 beats, relevé on half-toe, opening the working leg to the side at 45°. Repeat 4 frappés and close the working leg in fifth position back demi-plié. At the conclusion, open the working leg at 45°.

Doubles frappés: 8 to the side, each on 1 beat, and in 2 measures, développé attitude effacée.

5. RONDS DE JAMBE EN L'AIR. 8 measures in 2/4.

On 2 introductory chords, préparation temps relevé en dehors. Eight ronds de jambe en l'air, each on 1 beat; in 4 measures, développé attitude croisée. Execute the same en dedans, ending in a pose croisée front.

6. PETITS BATTEMENTS SUR LE COU-DE-PIED. 16 measures in 2/4.

Four petits battements (accent front), each on 1 beat; on 2 beats, a small pose croisée front, pointe tendue on the floor; on 2 beats, come up on half-toe and bring the foot of the working leg sur le cou-de-pied front. Four petits battements (accent back), each on 1 beat; on 2 beats, a small pose croisée back, pointe tendue on the floor; on 2 beats, come up on half-toe and bring the foot of the supporting leg sur le cou-de-pied back. Sixteen petits battements front (continuous, without accent) each on 1 beat.

7. BATTEMENTS DÉVELOPPÉS. 16 measures in 2/4.

First measure: développé front. Second measure: carry the working leg to the side. Third and fourth measures: carry the leg to the back. Fifth measure: passé to 90°. Sixth measure: développé écarté back. Seventh measure: maintain the position. Eighth measure: bring the working leg down in fifth position back. Execute the same en dedans, ending in a pose écartée front.

8. GRANDS BATTEMENTS JETÉS. 8 measures in 2/4.

Three grands battements pointés and 1 in fifth position, in effacé front; 3 pointés and 1 in fifth position, in écarté back; 3 pointés and 1 in fifth position, in second arabesque; 3 pointés and 1 in fifth position to the side, each on 1 beat.

Arabesque, with the arm in second position.

EXERCISES IN THE CENTER

1. 16 measures in 4/4.

Two measures: 2 grands pliés in fourth position croisée. Two measures: développé front (right leg) and demi-rond en dehors to second position. Two measures: passé at 90° (on 2 beats) in attitude croisée, ending in fifth position. Two measures: développé back and demi-rond en dedans to second position. Two measures: passé at 90° (on 2 beats) and pose croisée front at 90°, ending in fifth position. Two measures: développé third arabesque (left leg), holding the position, change arms to fourth arabesque. One measure: maintain the position. One measure: on the first and second beat, bring down the leg in fifth position and lower the arms in the preparatory (arm) position; on the third and fourth beats, open the arms in second (arm) position. Two measures: third port de bras, bending the body.

2. BATTEMENTS TENDUS AND BATTEMENTS TENDUS JETÉS. 12 measures in 4/4.

Right foot: 8 battements tendus, in a big pose croisée front, each on 1 beat; left foot: 8 battements tendus in third arabesque, each on 1 beat; right foot: 16 battements tendus in a big pose écartée back, each on 1 beat. Battements tendus jetés: left foot, 3 in croisé front, on half a beat each (pause on the fourth half beat). Repeat once more. Right foot, 3 in croisé back, each on half a beat. Repeat once more. Left foot, 3 in écarté back, each on half a beat. Repeat once more. One measure: right foot, end with a pose croisée front, pointe tendue on the floor.

3. RONDS DE JAMBE À TERRE. 8 measures in 4/4.

On 2 introductory chords, préparation en dehors. Six ronds de jambe à terre, each on 1 beat; on 2 beats, préparation en dehors. Six ronds de jambe à terre en dedans, each on 1 beat, and on 2 beats, préparation en dedans. Two measures: trace a half circle in plié en dedans and en dehors. Two measures: port de bras in a deep plié, bending the body.

4. BATTEMENTS FONDUS AT 45° AND FRAPPÉS. 16 measures in 2/4.

Two fondus front (right leg), each on 2 beats; 2 fondus back (left leg), each on 2 beats; 4 fondus to the side (right leg), each on 2 beats. Frappés: 8 to the side, each on 1 beat; 4 doubles frappés, each on 1 beat; on 2 beats, close the working leg in fifth position back; on 2 beats, a small pose croisée back, pointe tendue on the floor.

5. PETITS BATTEMENTS SUR LE COU-DE-PIED. 16 measures in 2/4.

Four petits battements (accent front), 4 (accent back), each on 1 beat; 7 petits battements front (continuous, without accent), each on 1 beat; on 1 beat, tombé on the supporting foot in fifth position front, the left leg open to the side at 45° (dégagé); 6 pas de bourrée from side to side, without changing feet, each on 2 beats; on 2 beats, soutenu in fifth position, half-toe (left foot front); on 2 beats, first arabesque on the diagonal toward corner 2, pointe tendue on the floor, in plié.

6. GRANDS BATTEMENTS JETÉS. 8 measures in 4/4.

Eight grands battements, croisé front (right leg); 8 in third arabesque (left leg); 8 in écarté back (right leg), each on 1 beat. Two measures: left leg, relevé lent to 90° in first arabesque.

7. ADAGIO. 16 measures in 4/4.

First measure: grand plié in fifth position. Second measure: relevé on half-toe. Third and fourth measures: développé effacé front (right leg). Fifth and sixth measures: attitude effacée (left leg). Seventh, eighth, and ninth measures: grand rond de jambe développé en dehors (left leg). Tenth measure: on the first and second beats, bring the working leg down in fifth position demi-plié, the right foot sur le cou-de-pied front; on the third and fourth beats, pas de bourrée en dedans, changing feet, ending in fifth position. Eleventh and twelfth measures: développé in first arabesque (right leg), holding the leg, change the arms to second arabesque. Thirteenth measure: maintain the position. Fourteenth measure: on the first and second beats, bring the working leg down in fifth position front, demi-plié, the left foot sur le cou-de-pied back; on the third and fourth beats, pas de bourrée en dehors, changing feet, ending in fifth position. Fifteenth and sixteenth measures: step forward on the left foot in a big pose croisée back, pointe tendue on the floor and through a wide circular movement, bring the arms, body, and head in fourth arabesque, pointe tendue on the floor.

ALLEGRO

1. 8 measures in 2/4.
Double assemblé with the right and left leg, each on 2 beats; 4 assemblés to the side, changing feet (forward), each on 1 beat. Repeat the combination once more. Execute the same in the reverse direction.

2. 4 measures in 4/4.
Fifth position, right foot front. Starting on the right foot, 4 glissades to the side, changing feet, each on 1 beat; 2 échappés, with and without changing feet in second position, each on 2 beats. Repeat the combination on the other leg. Execute in the reverse direction, starting the glissade with the back foot in fifth position.

3. 8 measures in 2/4.
Fifth position, left foot front. On 1 beat, glissade to the side (right foot) without changing feet; on 1 beat, jeté on thè right foot, ending with the left foot sur le cou-de-pied back; on 2 beats, pas de bourrée, changing feet and ending in fifth position. Repeat the combination once more, and execute the combination twice, starting on the left foot, in the reverse direction.

4. 8 measures in 2/4.
Sissonne ouverte to the side (ending with assemblé) on the right and left leg, each on 2 beats; 2 sissonnes fermées to the side, changing feet, each on 1 beat; on 1 beat, stretch the knees; on 1 beat, demi-plié; repeat the combination once more. Execute in the reverse direction.

5. 8 measures in 2/4.
Two pas de basque front, each on 2 beats; 2 petits changements de pieds, each on 1 beat; on 1 beat, stretch the knees; on 1 beat, demi-plié to repeat the combination once more. Execute in the same way pas de basque back.

6. 4 measures in 4/4, or 16 measures in 3/4 (Waltz).
Three grands échappés in second position, changing feet, each on 2 beats; on 1 beat, stretch the knees; on 1 beat, demi-plié to prepare for the next 3 échappés.

7. SISSONNE IN FIRST ARABESQUE AND PAS DE CHAT. 16 measures in 3/4 (Waltz).

From corner 6 to corner 2, on the diagonal; in 8 measures, execute 4 times sissonne in first arabesque with pas de chat; in 4 measures, 4 balancés (moving slightly backward); in 1 measure, step on the right foot in pose effacée back, pointe tendue on the floor; in the following 3 measures, maintain the position. Execute from corner 4 to corner 8, on the diagonal as well.

8. 8 measures in 2/4.

Sixteen petits changements de pieds, each on 1 beat.

SEVENTH EXAMPLE OF EXERCISES ON POINTES

1. 16 measures in 2/4.

Eight relevés in first and 8 relevés in second position, each on 2 beats.

2. 8 measures in 4/4.

Three doubles échappés in second position, each on 4 beats; 2 échappés in second position, changing feet, each on 2 beats. Repeat once more.

3. 16 measures in 2/4.

Seven sus-sous in pose croisée, traveling forward, each on 2 beats; on 2 beats, échappé in second position, changing feet. Repeat on the other leg; thereafter in the reverse direction.

4. 8 measures in 2/4.

Seven pas de bourrée from side to side, without changing feet, each on 2 beats. End the last pas de bourrée in fifth position. On 2 beats, step forward in fifth position, on pointes, lifting the arms in a big pose croisée.

5. 16 measures in 2/4.

Three sissonnes simples to the back, changing feet, each on 2 beats, and on 2 beats, relevé in fifth position. Repeat 4 times. Execute in the reverse direction, changing feet to the front.

6. 16 measures in 6/8.

Eight measures: pas couru on the diagonal forward and in 8 measures, pas couru on the diagonal, backward.

Battement tendu front, at the barre.

Eighth Lesson

EXERCISES AT THE BARRE

1. 12 measures in 4/4.

Two grands pliés in first, second, fourth, and fifth positions, each on 4 beats; 2 port de bras, bending the body, each in 2 measures.

2. BATTEMENTS TENDUS AND BATTEMENTS TENDUS JETÉS. 16 measures in 2/4.

One battement tendu in demi-plié, to the front, to the side, to the back and to the side, each on 2 beats (on 1 beat, battement tendu; on the second beat, continue in demi-plié). Two battements tendus front, side, back, and side, each on 1 beat. Execute the combination in the reverse direction. Battements tendus jetés: 4 front, each on 1 beat; 7 to the side, each on half a beat (pause on half a beat); 4 to the back, each on 1 beat; 7 to the side, each on half a beat (pause on half a beat).

3. RONDS DE JAMBE À TERRE. 16 measures in 2/4.

On 2 introductory chords, préparation en dehors. Eight ronds de jambe à terre, each on 1 beat, end the last one front, pointe tendue on the floor, in plié. In 4 measures: port de bras, bending the body. Eight ronds de jambe à terre en dedans, each on 1 beat, end the last back, pointe tendue on the floor, in plié. In 4 measures: port de bras, bending the body.

4. BATTEMENTS SOUTENUS, BATTEMENTS FONDUS AT 45° AND FRAPPÉS. 24 measures in 2/4.

One battement soutenu front, pointe tendue on the floor, to the side, to the back, and to the side, each on 2 beats; 1 battement fondu again in the same directions (en croix), each on 2 beats. Repeat battements soutenus and fondus in the reverse direction.

Frappés: 2 to the front, to the side, to the back and to the side, each on 1 beat. Doubles frappés: 8 to the side, each on 1 beat.

5. RONDS DE JAMBE EN L'AIR. 8 measures in 4/4.

On 2 introductory chords, come up on half-toe and open the working leg to the side at 45°, préparation. Six ronds de jambe en l'air en dehors, each on 1 beat; on 2 beats, plié-relevé. Six ronds de jambe en l'air en dedans, each on 1 beat; on 2 beats, plié-relevé. Four ronds de jambe en l'air en dehors and 4 en dedans, each on 1 beat; in 2 measures, développé in second arabesque.

6. PETITS BATTEMENTS SUR LE COU-DE-PIED. 16 measures in 2/4.

Three petits battements front, each on 1 beat; on 1 beat, pause. Repeat once more. Seven petits battements front, each on 1 beat, on the seventh, demi-plié on the supporting leg; on 1 beat, pause. Repeat the same to the back.

7. BATTEMENTS DÉVELOPPÉS. 16 measures in 2/4.

First measure: développé front. Second measure: carry the working leg to the side. Third and fourth measures: slow passé through first position back and relevé to 90° in second arabesque. Fifth measure: maintain the position. Sixth measure: passé at 90°. Seventh measure: développé to the side. Eighth measure: bring the working leg down in fifth position back. Ninth measure: développé back. Tenth measue: carry the working leg to the side. Eleventh and twelfth measures: slow passé through first position front and relevé to 90° in pose effacée front. Thirteenth measure: maintain the position. Fourteenth measure: passé at 90°. Fifteenth measure: développé to the side. Sixteenth measure: bring the working leg down in fifth position.

8. GRANDS BATTEMENTS JETÉS. 8 measures in 2/4.

One grand battement, 1 battement tendu front, each on 1 beat. Repeat once more, and continue to the side, to the back and to the side (en croix).

EXERCISES IN THE CENTER

1. 8 measures in 4/4.

First measure: grand plié in first position. Second measure: demi-plié and relevé on half-toe. Third and fourth measures: développé croisée front (right leg), passé at 90° and développé to the side. Fifth measure: grand plié in second position. Sixth measure: demi-plié and relevé on half-toe. Seventh and eighth measures: développé attitude croisée (right leg), passé at 90° and développé to the side.

2. BATTEMENTS TENDUS AND BATTEMENTS TENDUS JETÉS. 16 measures in 2/4.

Two battements tendus front, in demi-plié, to the side, to the back and to the side, each on 2 beats (on 1 beat, battement tendu; on 1 beat, continue in demi-plié). Four doubles battements tendus to the side, each on 2 beats; 3 battements tendus jetés to the side, each on half a beat (pause on the fourth half beat). Execute 4 times.

3. RONDS DE JAMBE À TERRE. 4 measures in 4/4.

On 2 introductory chords, préparation en dehors.

Eight ronds de jambe à terre, each on 1 beat, end the last in effacé front, pointe tendue on the floor, in plié, leaning the body slightly backward; on 2 beats, demi-rond en dehors, pointe tendue on the floor in écarté back, raising the right arm to third (arm) position and the left to second (arm) position; on 2 beats, pass onto the right extended leg to corner 4, in a small pose effacée back, pointe tendue on the floor; in 1 measure, remain on the extended supporting right leg (the left, pointe tendue) and turn to corner 8 (en dehors), in a big pose effacée front, pointe tendue on the floor. Execute separately ronds de jambe à terre en dedans, end the last one in effacé back, pointe tendue on the floor, in plié; demi-rond en dedans to écarté front; step on to the extended right leg to corner 2, turn to corner 6, in a small pose effacée front, pointe tendue, on the floor and remaining on the extended right leg, turn en dedans to corner 2 in a big pose effacée back, pointe tendue on the floor.

4. BATTEMENTS FONDUS AND FRAPPÉS. 16 measures in 2/4.

Two fondus front (right leg), 2 fondus back (left leg), 4 fondus to the side (right leg), each on 2 beats. Frappés: 6 to the side, on 1 beat each; on 2 beats, bring the working leg in fifth position back and in 4 measures execute the third port de bras.

5. RONDS DE JAMBE EN L'AIR. 4 measures in 4/4.

On 2 introductory chords, préparation temps relevé en dehors. Eight

Pose écartée back.

ronds de jambe en l'air, each on 1 beat, and in 2 measures, grand rond de jambe développé en dehors. Repeat en dedans separately.

6. ADAGIO. 12 measures in 4/4.

First measure: grand plié in fifth position, right foot front; at the end, raise the left arm to third (arm) position and the right to second (arm) position. Second measure: second port de bras. Third and fourth measures: développé effacé front (right leg), passé at 90° (on the fourth beat of the third measure) and développé attitude croisée; end in fifth position. Fifth and sixth measures: développé to the side (left leg), passé at 90° and développé in fourth arabesque; end in fifth position. Seventh and eighth measures: attitude effacée (left leg), passé at 90° and développé croisé front; end in fifth position. Ninth and tenth measures: développé in first arabesque, on the diagonal to corner 8 (right leg); end in fifth position, right foot front. Eleventh measure: starting on the right foot, pas de basque front and relevé in fifth position, half-toe. Twelfth measure: trace a half circle in plié en dehors (left foot, rond de jambe à terre); end in croisé back, pointe tendue on the floor, the arms raised in third (arm) position.

Position à la seconde en l'air (90°).

ALLEGRO

1. 8 measures in 4/4.

Four assemblés front, in turn on the right and left leg, each on 1 beat; on 2 beats, échappé in second position, changing feet; 2 assemblés in a small pose croisée front, each on 1 beat. Repeat on the other leg; subsequently in the reverse direction.

2. 8 measures in 2/4.

Three glissades croisées front, 1 to the side, changing feet, each on 1 beat; 2 échappés in fourth position croisée, each on 2 beats. Repeat on the other leg; subsequently in the reverse direction.

3. 8 measures in 2/4.

Sissonne ouverte croisée front and to the side, ending with assemblé, each on 2 beats; échappé in second position, ending on one leg (sur le cou-de-pied back) and on 2 beats, pas de bourrée en dehors, changing feet. Repeat on the other leg; subsequently in the reverse direction.

4. 4 measures in 4/4.

Two sissonnes fermées to the side, without changing feet, each on 1 beat; on 1 beat, stretch the knees; on 1 beat, demi-plié to prepare for the following jumps. Repeat 4 times.

5. 8 measures in 2/4.

Grand échappé in fourth position croisée and grand échappé in second position, changing feet, each on 2 beats. Four grands changements de pieds, each on 1 beat. Repeat on the other leg.

6. 16 measures in 3/4 (Waltz).

In a straight line, from side 7 to side 3, starting on the right leg: in 6 measures, 3 sissonnes in first arabesque and pas de chat; in 2 measures, step on the right leg in first arabesque, pointe tendue on the floor to side 3. Repeat the same on the left leg from side 3 to side 7.[1]

---

[1] It is recommended that students be divided into two groups so that they can execute sissonne–pas de chat simultaneously; one group moves from side 7 to side 3, the other from side 3 to side 7. Here, it is necessary to explain the stage rule of crossing to the opposite side; the group finding itself on the left side always crosses in front.

EIGHTH EXAMPLE OF EXERCISES ON POINTES

1. 32 measures in 3/4 (Waltz).
Four temps liés front, 4 to the back, each in 4 measures.

2. 16 measures in 4/4.
Two doubles échappés in fourth position croisée, 1 double échappé in second position, changing feet, each on 4 beats. Two sus-sous, traveling front in pose croisée, each on 2 beats. Repeat on the other leg; subsequently in the reverse direction.

3. 8 measures in 4/4.
Échappé in second position, ending on one leg (the other foot sur le cou-de-pied back), in turn on the right and left leg, each on 1 beat; 4 sissonnes simples, changing feet to the back, each on 2 beats. Repeat once more; subsequently in the reverse direction.

4. 16 measures in 3/4 (Waltz).
8 measures: starting on the right foot, pas de bourrée, front suivi in croisé, come down in demi-plié on the last measure. 8 measures: step forward on the right foot, bringing the arms to third arabesque position, and pas de bourrée suivi en tournant to the right side, 4 full turns.

Third Year

In the third year, the study of exercises on half-toe begins in the center of the studio. Easy exercises are done en tournant, and the study of tours (pirouettes) begins.

Battement tendu front, at the barre.

First Semester
First Lesson

EXERCISES AT THE BARRE

1. 16 measures in 4/4.
One demi-plié, 2 grands pliés, 1 relevé on half-toe in first, second, fourth, and fifth positions, each on 4 beats.

2. BATTEMENTS TENDUS. 24 measures in 2/4.

Two battements tendus in demi-plié; front, side, back, and side, each on 1 beat; 4 to the side, without plié, each on 1 beat; on 1 beat, execute the fifth battement and a half turn toward the barre, changing feet; at the end, open the left leg to the side, pointe tendue on the floor; on 1 beat, maintain the position; on 1 beat, half a turn toward the barre, changing feet; at the end open the right leg to the side, pointe tendue on the floor; on 1 beat, close the working leg in fifth position back. Repeat battements tendus in the reverse direction with half a turn away from the barre.

Battements tendus jetés: 3 to the front, each on half a beat. Repeat once more. Seven to the side, each on half a beat; 3 to the back. Repeat once more. Seven to the side, each on half a beat.

3. RONDS DE JAMBE À TERRE. 12 measures in 4/4.

On 2 introductory chords, préparation en dehors. Four ronds de jambe à terre, each on 1 beat, end the fourth to the front in demi-plié; on 4 beats, trace a half circle en dehors and en dedans. Repeat the same en dedans, and subsequently once more en dehors and en dedans. Two measures: 2 port de bras in deep plié, bending the body.

4. BATTEMENTS FONDUS AT 45° AND FRAPPÉS. 24 measures in 2/4.

On 2 beats, 1 fondu front in a small pose effacée front; on 2 beats, plié and relevé with demi-rond in écartée back. Repeat once more. Two fondus to the side, each on 2 beats; 4 frappés, each on 1 beat. Repeat fondus and frappés in the reverse direction.

Frappés: 4 in pose effacée front, 4 in pose écartée back, 4 in pose effacée back and 4 in pose écartée front, each on 1 beat.

5. RONDS DE JAMBE EN L'AIR. 8 measures in 4/4.

On 2 introductory chords, préparation temps relevé en dehors. Seven ronds de jambe en l'air, each on 1 beat; end the seventh rond de jambe in pose effacée front in plié, pointe tendue on the floor, and on 1 beat, close the working leg in fifth position, bringing the body (en face) facing front. On 1 beat, relevé lent to the side to 90°; on 2 beats, bring the working leg down in fifth position back and on 2 beats, préparation temps relevé en dedans. Seven ronds de jambe en dedans, each on 1 beat, end the seventh in a small pose effacée back in plié, pointe tendue on the floor; on 1 beat, close the working leg in fifth position. On 1 beat, relevé lent to the side to 90°; on 4 beats, come up on half-toe and bring the working leg down in fifth position.

6. DOUBLES FRAPPÉS AND PETITS BATTEMENTS SUR LE COU-DE-PIED. 16 measures in 2/4.

Eight doubles frappés, pointe tendue on the floor (coming up on half-toe, at the time of the stroke and transfer of the working foot sur le cou-de-pied, coming down on the full supporting foot at the end of each frappé), to the front, to the side, to the back, to the side, etc., each on 1 beat.

Petits battements: 2 with accent front, each on 1 beat; 3 without accent, each on half a beat; half a beat, pause; 2 petits battements with accent front, each on 1 beat; 2 without accent, each on half a beat; on 1 beat, come down on the full supporting foot and open the working leg to the side, pointe tendue on the floor. Repeat doubles frappés and petits battements in the reverse direction.

7. BATTEMENTS DÉVELOPPÉS. 16 measures in 4/4.

First measure: small pose effacée front in plié, pointe tendue on the floor and relevé to 90° in a big pose effacée front. Second measure: on the first and second beats, relevé on half-toe; on the third and fourth beats, bring the working leg down in fifth position. Third measure: small pose écartée back in plié, pointe tendue on the floor, and relevé to 90° in a big pose écartée back. Fourth measure: on the first and second beats, relevé on half-toe; on the third and fourth beats, bring the working leg down in fifth position. Fifth and sixth measures: grand rond de jambe développé en dedans, on the last 2 beats, relevé on half-toe. Seventh measure: bring down the working leg in fifth position demi-plié and make a turn on half-toe toward the barre, ending in demi-plié. Eighth measure: on the first and second beats, développé in second arabesque; on the third beat, relevé on half-toe; on the fourth beat, end the movement in fifth position. Repeat the same in the reverse direction; at the end, execute the développé coming up on half-toe in pose croisée front.

8. GRANDS BATTEMENTS JETÉS POINTÉS. 8 measures in 2/4.

Two grands battements pointés front, each on 1 beat; on the third battement, hold the working leg in the air, at 90° to the count of 3 half beats, and on 1 beat bring it down in fifth position. Repeat the same to the side, to the back, and to the side.

EXERCISES IN THE CENTER

1. SMALL ADAGIO AND BATTEMENTS TENDUS.[1] 16 measures in
4/4.

First and second measures: 2 grands pliés in first position. Third and
fourth measures: développé front (right leg), rising on half-toe. Fifth
and sixth measures: 2 grands pliés in second position. Seventh and eighth
measures: développé back (right leg), rising on half-toe. Ninth and tenth
measures: développé to the side (right leg), rising on half-toe. Eleventh
and twelfth measures: grand rond de jambe développé en dehors (left
leg). Thirteenth measure: trace a half circle in plié (rond de jambe à
terre) en dedans. Fourteenth measure: soutenu in fifth position half-
toe, raising the arms, the right to third (arm) position, the left to second
position (looking toward the right hand); on the last beat, come down
on both feet. Fifteenth measure: fifth port de bras. Sixteenth measure:
first arabesque, pointe tendue on the floor, in plié (left leg), in straight
line from side 7 to side 3, bending the body slightly. The right arm
up in third (arm) position, the head turned to the left. Battements tendus:
8 measures in 4/4: 16 battements tendus to the side (right foot), each
on 1 beat. Battements tendus jetés: 3 to the side, each on half a beat,
8 times consecutively.

2. BATTEMENTS FONDUS AT 45° ON FLAT FOOT AND ALSO
RISING ON HALF-TOE. 16 measures in 2/4.

On 2 beats, fondu in a small pose croisée front; on 2 beats, plié-relevé,
turning the body en face, the working leg remaining in front. On 2
beats, fondu in a small pose effacée front; on 2 beats, plié-relevé with
demi-rond to second position (this is done on the flat foot). Three fondus
to the side, rising on half-toe, each on 2 beats; on 2 beats, come down
in fifth position. On 2 beats, fondu in a small pose croisée back; on 2
beats, plié-relevé, turning the body en face, the working leg remaining
back. On 2 beats, fondu in a small pose effacée back; on 2 beats, plié-
relevé with demi-rond to second position (this is done on the flat foot).
Three fondus to the side rising on half toe, each on 2 beats. Stay on
half-toe for 2 beats, after the third fondu.

---

[1] The first adagio in the third year may be called conventionally small adagio for its
content and is distinguished from the grand adagio, which is executed at the conclusion
of exercises in the center. Battements tendus may be combined with the first adagio or
executed in a separate combination.

3. BATTEMENTS FRAPPÉS, RISING ON HALF-TOE. 8 measures in 2/4.

Six frappés to the side (at 45°), each on 1 beat; on 2 beats, come up on half-toe. Six frappés on half-toe, each on 1 beat, and on 2 beats, end the exercise in fifth position.

4. GRANDS BATTEMENTS JETÉS. 8 measures in 2/4.

Two grands battements jetés croisés front, 2 to the front, en face, 2 in effacé front, 2 to the side; 2 in écarté back, 2 in effacé back, 2 back en face (facing front) and 2 in croisé back, each on 1 beat.

5. GRAND ADAGIO. 16 measures in 4/4 or 48 measures in 3/4 (Slow Waltz).

First and second measures: starting on the right leg, take 7 steps forward and place yourself in fifth position (each step toward the designated place),[2] the right foot front, the arms open in second position.[3] Third and fourth measures: grand plié in fifth position and relevé on half-toe, raise the arms, the right to third (arm) position and the left to first (arm) position (the body bends slightly to the left, the head raised toward the right hand). Fifth measure: développé to the side (right leg). Sixth measure: turn slowly in first arabesque. Seventh measure: lower the right leg to fifth position front, in demi-plié, and make a full turn on half-toe to the left (détourné). Eighth and ninth measures: développé to the side (left leg) and a slow turn in effacé front. Tenth measure: on the first and second beats, plié in effacé; on the third and fourth beats, pas de bourrée en dedans, changing feet. Eleventh and twelfth measures: développé in attitude effacée (left leg) and a slow turn into attitude croisée; transfer the arms, the right to third (arm) position and the left to first (arm) position. The pose is similar to the pose, relevé on half-toe described in the beginning of this adagio. Thirteenth measure: passé at 90° and développé écarté back. Fourteenth measure: lower the leg to fifth position back in demi-plié and make a full turn on half-toe to the left; raise the arms to third (arm) position. Fifteenth and sixteenth measures: sissonne in first arabesque (left leg) run past corner 6, side 7, corner 8, step on the left foot in second arabesque, pointe tendue on the floor.

---

[2] Before the beginning of the adagio, the students should be at a certain distance from their respective places where the exercise begins, starting from fifth position.

[3] It is recommended that the steps be done with a fully extended and pointed foot, avoiding an excessive turn-out. In this way, the students prepare themselves for the conventional but correct gait on the stage.

ALLEGRO

1. 8 measures in 2/4.

Eight assemblés to the side, moving forward and changing feet, each on 1 beat; on half a beat, coupé and 8 assemblés to the side, moving backward and changing feet.

2. 8 measures in 2/4.

Fifth position, right foot front. On 2 beats, sissonne simple, ending with the left foot sur le cou-de-pied back, assemblé. Repeat the sissonne and assemblé once more. Sissonne simple, temps levé on 2 beats and on 2 beats, pas de bourrée en dehors, changing feet. Repeat the whole exercise on the left leg, and subsequently in the reverse direction.

3. 8 measures in 4/4.

Jeté to the side, 2 temps relevés, assemblé croisé back. Each jump is done on 1 beat. Repeat 4 times, in turn on the right and left leg, and subsequently in the reverse direction.

4. 16 measures in 2/4.

Two sissonnes ouvertes croisées front, ending with assemblé, each on 2 beats; 2 sissonnes fermées, traveling forward in a small pose croisée back, each on 1 beat; on 2 beats, petit échappé in second position, changing feet, with temps levé in second position, on half a beat.[4] Repeat on the other leg and subsequently in the reverse direction.

5. SISSONNE TOMBÉE CROISÉE FRONT, BACK AND SIDE. Musical measure 2/4.

Croisée front; on the upbeat, demi-plié and jump; on the first beat, end the jump in fourth position croisée; on the second beat, a sliding jump traveling forward, joining the legs together in fifth position demi-plié.[5] Repeat 4 times forward, and then 4 times backward. (In the following lessons, sissonne tombée is studied to the side, in a small pose effacée front and back.) Sissonne tombée can be done to the tempo of a waltz, each in 2 measures.

---

[4] Temps levé in second position must be short-spaced, resembling a springboard jump.
[5] The sliding jump is similar to the concluding jump in pas de basque.

6. 8 measures in 4/4.

Two grands échappés in second position, changing feet, each on 2 beats; on 4 beats, 1 grand échappé with 2 temps levés in second position. Repeat 4 times.

7. 8 measures in 2/4.

Two petits changements de pieds, each on 1 beat; 3 on half a beat each and on half a beat, pause. Repeat 4 times.[6]

FIRST EXAMPLE OF EXERCISES ON POINTES[7]

1. 16 measures in 2/4.

Four relevés in first position, each on 2 beats; 8 relevés each on 1 beat. Execute the same in second position.

2. 16 measures in 4/4.

Four échappés in second position, changing feet, each on 2 beats; on 4 beats, 1 double échappé and 4 échappés, changing feet, each on 1 beat. Repeat 4 times.

3. 16 measures in 2/4.

Three sissonnes simples, right, left, right foot, on 2 beats each; 2 sissonnes simples, left and right foot, each on 1 beat. Repeat 4 times, and execute in the reverse direction.

4. 16 measures in 2/4.

On the right leg: 4 jetés traveling forward in a small pose croisée, each on 2 beats. In 4 measures, with the right foot front, pas de bourrée suivi in a straight line to the right, ending with the transfer of the left foot front in fifth position. Repeat on the other leg.

5. Musical measure 2/4 (Polka).

On 2 introductory chords, come up in fifth position on pointes. Eight polka steps, moving front and 8 polka steps moving back. At the discretion of the teacher, the polka step forward can be executed in a small circle to the right and to the left side.

---

[6] Each lesson ends with the port de bras and the bending of the body.

[7] In the third year, it is recommended that the lesson be conducted on pointes twice a week, in place of the allegro.

Arabesque holding the barre.

Second Lesson

EXERCISES AT THE BARRE

1. 16 measures in 4/4.
Two grands pliés, each on 1 beat; on 4 beats, relevé on half-toe; 2 relevés, each on 2 beats. Execute in first, second, fourth, and fifth positions.

2. BATTEMENTS TENDUS. 32 measures in 2/4.
Six battements tendus front, each on 1 beat; execute the seventh battement with a half turn toward the barre, changing feet, on 1 beat, and open the left foot front, pointe tendue on the floor; on 1 beat, bring

the left foot into fifth position. Repeat the same with the left foot. Four doubles battements tendus to the side, on the right foot, each on 2 beats. Battements tendus jetés: 3 to the side, 3 to the front, 3 to the side, and 3 to the back, each on half a beat (half a beat, pause). Repeat the whole combination in the reverse direction; starting on the right foot to the back.

3. RONDS DE JAMBE À TERRE. 12 measures in 4/4.

On 2 introductory chords, préparation en dehors. Four ronds de jambe à terre, each on 1 beat; end the fourth rond de jambe à terre front, pointe tendue on the floor. A quick passé (passing movement) through first position with little throws of the leg to the back, front, back at 45° (tendu jeté), each on half a beat (half a beat, pause); continue front, back, front, as well on half a beat each. Continue the same with ronds de jambe à terre en dedans, and then repeat once en dehors and en dedans. Two measures: trace a half circle in plié en dedans, then en dehors; 2 measures; port de bras in a deep plié, bending the body.

4. BATTEMENTS FONDUS TOMBÉS. 32 measures in 2/4.

On 2 beats, fondu front; on 2 beats, tombé front in plié on the working right leg, bring the left foot sur le cou-de-pied back and fondu on the left leg back; on 2 beats, tombé back in plié on the left leg, bring the right foot sur le cou-de-pied front and fondu on the right leg front; 2 beats, maintain the position. Four fondus to the side (right leg), each on 2 beats. Repeat the same in the reverse direction, starting with the right leg to the back. Frappés to the side: 4, each on 1 beat; 3 and once more 3, each on half a beat (half a beat, pause). Repeat the combination of frappés 4 times.

5. RONDS DE JAMBE EN L'AIR. 8 measures in 4/4.

On 2 introductory chords, préparation temps relevé en dehors. Four ronds de jambe en l'air, each on 1 beat. Bring the working leg to fifth position back in demi-plié on 1 beat; on 1 beat, a full turn on half-toe away from the barre and on 2 beats, préparation temps relevé en dehors. Repeat the same once more and subsequently twice the same en dedans.

6. PETITS BATTEMENTS SUR LE COU-DE-PIED. 16 measures in 2/4.

Sixteen petits battements, each on 1 beat. In 4 measures: open the working leg to the side at 45°, lower to fifth position back and développé in attitude effacée, rising on half-toe; in 4 measures: développé in attitude croisée, rising on half-toe.

7. BATTEMENTS SOUTENUS AT 90°.[1] 8 measures in 4/4.

On the first beat, come up on half-toe; simultaneously raise the working leg, pointe tendue, to the knee of the supporting leg; on the second beat, demi-plié on the supporting leg, extend the working leg at 90° in any given direction; on the third beat, start lowering the working leg; and on the fourth beat, slide the working leg, joining the supporting leg in fifth position and simultaneously come up on half-toe. Execute twice to the front, to the side, to the back, and to the side.

8. GRANDS BATTEMENTS JETÉS. 8 measures in 2/4.

Four grands battements front, 4 in écarté back, 4 to the back, and 4 in écarté front, each on 1 beat.

9. PRÉPARATION FOR TOURS (PIROUETTES) FROM FIFTH POSITION EN DEHORS AND EN DEDANS.

For the men's lessons, préparation starts from fifth and from second position. Study each movement in one measure in 4/4.

EXERCISES IN THE CENTER

1. SMALL ADAGIO AND BATTEMENTS TENDUS. 8 measures in 4/4.

First and second measures: grand plié in fourth position effacée and relevé on half-toe. Third and fourth measures: développé front (right leg), turn the body in pose effacée front and come up on half-toe, ending by lowering the working leg in fifth position back. Fifth and sixth measures: développé back (right leg), turn the body in attitude effacée, come up on half-toe, and end in fifth position front. Seventh and eighth measures: développé back (left leg), demi-rond en dedans to the side, and turn in pose écartée front.

Battements tendus: 8 measures in 4/4. Four in croisé front, each on 1 beat; battements tendus jetés front in a pose croisée, 3 and once more 3, each on half a beat. Repeat the same to the side, then to the back in pose croisée back and to the side.

---

[1] In order to avoid overloading the exercise in the study of battements soutenus at 90° during the first lessons, it is also possible to substitute battements développés. Later, battements soutenus at 90° are done in place of battements fondus.

2. RONDS DE JAMBE À TERRE. 24 measures in 2/4.

On 2 introductory chords, préparation en dehors. Eight ronds de jambe à terre, each on 1 beat, end the eighth rond de jambe to the front, pointe tendue on the floor; on 2 beats, relevé to 90°; on 2 beats, demi-rond en dehors to the side; on 2 beats, come up on half-toe; on 2 beats, lower the working leg, pointe tendue on the floor in second position. Starting from this position, repeat all en dedans. Four measures: trace a half circle in plié, en dedans, then en dehors; 4 measures: port de bras in deep plié, bending the body toward the leg in croisé back, pointe tendue on the floor.

3. BATTEMENTS FONDUS AT 45° ON HALF-TOE.[2] 8 measures in 2/4.

Two fondus front, to the side, to the back and to the side, each on 2 beats.

4. PAS DE BOURRÉE DESSUS-DESSOUS.[3] Musical measure 2/4 or 3/4.

5. RONDS DE JAMBE EN L'AIR, RISING ON HALF-TOE.[4] 8 measures in 2/4.

Six ronds de jambe en l'air en dehors on the flat foot, each on 1 beat; on 2 beats, come up on half-toe. Six ronds de jambe en l'air en dehors on half-toe; on 2 beats, come down in fifth position. Execute en dedans separately.

6. PETITS BATTEMENTS SUR LE COU-DE-PIED, RISING ON HALF-TOE. Musical measure 2/4.

Six petits battements on the flat foot, each on 1 beat; on 2 beats, come up on half-toe. Six petits battements on half-toe, on 2 beats, open the working leg to the side at 45°, and come down in fifth position.[5]

7. PRÉPARATION FROM SECOND POSITION FOR TOURS (PIROUETTES) SUR LE COU-DE-PIED EN DEHORS AND EN DEDANS. Musical measure 4/4.

Each préparation is done in 2 measures. First measure: on the first

[2] Starting from this lesson, battements fondus and frappés are executed in the center of the studio, entirely on half-toe.
[3] In the beginning, pas de bourrée dessus-dessous is studied with pointe tendue on the floor, subsequently with the leg opening at 45°.
[4] After a few lessons, préparation temps relevé and ronds de jambe en l'air are executed entirely on half-toe.
[5] After a few lessons, préparation and petits battements are executed entirely on half-toe, without any acceleration of musical tempo.

beat, demi-plié in fifth position; on the second beat, spring up quickly in fifth position half-toe; on the third beat, remaining on the supporting leg, half-toe, open the other leg to the side at 45°; on the fourth beat, maintain the position. Second measure: on the first beat, demi-plié in second position; on the second beat, spring up quickly on the supporting leg, half-toe, bring the other leg sur le cou-de-pied front; on the third beat, maintain the position; on the fourth beat, come down in fifth position, demi-plié.

8. GRAND ADAGIO.[6] 8 measures in 4/4 or 32 measures in 3/4 (Slow Waltz).

Fifth position, right foot front. First measure: 2 glissades to the right side, changing feet, and relevé on half-toe. Second measure: grand plié in fifth position. Third and fourth measures: développé croisé front, (right leg), the right arm raised to third (arm) position, the left to second (arm) position, and demi-rond in écarté front, ending in fifth position. Fifth and sixth measures: développé écarté back (left leg) and demi-rond in third arabesque. Seventh measure: from third arabesque, without lowering the leg, move arms and body to fourth arabesque. Eighth measure: lower the working leg in fifth position and follow with pas de basque front.

ALLEGRO

1. 8 measures in 4/4.

Assemblé front to the side, changing feet, and 3 assemblés croisées front, each on 1 beat. Repeat 4 times, on the right and left leg in turn and subsequently in the reverse direction.

2. 8 measures in 2/4.

Jeté to the side, temps levé, in turn on the right and left leg. Each jump is done on 1 beat. Repeat 4 times, then coupé on half a beat, and continue, repeating the whole exercise in the reverse direction.

3. JETÉ TRAVELING FRONT IN CROISÉ, TO THE BACK AND TO THE SIDE. Musical measure 4/4.

Croisé front. On the first beat, demi-plié; jump between the first and

---

[6] Taking into account the length of this exercise in the center of the studio, one can transfer the grand adagio to the following lesson and execute the allegro combinations immediately after préparation for tours from second position.

second beats, traveling front on the right leg; on the second beat, end the jump in demi-plié, the left foot sur le cou-de-pied back; on the third beat, assemblé; on the fourth beat, stretch the knees. Repeat 4 times. Execute the same to croisé back and to the side.[7]

4. 8 measures in 2/4.

Two pas de basque front, each on 2 beats; 3 sissonnes fermées, traveling forward, in a small pose croisée, and 1 sissonne to the side, each on 1 beat. Repeat on the other leg and thereafter in the reverse direction.

5. 16 measures in 2/4 or 32 measures in 3/4 (Waltz).

Sissonne tombée croisée front and to the side, in 1 measure in 2/4, or in 2 measures of a waltz. (Temps lié sauté). Execute 4 times to the front and 4 times to the back.

6. BALLONNÉ TO THE SIDE WITHOUT TRAVELING. Musical measure 4/4.

On the first beat, demi-plié; jump, between the first and second beats; on the second beat, end the jump in demi-plié; on the third beat, assemblé; on the fourth beat, stretch the knees. Repeat 4 to 8 times.[8]

7. 4 measures in 4/4.

Two grands changements de pieds, each on 1 beat; 3 petits changements de pieds, each on half a beat. Repeat 4 times.

8. GRANDS BATTEMENTS JETÉS. 8 measures in 2/4.

Eight grands battements to the side, in turn with the right and left leg, bringing down the working leg each time in fifth position back (moving backward). Eight grands battements to the side, bringing down the working leg in fifth position front (moving forward), each on 1 beat.

SECOND EXAMPLE OF EXERCISES ON POINTES

1. 8 measures in 2/4.

Eight relevés in first position, 8 relevés in second position, each on 1 beat.

---

[7] According to the ability of the students, jeté with a traveling motion is done on 1 beat.

[8] Ballonné is studied facing the barre for a period of a week, then in the center of the studio, to the side and in croisé front and back. Depending on the ability of the students in this exercise, each step is done on 1 beat.

2. 16 measures in 2/4.

Two sus-sous, traveling front, right foot front, each on 2 beats; 4 sus-sous, each on 1 beat. On the first sus-sous, the arms are in first (arm) position, on the second sus-sous, the right arm in third (arm) position and the left in second (arm) position. On the following sus-sous, open the arms gradually and lower into the preparatory (arm) position. Two sus-sous, traveling back, each on 2 beats; 4 sus-sous, each on 1 beat. The position of the arms is similar to the one in sus-sous front, only the left arm rises to third (arm) position. Four jetés on the right leg, traveling to the right side, each on 2 beats. Two relevés in fifth position, each on 2 beats. On the first relevé, the right arm in second (arm) position, the left arm in first (arm) position; on the second relevé, the left arm in second position, the right arm in first position. On 2 beats, step forward on pointes in fifth position, raising the arms in third (arm) position; on 2 beats, come down in demi-plié in the pose third arabesque, the left foot back, pointe tendue on the floor.

3. PAS DE BOURÉE DESSUS-DESSOUS, POINTE TENDUE ON THE FLOOR. Musical measure 2/4 or 3/4.

Execute 8 times on the right and left foot.

4. 8 measures in 4/4.

Two échappés in second position, ending on one leg, the other sur le cou-de-pied back, in turn on the right and left leg, each on 1 beat. In 2 measures, 1 échappé on the right leg, ending on one foot, with an additional relevé on the left foot, and relevé in fifth position. Repeat on the other leg. Execute the same in the reverse direction.

5. 16 measures in 2/4 or 32 measures in 3/4 (Waltz).

Sissonne simple on the left leg, the right foot sur le cou-de-pied front (without changing feet). Sissonne simple on the right foot, the left foot sur le cou-de-pied back (without changing feet), each on 2 beats. Repeat 4 times. In 8 measures, pas couru on the right foot to croisé front, gradually lift the arms to third (arm) position and bring them down in the preparatory (arm) position.

Leg in second position, at the barre.

Third Lesson

EXERCISES AT THE BARRE

1. 16 measures in 4/4.

Two demi-pliés, each on 2 beats; 2 grands pliés, each on 4 beats, and on 4 beats, relevé on half-toe in first, second, fourth, and fifth positions.

2. BATTEMENTS TENDUS. 24 measures in 2/4.

Four battements tendus front (right foot), gradually lifting the arms in third (arm) position; 4 battements tendus back (left foot), lowering the arms from third position to arabesque position; 8 battements tendus to the side (right foot), each on 1 beat. Repeat in the reverse direction, starting with the right foot back. Battements tendus jetés: 6 front, each on half a beat, the seventh in demi-plié, on 1 beat. Repeat the same jetés to the side, to the back and to the side.

3. RONDS DE JAMBE À TERRE. 24 measures in 2/4.

On 2 introductory chords, préparation en dehors. Eight ronds de jambe à terre, each on 1 beat; 2 on 1 beat, 3 on half a beat each (half a beat, pause); 2 on 1 beat, 3 on half a beat (half a beat, pause). Repeat en dedans. Four measures: trace a half circle in plié en dedans–en dehors; 4 measures: port de bras in deep plié, bending the body.

4. BATTEMENTS DOUBLES FONDUS AT 45°. 16 measures in 4/4.

On the first beat, demi-plié, the working leg in position sur le cou-de-pied; on the second beat, relevé on half-toe, on the supporting leg; the working leg remains sur le cou-de-pied; on the third beat, demi-plié on the supporting leg; the working leg begins to open in the given direction; on the fourth beat, come up on half-toe on the supporting leg, and simultaneously stretch the working leg.[1] Execute twice to the front, to the side, to the back, and to the side.

Frappés to the side: 2, each on 1 beat; 3, each on half a beat (half a beat, pause). Repeat 4 times. Doubles frappés: effacé front, effacé back, effacé front, effacé back, and 4 to the side, each on 1 beat; on 1 beat, lower the working leg in fifth position back, make a half turn on half-toe away from the barre and with the left foot back, take a pose effacée back, pointe tendue on the floor, in plié; on 4 beats, relevé to 90° in attitude effacée.

5. RONDS DE JAMBE EN L'AIR. 8 measures in 4/4.

On 4 beats, préparation from fifth position for tour sur le cou-de-pied en dehors, on the fourth beat open the working leg to the side at 45°; 11 ronds de jambe en l'air en dehors, each on 1 beat, and on 1 beat, bring the working leg down to fifth position back. Repeat the same en dedans.

6. PETITS BATTEMENTS SUR LE COU-DE-PIED. 16 measures in 2/4.

Six petits battements front, each on 1 beat, on the sixth petit battement, the arm in second position comes down to the preparatory (arm) position. On 1 beat, tombé to fifth position front, on the right working leg in demi-plié, the left sur le cou-de-pied back. On 1 beat, make a half turn on the right foot half-toe toward the barre, and bring the left foot sur le cou-de-pied front. Repeat the same on the left leg, and

---

[1] Students beginning the study of the battement fondu, should execute it on 4 beats. After the students have developed some facility in the step (one or two weeks), it should be executed on 2 beats.

subsequently execute petits battements on the right and left foot and tombé back with a half turn away from the barre. (Before tombé back, the arm remains in second position.)[2]

7. BATTEMENTS DÉVELOPPÉS. 16 measures in 4/4.

First measure: développé front and demi-rond en dehors to the side. Second measure: demi-rond en dedans front and relevé on half-toe (on the third and fourth beats). Third measure: passé through first position back and relevé to 90°, in second arabesque demi-plié. Fourth measure: demi-rond en dedans (stretching the supporting leg) to pose écartée back and end in fifth position. Fifth measure: développé back and demi-rond en dedans to the side. Sixth measure demi-rond en dehors back and relevé on half toe (on the third and fourth beats). Seventh measure: passé through first position front and relevé front to 90°, in demi-plié. Eighth measure: demi-rond en dehors (stretching the supporting leg) to pose écartée front. Repeat the whole exercise from the beginning.

8. GRANDS BATTEMENTS JETÉS. 16 measures in 2/4.

Six grands battements front, each on 1 beat, end the sixth battement in fifth position, demi-plié; on 2 beats, make a full turn in fifth position, half-toe, to the barre, and come down on both feet. Six grands battements back, each on 1 beat, end the sixth battement in fifth position, demi-plié; on 2 beats, make a full turn in fifth position half-toe, away from the barre and come down on both feet. Eight grands battements to the side, each on 1 beat, and in 4 measures, third port de bras, bending the body.

EXERCISES IN THE CENTER

1. SMALL ADAGIO AND BATTEMENTS TENDUS. 8 measures in 4/4.

First and second measures: grand plié in fifth position (right foot front) and relevé on half-toe. Third and fourth measures: grand rond de jambe développé en dehors concluding with a rise on half-toe and ending in fifth position. Fifth measure: by means of a petit battement sur le cou-de-pied, bring the left foot back, développé attitude croisée, raise the right arm to third (arm) position; subsequently change the arms, opening

---

[2] This combination of petits battements is done on both legs, without repeating separately on the left leg, but it can be grouped together on the right and left foot in a separate combination.

the right in second position and raising the left in third position. Sixth and seventh measures: stretch the left leg croisé back and make a grand rond de jambe développé en dedans concluding with a rise on half-toe and ending in fifth position. Eighth measure: first arabesque (left leg) pointe tendue on the floor, bending the body. Battements tendus: 8 measures in 4/4. Right foot, in a big pose effacée front: 2 in demi-plié, 2 on the straight leg, each on 1 beat; left foot, in a big pose effacée back: 2 in demi-plié, 2 on the straight leg, each on 1 beat; right foot, 8 tendus to the side, each on 1 beat. Battements tendus jetés: 7 to the side in first position and 7 once more, each on half a beat. End the last battement tendu jeté in fifth position front and in 2 measures, préparation from second position for tour sur le cou-de-pied en dehors.

2. BATTEMENTS SOUTENUS. 8 measures in 4/4.

Two soutenus front, pointe tendue on the floor, each on 2 beats, 1 soutenu at 90°, on 4 beats. Repeat the same to the side, to the back, and to the side.

3. BATTEMENTS FRAPPÉS. 4 measures in 4/4.

On 2 introductory chords, come up on half-toe and open the working leg to the side at 45°. Seven frappés, each on 1 beat; bring the working leg down to fifth position front on 1 beat, and make a préparation from second position for tour sur le cou-de-pied en dedans in 2 measures.

4. RONDS DE JAMBE EN L'AIR. 4 measures in 4/4.

On 2 introductory chords, préparation temps relevé en dehors. Eight ronds de jambe en l'air, each on 1 beat; on the eighth rond de jambe, demi-plié; 2 pas de bourrée dessus-dessous, in 2 measures. Repeat the same with ronds de jambe en l'air en dedans and pas de bourrée dessus-dessous.

5. PRÉPARATION FROM FIFTH POSITION FOR TOURS SUR LE COU-DE-PIED EN DEHORS AND EN DEDANS. Musical measure 4/4.

Execute each préparation in 1 measure. On the first beat, demi-plié; on the second beat, spring up on half toe on the supporting foot and place the other foot sur le cou-de-pied; on the third beat, maintain the position; on the fourth beat, come down in fifth position demi-plié.

6. GRANDS BATTEMENTS JETÉS POINTÉS. 8 measures in 4/4.

Execute each grand battement on 1 beat. Right leg: 6 grands battements jetés pointés and 1 in fifth position in effacé front; join the arms in first (arm) position on 1 beat. Left leg: 6 grands battements jetés pointés and 1 in fifth position, in first arabesque to corner 2; on the last battement, lower the arms in the preparatory (arm) position, and open them in second (arm) position on 1 beat. Right leg: 8 grands battements jetés to the side in fifth position, then relevé in first arabesque to 90° on the left leg in 1 measure, and in 1 measure come down in demi-plié, taking a pose in second arabesque.

7. GRAND ADAGIO. 12 measures in 4/4.

Right foot front. First and second measures: grand plié in fourth position effacée and relevé on half-toe. Third measure: développé in effacé front (right leg), demi-rond en dehors in écarté back. Fourth measure: move to attitude effacée. Fifth measure: plié in attitude, on 2 beats, and pas de bourrée en dehors (changing feet) on 2 beats. Sixth measure: développé attitude effacée (left leg), and without lowering the leg, move to first arabesque facing corner 2. Seventh measure: relevé on half-toe in arabesque, ending in fifth position. Eighth measure: développé to the side (right leg), raising the arms to third (arm) position. Ninth measure: move into second arabesque. Tenth measure: passé at 90° in croisé front. Eleventh measure: come up on half-toe and bring the working leg down to fifth position. Twelfth measure: from fifth position half-toe, turn to the left side into a small pose croisée front (plié) left foot, pointe tendue on the floor.

ALLEGRO

1. 16 measures in 2/4.

Two doubles assemblés on the right and left leg, each on 2 beats; échappé in second position, changing feet, on 2 beats and sissonne tombée croisée front, on 2 beats. Repeat on the other leg and in the reverse direction.

2. 4 measures in 4/4.

Jeté to the side, 2 temps levé, assemblé croisée back. Repeat on the other leg. Four jetés in turn on the right and left leg (each jump on 1 beat) and 2 pas de bourrée changing feet en dehors, each on 2 beats. Repeat the same in the reverse direction.

3. 8 measures in 2/4.

Fifth position, left foot front. Jeté, traveling to the side on the right leg (without changing feet), ending assemblé croisé front. Jeté, traveling to croisé front on the left leg, ending assemblé croisé back. Execute each jump on 1 beat. Repeat 4 times and 4 times on the other leg and subsequently in the reverse direction.

4. 8 measures in 2/4.

Three ballonnés to the side, ending the first ballonné sur le cou-de-pied front, the second to the back, the third to the front, each on 1 beat; assemblé to the side, ending in fifth position back, on 1 beat. Repeat 4 times, in turn on the right and the left leg.

5. 8 measures in 2/4.

Three ballonnés croisés front, each on 1 beat; assemblé to the side, ending in fifth position back, on 1 beat. Repeat 4 times, in turn, on the right and the left leg, and subsequently in the reverse direction.

6. PAS DE CHAT WITH A THROW OF THE LEGS TO THE BACK. Musical measure 4/4.

a) Fifth position, left foot front. On the first beat, demi-plié and simultaneously throw the right leg croisé to the back (half bent) at 45°; between the first and second beats, jump forward, throwing the left leg effacé back (half bent) at 45°; on the second beat, end the jump in fifth position, demi-plié; on the third and fourth beats, stretch the knees. Repeat 4 times.

b) On the first beat: demi-plié in fifth position; jump between the first and second beats, ending the jump on the second beat; on the third and fourth beats, stretch the knees. Repeat 4 to 8 times.[3]

7. Musical measure 3/4 (Waltz).

A quick run on pointed feet on the diagonal from corner 6 to corner 2, thereafter from corner 4 to corner 8.[4]

8. 8 measures in 2/4.

Grand échappé in fourth position croisée, grand échappé in second position, changing feet, each on 2 beats; 4 grands changements de pieds, each on 1 beat. Repeat on the other leg.

9. 8 measures in 2/4.

Seven big temps levés in first position (as from a springboard), each on half a beat, and pause in demi-plié on half a beat. Repeat 4 times.[5]

[3] According to the mastery, the pas de chat back is executed on 2 beats; on the upbeat, demi-plié and jump; on the first beat, end the jump in demi-plié; on the second beat, maintain the position in demi-plié. After six months' training, execute the pas de chat on 1 beat.

[4] During the run, it is necessary to keep the body slightly back, as if "set apart" from the legs. The body is not allowed to lean forward or bob up and down during the run. The steps are taken with the foot fully extended, striding from the pointed toe to the heel and with the greatest smoothness possible. The position of the arms may be very varied, according to the instruction of the teacher.

[5] Execute in a quick tempo.

10. 4 measures in 4/4.

Two petits changements de pieds, each on 1 beat; 3 changements de pieds, each on half a beat. Repeat 4 times.

THIRD EXAMPLE OF EXERCISES ON POINTES

1. 16 measures in 2/4.

Sixteen relevés in first position, 16 in second position, each on 1 beat.

2. 8 measures in 2/4.

Right foot front. Eight échappés in second position, changing feet. Eight échappés, the first en tournant to the right side to side 3 (a quarter turn), the second en face to side 3; continue with the following échappés, the third, en tournant, the fourth en face to side 5, and likewise to side 7 and side 1, each on 2 beats.

3. 16 measures in 2/4.

Four sissonnes simples, in turn on the right and left leg, changing feet to the back; 4 sissonnes simples on the left leg, starting with the right leg, changing to the back, then to the front, to the back and to the front, each on 2 beats. On those last 4 sissonnes, the body bends slightly to the right, the right arm in first (arm) position, the left arm in second (arm) position. Repeat once more.

4. JETÉ FONDU ON THE DIAGONAL FRONT AND BACK (COMING DOWN SOFTLY THROUGH THE BALL OF THE FOOT, ON EACH STEP). Musical measure 2/4.

Eight jetés fondus front (starting on the right leg) from corner 6 to corner 2, each in 1 measure. Repeat on the left leg, from corner 4 to corner 8, and subsequently in the reverse direction.

5. 16 measures in 3/4 (Waltz).

Two échappés in second position, changing feet, each in 2 measures; 2 pas de basque front, each in 2 measures. Repeat once more, and subsequently with pas de basque to the back.

Class in courtly dances.

Fourth Lesson

EXERCISES AT THE BARRE[1]

1. 8 measures in 4/4.

Two grands pliés in first, second, fourth, and fifth positions, each on 4 beats.

[1] As seen in previous examples, in this lesson certain movements are executed not only on 1 beat, but also on half a beat. In the first three lessons of this year, when 3 movements are executed on half a beat each, a pause is thereafter indicated on the half beat: 7 movements on half a beat each, and on half a beat, pause, etc. In the subsequent development, it is not necessary to spell out such detailed indications, as an odd number of movements, whether executed on half a beat or a quarter of a beat, will generally be followed by a pause.

2. BATTEMENTS TENDUS. 32 measures in 2/4.

Six battements tendus front, each on 1 beat; on the sixth battement tendu, end in demi-plié, then on 1 beat, from fifth position half-toe, make a half turn toward the barre, and again on 1 beat, make a half turn toward the barre. Four battements tendus doubles to the side, each on 2 beats. Repeat in the reverse direction, starting on the right foot back with the half turns away from the barre. Battements tendus jetés: 3 front, each on half a beat; on the third, end in demi-plié. Repeat once more. Seven battements tendus jetés to the side, each on half a beat; on the seventh, end in demi-plié. Repeat the same to the back and to the side. Sixteen tendus jetés to the side in first position, each on half a beat.

3. RONDS DE JAMBE À TERRE. 24 measures in 2/4.

On 2 introductory chords, préparation en dehors. Two ronds de jambe à terre, each on 1 beat, 3 on half a beat, each. Repeat 4 en dehors and 4 times en dedans. In 4 measures: trace a half circle en dedans, in plié, then en dehors; in 4 measures, port de bras, in deep plié, bending the body. At the conclusion of the port de bras, on the last 2 beats, demi-plié in fifth position, come up on half-toe and make a half turn away from the barre.

4. BATTEMENTS SOUTENUS. 12 measures in 4/4.

Soutenus front at 90°: 1 on 4 beats, 2 on 2 beats, each. Repeat the same to the side, to the back and to the side. Frappés: 4 front, each on 1 beat, to the side, 3 and again 3, each on half a beat; 4 to the back, each on 1 beat, to the side, 3 and again 3, each on half a beat.

5. RONDS DE JAMBE EN L'AIR. 16 measures in 2/4.

On 2 introductory chords, préparation temps relevé en dehors. Seven ronds de jambe en l'air, each on 1 beat, end the seventh in a small pose effacée front, pointe tendue on the floor, in plié and on 1 beat, come up on half-toe, bringing the working leg to the side at 45°. Repeat the same once more and twice en dedans, in a small pose effacée back.

6. PETITS BATTEMENTS SUR LE COU-DE-PIED. 8 measures in 4/4.

Twelve petits battements front, each on 1 beat; then on 4 beats, préparation, from fifth position for tour en dehors sur le cou-de-pied. Twelve petits battements back, each on 1 beat and on 4 beats, préparation from fifth position for tour en dedans.

7. BATTEMENTS DÉVELOPPÉS. 8 measures in 4/4 or 32 measures in 3/4 (Waltz).

First and second measures: grand rond de jambe développé en dehors, and at the end, relevé on half-toe. Third measure: développé in attitude croisée; on the fourth beat, passé at 90° and simultaneously relevé on half-toe on the supporting leg. Fourth measure: come down from half-toe onto the flat foot; simultaneously open the working leg in pose écartée front. Fifth and sixth measures: grand rond de jambe développé en dedans, and at the end, relevé on half-toe. Seventh measure: développé in pose croisée front, and on the fourth beat, passé at 90° and relevé on half-toe. Eighth measure: come down onto the flat foot and open the working leg in pose écartée back.

8. GRANDS BATTEMENTS JETÉS. 16 measures in 4/4.

Four grands battements front (right leg); 4 grands battements back (left leg); 4 grands battements to the side (right leg) each on 1 beat and on 4 beats, bend the body to the side (toward the barre) raising the arms from second (arm) position to third (arm) position. Repeat in the reverse direction, starting on the right leg back.

EXERCISES IN THE CENTER

1. SMALL ADAGIO AND BATTEMENTS TENDUS. 12 measures in 4/4.

First and second measures: grand plié in fifth position (right foot front), demi-plié, and relevé on half-toe, raising the right arm into third (arm) position and the left arm in second position allongée.[2] Third and fourth measures: développé croisé front (right leg), passé at 90° into first arabesque facing corner 8 and relevé on half-toe, ending in fifth position, right foot front. Fifth measure: développé in third arabesque (left leg), without lowering the leg, move into attitude croisée. Sixth measure: keeping this pose, come down in demi-plié, changing the right arm to

---

[2] It is recommended in the third lesson to introduce the position of arms in allongé, with poses of either leg extended, pointe tendue on the floor, as well as at 90°. In attitude effacée, the position of arms in allongé is taken before lowering the arms into the preparatory (arm) position.

third (arm) position and the left to first (arm) position and end in fifth
position (feet). Seventh measure: développé to the side (left leg). Eighth
measure: relevé on half-toe; end by bringing the left leg down in fifth
position front. Ninth measure: open the right arm to third (arm) position
and the left to first (arm) position. Tenth measure: fifth port de bras.
Eleventh and twelfth measures: pose croisée back in demi-plié with a
slight bending of the body, the right leg back, pointe tendue on the
floor, right arm in third (arm) position and the left arm in second position
allongée.

Battements tendus: 8 measures in 4/4. Four battements tendus (left
foot) in a small pose croisée front, 4 in a small pose croisée back (right
foot); 4 to the side (right foot), each on 1 beat. Tendus jetés: 7 to the
side, each on half a beat. In 2 measures, préparation for tour sur le
cou-de-pied en dehors from second position; in 2 measures, préparation
for tour sur le cou-de-pied en dedans from second position.

2. BATTEMENTS FONDUS AT 45°. 16 measures in 2/4.

Right leg: 2 fondus croisés front, each on 2 beats; tombé front and 2
fondus croisés back (left leg), each on 2 beats; tombé back and 2 fondus
to the side (right leg), tombé to the side and 2 fondus to the side (left
leg), each on 2 beats. Coupé on a quarter of a beat, through half-toe,
bring the right foot front, and battements frappés to the side (right
leg), 2 on 1 beat each, 3 on half a beat each. Repeat the frappés once
more and follow with 8 doubles frappés to the side, each on 1 beat.

3. RONDS DE JAMBE EN L'AIR. 8 measures in 2/4.

On 2 introductory chords, préparation temps relevé en dehors. Eight
ronds de jambe en l'air, each on 1 beat; on 4 beats, développé front
and demi-rond en dehors to the side; on 4 beats, passé at 90° in attitude
croisée, ending relevé, half-toe. Execute en dedans separately.

4. GLISSADE EN TOURNANT IN HALF TOUR. Musical measure 4/4.

Fifth position, right foot front. On the upbeat, demi-plié; on the first
beat, starting on the right foot, glissade on half-toe to the right side
(half a turn). At the end of the glissade, the right foot remains front,
the left arm in first (arm) position, the right in second (arm) position.
On the second beat, come down in demi-plié. On the third beat, glissade
to the side, on half-toe, starting on the left foot with half a turn to
the right, back to the starting position facing corner 1. At the end of
the glissade, the right foot remains front, the right arm in first (arm)
position, the left in second (arm) position. On the fourth beat, come
down in demi-plié. Execute the exercise 8 times in a straight line from
side 7 to side 3.

5. FOURTH PORT DE BRAS (GRAND PORT DE BRAS).

Study in 2 measures, each in 4/4, then, at the end of the first year, in 1 measure.

6. GRAND ADAGIO. 12 measures in 4/4.

Fifth position, right foot front. Open the arms to second position on 2 introductory chords and bring the left foot in position sur le cou-de-pied back, pointe tendue on the floor. First measure: come down in slight plié onto the left leg, closing the arms, the right to third (arm) position and the left in first (arm) position while bending the body slightly to the left; on the fourth beat, step quickly on the right leg in first arabesque to corner 2. Second measure: plié in pose arabesque, step back on the left leg, passé through first position back and relevé in attitude croisée (right leg). Third measure: from pose attitude, demi-rond en dedans in pose écartée back. Fourth measure: bring the working leg down in fifth position and développé in effacée front (left leg). Fifth measure: from pose effacée, demi-rond en dehors in pose écartée back. Sixth measure: from écartée, move into first arabesque, facing corner 2. Seventh measure: passé at 90° in pose croisée front. Eighth measure: from pose croisée, demi-rond en dehors in pose écartée front. Ninth measure: brush the left foot through first position demi-plié to the front, and step on the left foot in croisée, the right foot back, pointe tendue on the floor. Tenth measure: relevé to 90° in fourth arabesque. Eleventh measure: bring the working leg down in fifth position, demi-plié, and make a turn on half-toe to the right side. Twelfth measure: right leg, sissonne tombée effacée front, step on the right leg in effacé back, pointe tendue on the floor, (left foot) the arms in second and third (arm) positions allongées.

ALLEGRO

1. 8 measures in 2/4.

Starting with the right foot: 2 glissades to the side, changing feet, each on 1 beat, 3 glissades to the side, changing feet, each on half a beat. Repeat 4 times, in turn on the right and left side.

2. 4 measures in 4/4.

Fifth position, left foot front. Glissade (right foot) without changing feet, assemblé to the side, ending right foot front, sissonne ouverte croisée front, assemblé. Execute each jump on 1 beat. Repeat 4 times, in turn on the right and left leg and then separately in the reverse direction.

3. 4 measures in 4/4.

Right leg: jeté traveling to the side, temps levé; left leg: jeté traveling croisé front, assemblé croisée back. Repeat 4 times. Execute each jump on 1 beat and execute separately in the reverse direction.

4. 8 measures in 4/4.

Three ballonnés croisés front, each on 1 beat; then, assemblé to the side, on 1 beat and 2 grands échappés in second position, on 2 beats each. Repeat on the other leg and separately in the reverse direction.

5. 8 measures in 2/4.

Three pas de chat back, each on 1 beat; pas de bourrée, changing feet en dehors, on 1 beat. Repeat 3 times in turn on the right and left leg. Two pas de chat front, each on 1 beat, and on 2 beats, pause.

6. CHANGEMENTS DE PIEDS EN TOURNANT. Musical measure 2/4.

a) An eighth of a turn. Fifth position, right foot front. First jump turning to corner 2, second jump to side 3 and continue to corners and sides 4, 5, 6, 7, 8, and 1, each on 1 beat.

b) A quarter of a turn. First, jump turning to side 3; second, jump to side 5; and continue to side 7 and 1.[3]

7. 8 measures in 2/4.

Eight grands changements de pieds, each on 1 beat; 7 and once more 7 petits changements de pieds, each on half a beat.

FOURTH EXAMPLE OF EXERCISES ON POINTES

1. 16 measures in 2/4.

Four relevés in first position, each on 2 beats; 8 relevés, each on 1 beat. Execute the same in second position.

[3] For a better assimilation of jumps en tournant, one can alternate with jumps without turns.

2. 8 measures in 4/4.

Two échappés in fourth position croisée, each on 2 beats; double échappé in second position, changing feet, on 4 beats. Repeat 4 times.

3. GLISSADE EN TOURNANT IN HALF TURN.

Execution similar to that in the exercise on half-toe.

4. 16 measures in 3/4 (Waltz).

Fifth position, left foot front, moving diagonally from corner 6 to corner 2. Seven jetés fondus front (starting on the right leg), each in 1 measure. The seventh time, tombé front on the left leg, open the right leg in écarté front, pointe tendue on the floor to corner 2, turn the body with the right shoulder toward corner 2 and slightly bend toward the foot. In 8 measures: pas de bourrée suivi upward on the diagonal to corner 6; right foot front, the body facing with the right shoulder, corner 2, and with the left shoulder corner 6, the right arm in first (arm) position, the left arm in second (arm) position.

5. 8 measures in 2/4.

Eight sissonnes simples, in turn on the right and left leg, changing feet to the back; then 8 sissonnes simples, changing feet to the front, each on 1 beat.

6. PRÉPARATION FROM FIFTH POSITION FOR TOURS SUR LE COU-DE-PIED EN DEHORS AND EN DEDANS.

En dehors. Fifth position, right foot front. On the upbeat, demi-plié. On the first beat, spring up quickly on toe, on the left foot, the right foot sur le cou-de-pied front, the right arm in first (arm) position, the left in second (arm) position; on the second beat, maintaining the same arm position, come down in fifth position, demi-plié; on the third beat, spring up quickly on toe, on the left foot, the right foot sur le cou-de-pied front, both arms meeting in first (arm) position; on the fourth beat, come down in fifth position, demi-plié, bringing the right foot back. En dedans. Fifth position, right foot front. On the upbeat, demi-plié. On the first beat, spring up quickly on toe, on the right foot, the left foot sur le cou-de-pied back, the right arm in first (arm) position, the left arm in second (arm) position; on the second beat, demi-plié in fifth position; on the third beat, spring up quickly on toe, on the right foot, the left foot sur le cou-de-pied front, both arms meet in first (arm) position; on the fourth beat, come down in fifth position, demi-plié, bringing the left foot front.

Position à la seconde en l'air, on pointes.

Second Semester
Fifth Lesson

EXERCISES AT THE BARRE

1. 12 measures in 4/4.

Two grands pliés in first, second, fourth, and fifth positions, on 4 beats each; 2 ports de bras, bending the body, each in 2 measures.

2. BATTEMENTS TENDUS. 32 measures in 2/4.

Four battements tendus front, demi-plié on the fourth battement. Repeat the same to the side, to the back and to the side. Two battements tendus front (right foot), 2 battements tendus back (left foot), 4 to the side (right foot). Two battements tendus back (right foot), 2 battements tendus front (left foot), 4 to the side (right foot), each on 1 beat. Battements tendus jetés: 7 to the front, each on half a beat, on the seventh, demi-plié. Repeat the same to the side, to the back and to the side. Seven battements tendus jetés in first position, each on half a beat, repeating 4 times.

3. RONDS DE JAMBE À TERRE. 16 measures in 2/4.

On 2 introductory chords, préparation en dehors. Four ronds de jambe à terre, each on 1 beat, ending front at 45°; on 2 beats, bring the working leg to the side, to the back and front through first position at 45°, and on another 2 beats, repeat the same once more. Execute the same, from the beginning of the exercise en dedans. In 2 measures, trace a half circle in plié, en dedans and en dehors; in 2 measures, port de bras in deep plié, bending the body; thereafter end in fifth position demi-plié, and on the last beat, make a half turn on half-toe, away from the barre.

4. BATTEMENTS FONDUS AT 45°. 32 measures in 2/4.

Two doubles fondus, 2 simples fondus front, each on 2 beats. Repeat the same to the side, to the back, and to the side. Frappés: 3 front, each on 1 beat, then on 1 beat, coupé, release the left foot back; 3 frappés with the left foot back, each on 1 beat, then coupé, opening the right leg to the side; 3 frappés and again 3 frappés to the side, each on half a beat; 4 doubles frappés, each on 1 beat. Repeat frappés in the reverse direction, starting with the right foot back.

5. RONDS DE JAMBE EN L'AIR. 8 measures in 2/4.

On 2 introductory chords, préparation temps relevé en dehors. Two ronds de jambe en l'air, each on 1 beat; 3 ronds de jambe en l'air, each on half a beat. Repeat once more and separately in the reverse direction.

6. PETITS BATTEMENTS SUR LE COU-DE-PIED. 8 measures in 2/4.

Eight petits battements, each on 1 beat; 16 petits battements, each on half a beat.

7. BATTEMENTS DÉVELOPPÉS. 16 measures in 4/4.

First measure: relevé lent to 90°, to the side. Second measure: demi-rond en dedans, to the front. Third and fourth measures: passé at 90°, développé to the side, and on half-toe, demi-rond to the front, ending in fifth position. Fifth measure: relevé lent to 90° in effacé front. Sixth measure: demi-rond in écarté back. Seventh and eighth measures: passé at 90° in effacé front (half-toe) and demi-rond in écarté back, ending in fifth position. Ninth measure: relevé to 90° to the side. Tenth measure: demi-rond en dehors, to the back. Eleventh and twelfth measures: passé at 90°, développé to the side on half-toe and demi-rond to the back. Thirteenth measure: relevé lent to 90° in effacé back. Fourteenth measure: demi-rond, in écarté front. Fifteenth and sixteenth measures: passé at 90° in effacé back on half-toe and demi-rond in écarté front.

8. GRANDS BATTEMENTS JETÉS POINTÉS. 4 measures in 4/4.

Three grands battements pointés and 1 in fifth position, in effacé front, in écarté back, in effacé back and in écarté front, each on 1 beat.

EXERCISES IN THE CENTER

1. SMALL ADAGIO. 8 measures in 4/4.

Fifth position, right foot front, left arm in third (arm) position, the right arm in second (arm) position. First measure: grand plié with second port de bras. Second measure: fourth port de bras. Third measure: développé to the side and demi-rond to croisé front (left leg). Fourth measure: plié in the pose croisée and 1 step forward onto the left foot, taking a pose in attitude croisée. Fifth measure: plié in attitude and pas de bourrée, changing feet en dehors. Sixth and seventh measures: grand rond de jambe développé en dehors (right leg) and at the end relevé on half-toe. Eighth measure: relevé to 90° in first arabesque on half-toe (left leg).

2. BATTEMENTS TENDUS EN TOURNANT. Musical measure 2/4.

En dehors. Fifth position, right foot front. First battement to the side, with an eighth of a turn to corner 2, the second battement to the side, without any turn, facing again corner 2. Third battement, with an eighth of a turn to side 3, the fourth battement without any turn, facing again side 3 and so forth to corners and sides 4, 5, 6, 7, 8, and 1, each battement on 1 beat. In the execution en dedans, the position of the right foot beforehand is in fifth position back and the turns follow to corners and sides 8, 7, 6, 5, 4, 3, 2, and 1.

3. TOURS SUR LE COU-DE-PIED FROM SECOND POSITION EN DEHORS AND EN DEDANS. Musical measure 4/4.

The movement is distributed on musical beats, just as in the exercise of the first semester for the préparation for tours. All demi-pliés are done on the first beats of a measure, then toward the end of the year, all demi-pliés are done on the upbeat, which means on the half beat before the first beat of a measure. Tours are executed on the second and third beats of the second measure.

4. PRÉPARATION AND TOUR SUR LE COU-DE-PIED FROM FIFTH POSITION EN DEHORS AND EN DEDANS. Musical measure 4/4.

5. RONDS DE JAMBE À TERRE AND RONDS DE JAMBE EN L'AIR. 12 measures in 4/4.

On 2 introductory chords, préparation en dehors. Eight ronds de jambe à terre, each on 1 beat. End the last rond de jambe rising on half-toe on the supporting leg and simultaneously carry the working leg to the side at 45°. Eight ronds de jambe en l'air en dehors, each on 1 beat. Repeat the same en dedans. In 2 measures: trace a half circle in plié en dedans and en dehors (on the floor) and demi-rond en dedans, stretch the knee of the supporting leg on the last beat. In 1 measure: passé front, pointe tendue on the floor, through first position and simultaneously turn the body en dedans, facing corner 6, then raise the arms through the preparatory (arm) and first (arm) positions to the third (arm) position. In 1 measure, turn the body on the supporting leg en dedans, facing the mirror, and taking a pose in third arabesque, pointe tendue on the floor.

6. BATTEMENTS SOUTENUS. 16 measures in 2/4.

Two soutenus in a small pose croisée front, pointe tendue on the floor, 2 soutenus at 90° in a big pose croisée front, each on 2 beats. Repeat the same to the side, to croisé back and to the side.

7. PETITS BATTEMENTS SUR LE COU-DE-PIED. 8 measures in 2/4.

Fourteen petits battements, each on half a beat; then on 1 beat, bring the working right foot in fifth position front and come down in demi-plié; 4 glissades en tournant in half turns, starting to the right side, each on 2 beats.

8. GRAND ADAGIO. 12 measures in 4/4.

On 2 introductory chords, step forward on the right foot in a big pose croisée back, pointe tendue on the floor. First and second measures: fourth port de bras (grand port de bras). Third measure: relevé to 90°

in third arabesque (left leg). Fourth measure: relevé on half toe, ending in fifth position. Fifth measure: développé to the side and without lowering the leg, move into a pose écartée back (right leg). Sixth measure: plié in pose écartée back and pas de bourrée en dehors, changing feet. Seventh measure: développé to the side, and without lowering the leg, move into a pose écartée front (left leg). Eighth measure: plié in pose écartée front and pas de bourrée en dedans, changing feet. Ninth and tenth measures: développé effacé front, relevé on half-toe, ending in fifth position. Eleventh and twelfth measures: développé attitude effacée and relevé on half-toe.

ALLEGRO

1. 8 measures in 4/4.
Starting with the right leg: assemblé croisé front, to the side, croisé back and to the side, each on 1 beat; échappé in fourth position croisé, échappé in second position, changing feet, each jump on 2 beats. Repeat 4 times, in turn on the right and left leg.

2. 4 measures in 4/4.
Fifth position, left foot front. Starting on the right foot: glissade to the side, without changing feet, then jeté on the right leg to the side, bringing the left foot sur le cou-de-pied back, the right arm in third (arm) position and the left arm in second (arm) position. Execute temps levé, opening the right arm to second (arm) position, then assemblé croisé back. Each jump on 1 beat; repeat 4 times, in turn on the right and left leg.

3. Musical measure 2/4.
a) On 1 beat, ballonné traveling to the side; on 1 beat, assemblé. Repeat 4 times, in turn on the right and left leg.
b) Repeat the same exercise in the poses effacées front and back.[1]

---

[1] Starting with this lesson, ballonné in all directions is executed only with a traveling movement.

4. 8 measures in 2/4 or 16 measures in 3/4 (Waltz).

Right leg: sissonne tombée effacée front, end in fifth position, left foot front; left leg: sissonne tombée effacée front, end in fifth position, right foot front, each on 2 beats. On 2 beats, pas de basque front, starting on the right leg. In the execution of demi-rond en dehors, the right arm is in third (arm) position, the left in second (arm) position; on pas de basque, the right arm opens to second (arm) position, the left lowers to the preparatory (arm) position and comes up through first position to third (arm) position at the end of the jump. On 2 beats, 2 petits changements de pieds, bringing the arms down to the preparatory arm position. Repeat on the other leg and separately in the reverse direction.

5. ÉCHAPPÉS BATTUS. Musical measure 4/4.

On the first beat, demi-plié; jump between the first and second beats; on the second beat, end the jump in second position demi-plié; jump with battu, between the second and third beats; on the third beat, end the jump in fifth position demi-plié; on the fourth beat, stretch the knees. Repeat 8 times.

6. 8 measures in 2/4.

On 2 beats, grand échappé in second position, changing feet; 2 grands changements de pieds, each on 1 beat. Repeat 4 times.

7. 8 measures in 2/4.

Seven petits changements de pieds, each on 1 beat. Repeat 4 times.

FIFTH EXAMPLE OF EXERCISES ON POINTES

1. 16 measures in 2/4.

Six relevés in first position, each on 2 beats; 4 relevés, each on 1 beat. Repeat the same in second position.

2. 8 measures in 4/4.

Two doubles échappés in second position, each on 4 beats; 4 échappés in second position, changing feet, each on 2 beats. Two doubles échappés in second position, 4 échappés in second position en tournant in a quarter of a turn.

3. 16 measures in 3/4 (Waltz).

Starting on the right leg, 2 temps liés front, each in 4 measures; 3 jetés on the right leg in a small pose effacée back, traveling on the diagonal front to corner 2, each in 2 measures. On the third jeté, come down on the right leg in plié and open the left leg back at 45°, in a small second arabesque pose, then in 2 measures, pas de bourrée en dehors, changing feet. Repeat the same in the reverse direction.

4. 32 measures in 2/4.

Four glissades en tournant in half a turn, each on 2 beats; 2 sissonnes simples, changing feet to the back, each on 2 beats; 3 sissonnes simples, each on 1 beat and on 1 beat, a pause in demi-plié. Repeat 4 times, in turn on the right and left leg.

5. 8 measures in 6/8.

In 2 measures: on the right foot, pas de bourrée suivi in a straight line across to the right, ending in demi-plié, the left leg croisé front, pointe tendue on the floor. In 2 measures: execute the same with the left foot front to the left side and in 2 measures, with the right foot to the right side, ending in fifth position, the left foot front. In 2 measures: with the left foot, pas de bourrée suivi front croisé, plié in fifth position and pas de chat back. (Execute pas de bourrée suivi in a quick tempo.)

Grand plié in fourth position, croisé.

Sixth Lesson

EXERCISES AT THE BARRE

1. 16 measures in 4/4.

Two demi-pliés, 2 grands pliés, each on 4 beats in first, second, fourth, and fifth positions.

2. BATTEMENTS TENDUS. 24 measures in 2/4.

Two battements tendus front, to the side, to the back and to the side, each on 1 beat; 3 battements tendus doubles, each on 2 beats, on the third, demi-plié and on 2 beats, make a full turn on half-toe toward the barre. Repeat in the reverse direction, starting with the right foot to the back, with a full turn away from the barre. Battements tendus jetés: 3 front, to the side, to the back and to the side, each on half a beat. Repeat jetés once more.

3. RONDS DE JAMBE À TERRE AND RONDS DE JAMBE EN L'AIR. 12 measures in 4/4.

On 2 introductory chords, préparation en dehors. Four ronds de jambe à terre, each on 1 beat, then 3 ronds de jambe and again 3, each on half a beat; 4 ronds de jambe en l'air en dehors, each on 1 beat, then 3 ronds de jambe en l'air and again 3, each on half a beat. Repeat the same en dedans. In 2 measures: trace a half circle in plié, en dehors and en dedans; in 2 measures: port de bras, bending the body, and end in fifth position demi-plié. On the last beat, make a half turn on half-toe toward the barre.

4. BATTEMENTS FONDUS AT 45°. 8 measures in 4/4.

On 2 beats: fondu front; on 2 beats, plié relevé with a demi-rond to the side. Repeat 2 more times. On 4 beats, tour en dehors sur le cou-de-pied from fifth position. Repeat fondus in the reverse direction with tour en dedans.

5. BATTEMENTS FRAPPÉS. 16 measures in 2/4.

To the side: 3 frappés, 3 times in a row, each on half a beat; make a half turn on the right foot (half-toe) toward the barre, and at the end, extend the left leg to the side at 45° on 1 beat; maintain the position on 1 beat. Repeat the same on the left side and subsequently continue with frappés on the right and left leg, with the half turns away from the barre.[1]

6. PETITS BATTEMENTS SUR LE COU-DE-PIED. 8 measures in 2/4.

Twelve petits battements, each on half a beat; on 1 beat, a small pose effacée front in plié, pointe tendue on the floor; on 1 beat, rise on half-toe on the supporting foot, the working leg opened to the side at 45°. Repeat petits battements in the reverse direction and end in a small pose effacée back in plié, pointe tendue on the floor.

7. BATTEMENTS DÉVELOPPÉS. 16 measures in 4/4.

First measure: développé to the side. Second measure: plié, stretch the

[1] It is recommended that half turns raised on half-toe be studied separately first, and battements frappés, ronds de jambe en l'air, etc., added later.

knee of the supporting leg while the working leg remains in the position développé at 90°. Third measure: demi-rond to the front. Fourth measure: relevé on half toe, ending in fifth position. Fifth measure: développé in pose croisée front. Sixth measure: plié, stretch the knee of the supporting leg, maintaining the pose croisée. Seventh measure: demi-rond to the side. Eighth measure: relevé on half-toe, end in fifth position. Ninth and tenth measures: développé to the side, plié, stretch the knee of the supporting leg. Eleventh and twelfth measures: demi-rond to the back, relevé on half-toe and end in fifth position. Thirteenth and fourteenth measures: développé in attitude croisée, plié and stretch the knee of the supporting leg. Fifteenth and sixteenth measures: demi-rond to the side and relevé on half-toe.

8. GRANDS BATTEMENTS JETÉS. 16 measures in 2/4.

Four grands battements front, side, back and side, each on 1 beat. Two grands battements front, each on 1 beat; then on the third battement, hold the working leg at 90° for 1½ beats, and on 1 beat, bring the leg down in fifth position. Repeat the same to the side, back and side.

EXERCISES IN THE CENTER

1. SMALL ADAGIO AND BATTEMENTS TENDUS. 8 measures in 4/4.

First measure: grand plié in second position, ending with the right arm in third (arm) position and the left arm in second (arm) position. Second measure: turn the body to the right and step on the right leg in second arabesque, the left foot back, pointe tendue on the floor. Third measure: relevé to 90° in second arabesque. Fourth and fifth measures: bring the left working leg to the side at 90°, relevé on half-toe, and end in fifth position front. Sixth measure: développé to the side and demi-rond to the back (right leg). Seventh measure: passé at 90° in pose effacée front and relevé on half-toe. Eighth measure: bring the working leg down in fifth position front; maintaining the épaulement effacé, take a pose effacée back on the right leg in plié, the left foot back, pointe tendue on the floor, the left arm in third (arm) position, the right arm in second (arm) position allongé.

Battements tendus: 8 measures in 4/4. Starting with the right foot, 2 to the front; on the left foot, 2 to the back; on the right foot, 4 to the side en tournant en dehors, each on one eighth of a turn with the right foot; 2 to the front, with the right foot 2 to the back (facing side 5), with the left foot, 4 to the side en tournant en dehors each on one eighth of a turn and on 1 beat each. Battements tendus jetés: 3 front, 3 side, 3 back, 3 side, repeat once more, each on half a beat. In 2 measures: préparation for tour sur le cou-de-pied en dedans from second position; in 2 measures, tour en dedans from second position.

2. RONDS DE JAMBE À TERRE EN TOURNANT. 12 measures in 4/4.

On 2 introductory chords, préparation en dehors. Eight ronds de jambe à terre en face, 8 en tournant en dehors starting to turn on the first rond de jambe, facing corner 2, on the second rond de jambe, facing side 3 and further facing corners and sides, 4, 5, 6, 7, 8, and 1, each on 1 beat. Repeat the same en dedans. In 2 measures: trace a half circle in plié en dedans and en dehors, ending in a big pose croisée back, pointe tendue on the floor, on a straight supporting leg; in 2 measures, grand port de bras (fourth port de bras).

3. BATTEMENTS FONDUS AT 45°. 16 measures in 2/4.

Three fondus in a small pose effacée front, each on 2 beats, then on 2 beats, tombé front in first arabesque at 45° and pas de bourrée en dehors, changing feet. Repeat 4 times, in turn on the right and on the left leg and separately in the reverse direction.

4. BATTEMENTS FRAPPÉS. 8 measures in 4/4.

Right leg: 7 frappés in a small pose effacée front, each on 1 beat; on 1 beat, coupé and open the left leg to the back in pose effacée at 45°; 7 frappés in a small pose effacée back (left leg), each on 1 beat, then on 1 beat coupé and open the right leg to the side at 45°; 4 frappés to the side (right leg) each on 1 beat, then 3 and again 3, each on half a beat; on 4 beats, tour sur le cou-de-pied en dedans from fifth position to the right side; on 4 beats, step on the left foot front in fifth position, on half-toe, the left arm to first (arm) position and the right to third (arm) position, hands stretched out in position allongée.

5. TOURS GLISSADES EN TOURNANT. Musical measure 2/4.

a) Execute in a straight line, with the right foot from side 7 to side 3 and with the left foot from side 3 to side 7.

b) In a straight line from side 5 to side 1, with the right and left foot, each tour on 2 beats.[2]

6. PRÉPARATION FOR TOURS EN DEHORS AND EN DEDANS FROM FOURTH POSITION. Musical measure 4/4.

a) En dehors. On 2 introductory chords, from fifth position step in fourth position croisée for préparation en dehors, the left foot front. On the first beat, demi-plié; on the second beat, spring up quickly on the left foot (half-toe), the right foot sur le cou-de-pied front; on the third beat, maintain the position; on the fourth beat, come down in fifth position demi-plié, right foot front.

b) On the first beat, demi-plié in fifth position; on the second beat, spring up on the left foot (half-toe), the right foot sur le cou-de-pied front; simultaneously turn, facing corner 2; on the third beat, maintain the position; on the fourth beat, come down in fourth position croisée, the left leg in demi-plié and the right fully stretched to the back, on flat foot. On the following 4 beats, plié on both legs and préparation, as described in paragraph "a." Execute préparation en dedans in the same musical tempo.[3]

7. GRAND ADAGIO. 12 measures in 4/4.

First measure: right foot: glissade croisée front; left foot: glissade croisée back and relevé on half-toe. Second measure: développé front and demi-rond to the side (right leg). Third and fourth measures: turn the body to first arabesque and back again to the side, relevé on half-toe, end in fifth position. Fifth and sixth measures: développé in pose écartée back, demi-rond to third arabesque. Seventh measure: from third arabesque, take a pose in fourth arabesque, coming down in plié. Eighth measure: bring the working leg down in fifth position and développé to the side (right leg). Ninth measure: demi-rond to the back, relevé on half-toe, end in fifth position. Tenth measure: starting on the left foot, step into a big pose croisée back, pointe tendue on the floor, the left arm in third (arm) position, the right in second (arm) position; subsequently open the left arm in second (arm) position and the right in third (arm) position. Eleventh and twelfth measures: grand port de bras.

---

[2] These tours also bear another name: tours soutenus en dedans. The term soutenu defines only a strong tension of the legs in the turns in fifth position; essentially these tours appear to be typical glissades en tournant from which each tour starts.

[3] At the end of the school year, all demi-pliés are executed on the upbeat. In this manner, the duration of staying power on half-toe which comes on the first, second, and third beats, increases.

ALLEGRO

1. 8 measures in 2/4.
Four doubles assemblés traveling front, 4 doubles assemblés traveling back, each on 2 beats.

2. 8 measures in 2/4.
On 1 beat, jeté to the side, ending sur le cou-de-pied back; 2 temps levés, each on half a beat. Repeat 4 times; follow with a coupé and execute the same in the reverse direction.

3. 4 measures in 4/4.
Right leg: 2 ballonnés in effacé front, each on 1 beat; on 1 beat, jeté, traveling in effacé front (ending the jeté with the left leg stretched to the back at 45°) and on 1 beat, pas de bourrée en dehors, changing feet; right leg: 2 sissonnes tombées croisées back, each on 2 beats. Repeat the same on the other leg and separately in the reverse direction.

4. 8 measures in 2/4, or 16 measures in 3/4 (Waltz).
On 1 beat, pas de chat front; on 1 beat, pas de bourrée en dehors, changing feet. Execute 8 times. During the execution of the first 4 pas de chats, the arms are positioned in a small pose (according to the instructions of the teacher), then in the following pas de chats, the arms come up to third (arm) position, for each jump, and on pas de bourrée, come down in the preparatory (arm) position.

5. CHANGEMENTS DE PIEDS EN TOURNANT IN HALF TURN. Musical measure 4/4.
On the first beat, demi-plié; jump, turning the body in the air, between the first and second beats; on the second beat, end the jump in demi-plié; on the third and fourth beats, stretch the knees. Repeat 4 times with turns to the right side and 4 times with turns to the left side.

6. TOUR EN L'AIR FOR THE MEN'S CLASS. Musical measure 4/4.
Fifth position, right foot front. On the upbeat, demi-plié; on the first beat, relevé on half-toe in fifth position (préparation); on the second beat, demi-plié; between the second and third beats, tour en l'air to

the right side; on the third beat, end the tour, landing in demi-plié; on the fourth beat, stretch the knees. In the following measure, change the foot through battement tendu for the repetition of tour en l'air to the right side.

7. ÉCHAPPÉ BATTU.
Similar execution as in the fifth lesson, each on 4 beats, then according to the mastery of the step on 2 beats each.

8. ROYALE. Musical measure 4/4.
Study facing the barre. On the first beat, demi-plié; jump and beat, between the first and second beats; on the second beat, end the jump in fifth position, demi-plié; on the third and fourth beats, stretch the knees. Repeat 8 times.[4]

9. 4 measures in 2/4.
Sixteen petits changements de pieds, each on half a beat.

SIXTH EXAMPLE OF EXERCISES ON POINTES

1. 16 measures in 2/4.
Three relevés in fifth position, each on 2 beats; on 2 beats, échappé in second position, changing feet. Repeat 4 times, in turn on the right and left leg.

2. 8 measures in 4/4.
Four sus-sous, traveling front in a small pose croisée, each on 2 beats; on 4 beats, double échappé in second position, without changing the feet; 2 échappés en tournant, in second position, changing feet, in a

[4] Before starting to study the royale and entrechat-quatre, it is recommended to approach training in the beating steps as follows: a jump from fifth position with a small and quick opening of the feet in the air to the side; and a quick closing of the feet in fifth position, demi-plié.

quarter turn each and on 2 beats. Four sus-sous, traveling back, with the back facing corner 1, in a small pose croisée, each on 2 beats; then on 4 beats, double échappé in second position and 2 échappés en tournant in second position, in a quarter turn each and on 2 beats.

3. 8 measures in 4/4.

Four sissonnes simples, changing feet to the back, each on 2 beats; 4 sissonnes simples, on 1 beat each and on 4 beats, pas couru front in first position. Repeat the whole exercise.

4. 8 measures in 2/4.

Sissonnes simples en tournant, each in a quarter of a turn, and on 2 beats, 8 sissonnes, starting on the right leg to the right side and separately on the left leg to the left side.

5. PRÉPARATION AND TOUR EN DEHORS AND EN DEDANS FROM FIFTH POSITION. Musical measure 4/4.

On the upbeat, demi-plié. On the first beat, spring up quickly on pointes on the supporting foot, the other foot sur le cou-de-pied front, the arms in first, then in second (arm) position (préparation); on the second beat, demi-plié in fifth position; on the third beat, tour; on the fourth beat, end the tour in fifth position, demi-plié. Repeat 4 times on each leg en dehors and 4 times en dedans.

Second position, on pointes, arms in first position.

Seventh Lesson

EXERCISES AT THE BARRE

1. 16 measures in 4/4.

Two grands pliés, 2 relevés on half-toe, each on 4 beats in first, second, fourth, and fifth positions.

2. BATTEMENTS TENDUS. 24 measures in 2/4.

Eight battements tendus front, to the side, to the back, and to the side, each on 1 beat. Battements tendus jetés: 4 front, each on half a beat; on the fourth jeté, hold the working leg off the floor at 45° for half a beat. Continue the following 4 jetés to the side, to the back, and to the side, starting at 45°.

3. RONDS DE JAMBE À TERRE. 12 measures in 4/4.

On 2 introductory chords, préparation en dehors. Six ronds de jambe à terre, each on 1 beat; then on 2 beats, préparation en dehors; 2 ronds de jambe à terre, each on 1 beat, 3 on half a beat each; 2 on 1 beat each and again 3 on half a beat each. Repeat the same en dedans. In 2 measures: trace a half circle in plié en dedans, then en dehors; in 2 measures, port de bras in deep plié, bending the body, end in fifth position demi-plié, and on the last beat, make a half turn on half-toe away from the barre.

4. BATTEMENTS SOUTENUS AT 90°. 24 measures in 2/4.

Two soutenus in pose effacée front at 90°, 2 in pose écartée back, 2 in pose effacée back and 2 to the side, each on 2 beats; on the last soutenu, bring the working leg down from 90° to 45°, and simultaneously come up on half-toe on the supporting leg. Frappés: 2 to the front, each on 1 beat, then 3, each on half a beat. Repeat the same to the side, to the back and to the side. Doubles frappés: 8 to the side, each on 1 beat. In 4 measures: bring the working leg down in fifth position front and continue with port de bras and bending of the body.

5. RONDS DE JAMBE EN L'AIR. 8 measures in 4/4.

On 2 introductory chords, préparation temps relevé en dehors. Two ronds de jambe en l'air, each on 1 beat, then 3 on half a beat each. Repeat once more. In 4 measures: tour sur le cou-de-pied en dehors, from fifth position, ending with the opening of the working leg to the side at 45°. Three ronds de jambe en l'air en dehors, each on 1 beat, end the third rond de jambe in a small pose effacée front in plié, pointe tendue on the floor, and come up on half-toe, on 1 beat, while the working leg is open to the side at 45°. Repeat the whole exercise en dedans.

6. PETITS BATTEMENTS SUR LE COU-DE-PIED. 16 measures in 2/4.

Twelve petits battements, each on half a beat, then on 2 beats, take a small pose croisée front in plié, pointe tendue on the floor. Repeat 12 petits battements, and on 2 beats, take a small pose effacée front in plié, pointe tendue on the floor. Repeat petits battements to the back in small poses croisées and effacées back.

7. BATTEMENTS DÉVELOPPÉS. 8 measures in 4/4.

First and second measures: développé front, come up on half-toe, demi-rond to the side and demi-rond to the front, ending in fifth position. Third and fourth measures: développé to the side, come up on half-toe, demi-rond to the front and demi-rond to the side, ending in fifth position. Fifth and sixth measures: développé back, come up on half-toe, demi-rond to the side and demi-rond to the back, ending in fifth position. Seventh and eighth measures: développé to the side, come up on half-toe, demi-rond to the back and demi-rond to the side.

8. GRANDS BATTEMENTS JETÉS. 8 measures in 2/4.

Four grands battements front, to the side, to the back and to the side, each on 1 beat.

EXERCISES IN THE CENTER

1. SMALL ADAGIO AND BATTEMENTS TENDUS. 8 measures in 4/4.

First and second measures: 2 grands pliés in first position. Third and fourth measures: développé to the side (right leg), passé at 90° front, relevé on half-toe, end in fifth position. Fifth and sixth measures: développé to the side (right leg), passé at 90° to the back, relevé on half-toe, end in fifth position. Seventh and eighth measures: grand rond de jambe développé en dehors (left leg) and at the end, relevé on half-toe. Battements tendus: 8 measures in 4/4. Right foot: 2 battements tendus front in demi-plié, to the side, to the back and to the side, each on 1 beat; left foot: 8 battements tendus en tournant en dedans on one eighth of a turn, each on half a beat. Battements tendus jetés: right foot, 3 in a small pose croisée front, to the side, to croisée back, to the side, each on half a beat; 16 battements tendus jetés in first position, each on half a beat. In 2 measures: préparation for tour sur le cou-de-pied en dehors from second position; in 2 measures, tour en dehors from second position.

2. BATTEMENTS FONDUS AT 45°. 16 measures in 2/4.

On 2 beats, fondu in a small pose effacée front; on 2 beats, plié-relevé. Repeat once more, and continue the same in a small pose écartée back and effacée back. On 2 beats, 1 fondu to the side; 2 frappés, each on 1 beat, 3 frappés and again 3 frappés, each on half a beat.

3. RONDS DE JAMBE EN L'AIR. 4 measures in 4/4.

On 4 beats, tour sur le cou-de-pied en dehors from fifth position; at the end open the working leg to the side at 45°. Four ronds de jambe en l'air en dehors, each on 1 beat, 3 ronds de jambe en l'air and again 3 ronds de jambe en l'air, each on half a beat. End the last rond de jambe in plié and on 4 beats, pas de bourrée dessous-dessus. Repeat the same en dedans and at the end, pas de bourrée dessus-dessous.

4. PETITS BATTEMENTS SUR LE COU-DE-PIED. 8 measures in 2/4.

Twelve petits battements, each on half a beat; on 2 beats, take a small pose croisée front in plié, pointe tendue on the floor. Repeat 12 petits battements, then on 1 beat, take a small pose effacée back in plié, pointe tendue on the floor and on 1 beat, pas de bourrée en dehors, changing feet.

5. PRÉPARATION FOR TOURS EN DEHORS AND EN DEDANS FROM FOURTH POSITION.

Execution similar to that described in the sixth lesson.

6. GRANDS BATTEMENTS JETÉS POINTÉS. 8 measures in 2/4.

Three grands battements pointés in croisé front, fourth battement in fifth position, each on 1 beat. Repeat the same to the side, then to the back in third and fourth arabesque poses, and again to the side.

7. TOURS GLISSADES EN TOURNANT.[1] 8 measures in 2/4.

Eight tours in a straight line from side 5 to side 1, starting on the right foot, each on 2 beats. End the last tour in fifth position, the right foot back. Repeat on the left foot.

ALLEGRO

1. 16 measures in 2/4.

Fifth position, right foot front. Starting on the right side: 3 glissades to the side, changing feet, each on 1 beat; then on 1 beat, assemblé to the side (bring the right foot front), échappé in fourth position croisée and échappé in second position, changing feet, each on 2 beats. Repeat all together 4 times, in turn on the right and left foot, and separately in the reverse direction. Start the glissades to the right side, with the right foot in fifth position back (starting position).

---

[1] In this lesson, the grand adagio is omitted; instead execute the tours glissades en tournant.

2. 8 measures in 2/4.

Sissonne ouverte in a small pose écartée back, assemblé and close the leg in fifth position back; 2 sissonnes fermées traveling forward, in a small pose croisée back. Execute each jump on 1 beat. Repeat 4 times in turn on the right and left leg, and subsequently in the reverse direction.

3. 8 measures in 2/4.

Three jetés traveling forward in a small pose croisée, each on 1 beat and with a short coupé between the second and third jeté; on 1 beat, assemblé croisé back. Échappé in second position, without changing feet and échappé battu, changing feet, each on 2 beats. Repeat on the other leg, and in the reverse direction.

4. 8 measures in 4/4.

Three ballonnés to the side, each on 1 beat; on 1 beat, assemblé to the side; 2 grands échappés in second position, changing feet, each on 2 beats. Repeat 4 times, in turn on the right and left leg.

5. 8 measures in 4/4.

Three échappés battus, each on 2 beats; on 1 beat, stretch the knees; on 1 beat, demi-plié for the following échappés. Repeat 4 times.

6. ROYALE IN THE CENTER. Musical measure 4/4.

Execution similar to that described in the sixth lesson.

7. ENTRECHAT-QUATRE.

Study facing the barre, and then according to the mastery of the step, in the center of the studio, each on 4 beats.

8. TOUR EN L'AIR FOR THE MEN'S CLASS.

Execution similar to that described in the sixth lesson.

9. 16 measures in 3/4 (Waltz).

Three pas de chat backward, with the right leg, each in 1 measure; in 1 measure, pas de bourrée en dehors, changing feet. Repeat on the left leg. Four balancés in a small pose in second arabesque, each on 1 beat; in 4 measures: a big scenic sissonne on the right leg in first arabesque and a big run forward to corner 2.

10. 8 measures in 2/4.

Seven petits changements de pieds, each on half a beat. Repeat 4 times.

SEVENTH EXAMPLE OF EXERCISES ON POINTES

1. 8 measures in 2/4.

Eight relevés in first position, each on 2 beats; on the eighth relevé, stay on pointes, without coming down in demi-plié. Repeat the same in second position.

2. 16 measures in 2/4.

Two pas de bourrée en dehors, changing feet; 4 pas de bourrée ballottés in croisé, step back in fifth position on pointes, plié-relevé in fifth position and dégagé to the side; 4 pas de bourrée dessus-dessous, step to the side in fifth position on pointes, plié-relevé in fifth position, coupé front and 2 pas de bourrée en dedans, changing feet. Each pas de bourrée, relevé with dégagé, relevé with coupé, on 2 beats.

3. 8 measures in 4/4.

Two échappés in second position, ending on one leg (the other sur le cou-de-pied back), each on 4 beats, in turn on the right and left leg. Four sissonnes simples en tournant, in a quarter turn to the right side, each on 2 beats. Two échappés in second position, ending on one leg (the other sur le cou-de-pied front), each on 4 beats; 4 sissonnes simples en tournant, in a quarter turn to the right side.

4. 8 measures in 2/4.

Move on the diagonal from corner 6 to corner 2. In 2 measures: dégagé (right leg) at 45° and pas de bourrée suivi, right foot front, in écarté position front, the right shoulder toward corner 2, the left shoulder toward corner 6. Raise the arms gradually from the preparatory (arm) position, the right arm to third (arm) position and the left arm to second (arm) position allongé. In 2 measures: 4 sissonnes simples (right leg), the right shoulder toward corner 2 in écarté front and changing in turn the right foot to fifth position back, front, back, front, each on 1 beat. Repeat from the beginning. Execute the combination in a quick tempo.

5. CHANGEMENTS DE PIEDS. Musical measure 2/4.

On 2 introductory chords, demi-plié and spring up quickly on pointes. Four changements de pieds, each on 1 beat. On the fourth changement de pieds, come down in demi-plié on both feet. Repeat once more.[2]

[2] It is recommended that study of the changements de pieds be made gradually, starting with no more than 4 consecutive jumps, then, as the step is mastered, 6 consecutive jumps, and at the end of the school year, 8 consecutive jumps.

Fourth position croiseé, pointe tendue, in demi-plié.

Eighth Lesson

EXERCISES AT THE BARRE

1. 16 measures in 4/4.

Two demi-pliés, each on 2 beats; 2 grands pliés, each on 4 beats; then on 4 beats, 1 relevé on half-toe in first, second, fourth, and fifth positions.

2. BATTEMENTS TENDUS. 24 measures in 2/4.

Four battements tendus front, each on 1 beat; execute the fifth battement tendu with half a turn on half-toe toward the barre, on 1 beat, and at the end open the left foot to the front, pointe tendue on the floor; maintain the position, on 1 beat; on 1 beat, make a half turn on half-toe toward the barre and at the end open the right foot to the front,

pointe tendue on the floor; maintain the position on 1 beat. Eight battements tendus to the side, each on 1 beat. Repeat in the reverse direction,
starting with the right foot to the back, with half turns away from the
barre. Battements tendus jetés: 7 to the side, each on half a beat, on
the seventh battement tendu jeté, demi-plié, repeating the tendus jetés
section 4 times.

3. RONDS DE JAMBE À TERRE. 12 measures in 4/4.

On 2 introductory chords, préparation en dehors. Six ronds de jambe
à terre, each on 1 beat; 3 ronds de jambe on half a beat each, ending
to the front, pointe tendue on the floor; on 4 beats, relevé lent on
half-toe to 90°; on 4 beats, demi-rond to the side and bring the working
leg down in second position, pointe tendue on the floor. Repeat en
dedans with relevé back to 90° and demi-rond to the side. In 2 measures:
trace half a circle en dehors–en dedans, ending in fifth position, knees
straight; in 2 measures, port de bras, bending the body.

4. BATTEMENTS FONDUS AT 45°. 12 measures in 4/4.

Double fondu front, double fondu front with a demi-rond to the side,
each on 2 beats. Repeat once more, then double fondu back, double
fondu back with a demi-rond to the side, each on 2 beats. Repeat once
more. Frappés: 2 to the side, each on half a beat; 3 to the side, each
on half a beat; 2 to the side, on 1 beat each and on 2 beats, take a
small pose effacée front in plié, pointe tendue on the floor. Repeat
the frappés, and take a small pose effacée back in plié, pointe tendue
on the floor. Four doubles frappés to the side, each on 1 beat; on 1
beat, make a half turn on half-toe toward the barre, and at the end
open the left leg to the side at 45°; maintain the position for 1 beat;
on 2 beats, bring the left leg down in fifth position back; on 4 beats,
relevé in second arabesque (left leg) to 90°; on 4 beats, relevé again
on half-toe in arabesque.

5. RONDS DE JAMBE EN L'AIR. 4 measures in 4/4.

On 2 introductory chords, préparation temps relevé en dehors. Six ronds
de jambe en l'air, each on 1 beat; on 1 beat, demi-plié in fifth position
(working leg in the back); on 1 beat, rise on half-toe on the supporting
leg and open the working leg to the side at 45°. Repeat en dedans,
and bring the working leg to the front in fifth position demi-plié.

6. PETITS BATTEMENTS SUR LE COU-DE-PIED. 16 measures in
2/4.

Twelve petits battements, each on half a beat; on 1 beat, tombé in
plié, on the working right foot to fifth position front, the left foot sur
le cou-de-pied back; on 1 beat, make a half a turn on half-toe toward

the barre, bringing the left foot sur le cou-de-pied front. Continue petits battements and tombé with half a turn toward the barre, with the left foot; then repeat the same on the right and left foot with half turns away from the barre. Start this combination with the right foot, then with the left foot, without any stop.

7. BATTEMENTS DÉVELOPPÉS. 8 measures in 4/4.

First and second measures: grand rond de jambe développé en dehors. Third and fourth measures: passé at 90°, half-toe in effacée front and passé at 90° in attitude effacée. Fifth, sixth, seventh, and eighth measures: repeat the same en dedans.

8. GRANDS BATTEMENTS JETÉS. 8 measures in 2/4.

Four grands battements in effacé front, écarté back, second arabesque, and écarté front, each on 1 beat.

EXERCISES IN THE CENTER

1. SMALL ADAGIO AND BATTEMENTS TENDUS. 8 measures in 4/4.

First and second measures: grand plié in fifth position, right foot front, ending with the right arm in second (arm) position and the left arm in third (arm) position; fourth port de bras. Third and fourth measures: grand rond de jambe développé en dehors (right leg) and passé at 90°, on half-toe. Fifth measure: développé écarté front (on the flat foot), end in fifth position, right foot front. Sixth and seventh measures: grand rond de jambe développé en dedans (left leg) and passé at 90°, on half-toe. Eighth measure: développé écarté back (on the flat foot). Battements tendus: 8 measures in 4/4. Six battements tendus croisés front (right foot), the right arm in third (arm) position, the left arm in first (arm) position, each on 1 beat; on the sixth battement, demi-plié and on 2 beats, make a full turn on half-toe in fifth position to the left side; 6 battements tendus in croisé back (right foot), the right arm in first (arm) position, the left arm in third (arm) position, each on 1 beat; on 2 beats, make a full turn on half-toe to the right side; 8 battements tendus to the side, each on 1 beat. Battements tendus jetés: 15 to the side, each on half a beat; pause, on half a beat, in fifth position. In 2 measures: tour sur le cou-de-pied en dehors to the right side, from second position; in 2 measures: tour sur le cou-de-pied en dedans, to the left side, from second position.

2. RONDS DE JAMBE À TERRE. 12 measures in 4/4.

On 2 introductory chords, préparation en dehors. Eight ronds de jambe à terre (en face, facing front), 8 en tournant en dehors, each on 1 beat. Repeat the same en dedans. In 2 measures: trace half a circle in plié, en dedans–en dehors, ending in a big pose croisée back, pointe tendue on the floor on the straight supporting leg. In 2 measures: 2 grands ports de bras, each in 1 measure.

3. BATTEMENTS SOUTENUS AT 90°. 8 measures in 4/4.

Two soutenus at 90° in effacé front (right leg), 2 in effacée back (left leg), 2 in écarté back (right leg), and 2 in third arabesque, each on 2 beats. End in fifth position, half-toe, and open the working leg to the side at 45°. Frappés: 3 frappés to the side, each on half a beat, execute 4 times; 4 doubles frappés, each on 1 beat and on 4 beats, tour sur le cou-de-pied en dehors from fifth position, to the right side.

4. GRANDS BATTEMENTS JETÉS. 8 measures in 2/4.

Four grands battements in effacé front (right leg), 4 grands battements in effacé back (left leg), 4 grands battements in écarté back (right leg) and 4 grands battements in third arabesque.

5. GRAND ADAGIO. 16 measures in 4/4.

First measure: grand plié in fourth position croisée. Second measure: développé in first arabesque facing corner 2 (left leg). Third and fourth measures: from arabesque, move in attitude effacée, relevé on half-toe, ending in fifth position, left foot front. Fifth and sixth measures: développé to the side (right leg), both arms in third (arm) position, passé through first position to the back in third arabesque plié. Seventh and eighth measures: step backward, développé in écarté back (left leg) and demi-rond in fourth arabesque. Ninth measure: plié in fourth arabesque and pas de bourrée en dehors, changing feet. Tenth and eleventh measures: développé in écarté front (right leg) and demi-rond in attitude effacée. Twelfth and thirteenth measures: from the pose attitude, demi-rond to the side, plié and pas de bourrée dessus. Fourteenth measure: préparation from fifth position to fifth position. Fifteenth measure: tour sur le cou-de-pied en dehors to the left side, from fifth position. Sixteenth measure: on the right foot: 2 glissades to the side, changing feet, and step on the right foot forward in fifth position, on half-toe, the arms in third arabesque position.

ALLEGRO

1. 8 measures in 2/4.

Six assemblés to the side, changing feet forward; 2 jetés to the side, each on 1 beat, then a short coupé. Repeat the same in the reverse direction.

2. 8 measures in 2/4.

Sissonne ouverte in a small pose effacée front, assemblé, in turn on the right and left leg; échappé in second position, landing on one leg (sur le cou-de-pied back), temps levé, assemblé croisé back. Execute each jump on 1 beat. Repeat the same on the other leg, and separately in the reverse direction.

3. 16 measures in 2/4.

Two sissonnes fermées traveling forward in a small pose croisée back; 2 sissonnes fermées traveling backward in a small pose croisée front, each on 1 beat. In 2 measures, pas de basque front and 2 pas de chat back, each on 1 beat. Repeat 4 times, in turn on the right and left leg, and subsequently repeat in the reverse direction.

4. 8 measures in 2/4.

On the upbeat, coupé with the left foot back and 3 ballonnés effacés front with the right leg, each on 1 beat; then on 1 beat, assemblé to the side, ending with the right foot back. On the left leg: 2 sissonnes fermées to corner 8 in a small second arabesque, each on 1 beat. End the first sissonne in fifth position, the right foot back and on the second, the right foot front. On 2 beats, from fifth position, half-toe, make a turn to the left side, ending in demi-plié on the left foot and the right foot sur le cou-de-pied back. Coupé and repeat the exercise on the other leg, and subsequently repeat in the reverse direction.

5. 4 measures in 4/4.

Two royale, each on 1 beat; then stretch the knees, on 1 beat and demi-plié on 1 beat, preparing for the following jump. Repeat 4 times.

6. ENTRECHAT-QUATRE.

Execution similar to that in the royale, 4 times on the right and left side.

7. 8 measures in 2/4.

Eight petits changements de pieds, each on 1 beat; 16 petits changements de pieds, each on half a beat.

EIGHTH EXAMPLE OF EXERCISES ON POINTES

1. 32 measures in 3/4 (Waltz).

Three glissades in a small pose croisée front, 1 glissade to the side, changing feet, each in 2 measures. Repeat 4 times, in turn on the right and left foot, and subsequently in the reverse direction.

2. 8 measures in 4/4.

Four échappés in second position, changing feet, each on 2 beats; then on 4 beats, double échappé, landing on one foot (the other sur le cou-de-pied back), and on 4 beats, 2 pas de bourrée en dehors, changing feet. On 4 beats, double échappé, landing on one foot (the other sur le cou-de-pied front) and on 4 beats, 2 pas de bourrée en dedans, changing feet. Four échappés en tournant in second position, in a quarter turn to the right side, each on 2 beats.

3. 16 measures in 2/4.

Four sissonnes simples to the back, changing feet, each on 2 beats, 8 sissonnes simples to the back, changing feet, each on 1 beat. Repeat in the reverse direction.

4. 32 measures in 3/4 (Waltz).

Fifth position, left foot front, moving on the diagonal from corner 6 to corner 2. Seven jetés fondus front, starting on the right leg, each in 1 measure. End the seventh jeté fondu with tombé balancé on the left foot, in the eighth measure. Six balancés to the side, traveling backward, in turn on the right and left foot, each in 1 measure; dégagé to the side (right foot) in 1 measure, and assemblé soutenu, ending with the right foot front, in 1 measure. Continue the exercise on the other leg, moving toward corner 8.

5. 16 measures in 2/4.

Two sissonnes simples to the back, changing feet, each on 2 beats; on 2 beats, préparation en dehors from fifth position for tour sur le cou-de-pied en dehors; on 2 beats, tour en dehors from fifth position. Repeat 4 times in turn on the right and left leg, and subsequently in the reverse direction, with tour en dedans.

6. 16 measures in 3/4 (Slow Waltz).

14 measures: On the right foot, slow pas de bourrée suivi, in croisé front, the right arm in third (arm) position, the left arm in second (arm) position. In 2 measures: come down from pointes in first arabesque pose at 90°, in plié, facing corner 2. The right arm lowers from third to first (arm) position and extends forward in the arabesque pose.

Fourth Year

This period of study involves strengthening the stability in various turns, while performing the exercises on half-toe and full-toe (on pointes); furthermore, developing the smooth connection of movements of the arms and body.

Fifth position on pointes, arms in first position.

First Semester
First Lesson

EXERCISES AT THE BARRE

The combination of exercises becomes more complicated. The half turns are performed on one leg.

1. 16 measures in 4/4.
Two grands pliés, each on 4 beats; 1 relevé, on 4 beats; 2 relevés, on 2 beats, each in first, second, fourth, and fifth positions.

2. BATTEMENTS TENDUS. 24 measures in 2/4.

Four battements tendus to the front (right foot), 4 battements to the back (left foot), 8 battements to the side (right foot), each on 1 beat. Repeat in the reverse direction, starting to the back with the right foot. Battements tendus jetés: 3 to the side, each on half a beat; flic-flac en dehors en face, on 2 beats; 3 battements tendus jetés to the side and flic-flac en dedans en face. Repeat battements tendus jetés and flic-flac 2 more times.[1]

3. RONDS DE JAMBE À TERRE. 12 measures in 4/4.

On 2 introductory chords, préparation en dehors. Two ronds de jambe à terre, each on 1 beat, followed by préparation en dehors, on 2 beats. Repeat once more. Seven ronds de jambe à terre and again 7 ronds de jambe à terre, each on half a beat. Repeat en dedans. In 2 measures: trace a half circle in plié en dehors, ending in a pose second arabesque, pointe tendue on the floor; make a half turn away from the barre and bring the working leg to fifth position half-toe; in 2 measures, port de bras on half-toe, bending the body.

4. BATTEMENTS FONDUS AT 45°. 16 measures in 2/4.

Fondu front, side, and front, each on 2 beats; on 2 beats, plié and relevé with a half turn toward the barre, ending the half turn with the working leg to the back. Repeat the same with the left leg, then pass on to the left leg in plié, and simultaneously do a petit battement to the back. Resume with fondu to the back, to the side, and to the back, plié, and relevé with a half turn away from the barre, ending the half turn with the working leg to the front. Repeat with the left leg. This combination of fondus is done at once with the right and left leg.

5. BATTEMENTS FRAPPÉS. 8 measures in 2/4.

Seven frappés to the side, each on half a beat; 4 doubles frappés front, side, back, and side, each on half a beat. Repeat once more.

6. RONDS DE JAMBE EN L'AIR. 8 measures in 4/4.

Four ronds de jambe en l'air en dehors, each on 1 beat; execute the third and fourth rond de jambe with plié-relevé on the supporting leg. Repeat once more. Ten petits battements sur le cou-de-pied, each on half a beat; on 1 beat, demi-plié in fifth position and on 2 beats, tour sur le cou-de-pied en dehors, opening the working leg to the side at 45° at the end. Repeat the whole exercise en dedans.

---

[1] Flic-flac is combined with battements tendus jetés and other exercises, after the exercise is separately studied at the end of exercises at the barre.

7. BATTEMENTS DÉVELOPPÉS WITH PLIÉ-RELEVÉ. 16 measures in 4/4.

First measure: développé front. Second measure: plié on the first beat, relevé on half-toe on the second beat; bring the leg down to the preparatory position on the third and fourth beats. Repeat once more and follow with battements développés to the side, to the back and to the side.

8. GRANDS BATTEMENTS JETÉS RISING ON HALF-TOE. 8 measures in 2/4.

Two grands battements front, side, back, and side, each on 1 beat, then 2 grands battements in the same directions rising on half-toe, each on 1 beat.[2]

EXERCISES IN THE CENTER

1. SMALL ADAGIO AND BATTEMENTS TENDUS. 8 measures in 4/4.

First measure: grand plié in fourth position croisée. Second measure: fourth port de bras. Third measure: développé front (right leg). Fourth measure: plié on the first beat; relevé on half-toe on the second beat; bring the leg down to the preparatory position on the third and fourth beats. Fifth and sixth measures: développé plié-relevé (left leg back). Seventh and eighth measures: développé plié-relevé to the side (right leg). Battements tendus and tours (turns), 8 measures in 4/4. On the right foot, first battement tendu en tournant en dehors (a quarter turn to side 3), second battement en face (facing) side 3. Execute 8 battements tendus en tournant and en face, each on 1 beat. Battements tendus jetés: 8 battements tendus jetés en tournant en dehors on the right foot, each on 1 beat (in an eighth of a turn, starting to corner 2, side 3, corner 4, side 5, corner 6, side 7, corner 8, and facing side 1); 7 battements tendus jetés to the side en face, on the left foot and again 7 battements jetés, each on half a beat. In 1 measure: préparation from fifth to fourth position and in 1 measure: tour sur le cou-de-pied en dehors.

---

[2] The rising on half-toe on the supporting leg takes place at the moment of the controlled throw of the working leg (jeté). End each grand battement by coming down from half-toe on both feet.

2. RONDS DE JAMBE À TERRE. 12 measures in 4/4.

On 2 introductory chords, préparation en dehors. First rond de jambe à terre en tournant, a quarter turn, the second rond de jambe, en face, etc. . . . Execute 8 ronds de jambe in this manner, each on 1 beat. Repeat the same en dedans. In 2 measures: trace half a circle in plié, en dedans, then en dehors, ending in a big pose croisée back, pointe tendue on the floor, on a stretched supporting leg. In 2 measures: 2 grands port de bras, end the second port de bras in fourth position in a wide préparation for tour en dehors. In 2 measures: 2 préparations for tours in attitude croisée. In 2 measures: grand rond de jambe développé en dehors on half-toe (left leg).

3. BATTEMENTS FONDUS AT 45°. 8 measures in 4/4.

Tour sur le cou-de-pied from fifth position en dehors, on 2 beats. Battement fondu front on 2 beats; repeat the tour and battement fondu to the side. Double fondu front and side, each on 2 beats; 7 frappés to the side, each on half a beat. Repeat the whole exercise in the reverse direction with tours en dedans, ending with 4 doubles frappés, each on 1 beat.

4. RONDS DE JAMBE EN L'AIR. 8 measures in 2/4.

Four ronds de jambe en l'air en dehors, each on 1 beat, then 3 ronds de jambe and again 3 ronds de jambe on half a beat. In 1 measure: développé to the side. In 2 measures: a slow turn en dehors with passé at 90°. In 1 measure: follow the turn with développé croisé front on half-toe. Execute en dedans separately and end the slow turn en dedans in attitude croisée on half-toe.

5. PAS DE BOURRÉE BALLOTTÉ IN EFFACÉ, EN TOURNANT. 8 measures in 2/4.

Préparation on the right leg, the left foot stretched to the back, pointe tendue on the floor. On the upbeat, on 2 half beats, plié on the right foot and bend the left foot sur le cou-de-pied back. On 2 beats, pas de bourrée ballotté front in effacé, turning to corner 4; on 2 beats, pas de bourrée ballotté back in effacé, facing corner 4. Execute the following pas de bourrée ballotté in the same manner to corner 6, 8, and 2.

6. TOURS LENTS (SLOW TURNS) À LA SECONDE (TOUR DE PROMENADE). INITIAL STUDY IN HALF TURN. Musical measure 2/4.

First measure: développé to the side (right leg). Second and third measures: a slow turn à la seconde en dehors,[3] turning to corner 2, side 3, corner 4 and side 5, on each beat. Fourth measure: bring the working leg down to the preparatory-position. Fifth measure: développé to the side. Sixth and seventh measures: a slow turn à la seconde en dehors, turning to corner 6, side 7, corner 8 and side 1, on each beat. Eighth measure: bring the working leg down in fifth position back.[4]

7. PRÉPARATION FOR TOUR À LA SECONDE FROM SECOND POSITION. Musical measure 4/4.

En dehors. Fifth position, right foot front. On the upbeat, demi-plié. First measure: come up with a slight jump to fifth position, half-toe, the arms in first (arm) position. Hold the position on the second beat. Grand battement to the side (right leg) on the third beat, and open the arms to second (arm) position. Hold the position on the fourth beat. In the second measure: on half a beat, demi-plié in second position (on the upbeat), bring the right arm to first (arm) position while the left arm remains in second; on the first beat, spring onto the left leg (half-toe) while raising the right leg in grand battement to the side, the arms in second position; on the second and third beats, hold the position; on the fourth beat, end in fifth position, right foot back. Repeat 4 times, on the right and left leg, in turn. Execute en dedans in the same manner.

ALLEGRO

1. 16 measures in 2/4.

Four glissades to the side, changing feet, starting right foot front; 1 glissade croisée front (right foot); 1 glissade croisée back (left foot),

---

[3] In this instance, the particular term *à la seconde* implies a continuous hold of the leg in second position, when it applies to slow turns, tours at 90° from second position, as in the men's grandes pirouettes, pirouettes à la seconde, where the working leg is raised to the side at 90°. In battements développés, grands battements jetés to the side, the term à la seconde is hardly ever applied in this sense.

[4] The study of tours lents—tour de promenade—(slow turns) is carried out in this way: en dehors in attitude croisée and en dedans in a pose croisée front. According to the mastery of the step, full turns are executed, first to 2 measures in 4/4, or 8 measures in 2/4, thereafter to 1 measure in 4/4. Tours lents in other poses are studied later.

each on 1 beat; on 2 beats, échappé battu, changing feet. Repeat 4 times, in turn on the right and left foot.

2. 8 measures in 2/4.

Four assemblés to the side, moving front and changing feet, each on 1 beat; a short coupé front and on 1 beat, assemblé traveling to the side and bringing the working leg front; on 1 beat, stretch the knees; on 1 beat, demi-plié to resume the combination on the other leg. Execute in the reverse direction.

3. 8 measures in 2/4.

Fifth position, left foot front. On 1 beat, jeté on the right leg, traveling to the side, ending with the left foot sur le cou-de-pied front; on 1 beat, temps levé; jeté croisé traveling front, coupé-jeté, coupé-jeté, coupé-jeté croisé front, assemblé croisé back, each jump on 1 beat and on 1 beat, royale. Repeat on the other leg, and separately in the reverse direction.

4. 16 measures in 2/4.

Three échappés battus, changing feet, each on 2 beats; 2 entrechats-quatre, each on 1 beat. Repeat 4 times, in turn on the right and left leg.

5. COMPLEX ÉCHAPPÉ BATTU.[5] Musical measure 4/4.

On the first and second beats, execute the complex échappé battu; on the third beat, stretch the knees; on the fourth beat, demi-plié for the subsequent jump. Repeat from 4 to 8 times. Depending on the mastery of the step, execute each échappé battu without pause on 2 beats.

6. 4 measures in 4/4.

Two grands changements de pieds, each on 1 beat; 3 petits changements de pieds, each on half a beat. Repeat 4 times.[6]

---

[5] In the complex échappé battu, a beat of the feet is executed in the first jump, from fifth position to second and again in the second jump, from second position to fifth. In the simple échappé battu, the breakdown of the movement follows this example: right foot front fifth position, demi-plié, jump, holding the feet crossed in fifth position, land in second position plié, then in the second jump from second position plié, jump, bringing the right foot front with a beat and change feet in the air, landing in fifth position, right foot back.

[6] Each lesson ends with port de bras, bending the body.

FIRST EXAMPLE OF EXERCISES ON POINTES

1. 16 measures in 2/4.
Eight échappés in second position, changing feet, each on 2 beats; 8 échappés in second position, traveling to the back. The traveling movement to the back takes place when jumping on pointes in second position, and conclude the échappé in fifth position demi-plié, without any traveling movement. Repeat 8 échappés on the same spot and 8 échappés, traveling forward.

2. 8 measures in 2/4.
Fifth position, right foot front. On 2 beats, 1 sus-sous traveling forward in pose croisée, 2 sus-sous, each on 1 beat. On 2 beats, 1 sus-sous, traveling to the back in pose croisée, 2 sus-sous, each on 1 beat. Four échappés en tournant in fourth position effacée, in a quarter turn, each on 2 beats. The first turn, to the right side, faces corner 4, the second corner 6, the third corner 8 and the last corner 2. End the last échappé in fifth position, right foot back.

3. COUPÉ BALLONNÉ IN SECOND POSITION. 16 measures in 3/4 (Slow Waltz).
Préparation on the right leg, the left foot is stretched croisé back, pointe tendue on the floor. On the upbeat, demi-plié, the left foot moves sur le cou-de-pied back. First measure: coupé and come up on the left foot sur les pointes, while stretching the right leg to the side at 45°. Second measure: plié on the left leg, the right foot moves sur le cou-de-pied back. Coupé on the right foot and repeat ballonné on the left leg. Execute 8 ballonnés in this manner. Repeat ballonnés in the reverse direction, starting with préparation croisée front.

4. PAS DE BOURRÉE BALLOTTÉ IN EFFACÉ, EN TOURNANT.
Execution similar to that in the fifth exercise in the center.

5. 16 measures in 2/4.
Four measures: pas de bourrée suivi (starting on the right foot) in a straight line from side 7 to side 3, end in fifth position, demi-plié, left foot front. Two measures: 4 changements de pieds, each on 1 beat; on the last changement de pied, come down (off pointes), on both feet. Two measures: 2 jetés on the left leg, traveling forward in a small pose croisée. Eight measures: repeat the combination on the left foot.

Temps levé in first arabesque.

Second Lesson

EXERCISES AT THE BARRE

1. 12 measures in 4/4.

Two grands pliés in first, second, fourth, and fifth positions, each on 4 beats. Two ports de bras, bending the body, each on 4 beats. Four relevés on half-toe in fifth position, each on 2 beats.

2. BATTEMENTS TENDUS. 32 measures in 2/4.

Four battements tendus closing in demi-plié, to the front, side, back, and side, then 4 battements tendus without demi-plié, in all directions, each on 1 beat. Battements tendus jetés: 3 to the front, each on half a beat; on 2 beats, flic-flac en dedans en face with a pause (foot back, coupé); 3 battements tendus jetés back, and flic-flac en dehors en face with a pause front (foot front, coupé); 3 battements to the side, flic-flac en dehors; 3 battements to the side, flic-flac en dedans. Thirty-two battements tendus jetés in first position, each on half a beat.

3. RONDS DE JAMBE À TERRE AND RONDS DE JAMBE EN L'AIR. 12 measures in 4/4.

On 2 introductory chords, préparation en dehors. Four ronds de jambe à terre, each on 1 beat; 7 ronds de jambe à terre, each on half a beat; 4 ronds de jambe en l'air, each on 1 beat; 7 ronds de jambe en l'air, each on half a beat, ending the last rond de jambe en l'air in a small pose effacée front, pointe tendue on the floor. Repeat en dedans. In 2 measures: trace half a circle on the floor, in plié, en dedans, en dehors, ending with relevé on half-toe, the working leg raised to the back at 45°. In 1 measure, make a half turn on the supporting leg, away from the barre; the working leg, after the half turn, moves to the front; thereafter, another half turn in the reverse direction, the working leg reverting to the back. In 1 measure, plié in fifth position and half a turn on half-toe, away from the barre (détourné).

4. BATTEMENTS SOUTENUS, POINTE TENDUE ON THE FLOOR. 16 measures in 2/4.

Soutenu front, soutenu to the side, en tournant en dehors and 2 soutenus to the side, each on 2 beats. Repeat soutenus in the reverse direction. Frappés: 3 to the front, 3 to the side, each on half a beat; on 2 beats, from fifth position, tour sur le cou-de-pied en dehors and on 2 beats, fondu to the side. Repeat frappés and tour in the reverse direction.

5. PETITS BATTEMENTS SUR LE COU-DE-PIED. 8 measures in 4/4.

Four petits battements front, each on 1 beat, concluding each battement with plié on the supporting foot (half-toe during the battement). Seven petits battements each on half a beat, plié on the supporting foot, on the last battement. Repeat the whole exercise and subsequently in the reverse direction.

6. DÉVELOPPÉ BALLOTTÉ. 4 measures in 4/4.

First measure: développé ballotté front (right leg). Second measure: développé ballotté back (left leg). Third and fourth measures: repeat the same. Execute in the reverse direction: right leg to the back, left leg to the front.[1]

7. GRANDS BATTEMENTS JETÉS ON HALF-TOE. 8 measures in 2/4.

On 2 introductory chords, come up in fifth position half-toe. Four grands battements front, side, back, and side, each on 1 beat, and on the last battement come down from half-toe onto both feet.

EXERCISES IN THE CENTER

1. SMALL ADAGIO AND BATTEMENTS TENDUS. 8 measures in 4/4.

First measure: grand plié in fifth position, right foot front. Second measure: développé to the side (right leg) and passé at 90° into attitude croisée. Third and fourth measures: tour lent (slow turn) en dehors in attitude croisée. Fifth measure: relevé on half-toe in attitude croisée, close in fifth position, and développé (left leg) in effacé front. Sixth measure: from pose effacée, turn slowly en dehors with passé at 90°. Seventh measure: open the left leg in écarté back and relevé on half-toe. Eighth measure: plié in fifth position and a full turn on half-toe to the left side (détourné). Battements tendus: 8 measures in 4/4. Right foot: 16 to the side, each on 1 beat; on the fourth, eighth, twelfth, and sixteenth battements tendus, demi-plié. Battements tendus jetés: left foot: 7 in a small pose croisée front; right foot: 7 in a small pose croisée back, then 7 and again 7 to the side (right foot), each on half a beat. On 4 beats: from the left foot front, tour sur le cou-de-pied en dehors and tour en dedans from second position.

2. RONDS DE JAMBE À TERRE. 8 measures in 4/4.

On 2 introductory chords, préparation en dehors. Four ronds de jambe à terre en face, 4 en tournant a quarter turn each, each on 1 beat. Repeat en dedans. In 2 measures: développé attitude croisée, relevé on half-toe, come down in fourth position and préparation for tours

[1] Depending on the mastery of the step, développé ballotté is done together in one continuous movement, without any breakdown, on 2 beats to the front, and on 2 beats to the back.

en dehors in attitude croisée. In 2 measures: with the left foot, trace a half circle on the floor in plié, en dehors, and end in fourth arabesque (pose), pointe tendue on the floor, then relevé on half-toe in fourth arabesque at 90°.

3. BATTEMENTS FONDUS AT 45°. 8 measures in 2/4.

On 2 beats: fondu effacée front; on 2 beats, plié-relevé with rond en dehors in effacé back; 2 fondus to the side, each on 2 beats. Repeat the exercise and subsequently on the other leg. Repeat again in the reverse direction.

4. PETITS BATTEMENTS SUR LE COU-DE-PIED. 8 measures in 4/4.

Sixteen petits battements, gradually raising the arms from second position to third (arm) position; 14 petits battements, opening the arms to second (arm) position and lowering to the preparatory position, each on half a beat; on 1 beat, end in préparation fourth position for tours en dehors; on 4 beats, tour sur le cou-de-pied en dehors to the right side, end in fourth position; on 4 beats, repeat the tour and end in fifth position; on 4 beats, from fifth position (left foot front) préparation to fourth position for tours en dedans; on 4 beats, tour sur le cou-de-pied en dedans to the right side.

5. PAS DE BOURRÉE EN TOURNANT EN DEHORS AND EN DE-DANS, CHANGING FEET. Musical measure 2/4.

During the study of pas de bourrée en tournant, changing feet, it is recommended that the student do 1 pas de bourrée en face, the other en tournant, etc., no fewer than 8 pas de bourrée en dehors and 8 en dedans, each on 2 beats.

6. GRAND ADAGIO. 8 measures in 4/4.

First measure: grand plié in fifth position, right foot front and on the last half beat, relevé on half-toe. Second measure: dégagé the right foot in effacé front, in plié, pointe tendue on the floor; lean the body forward toward the right foot, lower the arms in the preparatory (arm) position and relevé to 90° in effacé front. Third measure: from pose effacée, turn en dedans to corner 6, in first arabesque. Fourth measure: relevé on half-toe, in arabesque, bring the working leg down in fifth position, and développé with the left leg in effacé front to corner 6. Fifth measure: from pose effacée, turn en dedans to corner 2 in first arabesque. Sixth measure: relevé on half-toe, in arabesque, bring the working leg down in fifth position front and with the right foot, soutenu en tournant en dedans to the left side. Seventh and eighth measures: left foot front, préparation à la seconde for tour en dedans from second position.

ALLEGRO

1. 16 measures in 2/4.

Doubles assemblés on the right and left leg, each on 2 beats; 2 échappés battus, changing feet, each on 2 beats. Repeat once more and subsequently in the reverse direction.

2. 8 measures in 4/4.

Two sissonnes fermées to the side, in turn on the right and left leg, each on 1 beat; 3 sissonnes fermées to the side, in turn on the right, left and right leg, each on half a beat. (The leg in fifth position front crosses, each time, to the back.) Left foot front: pas de basque front en tournant, in a quarter turn to side 7; pas de basque front en tournant, in a quarter turn to side 1.[2] Repeat on the other leg, and subsequently in the reverse direction.

3. 8 measures in 2/4.

Two ballonnés effacés front, each on 1 beat; 2 ballonnés effacés front, each on half a beat; on 1 beat, assemblé to the side. A short coupé front and assemblé, traveling to the side, in turn on the right and left leg, each on 2 beats. Repeat on the other leg and subsequently in the reverse direction.

4. PAS EMBOÎTÉ. Musical measure 2/4.

Eight emboîtés front, jumping on the same spot. Eight emboîtés back, jumping on the same spot. Later on, after several lessons, execute 8 emboîtés on the same spot and 8 traveling forward, in a straight line. Study the emboîté to the back in the same manner.

5. GRANDE SISSONNE OUVERTE TO THE SIDE. Musical measure 4/4.

a) On the first beat, demi-plié; sissonne ouverte, between the first and second beats; on the second beat, end the jump in demi-plié on the supporting leg, the working leg is opened to the side at 90°; on the third and fourth beats, bring the working leg in the preparatory fifth position and simultaneously stretch the supporting leg. Repeat 4 to 8 times.

[2] In pas de basque en tournant, the turn takes place at the time of the demi-rond de jambe à terre.

b) On the first beat, demi-plié; jump, between the first and second beats; on the second beat, end the jump in demi-plié, the working leg opened to the side at 90°; jump assemblé, between the second and third beats; on the third beat, end assemblé in fifth position demi-plié; on the fourth beat, stretch the knees.[3]

6. 8 measures in 4/4.

Four échappés battus, 4 complex échappés battus. Repeat once again for the men's lesson.

7. TOURS EN L'AIR FOR THE MEN'S LESSON. 4 measures in 4/4.

On the upbeat, demi-plié and relevé in fifth position, half-toe; on the first beat, demi-plié; between the first and second beats, tour en l'air; on the second beat, end tour en l'air in demi-plié; on the third and fourth beats, 3 petits changements de pieds, each on half a beat. Repeat 4 times.

8. 8 measures in 2/4.

Three petits changements de pieds and again 3, en face; 7 changements de pieds, en tournant, each on half a beat. Repeat. During changements de pieds en tournant, raise the arms from the preparatory position to third position, then gradually open to the side and lower into the preparatory position.

SECOND EXAMPLE OF EXERCISES ON POINTES

1. 8 measures in 2/4.

Eight relevés in first position, 8 in second position, each on 1 beat.

2. 8 measures in 4/4.

On 2 beats, échappé in second position, changing feet; 2 échappés, changing feet, each on 1 beat. Repeat. Sissonne simple, passing foot to the back, on 2 beats and 2 sissonnes simples, passing foot to the back, on 1 beat. Repeat once again the sissonnes and subsequently in the reverse direction.

---

[3] Grande sissonne ouverte in attitude croisée or croisée front, is studied in a similar manner, after a few lessons, in various other poses. At the end of the semester, grande sissonne ouverte is done on 1 beat and on 1 beat the closing assemblé.

3. 8 measures in 2/4.

Four coupés-ballonnés in second position, ending sur le cou-de-pied back, each on 2 beats; 3 pas de bourrée en dehors changing feet, en face, en tournant, en face, each on 2 beats; on 2 beats, relevé in fifth position, coupé, and in 4 measures, repeat the whole combination on the other leg. Execute in the reverse direction.

4. 16 measures in 2/4.

Four jetés on the right leg, traveling on the diagonal from corner 6 to corner 2 (the step jeté is done to the side, carrying the right shoulder to corner 2 and the left shoulder to corner 6), each on 2 beats; in 4 measures, pas de bourrée suivi, in small circle to the right. Four jetés on the left leg, traveling on the diagonal from corner 2 to corner 6, each on 2 beats; in 4 measures, pas de bourrée suivi, in a small circle to the left, end in fifth position, and on the last beat come up on pointes on the left foot, the right foot sur le cou-de-pied back, in a small pose croisée.

5. SISSONNE OUVERTE AT 45°. Musical measure 4/4.

To the side: on the first beat, demi-plié; on the second beat, come up on pointes, on one foot, the other open to the side at 45°; on the third beat, come down in fifth position, demi-plié; on the fourth beat, stretch the knees. Repeat 8 times, in turn on the right and left leg. Execute also in the reverse direction.[4]

6. JETÉS IN BIG POSES. 4 measures in 4/4 or 16 measures in 3/4 (Slow Waltz).

On the upbeat, plié on the left leg, and dégagé the right foot in croisé front at 45°. On the first beat, take a big step forward on the right foot, springing on pointes, in attitude croisée; on the second beat, hold the pose and come down on the right leg in plié; on the third and fourth beats, pas de bourrée en dehors, changing feet. Repeat 4 times, in turn on the right and left leg.[5]

[4] Sissonne ouverte is studied, at the beginning, facing the barre, sideways (2 or 3 lessons), and later in the center of the studio, to the side, in small poses croisées, effacées and écartées front and back. Depending on the mastery, it is executed on 2 beats each.

[5] The execution of jetés in a big pose third arabesque is done in a similar manner. Two jetés in first, second arabesques and attitude effacée dégagée are done in effacé. After mastering the preceding steps, jeté is studied in big poses croisées and effacées front. The term jeté on pointes carries the same meaning as piqué on pointes, with a thrust of the body either to the front, to the side, or to the back.

Second position, on pointes, arms in second position.

Third Lesson

EXERCISES AT THE BARRE

1. 16 measures in 4/4.
Two grands pliés in first, second, fourth, and fifth positions, each on 4 beats.

2. BATTEMENTS TENDUS. 24 measures in 2/4.
Two battements tendus front (right foot); 2 battements tendus back (left foot), each on 1 beat. Repeat once more. Four battements tendus doubles (right foot), each on 2 beats. Repeat in the reverse direction, starting on the right foot to the back. Battements tendus jetés: 7 to the front, to the side, to the back and to the side, each on half a beat.

3. RONDS DE JAMBE À TERRE. 12 measures in 4/4.

On 2 introductory chords, préparation en dehors. Four ronds de jambe à terre, each on 1 beat; 7 ronds de jambe à terre, each on half a beat, end foot front, pointe tendue. Four piqués front, each on a quarter beat; on 1 beat, bring the working leg to the side, pointe tendue on the floor; 4 piqués to the side, each on a quarter beat; on 1 beat, bring the working leg to the back, pointe tendue on the floor; 7 ronds de jambe à terre en dehors, each on half a beat. Repeat the whole combination en dedans. In 2 measures: trace half a circle in plié en dedans, en dehors; in 2 measures: port de bras, in a wide plié, bending the body.

4. BATTEMENTS FONDUS. 16 measures in 2/4.

One fondu at 45°, 1 fondu at 90°, to the front, to the side, to the back and to the side, each on 2 beats. Frappés: 3 to the side, each on half a beat, repeat 4 times; 8 doubles frappés, each on 1 beat.

5. RONDS DE JAMBE EN L'AIR. 16 measures in 4/4.

On 2 introductory chords, préparation temps relevé en dehors. Eight ronds de jambe en l'air, each on 1 beat, 7 ronds de jambe en l'air, each on half a beat; on 2 beats, demi-rond front at 45°; on 1 beat, half a turn (détourné), on the supporting left leg toward the barre (half-toe) concluding the turn, the working leg is back; on 1 beat, coupé, open the left leg to the side at 45°. Repeat the combination on the left leg, then without a pause, execute en dedans, in turn on the right and left leg.

6. PETITS BATTEMENTS SUR LE COU-DE-PIED. 8 measures in 4/4.

Sixteen petits battements front, 12 petits battements back, each on half a beat; on 1 beat, a quick développé in attitude effacée; on 1 beat, hold the position.

7. BATTEMENTS DÉVELOPPÉS. 8 measures in 4/4.

First measure: développé to the side, and demi-rond en dedans to the front. Second measure: a slow half turn on the flat foot (not rising) toward the barre. At the end of the turn, the working leg is in the back at 90°. Third measure: relevé on half-toe, plié in fifth position and a half turn toward the barre on half-toe (détourné). Fourth measure: développé on half-toe in écarté back, end in fifth position, the working leg back. Fifth measure: développé to the side and demi-rond en dehors to the back. Sixth measure: a slow half turn away from the barre, on the flat foot (not rising). At the end of the turn, the working leg is in the front at 90°. Seventh measure: relevé on half-toe, plié in fifth position and a half turn away from the barre, (détourné) on half-toe. Eighth measure: développé on half-toe in écarté front.

8. GRANDS BATTEMENTS (SMOOTH).[1] 8 measures in 2/4.

On 1 beat, a smooth grand battement; on 1 beat, pause in fifth position. Execute twice to the front, to the side, to the back and to the side.

EXERCISES IN THE CENTER

1. SMALL ADAGIO AND BATTEMENTS TENDUS. 8 measures in 4/4.

First measure: grand plié in first position. Second measure: développé to the side (left leg) and demi-rond en dedans in croisé front. Third measure: tour lent en dedans in pose croisée front. Fourth measure: relevé on half-toe, in croisé; at the end, bring the working leg down in fifth position and développé to the side (right leg). Fifth measure: tour lent en dedans à la seconde. Sixth measure: plié on the supporting leg, holding the working leg at 90°, and pas de bourrée dessus en tournant. Seventh and eighth measures: trace a half circle on the floor in plié (left leg, rond de jambe à terre), end in a pose fourth arabesque, pointe tendue on the floor in plié and relevé to 90°, rising on half-toe. Battements tendus and tours. 8 measures in 4/4. Right foot: 8 battements tendus en tournant en dehors in quarter turns in a big pose effacée front. The first battement with a turn to corner 4, the second en face (facing) corner 4. Execute the following 2 battements tendus in a similar way to corner 6, then to corner 8 and to corner 2, each on 1 beat. Execute battements tendus en tournant en dedans in a big pose effacée back in a similar manner, with the left foot with turns to corners 4, 6, 8, and 2. End the last battement in fifth position left foot front. Battements tendus jetés: right foot, 15 to the side, each on half a beat. In 2 measures: tours sur le cou-de-pied en dehors from second position.

2. BATTEMENTS SOUTENUS. 8 measures in 2/4 or 16 measures in 3/4 (Waltz).

Right foot: soutenu front pointe tendue on the floor in a small pose

---

[1] Smooth grands battements are done to the tempo of grands battements jetés in the way of a quick développé.

croisée; left foot: soutenu back in a small pose croisée; right foot: soutenu to the side en tournant en dehors; left foot: soutenu to the side en tournant en dedans; right foot: soutenu at 90° in a big pose croisée front; left foot: soutenu in pose third arabesque; right foot: 2 soutenus at 90° to the side, each on 2 beats.

3. RONDS DE JAMBE EN L'AIR. 8 measures in 4/4.

On 4 beats, tour sur le cou-de-pied en dehors from fifth position, ending with the working leg opened to the side at 45°. Two ronds de jambe en l'air en dehors, each on 1 beat, 3 ronds de jambe, each on half a beat. Repeat 2 more times. Préparation for tour à la seconde en dehors from second position on the right and left leg, each in 2 measures.

4. PAS COURU AND PETITS BATTEMENTS SUR LE COU-DE-PIED. 4 measures in 4/4.

Fifth position, left foot front. On the upbeat, on 4 quarters of a beat, pas couru in a diagonal from corner 6 to corner 2, starting on the right foot. End on the first beat on the left foot in a small pose effacée front in plié, right foot pointe tendue on the floor; on the second beat, step on half-toe on the right foot, execute a petit battement with the left foot and come down in plié in a small pose croisée front, left foot pointe tendue on the floor. (The step on half-toe is done on the first half beat, the pose croisée in plié on the second half beat.) Later, execute the same step with petit battement on the left foot and come down in plié in a small pose effacée front; step on the right foot and come down in plié in a pose croisée front, pass onto the left foot half-toe and execute 14 petits battements with the right foot, each on half a beat; on 1 beat, bring the right foot back in fourth position, préparation for tour en dehors, and on 4 beats, tour sur le cou-de-pied en dehors, ending in fourth position. Execute the same exercise in the reverse direction.

5. GRANDS BATTEMENTS JETÉS. 16 measures in 2/4.

Right leg: 6 grands battements in croisée front, each on 1 beat; on the sixth battement, demi-plié and on 2 beats, make a full turn on half toe to fifth position (détourné). Right leg: 6 grands battements in fourth arabesque, demi-plié and make a full turn on half-toe to fifth position; 4 grands battements to the side (right leg) and 4 grands battements to the side (left leg). In a straight line to the right side, tour glissade en tournant (3 times) each on 2 beats; on 2 beats, step forward on the right foot in attitude effacée, the arms in position allongé.

6. GRAND ADAGIO. 12 measures in 4/4.

First measure: grand plié in fifth position, right foot front. Second measure: relevé on the left foot, the right leg at 90° to the side (arms in third position) and turn to first arabesque. Third and fourth measures: tour lent en dedans in first arabesque. Fifth and sixth measures: plié in arabesque and pas de bourrée en dehors, en face and en tournant; end in fourth position, grande préparation for tour en dedans, right foot front. Seventh measure: préparation in first arabesque, then passé through first position to the front in fourth position, préparation for tour en dedans, left foot front. Eighth measure: préparation in attitude effacée; on the last beat, plié in attitude. Ninth measure: pas de bourrée en dehors, changing feet and step on the right foot forward in a big pose croisée back, pointe tendue on the floor. Tenth measure: grand port de bras. Eleventh measure: grand port de bras, ending in fourth position préparation for tour en dedans. Twelfth measure: préparation à la seconde en dedans.

ALLEGRO

1. 16 measures in 2/4.

Three assemblés to the side starting on the right, left and right leg; entrechat-quatre. Repeat 4 times and execute in the reverse direction. Each jump is done on 1 beat.

2. 8 measures in 4/4.

Right leg: sissonne ouverte in a small pose effacée front, temps levé, temps levé with demi-rond to the side, assemblé. Repeat on the left leg. Right leg: sissonne ouverte to the side, temps levé, pas de bourrée dessous en tournant, échappé in second position, changing feet and 2 sautés in fifth position, traveling forward. Repeat the whole exercise on the other leg. Each jump is done on 1 beat, pas de bourrée and échappé on 2 beats. Execute also in the reverse direction.

3. PAS CHASSÉ. 4 measures in 4/4 or 16 measures in 3/4.

Right leg: sissonne tombé croisée front, right arm in second position, left arm in third position; 2 chassés with big jumps traveling forward and a sliding jump without breaking contact with the floor in the same direction, on 1 beat or to 1 measure of a waltz, each. Left leg: sissonne tombée back, 2 chassés and a sliding jump on the floor, traveling backward. Execute also with the right leg in a big pose effacée front to corner 2 and on the left leg in a big pose effacée, to corner 6.

4. 8 measures in 2/4.

Fifth position, left foot front. Seven emboîtés, traveling forward in a diagonal to corner 2, each on 1 beat; on 1 beat, assemblé front. Seven emboîtés, traveling backward in a diagonal to corner 6; assemblé back.

5. 8 measures in 2/4.

On 1 beat: grande sissonne ouverte in croisé front; on 1 beat, assemblé; on 1 beat, grande sissonne ouverte to the side; on 1 beat, assemblé; 2 grands échappés in second position, changing feet, each on 2 beats. Repeat on the other leg, and subsequently in the reverse direction.

6. 16 measures in 2/4.

Échappé battu, landing on one foot, the other foot sur le cou-de-pied back; temps levé and assemblé croisé back. Repeat 4 times, in turn on the right and left leg and 4 times in the reverse direction. Each jump is done on 1 beat.

7. TOURS EN L'AIR FOR THE MEN'S LESSON.

8. 8 measures in 2/4.

Seven temps levés in a big bouncing jump in first position; 7 in second position, each on half a beat, end the last temps levé in fifth position; 7 and 7 more petits changements de pieds, each on half a beat.

THIRD EXAMPLE OF EXERCISES ON POINTES

1. 16 measures in 2/4.

Three échappés in second position, changing feet, each on 2 beats; on 2 beats, relevé in fifth position. Repeat on the other leg. Four échappés in second position, each on 2 beats; 8 échappés in second position, each on 1 beat.

2. 8 measures in 4/4.

Three échappés, landing on one foot, the other foot sur le cou-de-pied back, each on 4 beats; end the third échappé in plié on one leg; pas de bourrée en dehors en face and en tournant, changing feet, each on 2 beats. Repeat the whole exercise on the other leg, and subsequently in the reverse direction.

3. 16 measures in 2/4.

Three sissonnes ouvertes at 45°, in a small pose croisée front, 1 sissonne to the side, each on 2 beats. Repeat on the other leg. One sissonne ouverte in a small pose croisée front, 1 sissonne to the side and 2 sissonnes simples, changing feet to the back, each on 2 beats. Repeat on the other leg, and subsequently in the reverse direction.

4. 16 measures in 3/4 (Slow Waltz).

On the upbeat, plié on the left foot and dégagé the right foot in effacé front at 45°. First measure: jeté on the right leg in a big pose attitude effacée. Second measure: hold the pose; come down in plié on the right leg. Third and fourth measures: pas de bourrée en dehors, changing feet. Fifth, sixth, seventh, and eighth measures: repeat jeté in attitude effacée on the left leg. In the following 8 measures, execute as well the jetés on the right and left leg.

5. GRANDE SISSONNE OUVERTE. Musical measure 4/4.

To the side: on the first beat, demi-plié; on the second beat, grande sissonne ouverte to the side at 90°; on the third beat, come down in fifth position, demi-plié; on the fourth beat, stretch the knees. Repeat 4 times, in turn on the right and left leg, changing feet to the back, and 4 times in the reverse direction, changing feet to the front.[2]

6. 16 measures in 2/4.

In a straight line, from side 7 to side 3, starting on the right foot, 4 tours glissades en tournant, each on 2 beats; 4 sissonnes simples, changing feet to the back, each on 1 beat; on 2 beats, préparation from fifth position to fifth position, and on 2 beats, tour sur le cou-de-pied en dehors. Repeat on the other leg.

7. 8 measures in 2/4.

Fifth position, left foot front. On the diagonal from corner 6 to corner 2, 3 and 3 more changements de pieds on pointes, each on half a beat. Come down on both feet, on the last changement. Seven changements de pieds on pointes en tournant, starting the turn to the right side, each on half a beat. Follow through on the other leg in the direction to corner 8; changements de pieds on pointes en tournant starts to the left side.

---

[2] In the following lesson, the similar study of grandes sissonnes ouvertes in big poses croisées front, attitude croisée and attitude effacée, takes place. According to the mastery of the step, grandes sissonnes are done on 2 beats.

Pose écartée back.

Fourth Lesson

EXERCISES AT THE BARRE

1. 16 measures in 4/4.

Two demi-pliés, each on 2 beats; on 4 beats, 1 grand plié and 2 relevés on half-toe, each on 4 beats, in first, second, fourth, and fifth positions.

2. BATTEMENTS TENDUS. 16 measures in 2/4.

Sixteen battements tendus to the side, each on 1 beat, each time the working foot closes twice in front and twice in the back, in fifth position. Thirty-two battements tendus jetés to the side, each on half a beat, observing the same established order of changing feet in fifth position.

3. RONDS DE JAMBE À TERRE. 24 measures in 2/4.

On 2 introductory chords, préparation en dehors. Two ronds de jambe à terre, each on 1 beat; 3 ronds de jambe à terre, each on half a beat. Repeat once more and end with the foot front, pointe tendue on the floor. In 4 measures: relevé front to 90°, grand rond de jambe en dehors and passé through first position front, pointe tendue on the floor. Repeat the same en dedans, ending with the foot back, pointe tendue on the floor. In 4 measures: port de bras in wide plié, bending the body. In 4 measures: relevé lent to 90° in second arabesque and plié-relevé on half-toe.

4. BATTEMENTS FONDUS AT 45°. 16 measures in 2/4.

On 2 beats, fondu front; on 2 beats, plié-relevé with a half turn toward the barre; on 2 beats, plié-relevé again with a half turn toward the barre and on 2 beats, plié-relevé with demi-rond to the side. Frappés: 5 to the side, each on half a beat; on 3 half beats, flic-flac en dehors en face; 4 doubles frappés, each on 1 beat. Repeat the same in the reverse direction, starting with the right foot back.

5. RONDS DE JAMBE EN L'AIR. 8 measures in 4/4.

On 2 beats, tour sur le cou-de-pied en dehors from fifth position; on 1 beat, come down in plié in a small pose effacée front, pointe tendue on the floor; on 1 beat, relevé on half-toe on the supporting leg and open the working leg to the side at 45°. Four ronds de jambe en l'air en dehors, each on 1 beat, 3 and 3 more ronds de jambe en l'air, each on half a beat; end the third rond de jambe in effacé front, pointe tendue on the floor, in plié. On 4 beats, relevé to 90° in effacé front and at the end lower the working leg to fifth position back. Repeat the whole exercise en dedans.

6. PETITS BATTEMENTS SUR LE COU-DE-PIED. 16 measures in 2/4.

Fourteen petits battements front, each on half a beat; on the last, come down in demi-plié on the supporting leg and hold this position for 1 beat. Fourteen petits battements to the back and on the demi-plié, a small bend of the body to the back. Repeat 14 petits battements to the front and to the back.

7. BATTEMENTS DÉVELOPPÉS. 16 measures in 4/4.

First measure: développé front. Second measure: plié-relevé on half-toe and demi-rond to the side, end in fifth position. Third and fourth measures: développé to the side and plié-relevé with demi-rond to the front; end in fifth position. Fifth, sixth, seventh, and eighth measures: grand rond de jambe développé en dehors on half-toe, passé at 90° and again grand rond de jambe en dehors. Repeat in the reverse direction.

8. GRANDS BATTEMENTS JETÉS. 8 measures in 4/4.

Eight grands battements front, side and back, each on 1 beat; on 2 beats, port de bras, bending the body.

EXERCISES IN THE CENTER

1. SMALL ADAGIO. 16 measures in 4/4.

First and second measures: temps lié front at 90°. Third measure: without lowering the working leg, tour lent à la seconde en dedans. Fourth measure: demi-rond en dedans to croisé front, relevé on half-toe, at the end lower the working leg to fifth position. Repeat on the other leg and thereafter in the reverse direction with tours lents à la seconde en dehors and demi-rond en dehors in attitude croisée.

2. BATTEMENTS TENDUS. 12 measures in 4/4.

Eight battements tendus to the side (with 1 battement alternatingly on the right and left leg), changing feet to the back in fifth position; 8 battements changing feet to the front in fifth position, in this way moving backward and forward, on 1 beat each. The arms come up from the preparatory position to the second and meet in third position when one is traveling backward, and when one is traveling forward, the arms gradually open in second position. Battements tendus jetés: right foot to the side: 7 and again 7, each on half a beat. Repeat the same on the left foot. On 2 beats: right foot front: tour sur le cou-de-pied en dehors from second position; on 2 beats, left foot front: tour sur le cou-de-pied en dehors from second position.

3. BALLOTTÉ.[1] 8 measures in 4/4.

Ballotté in a big pose effacée front (right leg) and ballotté in a big pose effacée back allongée (left leg), each on 4 beats. Repeat once more. Four soutenus at 90° to the side, each on 2 beats, in turn on the right and left leg. On 2 beats: préparation for tour à la seconde en dehors (right leg).

4. JETÉS EN TOURNANT TRAVELING TO THE SIDE IN HALF TURNS. Musical measure 4/4.

Move in a straight line from side 7 to side 3. a) On the first beat, jeté en tournant on the right leg with a half turn en dedans; on the second beat, demi-plié on the right leg, the left leg is stretched to the side, pointe tendue on the floor; on the third beat, jeté en tournant on the left leg with a half turn en dehors, facing the mirror; on the fourth beat, demi-plié on the left leg, the right leg is stretched to the side, pointe tendue on the floor. Execute 8 jetés en tournant with half turns en dedans, en dehors; 8 jetés en tournant with half turns en dehors, en dedans in the same direction.

b) Each jeté en tournant is done on 2 beats, but at the end of each jeté, the leg opens to the side at 45°.[2]

5. GRAND ADAGIO. 8 measures in 4/4.

First measure: grand plié in second position with second port de bras; at the end, step on the right foot in second arabesque at 90°. Second measure: lean the body slightly and turn in pose écartée back. Third and fourth measures: from pose écartée, tombé in plié on the left leg to corner 6 in second arabesque and turn in pose effacée front to corner 2 (stretch the supporting leg), the right arm in third position, the left arm in first position with the hand and fingers stretched as in an arabesque position; relevé on half-toe, end in fifth position, right foot back. Fifth and sixth measures: développé in croisé front (left leg), relevé on half-toe, tombé on the left foot in plié (the right foot back, pointe tendue) and port de bras in a wide deep plié, bending the body; end in fourth position, grande préparation for tour en dedans. Seventh measure: préparation for tour in pose croisée front; on the last beat, come down in fourth position, grande préparation en dehors. Eighth measure: préparation for tour in effacé front.

---

[1] In this lesson, the ballotté at 90° replaces the combination of battements fondus. Depending on the mastery, the step is done on 2 beats.

[2] Depending on the mastery of the step, jeté en tournant is done on 1 beat. The half turn is done on the upbeat and the pause in demi-plié on the supporting leg, which ends each jeté, on 1 beat (the working leg is stretched to the side).

ALLEGRO

1. 16 measures in 2/4.

Assemblé to the side, right and left leg, changing feet to the front, each on 1 beat; on 2 beats, sissonne tombée croisée front, on the right leg, which is in fifth position back before the jump (during the jump the right leg moves forward). Repeat 4 times and subsequently in the reverse direction.

2. ASSEMBLÉ BATTU (initial study). Musical measure 4/4.

Each assemblé is done on 2 beats.

3. 16 measures in 2/4.

Jeté to the side on the right and left leg, each on 1 beat; on 2 beats, pas de bourrée en tournant en dehors changing feet; repeat on the other leg. On 1 beat, jeté to the side, 2 temps levés, each on half a beat; execute 4 times, in turn on the right and left leg; a short coupé and repeat the whole combination in the reverse direction.

4. 8 measures in 4/4.

Échappé battu, landing on one leg, the other foot sur le cou-de-pied back, temps levé, a short coupé and assemblé, traveling forward in croisé. Two ballonnés croisés front, assemblé to the side, royale. Each jump is done on 1 beat. Repeat on the other leg and in the reverse direction.

5. 8 measures in 2/4.

Grande sissonne ouverte in attitude croisée, end with assemblé; grande sissonne ouverte in attitude effacée, end with assemblé in fifth position front; 4 changements de pieds. Repeat on the other leg. All jumps are done on 1 beat. Execute also in the reverse direction.

6. 8 measures in 2/4.

Grande sissonne ouverte in first arabesque to corner 2, end with assemblé in fifth position front; grande sissonne ouverte in third arabesque, end with assemblé; 2 grands échappés in fourth position croisée. Repeat on the other leg. All jumps are done on 1 beat, grand échappé on 2 beats, each.

7. TOURS EN L'AIR FOR THE MEN'S LESSON.

One or 2 tours, depending on the ability of the students.

8. 4 measures in 4/4.

Three entrechats-quatre, 1 royale, each on 1 beat. Repeat 4 times.

9. 4 measures in 2/4.

Sixteen petits changements de pieds, each on half a beat.

FOURTH EXAMPLE OF EXERCISES ON POINTES

1. 16 measures in 2/4.

Two échappés in second position, changing feet, each on 2 beats; on 4 beats, 1 double échappé in second position. Execute 3 times. Échappé en tournant in half turn to side 5 and échappé en face to side 5; échappé en tournant in half turn to side 1 and échappé en face to side 1, each on 2 beats.

2. 8 measures in 4/4.

Two échappés in second position, ending on one leg, the other sur le cou-de-pied back, each on 4 beats; at the end of the second échappé, open the leg from the cou-de-pied to the side at 45°. On 4 beats, pas de bourrée dessus-dessous en face and on 4 beats, pas de bourrée dessus-dessous en tournant, end in fifth position. Jeté front in a small pose croisée with plié-relevé, each on 4 beats; execute 3 times. Concluding the third jeté, open the leg from sur le cou-de-pied to the side to 45° and on 4 beats, pas de bourrée dessus-dessous en tournant.

3. 8 measures in 4/4.

Four sissonnes ouvertes at 45° in a small pose effacée front, in turn on the right and left leg; end all sissonnes in fifth position back, each on 2 beats. Two sissonnes ouvertes to the side, on the right and left leg, each on 2 beats; on 4 beats, préparation from fifth position to fifth position and tour sur le cou-de-pied en dehors. Repeat the whole combination on the other leg and subsequently in the reverse direction.

4. 8 measures in 2/4.

Two grandes sissonnes ouvertes to the side, on the right and left leg; grande sissonne ouverte with the right leg in attitude croisée and attitude effacée, each on 2 beats. Repeat on the other leg, and subsequently in the reverse direction.

5. 4 measures in 4/4.

On 4 beats, préparation from fifth position to fourth and préparation for tour sur le cou-de-pied en dehors; end tour in fifth position. Execute 4 times, in turn on the right and left leg. Repeat the same with tours sur le cou-de-pied en dehors.

6. 32 measures in 3/4 (Slow Waltz).

8 measures: on the right foot, slow pas de bourrée suivi in a straight line from side 7 to side 3, right arm in third position, left arm in second position; in the last measure, bring the left foot in fifth position front, on pointes. 8 measures: remaining on pointes, execute a fourth port de bras. 8 measures: on the left foot, pas de bourrée suivi croisé front, right arm in third position, left arm in second position allongée. 8 measures: pas de bourrée suivi croisé back, lower the arms gradually in the preparatory position.

Position croisée front, pointe tendue on the floor.

Second Semester
Fifth Lesson

EXERCISES AT THE BARRE

1. 16 measures in 4/4.
Two demi-pliés, each on 2 beats; 2 grands pliés, each on 4 beats; on 4 beats, 1 relevé on half-toe in first, second, fourth, and fifth positions.

2. BATTEMENTS TENDUS. 48 measures in 2/4.
Six battements tendus front, each on 1 beat and on 2 beats, a full turn on half-toe in fifth position toward the barre. Six battements tendus back and a full turn on half-toe in fifth position away from the barre. Four doubles tendus to the side, each on 2 beats. On 4 beats: slide

212

the working leg to the side, pointe tendue on the floor and bend the body toward the barre, raising the arm in third position and ending in fifth position back. Repeat the whole exercise in the reverse direction. Battements tendus jetés: 7 in first position, 7 and again 7, each on half a beat; 5 piqués, and again 5 piqués, each on a quarter beat. Repeat tendus jetés and piqués.

3. RONDS DE JAMBE À TERRE. 24 measures in 2/4.

On 2 introductory chords, préparation en dehors. Four ronds de jambe à terre, each on 1 beat; 7 ronds de jambe à terre, each on half a beat, end in effacé front pointe tendue on the floor. In 2 measures: relevé lent to 90° in effacé front. In 2 measures: plié-relevé on half-toe and lower the working leg, pointe tendue on the floor. Repeat the same en dedans. Relevé lent to 90° and plié-relevé on half-toe in attitude effacée. On 4 beats: trace a half circle on the floor en dehors, en dedans, end in fifth position half-toe. On 4 beats: port de bras on half-toe, bending the body.

4. BATTEMENTS FONDUS AT 45°. 12 measures in 4/4.

Double fondu front and side, each on 2 beats; on 2 beats, fondu front and on 2 beats, plié-relevé with full rond de jambe en dehors, to the back. On half a beat, petit battement; on 2 beats, fondu front; plié-relevé with a half turn toward the barre, plié-relevé again on half-toe with a half turn toward the barre, plié-relevé with demi-rond de jambe to the side, each on 2 beats. Repeat the whole combination in the reverse direction, starting on the right foot back. Frappés: 3 to the side, each on half a beat; on 2 beats, come down in fifth position, demi-plié, the working leg in the back, then come up on half-toe, and open the working leg to the side at 45°; repeat frappés, then bring the working leg in fifth position front, in demi-plié; 8 doubles frappés to the side, each on 1 beat.

5. RONDS DE JAMBE EN L'AIR. 8 measures in 4/4.

On 4 beats, préparation for tour sur le cou-de-pied temps relevé en dehors; at the end open the working leg to the side at 45°. Four ronds de jambe en l'air, each on 1 beat; 7 ronds de jambe and again 7, each on half a beat. Repeat the same en dedans.

6. PETITS BATTEMENTS SUR LE COU-DE-PIED. 16 measures in 2/4.

Seven petits battements to the front, each on half a beat, end the seventh in demi-plié; 7 petits battements to the back, each on half a beat; 6 petits battements front, each on half a beat; on 1 beat, open the working leg to the front at 45°; on 1 beat, a half turn on half-toe on the supporting leg, toward the barre; on 1 beat, a half turn on half-toe away from the barre, and on 2 beats, demi-rond to the side. Repeat the whole combination in the reverse direction.

7. BATTEMENTS DÉVELOPPÉS. 16 measures in 4/4.

First and second measures: grand rond de jambe développé en dehors (on the flat foot); on the last 2 beats, passé at 90° and simultaneously plié on the supporting leg. Third and fourth measures: grand rond de jambe développé en dehors in plié; on the last 2 beats, passé at 90° and simultaneously relevé on half-toe on the supporting leg. Fifth and sixth measures: grand rond de jambe développé en dehors on half-toe, and passé at 90°. Seventh and eighth measures: développé in écarté back, passé at 90° in attitude effacée. Repeat en dedans.

8. GRANDS BATTEMENTS JETÉS. 8 measures in 2/4.

Four grands battements in effacé front, écarté back, effacé back and écarté front, each on 1 beat.

EXERCISES IN THE CENTER

1. SMALL ADAGIO AND BATTEMENTS TENDUS. 8 measures in 4/4.

First measure: grand plié in first position. Second measure: développé to the side, right leg. Third measure: on the first beat, hold the position, come up on half-toe; on the second beat, bring the leg in effacé front and lower the heel of the supporting leg; on the third beat, rise onto half-toe; on the fourth beat, bring the working leg to the side and lower the heel of the supporting leg. Fourth measure: plié-relevé in the same position (working leg to the side at 90°) and at the end, come down in second position. Fifth measure: grand plié in second position. Sixth measure: développé to the side, left leg. Seventh measure: come up on half-toe, bring the working leg in attitude effacée and lower the heel of the supporting leg; rise onto half-toe, in attitude effacée, carry the working leg to the side, and lower the heel of the supporting leg. Eighth measure: plié-relevé in the same position (working leg to the side at 90°), end in fifth position, left foot front. Battements tendus in 4 measures: 2 battements tendus front (left foot), each on 1 beat; 3 battements tendus jetés, each on half a beat. Repeat to the side, to the back, and to the side. In 2 measures: tour sur le cou-de-pied en dehors from second position; in 2 measures: tour sur le cou-de-pied en dedans from second position.

2. RONDS DE JAMBE À TERRE. 12 measures in 4/4.

On 2 introductory chords, préparation en dehors. Three ronds de jambe à terre en face, the fourth rond de jambe en tournant in a quarter turn. Execute 4 times. Repeat en dedans. Each rond de jambe is done on 1 beat. On 2 beats, trace a half circle on the floor en dedans, en dehors, end in fourth position croisée, grande préparation for tour en dehors; on 2 beats, 2 préparations for tours in attitude croisée.

3. JETÉS EN TOURNANT TRAVELING TO THE SIDE IN HALF TURNS. 8 measures in 4/4.

Six jetés en tournant, each on 1 beat; on half a beat, come up on half-toe and execute 3 frappés, each on half a beat; 7 frappés, each on half a beat, and on 4 beats, tour sur le cou-de-pied en dehors from fifth position. Follow through on the other leg, and subsequently in the reverse direction.

4. GRANDS BATTEMENTS JETÉS. 8 measures in 2/4.

Four grands battements in croisé front (right leg); 4 grands battements in third arabesque and 4 in fourth arabesque (left leg); 4 grands battements to the side (right leg), each on 1 beat.

5. GRAND ADAGIO. 12 measures in 4/4.

First measure: right foot front, grand port de bras. Second measure: relevé lent at 90° in third arabesque (left leg). Third measure: tour lent en dehors in third arabesque. Fourth measure: relevé on half-toe in arabesque, end in fifth position. Fifth and sixth measures: développé in écarté back (right leg), turn slowly en dehors with passé at 90°, and end in écarté back. Seventh measure: demi-rond en dehors in fourth arabesque, at the end, plié on the supporting leg. Eighth measure: step to the back, on the right foot, passé through first position, and relevé at 90° in first arabesque (left leg) to corner 2. Ninth measure: tour lent en dedans in first arabesque. Tenth measure: relevé on half-toe in arabesque and passé through first position to the front in fourth position, grande préparation en dehors. Eleventh measure: préparation for tour in third arabesque, end in fifth position. Twelfth measure: 2 glissades to the side, changing feet (starting on the left foot), step on the left foot to side 7 in plié, the right foot in the back, pointe tendue on the floor, right arm in third position, left arm in second position and bend backward. (The body faces a straight line toward side 7 and the back to side 3, the left shoulder is pulled back, the right arm in third position with the elbow pulled all the way front and the head turned to the right.)

ALLEGRO

1. 8 measures in 2/4.

Right leg: assemblé to the side, entrechat-quatre; left leg: assemblé to the side, royale; left leg: assemblé to the side, entrechat-quatre; right leg: assemblé royale. Repeat. Each jump is done on 1 beat. Execute in the reverse direction.

2. 8 measures in 2/4.

Two sissonnes fermées in a small pose écartée back, on the right and left leg, each on 1 beat; 3 sissonnes fermées to the side, on the right, left and right leg, each on half a beat; 2 sissonnes fermées traveling forward in a small pose croisée, each on 1 beat, and 3 sissonnes fermées traveling forward in a small pose croisée, each on half a beat. Repeat on the other leg, and subsequently in the reverse direction.

3. 4 measures in 4/4 or 16 measures in 3/4 (Waltz).

On the upbeat, développé on half-toe in croisé front (right leg); on the first beat, tombé, and on the following 3 beats, chassé front (as described in the third lesson). On the last quarter beat (on the upbeat), développé on half-toe in attitude croisée (left leg), tombé, and chassé back. Further on, développé on half-toe in effacé front (right leg) and chassé front; développé on half-toe in attitude effacée (left leg), and chassé back.

4. 8 measures in 2/4.

Right leg: grande sissonne ouverte to the side, assemblé, end in fifth position, right foot front; right leg: grande sissonne ouverte in écarté back, assemblé, end in fifth position, right foot back. Repeat on the left leg. Two grands échappés in second position, changing feet. Grande sissonne ouverte in écarté back and assemblé, on the right and left leg. Each jump is done on 1 beat. Execute in the reverse direction.

5. ENTRECHAT-TROIS AND ENTRECHAT-CINQ. Musical measure 4/4.

On the first beat, demi-plié; between the first and second beats, jump entrechat-trois back; on the second beat, end the jump in demi-plié; on the third beat, assemblé; on the fourth beat, stretch the knees. Repeat 4 times, in turn on the right and left leg, then execute entrechat-trois to the front. Entrechat-cinq is studied in the same way.[1]

---

[1] Depending on the mastery of the step, entrechat-trois and entrechat-cinq are done on 1 beat.

6. 16 measures in 2/4.

Two complex échappés battus, each on 2 beats; 3 entrechat-quatre, 1 royale, each on 1 beat. Execute 4 times, in turn on the right and left leg.

7. 32 measures in 3/4 (Waltz).

Fifth position, left foot front. Move on the diagonal from corner 6 to corner 2. Sissonne tombée in fourth position effacée (right leg), then immediately from fourth position, sissonne tombée in fourth position croisée (left leg). Execute 6 sissonnes tombées in this way, each in 1 measure. In sissonnes tombées in effacé, the right arm is in second position, the left in first position; in sissonnes tombées in croisée, the left arm is in second position, the right in first position. In effacé, the body leans slightly to the right; in croisé, the body is slightly thrown to the back. In 2 measures: step on the right foot, the left foot to the back, pointe tendue on the floor, in pose second arabesque. In 6 measures: moving on the diagonal upstage from corner 2 to corner 6; starting on the left foot, execute pas de basque en tournant, right arm in third position, left arm in second position, and balancé on the right foot in pose second arabesque toward corner 2. Execute 3 times. In 2 measures: a small step to the side, on the left foot, then a large step to the back, on the right foot in croisé front, left foot, pointe tendue on the floor. 8 measures: starting on the right leg, 3 pas de chat back and pas de bourrée en dehors, changing feet. Repeat pas de chat on the left leg. 8 measures: big sissonne in first arabesque (right leg), facing corner 8 and a quick run to corner 4.

8. 8 measures in 2/4.

Seven petits changements de pieds, each on half a beat. Repeat 4 times.

FIFTH EXAMPLE OF EXERCISES ON POINTES

1. 16 measures in 2/4.

Sixteen relevés in first position, 16 relevés in second position, each on 1 beat.

2. 16 measures in 2/4.

Four échappés in second position, changing feet, each on 1 beat; 2 doubles échappés, each on 2 beats. Repeat 4 times.

3. 16 measures in 2/4.

Four sissonnes simples, changing feet to the back, 2 sissonnes simples en tournant in half turns, each on 2 beats; 4 sissonnes simples, changing feet to the front, each on 1 beat. Repeat once more.

4. 32 measures in 3/4 (Waltz).

Préparation, left foot back in croisé, pointe tendue on the floor. On the upbeat, plié on the right leg and bring the left foot sur le cou-de-pied back. Four coupé-ballonnés to the side, ending sur le cou-de-pied back, each in 2 measures. On the first ballonné, open the arms in second position, when leaning the body to the left, raise the right arm in third position, and leave the left arm in second position. On the second ballon-né, when leaning the body to the right, raise the left arm in third position and leave the right arm in second position, etc. In 1 measure, bring the left foot front and step in fourth position croisée in demi-plié, lower the arms in the preparatory position. In 1 measure: spring onto pointes in attitude croisée, raising the arms in third position. In 2 measures: come down on the left foot demi-plié in fourth position and slowly open the arms in second position. In 4 measures: bring the right leg front in fourth position croisée and repeat the attitude croisée. Coupé and in 8 measures repeat 4 ballonnés; dégagé the left foot to the side, pointe tendue on the floor and in 8 measures, pas de bourrée suivi on the diagonal upstage to corner 4, left foot front. The left arm in first position, the right arm in second, hands and fingers stretched forward as in arabesque arms.

5. 16 measures in 3/4 (Waltz).

In 4 measures: jeté on the right leg in a big pose first arabesque to corner 2; plié and pas de bourrée en dehors, changing feet. In 4 measures: jeté on the left leg in first arabesque to corner 8, plié and pas de bourrée en dehors, changing feet. In 4 measures: jeté on the right leg in a big pose third arabesque, plié and pas de bourrée en dehors, changing feet. In 4 measures: left foot front, préparation from fifth position to fourth position and tour sur le cou-de-pied en dehors.

6. 4 measures in 4/4.

Préparation from fifth to fourth position and préparation for tour sur le cou-de-pied en dedans, end in fifth position. Repeat 4 times on the right leg and 4 times on the left leg. Execute also with tours sur le cou-de-pied en dedans.

Fourth position croisée, on half-toe.

Sixth Lesson

EXERCISES AT THE BARRE

1. 16 measures in 4/4.

Two demi-pliés, 2 grands pliés in first, second, and fourth position, each on 4 beats; 2 grands pliés in fifth position, each on 4 beats, and in 2 measures, port de bras, bending the body.

2. BATTEMENTS TENDUS. 16 measures in 2/4.

Four battements tendus front, each on 1 beat, 7 battements tendus jetés to the front, each on half a beat. Repeat to the side, to the back and to the side.

3. RONDS DE JAMBE À TERRE. 24 measures in 2/4.

On 2 introductory chords, préparation en dehors. Four ronds de jambe à terre, each on 1 beat, end pointe tendue front on the floor in plié; in 2 measures: trace a half circle on the floor in plié en dedans, en dehors. Four ronds de jambe à terre en dehors, each on 1 beat, then 3 ronds de jambe and again 3, each on half a beat. Repeat the same en dedans. In 4 measures: trace a half circle on the floor in plié en dedans and make a half turn toward the barre (the working leg remains on the floor, pointe tendue). Stretch the knee of the supporting leg. In 4 measures: port de bras in a wide plié, bending the body (left arm in third position).

4. BATTEMENTS SOUTENUS. 8 measures in 4/4.

Two soutenus front, pointe tendue on the floor, each on 1 beat; on 2 beats, soutenu at 90°. Repeat to the side, to the back and to the side. Frappés: 7 to the side, each on half a beat; on 4 beats, tour sur le cou-de-pied en dehors from fifth position; at the end, open the working leg to the side at 45°; 4 doubles frappés, each on 1 beat, and on 4 beats, tour sur le cou-de-pied en dedans from fifth position.

5. ROND DE JAMBE EN L'AIR. 8 measures in 4/4.

On 4 beats, préparation temps relevé en dehors for tour sur le cou-de-pied; at the end, open the working leg to the side at 45°. Four ronds de jambe en l'air, each on 1 beat; 7 ronds de jambe en l'air, each on half a beat, end in a small pose effacée front, pointe tendue on the floor, in plié; on 2 beats, soutenu en tournant en dedans, end in a small pose effacée back, pointe tendue on the floor in plié, and on 2 beats, relevé on half-toe, bringing the working leg to the side at 45°. Repeat en dedans.

6. PETITS BATTEMENTS SUR LE COU-DE-PIED. 16 measures in 2/4.

Six petits battements, each on half a beat; on 1 beat, lower the heel and open the working leg to the side, pointe tendue on the floor. Doubles frappés on the floor, rising onto half-toe, and lowering the heel after each frappé (to the front, to the back); a half turn toward the barre, then frappé to the front, a half turn again away from the barre and double frappé to the side, each on 1 beat. Repeat in the reverse direction (doubles frappés are done with half turns away from the barre). Repeat the whole combination from the beginning.

7. BATTEMENTS DÉVELOPPÉS. 16 measures in 4/4.

First measure: développé to the side and demi-rond front. Second and third measures: a half turn toward the barre and a half turn in the reverse direction (again toward the barre). Fourth measure: plié-relevé on half-toe and demi-rond to the side. Fifth measure: développé to the side and demi-rond to the back. Sixth and seventh measures: a half turn away from the barre and a half turn in the reverse direction (again toward the barre). Eighth measure: plié-relevé on half-toe with demi-rond to the side. Repeat the whole combination.

8. GRANDS BATTEMENTS JETÉS. 8 measures in 2/4.

Two grands battements (regular) and 2 grands battements (smooth) to the front, to the side, to the back and to the side, each on 1 beat.

EXERCISES IN THE CENTER

1. SMALL ADAGIO AND BATTEMENTS TENDUS. 16 measures in 4/4.

First measure: grand plié in first position. Second measure: développé in effacé front (right leg). Third measure: tour lent en dehors in effacé. Fourth measure: plié-relevé on half toe, end in first position and step into second position. Fifth measure: grand plié in second position. Sixth measure: développé in attitude effacée (right leg). Seventh measure: tour lent en dedans in attitude effacée. Eighth measure: plié-relevé on half-toe, end in fifth position, right foot front. Ninth measure: grand plié in fifth position. Tenth measure: développé in second arabesque (left leg). Eleventh measure: tour lent en dedans in second arabesque. Twelfth measure: plié, and relevé on half-toe, end in fifth position, left foot front. Thirteenth and fourteenth measures: grand rond de jambe développé en dehors on half-toe (left leg). Fifteenth and sixteenth measures: step forward on the right leg in fifth position half-toe, the left arm raised in third position, the right arm in second position and execute the fourth port de bras; at the end, bring the arms down in the preparatory position.

Battements tendus: 8 measures. Right foot: 8 battements tendus in a small pose croisée front; left foot: 8 battements tendus in a small pose croisée back, each on 1 beat. Battements tendus jetés: right foot: 7 to the side, each on half a beat, end the seventh battement in demi-plié, préparation for tour, and on 4 beats, tour sur le cou-de-pied en dehors from fifth position. Repeat battements tendus jetés; tour is done en dedans.

2. BATTEMENTS FONDUS AT 90°. 8 measures in 2/4.

Two fondus front, to the side, to the back and to the side, each on 2 beats.

3. RONDS DE JAMBE EN L'AIR. 8 measures in 2/4.

Eight ronds de jambe en l'air en dehors, each on 1 beat; end the eighth rond de jambe in demi-plié; 4 jetés en tournant traveling to the side, in half turns, each on 1 beat, and pas de bourrée dessous-dessus en tournant, each on 2 beats. Execute en dedans separately; jeté en tournant in the reverse direction, en dehors, en dedans, pas de bourrée en tournant dessus-dessous.

4. PETITS BATTEMENTS SUR LE COU-DE-PIED. 8 measures in 4/4.

Fourteen petits battements, each on half a beat; on 1 beat, bring the working leg sur le cou-de-pied back, demi-plié on the supporting leg; on 2 beats, pas de bourrée en tournant en dehors, changing feet; on 2 beats, pas de bourrée en dehors en face, changing feet. End in fourth position croisée in préparation for tour en dehors; on 4 beats, tour sur le cou-de-pied; at the end, open the working leg to the side at 45°. In the following 4 measures, repeat petits battements, pas de bourrée en dedans en tournant and en face, changing feet, tour from fourth position en dedans and end in fifth position demi-plié.

5. GRAND ADAGIO. 12 measures in 4/4.

First measure: fifth port de bras. Second measure: developpé in third arabesque and plié (left leg). Third measure: tour lent en dehors in third arabesque plié. Fourth measure: step back on the left foot, développé in croisé front (right leg), the right arm in third position and demi-rond to the side. Fifth measure: turn to second arabesque to corner 8, passé at 90° with half a turn en dedans to écarté front (the right shoulder facing corner 8). Sixth measure: plié in écarté and pas de bourrée en tournant en dedans, changing feet. Seventh measure: développé in attitude croisée (right leg) and demi-rond to the side. Eighth measure: hold the position and relevé on half-toe, passé through first position in demi-plié front and step on the right foot in a big pose croisée, the left foot back, pointe tendue on the floor. Ninth measure: grand port de bras, ending in fourth position for grande préparation for tour en dehors. Tenth measure: préparation in third arabesque. Eleventh measure: step forward on the right foot in fourth arabesque at 90°, end in fifth position. Twelfth measure: step on the right foot in fourth arabesque and relevé on half-toe. This adagio ends with a long sustained pause on half-toe in fourth arabesque.

ALLEGRO

1. 8 measures in 2/4.

Six assemblés to the side, changing feet to the front; 2 assemblés battus, in turn on the right and left leg, each on 1 beat. Repeat in the reverse direction.

2. 16 measures in 2/4.

Sissonne ouverte to the side at 45°, 2 temps levé assemblé; 2 sissonnes fermées traveling forward in a small pose croisée, 2 royales. Repeat 4 times, in turn on the right and left leg. Each jump is done on 1 beat. Execute also in the reverse direction.

3. 16 measures in 2/4.

Right leg: 4 ballonnés to the side, assemblé croisé back; entrechat-quatre, entrechat-cinq back, assemblé croisé back. Right leg: jeté traveling to the side; left leg: jeté croisé, traveling front, assemblé croisé back, entrechat-quatre, 2 entrechats-cinq back with assemblé. Repeat the same on the other leg. Each jump is done on 1 beat. Execute also in the reverse direction.

4. 16 measures in 3/4 (Waltz).

Three grands échappés in second position, changing feet, each in 2 measures; in 2 measures, grande sissonne ouverte in third arabesque, assemblé. Repeat on the other leg.

5. 4 measures in 4/4.

On the upbeat, développé to the side on half-toe (right leg); on the first beat, tombé and on the following 3 beats, chassé to the side, ending in fifth position, left leg front. Repeat pas chassé on the left and right leg. Four grands changements de pieds, each on 1 beat.

6. 8 measures in 2/4.

Two complex échappés battus, each on 2 beats; 7 petits changements de pieds, each on half a beat. Repeat.

7. TOURS EN L'AIR (for the men's lesson).

SIXTH EXAMPLE OF EXERCISES ON POINTES

1. 32 measures in 3/4 (Waltz).

Four temps liés, front, 4 times, each in 4 measures.

2. 16 measures in 2/4.

Four échappés in second position, changing feet, each on 1 beat; on 2 beats, entrechat-quatre and sissonne simple with the right foot, changing back; on 2 beats, entrechat-quatre and sissonne simple with the left foot. Repeat and execute 2 more times, changing feet in sissonnes simples to the front.

3. 16 measures in 3/4 (Slow Waltz).

Fifth position, left foot front. Move on the diagonal from corner 6 to corner 2. Six jetés fondus front, starting on the right leg, each in 1 measure. In 2 measures: step on the right foot (on pointes) in first arabesque at 45°, the right arm raised to the height of third arm position and without coming down from pointes, execute pas de bourrée en dehors, changing feet, end in fifth position in demi-plié; 4 jetés fondus to the back, starting on the right leg, each in 1 measure. In 2 measures: step back on the right foot and turn to the right side, in fifth position (on pointes), end in demi-plié, right foot front. In 2 measures: starting on the left foot: glissade (jumping) to the side without changing feet; jeté on the left leg in first arabesque at 90° and passé through first position, the right foot forward in a wide fourth position croisée, demi-plié on the right leg; the arms in the position of fourth arabesque.

4. 8 measures in 2/4.

Grande sissonne ouverte in first arabesque (on the right leg) to corner 2, grande sissonne ouverte in first arabesque (on the left leg) to corner

8, 2 grandes sissonnes ouvertes in écarté back (on the right leg). The first sissonne without changing feet; the second, changing feet, each on 2 beats. Repeat on the other leg, and execute in the reverse direction in effacé and écarté front.

5. 8 measures in 2/4.

Move on the diagonal from corner 6 to corner 2. In 2 measures: dégagé the right foot and pas de bourrée suivi (right foot front) in écarté front, the right shoulder facing corner 2, the left shoulder, corner 6. The arms gradually come up from the preparatory position, the right to third position, the left to second allongé. In 2 measures: 4 sissonnes simples en tournant to the right side, passing each time the right foot in fifth position back, front, back, front. Repeat the whole combination. This is done to a quick tempo.

6. 8 measures in 4/4.

On 2 beats: with the right foot front, préparation from fifth position to fourth, and on 2 beats, tour sur le cou-de-pied en dehors; 2 sissonnes simples, changing feet to the back, each on 2 beats. Repeat 4 times, in turn on the right and left leg. Execute the same with tours en dedans.

Arabesque on half-toe, arm in second position.

Seventh Lesson

EXERCISES AT THE BARRE

1. 16 measures in 4/4.
One demi-plié, 1 grand plié, each on 4 beats and 4 relevés on half-toe, each on 2 beats, in first, second, fourth, and fifth positions.

2. BATTEMENTS TENDUS. 32 measures in 2/4.
Four battements tendus in demi-plié, front, side, back, and side; 4 battements tendus on a straight supporting leg, front, side, back, and side, each on 1 beat. Battements tendus jetés: 7 to the front, 5 to the side, each on half a beat, and on 3 half beats, flic-flac en dehors en face; 7 battements tendus jetés to the back, 5 to the side, each on half a beat,

and on 3 half beats, flic-flac en dedans en face. Repeat battements tendus jetés and flic-flac.

3. RONDS DE JAMBE À TERRE. 32 measures in 2/4.

On 2 introductory chords, préparation en dehors. Three ronds de jambe à terre, each on 1 beat; 2 ronds de jambe à terre, each on half a beat. Repeat and end with the foot to the front, pointe tendue on the floor. Passé through first position to the back, to the front, to the back at 45° and front, back, front, each on half a beat, end on half-toe; on 1 beat, a half turn toward the barre; on 1 beat, coupé, open the left leg to the side at 45°, and on 2 beats, préparation en dehors on the left foot, ending to the side at 45°. Repeat the whole exercise on the left leg, after the half turn and coupé; repeat the combination on the right and left leg en dedans.

4. BATTEMENTS FONDUS. 24 measures in 2/4.

On 2 beats, fondu front at 90°; on 2 beats, plié-relevé. Repeat to the side. On 2 beats, fondu front at 45°; on 2 beats, plié-relevé with demi-rond to the side and 7 frappés, each on half a beat. Repeat the same in the reverse direction, starting on the right leg to the back. Doubles frappés: 16 to the side, each on 1 beat.

5. RONDS DE JAMBE EN L'AIR. 8 measures in 4/4.

On 2 beats, tour sur le cou-de-pied en dehors from fifth position. Repeat the tour. On 4 beats, préparation for tour temps relevé en dehors, at the end, open the working leg to the side at 45°. Four ronds de jambe en l'air en dehors, each on 1 beat; 7 ronds de jambe en l'air en dehors, each on half a beat. Repeat the whole combination en dedans.

6. PETITS BATTEMENTS SUR LE COU-DE-PIED. 8 measures in 4/4.

Eight petits battements, each on half a beat; on 4 beats, développé front. Repeat petits battements and follow with développé to the side. Sixteen petits battements, each on half a beat; on 4 beats, développé in second arabesque; on 4 beats, plié-relevé in attitude croisée.[1]

7. BATTEMENTS DÉVELOPPÉS. 16 measures in 4/4.

First and second measures: développé ballotté, right leg front, left leg back. Repeat. Third and fourth measures: développé to the side, plié-relevé on half-toe, plié-relevé in écarté back, end in fifth position. Fifth and sixth measures: développé ballotté, right leg back, left leg front. Repeat. Seventh and eighth measures: développé to the side, plié-relevé

---

[1] Execute all développés on the first beat of the measure, and hold the position for the last 3 beats.

on half-toe, plié-relevé in écarté front, end in fifth position. Repeat the whole combination.

8. GRANDS BATTEMENTS JETÉS POINTÉS. 16 measures in 2/4.

Seven grands battements pointés, the eighth grand battement in fifth position, effacé front, each on 1 beat. Follow through in écarté back, second arabesque and écarté front.

EXERCISES IN THE CENTER

1. SMALL ADAGIO AND BATTEMENTS TENDUS. 8 measures in 4/4.

First measure: grand plié in fifth position (right foot front). Second measure: développé to the side (right leg) and bring the leg to écarté back. Third measure: tour lent en dehors in écarté. Fourth measure: holding the position, plié on the supporting leg and pas de bourrée en tournant en dehors, changing feet. Fifth measure: développé to the side (left leg) and bring the leg to écarté front, right arm in third position, the left arm in second position. Sixth measure: tour lent en dedans in écarté. Seventh and eighth measures: from pose écarté, turn en dedans in first arabesque to corner 4 and continuing with the turn, end in fourth arabesque position.

Battements tendus: 8 measures. With the right foot: 6 battements tendus in a big pose croisée front, each on 1 beat; 3 battements tendus jetés, each on half a beat; on the left foot: 6 battements tendus in pose fourth arabesque, each on 1 beat; 3 battements tendus jetés, each on half a beat; with the right foot: 8 battements tendus to the side, each on 1 beat, then 7 battements tendus jetés and again 7, each on half a beat. In 2 measures: left foot front, préparation from fifth position to fourth (pass the left leg to the back) and tour sur le cou-de-pied en dedans to the right side, end in fourth position in préparation en dehors, left foot front. In 2 measures: préparation for tour en dehors and tour sur le cou-de-pied en dehors.

2. RONDS DE JAMBE À TERRE. 8 measures in 4/4.

On 2 introductory chords, préparation en dehors. Four ronds de jambe à terre en face, 4 en tournant en dehors in quarter turns, each on 1 beat. Repeat en dedans and end in fifth position, right foot front. In 2 measures: right foot front, préparation from second position for tour à la seconde en dehors. In 2 measures: left foot front, préparation for tour à la seconde en dedans.

3. BATTEMENTS FONDUS AT 45°. 16 measures in 2/4.

Three fondus in a small pose effacée front, each on 2 beats; on 2 beats, hold the pose on half-toe. Repeat the same in a small pose écartée back, effacée back and écartée front.

4. GRANDS BATTEMENTS JETÉS POINTÉS. 8 measures in 2/4.

Three grands battements pointés and 1 in fifth position effacée front, each on 1 beat; repeat the same in the poses écartées back, fourth arabesque, and écartées front.

5. GRAND ADAGIO. 12 measures in 4/4.

First measure: grand plié in fourth position croisée (right foot front). Second measure: développé in third arabesque (left leg) and bring the working leg to attitude croisée, the arms in third position. Third measure: tour lent en dehors in attitude. Fourth measure: plié in attitude, open the arms in allongé, end in fifth position. Fifth measure: développé to the side (right leg), plié, and take a wide step to the side on the right foot; raise the left leg to the side at 90°, as in a grand battement. Sixth measure: from this position, demi-rond in croisé front, the left arm in third position, the right arm in first position; on the last 2 beats, plié, holding the pose. Seventh measure: a quick passé through first position in first arabesque to corner 2, and pas de bourrée en dehors, changing feet, end in fourth position, grande préparation for tour en dehors. Eighth measure: préparation in attitude croisée, end in fifth position. Ninth and tenth measures: développés ballottés in effacé, left leg front and right leg back; repeat once more and end with passé through first position in fourth position croisée, grande préparation for tour en dedans. Eleventh measure: préparation in attitude effacée, end in fifth position, left foot front. Twelfth measure: starting on the right foot back, pas de basque en tournant to the back, in a quarter turn to side 7; right foot front, pas de basque en tournant to the front, in a quarter turn to side 1.

ALLEGRO

1. 16 measures in 2/4.

Two assemblés to the side, changing feet to the front, each on 1 beat; 3 assemblés to the side, changing feet to the front, each on half a beat, in turn on the right and left leg. Repeat 4 times and 4 times in the reverse direction.

2. 8 measures in 2/4.

On 1 beat, jeté to the side, 2 temps levés, each on half a beat; execute 3 times, in turn on the right and left leg; 2 jetés, each on 1 beat. Repeat once more and separately in the reverse direction.

3. 8 measures in 4/4.

On 2 beats, échappé battu, landing on one foot, the other sur le cou-de-pied back; on 2 beats, pas de bourrée en tournant en dehors, changing feet. Repeat. Three pas de chat back, each on 1 beat; on 1 beat, royale; 2 sissonnes tombées croisées front, each on 2 beats. Repeat the whole combination on the other leg and subsequently in the reverse direction.

4. 8 measures in 2/4.

On 1 beat, grande sissonne ouverte in croisé front (right leg); on 1 beat, assemblé; grande sissonne ouverte in attitude croisée (left leg), assemblé; grande sissonne ouverte in écarté back (right leg), assemblé; on 2 beats, grand échappé in fourth position croisée. Repeat on the other leg.

5. 4 measures in 4/4.

Three entrechats-quatre, 1 royale, each on 1 beat. Repeat 4 times, in turn on the right and left leg.

6. TOURS EN L'AIR (for the men's lesson).

7. 4 measures in 2/4.

Sixteen petits changements de pieds, each on half a beat.

SEVENTH EXAMPLE OF EXERCISES ON POINTES

1. 16 measures in 4/4.

Four échappés in second position, changing feet, each on 2 beats; on 4 beats, 2 doubles échappés and 8 échappés in second position, traveling to the back, each on 2 beats. Repeat from the beginning and execute 8 échappés traveling to the front.

2. 8 measures in 2/4.

Two sissonnes simples, changing feet to the back, each on 2 beats; 4

sissonnes simples, changing feet to the back, each on 1 beat, in turn on the right and left leg; 2 glissades en tournant en dehors, in a straight line to the left side, each on 2 beats. At the beginning of the glissade, the left arm is in third position, the right arm in first position; at the end, the left in second position, the right in third position. Four sissonnes simples, changing feet to the front (lower the arms gradually in the preparatory position), each on 1 beat, in turn on the left and right leg.

3. 16 measures in 2/4.

On 1 beat, sissonne ouverte at 45° (right leg) in a small pose effacée front; on 1 beat, tombé to corner 2, pas de bourrée en dehors en face and en tournant, changing feet, each on 2 beats; on 2 beats, sissonne ouverte at 45° (right leg) in a small pose effacée front, end in fifth position, right foot back. Three sissonnes ouvertes at 45°, in a small pose écartée back (left, right and left leg), each on 2 beats; on 2 beats, soutenu en tournant in fifth position, on pointes, end in plié and repeat on the other leg. Execute also in the reverse direction.

4. 16 measures in 3/4 (Slow Waltz).

Fifth position, left foot front. On the upbeat, glissade (jumping) to the side, starting on the right leg, without changing feet. First measure: jeté on the right leg in first arabesque at 90°. Second measure: passé through first position in a wide fourth position croisée, left foot front, in demi-plié, the arms in fourth arabesque position. Third and fourth measures: repeat glissade and with a step to the side, jeté on the right leg in attitude croisée (the arms in third position) and come down in demi-plié, in fourth position croisée, right foot front. In the following 4 measures: from this position, repeat the combination on the other leg. In 8 measures: step on the left foot and pas de bourrée suivi to the front in croisé, the left arm in third position, the right arm in second position. In the last measure: hold the position on pointes and bring the right foot in fifth position front, simultaneously open the left arm in second position, and raise the right arm from second to third position.

5. 4 measures in 4/4.

Grandes sissonnes ouvertes in écarté back on the right and left leg, each on 2 beats; on 4 beats, préparation from fifth position to fifth position and tour sur le cou-de-pied en dehors. Repeat on the other leg. Execute also in the reverse direction.

6. 8 measures in 2/4.

Three changements de pieds on pointes; again 3 and 7, each on half a beat; on the last changement, come down on both feet. Repeat.

Sissonne on pointes.

Eighth Lesson

EXERCISES AT THE BARRE

1. 16 measures in 4/4.

One demi-plié, 1 grand plié, 2 relevés on half-toe, each on 4 beats, in first, second, fourth, and fifth position.

2. BATTEMENTS TENDUS. 32 measures in 2/4.

Eight battements tendus front, each on 1 beat, demi-plié, on the fourth and eighth battements tendus; 4 doubles tendus to the side, each on 2 beats, lowering the heel twice in second position, on half beats. Repeat in the reverse direction, starting on the right foot back. Battements tendus jetés: 8 front, each on half a beat; 3 and again 3 to the side, each on half a beat, demi-plié on the third and sixth battement. Repeat battements tendus jetés in the reverse direction. Battements tendus jetés in first position: 7, 4 times in a row, each on half a beat.

3. RONDS DE JAMBE À TERRE AND RONDS DE JAMBE EN L'AIR. 16 measures in 4/4.

On 2 introductory chords, préparation en dehors. Two ronds de jambe à terre, each on 1 beat, then 3 and 7 ronds de jambe à terre, each on half a beat; at the end, come up on half-toe and open the working leg to the side at 45°. Two ronds de jambe en l'air en dehors, each on 1 beat; 3, 7, and 7 more ronds de jambe en l'air, each on half a beat, and 7 ronds de jambe à terre en dehors, each on half a beat, end foot front pointe tendue on the floor, in plié and in 2 measures, port de bras, bending the body. Repeat en dedans.

4. BATTEMENTS FONDUS AT 45°. 12 measures in 4/4.

On 2 beats: double fondu front; on 2 beats: plié-relevé. Repeat. On 2 beats: double fondu front with a full rond en dehors to the back; on 2 beats: plié-relevé; 2 doubles fondus to the side, each on 2 beats. Repeat in the reverse direction, starting with the right leg back. Frappés: to the side, 5 frappés, each on half a beat; on 3 half beats, flic-flac en face en dehors; 5 frappés and flic-flac en face en dedans. Eight doubles frappés to the side, each on 1 beat.

5. PETITS BATTEMENTS SUR LE COU-DE-PIED. 8 measures in 4/4.

Seven petits battements front, each on half a beat; on 2 beats: tombé in fifth position front, on the working right foot in demi-plié, the left foot sur le cou-de-pied back; a half turn toward the barre, on half-toe, and bring the left foot sur le cou-de-pied front; on 2 beats: tombé in fifth position on the left foot and a half turn again toward the barre, on half-toe. Seven petits battements front, each half a beat: on 4 beats: tour sur le cou-de-pied en dehors from fifth position, end in a small pose écartée back, pointe tendue on the floor, in plié. Repeat the whole combination in the reverse direction and tombé in fifth position back and execute the half turns on half-toe away from the barre.

6. BATTEMENTS DÉVELOPPÉS. 8 measures in 4/4.

First measure: relevé lent to 90° front; at the end, come up on half-toe. Second measure: from the preceding position, grand rond de jambe en dehors, on half-toe. Third and fourth measures: hold the position, and passé at 90° in effacé front, then demi-rond in écarté back, and move to attitude effacée, end in fifth position. Fifth measure: relevé lent to 90° back, come up on half-toe. Sixth measure: from the preceding position, grand rond de jambe en dedans, on half-toe. Seventh and eighth measures: hold the position on half-toe, passé at 90° in attitude effacée, demi-rond in écarté front and move to effacé front.

7. GRANDS BATTEMENTS JETÉS. 16 measures in 2/4.

Four grands battements front (right leg), 4 grands battements back (left leg), 4 grands battements to the side, and 4 in écarté back (right leg), each on 1 beat. Repeat in the reverse direction, starting right leg back.

EXERCISES IN THE CENTER

1. SMALL ADAGIO AND BATTEMENTS TENDUS. 8 measures in 4/4.

First measure: grand plié in second position, and relevé on half-toe. Second measure: développé to the side (right leg), raise the arms in third position and turn to second arabesque in plié. Third measure: tour lent en dedans in arabesque. Fourth measure: passé at 90°, in croisé front, relevé on half-toe and come down in fourth position croisée, grande préparation for tour en dehors. Fifth measure: préparation in attitude croisée; while holding the position, come down in plié, on the last beat. Sixth measure: pas de bourrée en tournant en dehors, changing feet and pas de bourrée en dehors en face, changing feet; end in fourth position croisée, grande préparation for tour en dedans. Seventh measure: préparation à la seconde (the arms in third position), end in fifth position, left foot front. Eighth measure: développé on half-toe in écarté back (left leg). Battements tendus: 8 measures. With the right foot: 8 battements tendus croisés front, raise the arms gradually in third position; with the left foot: 8 battements tendus croisés back, open the arms gradually in second position; with the right foot: 8 battements tendus to the side, each on 1 beat. Tendus jetés: right foot, to the side: 7 and 7 more each on half a beat. In 2 measures, on the left leg: tour sur le cou-de-pied en dehors from second position; on 2 beats, on the right leg: tour sur le cou-de-pied en dedans from second position.

2. BATTEMENTS FONDUS AT 45°. 8 measures in 4/4.

Three fondus in a small pose effacée front, each on 2 beats; on 2 beats, plié-relevé in a small pose écartée front; 2 fondus to the side at 45°, 1 fondu at 90°, each on 2 beats, and hold the pose on half-toe for 2 beats. Repeat in the reverse direction with plié-relevé from effacé back to écarté back and so forth.

3. RONDS DE JAMBE EN L'AIR. 8 measures in 4/4.

On 4 beats: pas de bourrée dessus-dessous en tournant, end in fifth position, préparation for tour sur le cou-de-pied en dehors; on 4 beats: tour en dehors; at the end, open the working leg to the side at 45°; ronds de jambe en l'air en dehors: 3, 3, 3 more, each on half a beat; 14 petits battements sur le cou-de-pied, each on half a beat; on 1 beat: come down in fifth position, demi-plié; on 4 beats: pas de basque to the front, ending in fourth position croisée, in préparation for tour, and tour sur le cou-de-pied en dehors; on 4 beats: step forward in fifth position half-toe, the arms in second and third position allongées. Execute in the reverse direction.

4. GRANDS BATTEMENTS JETÉS. 8 measures in 4/4.

Two grands battements front (right leg), 2 grands battements back (left leg), 2 grands battements to the side (right leg), each on 1 beat; on 2 beats, préparation from second position for tour à la seconde en dehors

Grand plié in fourth position croisé.

(left leg). Repeat the same, starting left leg back and execute the préparation à la seconde en dedans.

5. GRAND ADAGIO. 8 measures in 4/4.

First measure: right foot front, grand port de bras. Second measure: grand port de bras, ending in fourth position, grande préparation for tour en dedans. Third measure: préparation in pose croisée front. Fourth measure: plié in croisé and pas de bourrée en tournant en dedans, changing feet; on the third and fourth beats, step on the right foot in attitude effacée to corner 4. Fifth measure: from the pose attitude, lean the body slightly forward (stretch the knee of the working leg) and turn the body toward the working leg in pose écartée front to corner 8. Sixth measure: relevé on half-toe in écarté, tombé on the left foot in plié, in effacé front, the right foot, pointe tendue on the floor, the arms in position allongée, and pas de bourrée en dehors, changing feet, end in fourth position, grande préparation for tour en dehors. Seventh measure: préparation in effacé front, end in fifth position, right foot back. Eighth measure: 2 petits changements de pieds and a half turn to the right side in fifth position half-toe. The arms open through second position to fourth arabesque position, left leg back, the head turned to the right. The student is with her back to the mirror, when executing the last half turn on half-toe, which ends the adagio.

ALLEGRO

1. 8 measures in 2/4.

Four assemblés to the side, changing feet to the front, 4 assemblés battus, each on 1 beat. Repeat in the reverse direction.

2. 8 measures in 2/4.

Two ballonnés effacés front, 1 to the side, assemblé croisé back. Jeté in croisé, traveling forward, assemblé back; jeté in croisé, traveling forward, a short coupé and assemblé croisée, traveling forward. Repeat on the other leg. Each jump is done on 1 beat. Execute also in the reverse direction.

3. 16 measures in 2/4.

Move on the diagonal from corner 6 to corner 2. Fifth position, right foot front. Twelve emboîtés front, traveling to corner 2; 8 emboîtés front, traveling in a small half circle to corner 4; 8 emboîtés front, traveling in a small half circle to corner 8, each on 1 beat. On 1 beat, assemblé croisé front; on 1 beat, pause; on 1 beat, pas de chat front; on 1 beat, pause.

4. 4 measures in 4/4.

Two grandes sissonnes ouvertes in attitude croisée (right leg), end with assemblé; grande sissonne ouverte in écarté back, assemblé, 2 changements de pieds. Left leg: 2 grandes sissonnes ouvertes in croisé front, end with assemblé; grande sissonne ouverte in écarté front, assemblé and grand échappé in second position, changing feet. Each jump is done on 1 beat.

5. 16 measures in 3/4 (Waltz).

On the upbeat, développé on half-toe in écarté back (right leg). In 4 measures: tombé and pas chassé to corner 4, end in fifth position, left foot front. In 4 measures: développé on half-toe in croisé front (left leg), tombé and pas chassé front. In 4 measures: développé on half-toe in attitude croisée (right leg), tombé and pas chassé back. In 4 measures: big sissonne in first arabesque (left leg) and a big run to corner 8. At the end, step on the left foot in second arabesque to 90°, in plié.

6. TOURS EN L'AIR (for the men's lesson).

7. 8 measures in 2/4.

Three entrechats-cinq back, end with assemblé, 1 entrechat-trois, assemblé. Repeat on the other leg. Each jump is done on 1 beat. Repeat in the reverse direction.

8. 8 measures in 2/4.

Eight grands changements de pieds, each on 1 beat, 16 petits changements de pieds, each on half a beat.

EIGHTH EXAMPLE OF EXERCISES ON POINTES

1. 8 measures in 4/4.

Four échappés in second position, changing feet; 4 échappés en tournant in half turns, each on 2 beats, and on 4 beats, double échappé in second position, changing feet. Repeat on the other leg.

2. 16 measures in 2/4.

On 2 beats: starting on the right foot front, glissade forward in a small pose croisée; on 2 beats: turn in fifth position on pointes to the left side (détourné sur pointes). Repeat from the beginning on the left foot. Two sissonnes simples, changing feet to the back, each on 2 beats, and 4 sissonnes simples, each on 1 beat. Repeat the whole exercise and subsequently in the reverse direction.

3. 8 measures in 4/4.

Préparation: right foot back croisé, pointe tendue on the floor. On 2 beats: pas couru (4 steps) on the diagonal forward, end in demi-plié on the left foot; dégagé the right foot front, in effacé, pointe tendue on the floor, bend the body forward toward the foot, the left arm in second position at 45°, the right arm stretched forward in the direction of the right foot. On 2 beats: turn in effacé back, in plié, and simultaneously execute a rond de jambe à terre en dehors with the right foot to the pose effacée back; raise the right arm to third position, the left in second position allongée; raise the right foot slightly off the floor, and, while lowering the arms into the preparatory position, execute 1 emboîté back. Repeat the whole exercise on the other leg. From the preceding position, on 2 beats, pas de chat back and pas de bourrée en dehors, changing feet; on 2 beats, starting on the left foot back, 2 pas de chat back, and on 4 beats, starting on the right foot, pas de bourrée suivi in a straight line to the right side, the right arm in third position, the left arm in second position allongée. Repeat the whole combination. This is done to a quick tempo.

4. 8 measures in 2/4.

On the diagonal from corner 6 to corner 2, starting on the right foot: 4 tours glissades en tournant, each on 2 beats, end the last tour in fifth position, right foot back; on 2 beats: left foot front, préparation for tour sur le cou-de-pied en dehors from fifth position to fourth position; on 2 beats: tour en dehors; on 2 beats: soutenu en tournant en dedans (starting on the left foot); on 2 beats: plié in fifth position and grande sissonne ouverte in attitude croisée on the right leg.

5. 8 measures in 2/4.

On 2 beats, right foot front: préparation from fifth position to fifth position; on 2 beats: tour sur le cou-de-pied en dehors. Repeat on the other leg. Four grandes sissonnes ouvertes in first arabesque, in turn on the right and left leg, each on 2 beats. Repeat in the reverse direction with grandes sissonnes ouvertes in effacé front.

6. 8 measures in 2/4.

Eight sissonnes simples changing feet to the back, 8 sissonnes simples changing feet to the front, each on 1 beat. Execute to a quick tempo.

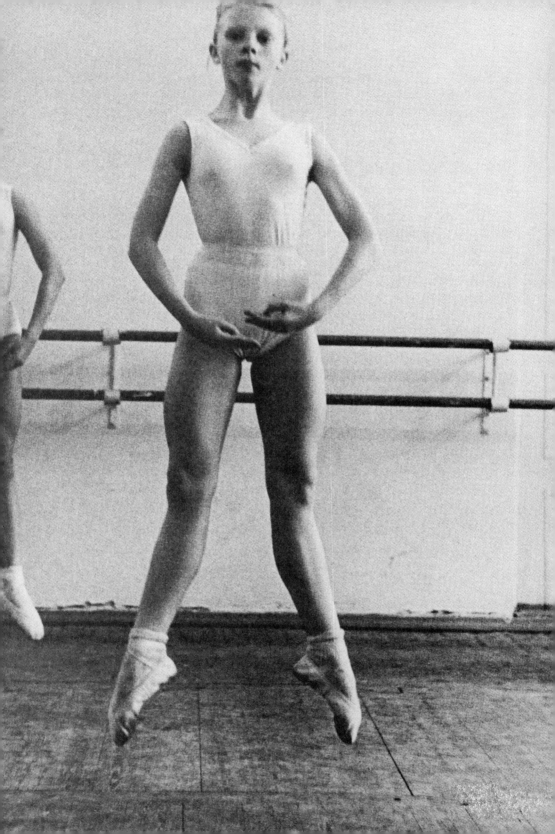

Fifth Year

The following elements will be stressed in the fifth year of study: mastering the technique of beats (beating steps); various turns in various ways; starting the study of tours in big poses; developing the smoothness of graceful movements and suppleness, when passing from one pose to another, in a harmonious movement; introducing more complicated forms of adagio, and developing elevation in the big jumps.

Position à la seconde en l'air (90°).

First Semester
First Lesson

EXERCISES AT THE BARRE

1. 16 measures in 4/4.
Two demi-pliés, 2 grands pliés, each on 4 beats, in first, second, fourth, and fifth positions.

2. BATTEMENTS TENDUS. 32 measures in 2/4.
Six battements tendus front, each on 1 beat; 3 battements tendus front, each on half a beat. Repeat the same to the side. Battements tendus jetés: 5 to the front, each on half a beat and on 3 half beats, flic-flac en tournant en dedans in a half turn; at the end, the working leg is in

the back at 45°. Five battements tendus jetés to the back, each on half a beat, and on 3 half beats, flic-flac en tournant en dehors, in a half turn; at the end the working leg is in front at 45°; 7 battements tendus jetés to the front, 7 to the side, each on half a beat. Repeat the whole exercise in the reverse direction.

3. RONDS DE JAMBE À TERRE AND GRANDS RONDS DE JAMBE JETÉS. 16 measures in 4/4.

On 2 introductory chords, préparation en dehors. Eight ronds de jambe à terre, each on 1 beat; 2 grands ronds de jambe jetés, each on 4 beats.[1] Repeat. Execute also en dedans.

4. BATTEMENTS FONDUS AT 45°. 8 measures in 4/4.

On 2 beats, fondu front; 2 fondus front, each on 1 beat. Execute to the side, to the back and to the side. Frappés: 7 to the side, and 7 more, each on half a beat, and 4 doubles frappés, each on 1 beat. On 2 beats, développé on half-toe, in écarté back and on 2 beats, a wide tombé with a half turn away from the barre in second arabesque plié at 90°.

5. RONDS DE JAMBE EN L'AIR. 8 measures in 4/4.

On 4 beats, tour temps relevé en dehors; on the last beat, open the working leg to the side at 45°; 4 ronds de jambe en l'air en dehors with plié-relevé on half-toe, each on 1 beat; 7 and 5 more ronds de jambe en l'air en dehors, each on half a beat, and on 1 beat, come down on the supporting leg, lowering the heel from half-toe, and come up again on half-toe. Repeat the whole exercise en dedans.

6. PETITS BATTEMENTS SUR LE COU-DE-PIED. 16 measures in 2/4.

Twelve petits battements front, each on half a beat; on 2 beats, tombé in fifth position on the working leg, in plié; stretch the left leg to the back, pointe tendue on the floor, bend the body back quickly, raise the right arm to third position; a short coupé on half-toe, open the working leg to the side at 45°. Repeat petits battements back; tombé in plié on the right foot, stretch the left leg to the front, pointe tendue on the floor. Repeat the whole exercise.

7. BATTEMENTS DÉVELOPPÉS WITH A SHORT BALANCÉ. 8 measures in 4/4.

First measure: on the first beat, développé front on half-toe; on the

[1] Grand rond de jambe jeté on 4 beats is not performed in its final form (a movement with a thrown leg [jeté]), but is executed, for two to three lessons, in a slower tempo in order to master this difficult step. Thereafter, it is done on 2 beats and 1 beat.

second beat, hold the position; after the second beat and before the third beat, a short balancé[2]; on the third beat, hold the position at 90°; on the fourth beat, end développé in fifth position. Second measure: repeat the same to the front. Execute to the side, to the back and to the side.

8. GRANDS BATTEMENTS JETÉS. 8 measures in 2/4.

Three grands battements to the front, each on 1 beat; 2 battements tendus, each on half a beat. Execute to the side, to the back and to the side.

EXERCISES IN THE CENTER

1. SMALL ADAGIO AND BATTEMENTS TENDUS. 8 measures in 4/4.

First measure: grand plié in first position; from the deep plié, préparation for tour sur le cou-de-pied en dehors, on the left leg. Second measure: grand plié in first position; from the deep plié, tour sur le cou-de-pied en dehors. Third and fourth measures: after the tour, stay on half-toe, and execute a grand rond de jambe développé en dehors, ending in first position. In the following 4 measures, repeat the whole exercise en dedans.

Battements tendus: 4 measures in 4/4. On the right foot: 8 battements tendus to the side, each on 1 beat; 5 battements tendus jetés, each on half a beat, and on 3 half beats, flic-flac en dehors en face, end to the side at 45°. Repeat battements tendus jetés, flic-flac en dedans. In 2 measures: tour sur le cou-de-pied en dehors, from second position, end in fourth position, préparation en dehors. In 2 measures: 1 and 2 tours sur le cou-de-pied en dehors, to the right side.

2. RONDS DE JAMBE À TERRE AND RONDS DE JAMBE EN L'AIR. 12 measures in 4/4.

On 2 introductory chords, préparation en dehors. Eight ronds de jambe à terre, each on 1 beat; 4 ronds de jambe en l'air, each on 1 beat; 7

---

[2] For more convenience and correct musical accompaniment of this balancé, add 2 dots after the second beat in the music. In this way, the balancé is done in one sixteenth note.

ronds de jambe en l'air, each on half a beat. Repeat en dedans. In 2 measures: développé in écarté back (left leg), a quick passé through first position in fourth arabesque, plié-relevé on half-toe in attitude croisée, the right arm in third position, the left arm in second position; end in fifth position. On 2 beats, développé in effacé front (right leg), a quick passé through first position into third arabesque, plié-relevé on half-toe in attitude croisée, the arms raised to third position.

3. TEMPS LIÉ À TERRE WITH TOUR SUR LE COU-DE-PIED. Musical measure 4/4.

Four temps lié to the front with tours sur le cou-de-pied en dehors, 4 temps lié to the back with tours sur le cou-de-pied en dedans, each in 2 measures.

4. BATTEMENTS FRAPPÉS. 8 measures in 2/4.

Seven and again 7 frappés to the side, each on half a beat; 8 frappés en tournant en dehors, each on 1 beat. Repeat en dedans.[3]

5. GRANDS BATTEMENTS JETÉS. 8 measures in 2/4.

Four grands battements in croisé front (right leg), the right arm in third position, the left arm in second position; 4 grands battements in third arabesque (left leg), 6 grands battements to the side (right leg), each on 1 beat. On the sixth grand battement, hold the working leg at 90° for 2 beats, and lower the leg in fifth position, on the last beat.

6. PRÉPARATION AND TOUR À LA SECONDE EN DEHORS FROM SECOND POSITION. Musical measure 4/4.

In 2 measures: right foot front; préparation for tour à la seconde en dehors from second position; execute in the same manner as in the fourth-year lesson, and end in fifth position, right foot front. In 2 measures: tour à la seconde en dehors to the right side, end in fifth position, right foot back. Repeat on the other leg. Execute the same way en dedans.

7. GRAND ADAGIO. 8 measures in 4/4.

First measure: grand plié in fifth position, right foot front; from the deep plié, préparation for tour sur le cou-de-pied en dehors. Second measure: développé in attitude croisée (right leg) and turn en dehors to corner 6, in effacé front. Third measure: relevé on half-toe, in effacé; end in fifth position and développé in third arabesque (left leg). Fourth measure: from arabesque position, turn en dedans to corner 8, in écarté front; relevé on half-toe and a wide tombé in first arabesque plié. Fifth

---

[3] It is recommended that study of battements frappés en tournant be done on the flat foot for a period of two to three lessons; thereafter execute it on half-toe.

measure: tour lent en dedans in first arabesque plié. Sixth measure: stretch the knee of the supporting leg; bring the working leg to the side at 90°, relevé on half-toe, and passé through first position to the front into fourth position, grande préparation for tour en dehors. Seventh measure: tour tire-bouchon en dehors,[4] the arms in third position, end in fourth position, préparation for tour sur le cou-de-pied en dehors. Eighth measure: 2 tours en dehors, end in fourth position, the left arm in third position, the right arm in second position allongée.

ALLEGRO

1. 16 measures in 2/4.

Two doubles assemblés (the first assemblé: simple; the second: battu), each on 2 beats; 4 assemblés battus, each on 1 beat. Repeat and subsequently in the reverse direction.

2. 16 measures in 2/4.

Two sautés in fifth position, traveling forward (soubresaut), each on 2 beats; 2 sautés, each on 1 beat, and on 2 beats, échappé battu (complex) changing feet. Repeat on the other leg, and subsequently in the reverse direction.

3. 8 measures in 2/4.

Fifth position, right foot front. On the left leg: 3 jetés fermés to the side, without changing feet, each on 2 beats and on 2 beats, 2 entrechats-quatre. Repeat on the other leg.

4. 8 measures in 2/4.

Three grandes sissonnes ouvertes in attitude croisée, traveling forward, and end with assemblé; grande sissonne ouverte in attitude effacée, traveling forward, end with assemblé. Repeat on the other leg. Each jump is done on 1 beat. Execute also in croisé and effacé front.[5]

---

[4] The term tire-bouchon, from the French, denotes "corkscrew," used in the Soviet ballet terminology. It describes the position of the working leg, the thigh turned out in second position and the toe of the working foot touching the knee of the supporting leg.

[5] Starting with this lesson, grandes sissonnes ouvertes in big poses are done with a traveling movement. It will no longer be mentioned in the textbook.

5. 8 measures in 2/4.

Seven entrechats-quatre, 1 royale, traveling to the back. Repeat on the other leg, each on 1 beat. Execute also the combination traveling forward.

6. 4 measures in 4/4.

Four grands échappés in second position, changing feet, each on 2 beats; 8 grands changements de pieds, each on 1 beat.

7. 4 measures in 2/4.

Sixteen petits changements de pieds, each on half a beat.[6]

FIRST EXAMPLE OF EXERCISES ON POINTES

1. 16 measures in 2/4.

Sixteen relevés in first and second positions, each on 1 beat.

2. 16 measures in 2/4.

Move in a straight line from side 7 to side 3. Fifth position, right foot front. Six jetés en tournant, traveling to the side in half turns, each on 1 beat; on 2 beats, step on the right foot, on pointes, to the right side and execute tour sur le cou-de-pied en dedans, ending in fifth position, left foot front. Eight sissonnes simples, changing feet to the back, each on 1 beat. Repeat the whole combination on the other leg. Execute in the reverse direction, the first jeté in a half turn, with a turn en dehors, the second, en dehors, etc.

3. 16 measures in 2/4.

Four sissonnes ouvertes to the side at 45°, in turn on the right and left leg, each on 2 beats; 4 ronds de jambe en l'air en dehors from fifth position, in turn on the right and left leg, each on 2 beats. Repeat and subsequently en dedans.

4. 8 measures in 4/4.

Grande sissonne ouverte à la seconde, on the right and left leg, each

---

[6] Each lesson ends with port de bras and a full bending of the body.

on 2 beats; on 2 beats, jeté on the right leg in third arabesque at 90°, come down in plié; on 2 beats, pas de bourrée en tournant en dehors, changing feet; on the left leg: 4 grandes sissonnes ouvertes in attitude croisée,[7] traveling forward, each on 2 beats. Repeat on the other leg and subsequently in the reverse direction.

5. 32 measures in 3/4 (Waltz).

In 4 measures: jeté on the right leg in first arabesque at 90°, to corner 2; plié-relevé in arabesque, end in fifth position, left foot front. In 4 measures: on the left foot: pas de bourrée suivi in croisé to the front, the right arm in third position, the left arm in first position (arabesque arm position, fingers stretched forward). Repeat on the other leg and execute in the reverse direction: jeté with plié-relevé in a big pose effacée front.

[7] Grandes sissonnes ouvertes on pointes in attitude and the 4 grandes sissonnes ouvertes in arabesque are performed with a traveling movement going forward. To the side, in poses in croisé, effacé front, écarté back, and écarté front, without traveling.

Position à la seconde en l'air (120°).

Second Lesson

EXERCISES AT THE BARRE

1. 16 measures in 4/4.
First position: on 4 beats, demi-plié; on 4 beats, 2 relevés on half-toe; 2 grands pliés, each on 4 beats. Second position: on 4 beats, demi-plié; on 4 beats, bend the body to the side toward the barre, the arm in third position; 2 grands pliés, each on 4 beats. Fourth position: on 4 beats, demi-plié; on 4 beats, 2 relevés on half-toe; 2 grands pliés, each on 4 beats. Fifth position: on 4 beats, demi-plié; on 4 beats, bend the body to the side away from the barre, the left arm in third position; 2 grands pliés, each on 4 beats.

2. BATTEMENTS TENDUS. 24 measures in 2/4.

Four battements tendus front (right foot), 4 battements tendus back (left foot), and 4 battements tendus to the side (right foot), each on 1 beat; 2 doubles tendus to the side in second position, lowering the heel on the floor at each battement, each on 2 beats. Repeat in the reverse direction, starting on the right foot to the back. Battements tendus jetés: 5 to the front, each on half a beat, demi-plié on the fifth battement; on 3 half beats, a full turn on half-toe toward the barre; end in demi-plié. Repeat battements tendus jetés to the back with a full turn away from the barre and follow through with battements tendus jetés to the side twice with a full turn toward the barre and a full turn away from the barre.

3. RONDS DE JAMBE À TERRE. 8 measures in 4/4.

On 2 introductory chords, préparation en dehors. Three ronds de jambe à terre en dehors, 3 en dedans, 7 en dehors, 3 en dedans, 3 en dehors, 7 en dedans, each on half a beat. In 2 measures: trace a half circle on the floor en dehors, en dedans and relevé front to 90°, rising on half-toe. In 2 measures: a half turn on half-toe, on the supporting leg toward the barre; the working leg is in the back at 90° after the turn; plié and relevé on half-toe straight up in attitude, the left arm in third position.

4. BATTEMENTS SOUTENUS AT 90°. 12 measures in 4/4.

Four soutenus front, side, back and side, each on 2 beats. Frappés: 15 to the side, each on half a beat; 4 doubles frappés to the side, each on 1 beat; on 2 beats, plié in fifth position and half a turn on half-toe away from the barre; on 2 beats, développé on half-toe in second arabesque (left leg).

5. RONDS DE JAMBE EN L'AIR AND PETITS BATTEMENTS SUR LE COU-DE-PIED. 8 measures in 4/4.

On 4 beats: assemblé front, tour sur le cou-de-pied en dehors from fifth position; end in a small pose effacée front, pointe tendue on the floor in plié; come up on half-toe and open the working leg to the side at 45°. Ronds de jambe en l'air en dehors: 3 and 3 more, each on half a beat; 14 petits battements front, each on half a beat; on 1 beat, come down in fifth position demi-plié, right foot back. Repeat the whole combination en dedans.

6. BATTEMENTS DÉVELOPPÉS. 8 measures in 4/4.

First measure: développé to the side and demi-rond en dedans to the front. Second measure: plié-relevé on half-toe and half a turn toward the barre; on the last beat, end in fifth position. Third and fourth measures: repeat the same on the left leg. In the following 4 measures: repeat the whole exercise in the reverse direction: développé to the side, demi-rond en dehors to the back, and plié-relevé with a half turn away from the barre.

7. GRANDS RONDS DE JAMBE JETÉS. 16 measures in 2/4.

Eight en dehors and 8 en dedans, each on 2 beats.

EXERCISES IN THE CENTER

1. SMALL ADAGIO AND BATTEMENTS TENDUS. 8 measures in 4/4.

First measure: grand plié in second position; from a deep plié, préparation on the left leg for tour sur le cou-de-pied en dehors. Second measure: grand plié in second position; from a deep plié, tour sur le cou-de-pied en dehors. Third and fourth measures: développé in effacée front (right leg), tour lent en dehors and demi-rond to pose écartée back. Fifth measure: from pose écartée, turn to corner 8 in first arabesque, end in plié. Sixth and seventh measures: passé on half-toe to croisé front (90°), the arms in second position; a wide tombé on the right leg in plié, the left leg in the back, pointe tendue on the floor and port de bras, bending the body; end in fourth position, grande préparation for tour en dedans. Eighth measure: tour tire-bouchon en dedans, the arms in third position. Battements tendus: 4 measures in 4/4. With the right foot: 3 battements tendus to the side, 1 en tournant en dehors in a half turn to side 5, 3 to the side facing side 5 and 1 en tournant en dedans in a half turn to side 1, each on 1 beat. Battements tendus jetés: on the left foot: 5 in a small pose croisée front, each on half a beat; on 3 half beats, flic-flac en dedans en face, end in a small pose croisée back, 5 battements tendus jetés in croisé back, each on half a beat; on 3 half beats, flic-flac en dehors en face, end with foot to the front in fourth position, préparation for tour sur le cou-de-pied en dedans. In 2 measures: 1 and 2 tours en dedans to the left side.

2. BATTEMENTS FONDUS AT 45°. 8 measures in 4/4.

On 2 beats, fondu in a small pose effacée front; on 2 beats, remain on half-toe and execute a full rond de jambe in a small pose effacée back. Repeat, bringing the working foot through petit battement in the sur le cou-de-pied front position. Two fondus in a small pose effacée front, each on 2 beats; on 4 beats, a wide tombé and tour sur le cou-de-pied en dedans; at the end, a short coupé on half-toe on the left foot, and open the right leg to the side at 45°. Frappés: 4 sets of 3 frappés to the side, each on half a beat; 8 frappés en tournant en dedans, each on 1 beat. Execute also in the reverse direction with tombé, with tour en dehors and frappés en tournant en dehors.

3. GRAND FOUETTÉ EFFACÉ FRONT AND BACK.

a) In 1 measure in 4/4. From fifth position, study the breakdown of the fouetté to the front and to the back, on a flat foot.

b) Préparation on the right leg, the left leg stretched in croisé back, pointe tendue on the floor. On the upbeat, plié on the right leg and coupé on half-toe on the left foot. On the first beat, demi-plié on the left leg, épaulement effacé; on the second and third beats, grand fouetté effacé front (en dehors) on half-toe; on the fourth beat, end fouetté in attitude effacée, demi-plié. Repeat 4 times on the right and left leg, to the front and to the back, en dehors and en dedans.[1]

4. GRAND ADAGIO. 8 measures in 4/4.

First measure: grand plié in first position; from a deep plié, préparation on the left leg for tour à la seconde en dehors. Second measure: tour lent à la seconde en dehors. Third measure: demi-rond in attitude croisée; plié; on the fourth beat, pas de bourrée en tournant en dehors, changing feet. Fourth measure: développé to the side and demi-rond in croisé front (left leg). Fifth measure: a slow turn en dedans from the pose croisée in attitude croisée. Sixth measure: demi-rond en dedans to the side, plié and pas de bourrée en dedans, changing feet; end in fourth position, grande préparation for tour en dehors. Seventh measure: tour en dehors in attitude. Eighth measure: lower the working leg in fifth position, demi-plié and execute 2 sissonnes fermées in second arabesque at 45°, on the right and left leg.

---

[1] As an example, this fouetté will be called effacé en dehors and effacé en dedans, as is the rule in the lessons. In the syllabus of instruction, it is called fouetté to the front and to the back.

ALLEGRO

1. 8 measures in 2/4.

Four doubles assemblés battus, in turn on the right and left leg, changing feet to the front; 4 doubles assemblés battus, changing feet to the back, each on 2 beats.

2. 8 measures in 2/4.

Eight doubles assemblés (without beats) changing feet to the front, 8 doubles assemblés, changing feet to the back, each on 1 beat.[2]

3. 8 measures in 2/4.

Ballonnés battus to the side, ending sur le cou-de-pied back and assemblé back, in turn on the right and left leg; 3 ballonnés to the side, traveling to the side, assemblé to the side (right leg). Repeat on the other leg. Each jump is done on 1 beat. Repeat the combination, ending ballonnés battus sur le cou-de-pied front.

4. 16 measures in 2/4.

Three jetés fermés croisés front, each on 2 beats; on 2 beats, entrechat-trois back, assemblé. Repeat on the other leg and subsequently in the reverse direction.

5. 8 measures in 2/4.

Sissonne ouverte to the side at 45°, temps levé, rond de jambe en l'air sauté en dehors, assemblé to the side. Repeat 4 times, in turn on the right and left leg. Each jump is done on 1 beat. Execute also en dedans.

6. 8 measures in 2/4.

On the right leg: 2 grandes sissonnes ouvertes in first arabesque, traveling on the diagonal to corner 2; end the first sissonne with assemblé, left foot back, and the second sissonne, with the left foot front. Repeat on the other leg. Six grands changements de pieds and turn on half-

---

[2] In this double assemblé, the first assemblé is performed on the upbeat (on half a beat), the second on the first beat, and the subsequent assemblés, on half a beat each.

toe in fifth position (détourné). Each jump is done on 1 beat, the turn on half-toe (détourné) on 2 beats.

7. 32 measures in 3/4 (Waltz).

Move in a straight line from side 7 to side 3. Starting on the right leg: 4 grandes sissonnes tombées to the side, ending with quick passing pas de bourrée dessous without changing feet, each in 2 measures; in 8 measures: a big (scenic) sissonne in first arabesque on the right leg, a big (scenic) run to corner 4 and step in fifth position, left foot front. On the left leg: 4 grandes sissonnes tombées with pas de bourrée on the diagonal from corner 4 to corner 8, each in 2 measures. Moving in a small circle to the left side: 4 glissades, without changing feet, and jeté, ending sur le cou-de-pied back, in turn on the left and right leg, each in 2 measures. The last glissade and jeté is done in a straight line from side 7 to side 3.

8. PAS FAILLI TO THE BACK AND TO THE FRONT. Musical measure 4/4.

On 2 beats, pas failli to the back; on 2 beats, turn on half-toe in fifth position (détourné) and demi-plié for the subsequent jump. Repeat 4 times and execute also pas failli to the front.[3]

9. 4 measures in 2/4.

Sixteen petits changements de pieds, each on half a beat.

10. TOURS EN L'AIR (for the men's lesson). 4 measures in 4/4.

Three petits changements de pieds, each on half a beat; on 1 beat, relevé in fifth position half-toe; on 1 beat, tour en l'air. Repeat 4 times. Execute also on the other leg.

SECOND EXAMPLE OF EXERCISES ON POINTES

1. 8 measures in 4/4.

Four échappés in second position, changing feet, each on 2 beats; double échappé in fourth position croisée and in fourth position effacée, each on 4 beats. Repeat on the other leg.

---

[3] In this instance, the tour on half-toe in fifth position is applied only for the reason that, in its initial study, pas failli is done several times in a row with the same leg.

2. 16 measures in 3/4 (Waltz).

In 8 measures: 4 sissonnes simples en tournant in a half turn to the right side, to side 3, 5, 7, and 1. First sissonne: on the right leg, the left foot sur le cou-de-pied back, the left arm in third position, the right arm in second position, the body leans to the right. Second sissonne: on the left leg, the right foot sur le cou-de-pied front, the right arm in third position, the left arm in second position, the body leans to the left. Third and fourth sissonnes: similar execution as in the first and second sissonnes. Sissonne ouverte in a small pose in second arabesque, on the right and left leg, each in 2 measures. In 4 measures: on the right leg: sissonne ouverte in a small pose effacée front, tombé and tour sur le cou-de-pied en dedans.

3. 8 measures in 2/4.

Fifth position, right foot front. Eight jetés en tournant, traveling to the side in half turns on the diagonal from corner 6 to corner 2, each on 1 beat; on 2 beats, step on pointes on the right foot and execute tour sur le cou-de-pied en dedans, end in fifth position, left foot front; on 2 beats, grande sissonne ouverte in third arabesque; on 2 beats, préparation from fifth position to fourth position for tour sur le cou-de-pied en dedans; on 2 beats, tour en dedans.

4. 8 measures in 4/4.

Three grandes sissonnes ouvertes in attitude croisée, traveling forward, each on 2 beats; on 2 beats, rond de jambe en l'air en dehors. Repeat 4 times, in turn on the right and left leg. Execute also in the reverse direction.

5. 4 measures in 4/4.

On 2 beats, préparation from fifth position to fourth position for tour sur le cou-de-pied en dehors; on 2 beats, tour en dehors. Repeat 4 times, in turn on the right and left leg. Execute also with 2 tours.

6. 8 measures in 2/4.

On 2 introductory chords: demi-plié and come up on pointes in fifth position. Right leg: 4 grands battements jetés front, 4 grands battements jetés to the side, each on 1 beat. Repeat on the other leg. Execute separately in the reverse direction.

Pose in écartée back.

Third Lesson

EXERCISES AT THE BARRE

1. 8 measures in 4/4.
Two grands pliés in first, second, fourth, and fifth positions, each on 4 beats.

2. BATTEMENTS TENDUS. 24 measures in 2/4.
Eight battements tendus front, 7 to the side, each on 1 beat; on 1 beat, on the seventh battement, make a half turn on half-toe toward the barre;

at the end open the left leg to the side, pointe tendue on the floor; on 1 beat, a half turn on half-toe toward the barre; at the end open the right leg to the side, pointe tendue on the floor. On the upbeat, a quick demi-rond à terre to the back and repeat again the battements tendus in the reverse direction. Battements tendue jetés: 7 to the front, to the side, to the back, and to the side, each on half a beat; on the last battement tendu jeté, come up on half-toe and hold the working leg to the side at 45°.

3. RONDS DE JAMBE À TERRE AND GRANDS RONDS DE JAMBE JETÉS. 12 measures in 4/4.

On 2 introductory chords, préparation en dehors. Four ronds de jambe à terre, each on 1 beat; 2 grands ronds de jambe jetés, each on 2 beats. Repeat and execute en dedans. In 2 measures: trace a half circle on the floor in plié, en dedans, en dehors, end in fifth position. In 2 measures: développé in attitude effacée on half-toe, plié-relevé on half-toe with a half turn away from the barre; at the end of the turn, the working leg is in front at 90°.

4. BATTEMENTS FONDUS AT 45°. 12 measures in 4/4.

On 2 beats, fondu front; on 2 beats, plié-relevé with a demi-rond to the side; on 4 beats, plié, and from 45°, tour sur le cou-de-pied en dehors; at the end, open the working leg to the side at 45°. Repeat from the beginning; execute in the reverse direction with tour en dedans. Frappés: 3 in a small pose effacée front, 3 in écarté back, 3 in effacé back and 3 in écarté front, each on half a beat. Doubles frappés: 4 in a small pose effacée front and back and 4 to the side, each on 1 beat.

5. RONDS DE JAMBE EN L'AIR. 8 measures in 2/4.

Three ronds de jambe en l'air en dehors, 3 en dedans, 7 en dehors, each on half a beat. Repeat in the reverse direction.

6. PETITS BATTEMENTS SUR LE COU-DE-PIED. 8 measures in 4/4.

Twenty-four petits battements to the front, each on half a beat; on 4 beats, grand rond de jambe développé en dehors on half-toe. Repeat in the reverse direction.

7. BATTEMENTS DÉVELOPPÉS. 8 measures in 4/4.

Two développés tombés front, side, back, and side, ending sur le cou-de-pied, each on 4 beats.

8. GRANDS BATTEMENTS JETÉS. 4 measures in 4/4.

Four grands battements on half-toe in effacé front, side, effacé back and side, each on 1 beat.

EXERCISES IN THE CENTER

1. SMALL ADAGIO AND BATTEMENTS TENDUS. 8 measures in 4/4.

First measure: grand plié in fifth position, right foot front; from deep plié, préparation right foot front for tour en dedans in attitude effacée. Second measure: come down from half-toe onto the flat foot and tour lent en dedans in attitude. Third and fourth measures: from the pose in attitude, grand rond de jambe en dedans in effacé front and relevé on half-toe; end in fifth position, left foot front. Fifth and sixth measures: développé in third arabesque (right leg) and a half turn en dehors to side 5; tour lent en dehors (position à la seconde) to side 1, plié and a large step on the right foot in first arabesque at 90°. Seventh measure: passé at 90° in croisé front, relevé on half-toe and come down in fourth position croisée, grande préparation for tour en dehors. Eighth measure: tour en dehors in attitude croisée.

Battements tendus: 8 measures in 4/4. On the left foot: 8 battements tendus in a small pose croisée front; on the right foot: 8 battements tendus in pose third arabesque and 8 battements tendus to the side, each on 1 beat. Tendus jetés: on the right foot: 7 to the side en tournant en dedans to side 5 and 7 en tournant to side 1, each on half a beat. In 2 measures: on the left leg: tour sur le cou-de-pied en dehors from second position. In 2 measures: 2 tours en dehors from second position.

2. BATTEMENTS FONDUS AT 45°. 8 measures in 4/4.

Two fondus in a small pose croisée front (right leg), each on 2 beats; on 4 beats, a wide tombé front and tour sur le cou-de-pied en dehors; 2 fondus in a small pose croisée back (left leg), each on 2 beats; on 4 beats, a wide tombé back and tour sur le cou-de-pied en dedans; 4 fondus to the side (right leg), each on 2 beats. Frappés: 3 to the side en tournant en dehors with a half turn to side 3, 3 to side 5, 3 to side 7, and 3 to side 1, each on half a beat. Repeat the combination in the reverse direction.

3. RONDS DE JAMBE EN L'AIR. 8 measures in 4/4.

On 4 beats, assemblé croisée front (right leg) and tour sur le cou-de-pied en dehors from fifth position; at the end, open the working leg to the side at 45°; 4 ronds de jambe en l'air en dehors, each on 1 beat; 7 ronds de jambe en l'air en dehors, each on half a beat; on 4 beats, a wide tombé to the side and tour sur le cou-de-pied en dedans, end in fifth position, left foot front. Repeat the combination on the other leg. Execute also en dedans, with the final tour from tombé en dehors.

4. GRAND FOUETTÉ EFFACÉ. 8 measures in 4/4.

On the diagonal from corner 6 to corner 2. Fifth position, left foot front. On the upbeat: a big step on the right foot, half-toe, to corner 2; on 4 beats, grand fouetté effacé en dehors (left leg); on 2 beats, pas de bourrée en dehors, changing feet, and on 2 beats, pause. Repeat 4 times. For the execution of the fouetté effacé en dedans, traveling from corner 6 to corner 2, stand in fifth position, right foot front and take a step on half-toe to corner 2 on the right foot.

5. FOUETTÉ AT 45°. Musical measure 2/4.

a) On the upbeat: demi-plié, open the working leg to the side at 45°. Eight fouettés en dehors en face, each on 2 beats.

b) Four tours fouettés, each on 2 beats.

c) Fourth position en face. On the upbeat: tour sur le cou-de-pied en dehors, end on the first beat in demi-plié, open the working leg to the side at 45° and execute 3 tours fouettés en dehors, each on 1 beat; end in fourth position, épaulement croisé.

6. BATTEMENTS DIVISÉS EN QUARTS (BATTEMENTS IN QUARTER TURNS). Musical measure 4/4.

En dehors front: first measure: on the first beat, développé front (right leg); on the second beat, demi-plié; on the third beat, turn en dehors to side 3 with relevé on half-toe; simultaneously bring the working leg to the side; on the fourth beat, come down onto the flat foot (lower the heel) and bend the working leg in position passée at 90°. In the second, third, and fourth measures, repeat the battements with turns to side 5, 7, and 1. End the last battement in fifth position. Execute also en dehors to the back. Execute the battements divisés en quarts en dedans to the front and to the back in the following lessons.[1]

---

[1] It is recommended that in the fifth girls' lesson the battements divisés en quarts be performed at the end of the exercises on pointes. These battements require a particularly great muscular effort. Combined with the allegro exercises, they may result in undesirable overwork.

ALLEGRO

1. 8 measures in 2/4.

Fifth position, right foot front. Four assemblés to the side (right leg), in a quarter turn to the right, each time changing the right foot to the back, to the front, to the back, to the front, each on 1 beat; on 2 beats, échappé battu, changing feet and 2 sissonnes fermées to the side, with the left and right leg, changing to the back, each on 1 beat. Repeat on the other leg; execute sissonnes fermées, changing feet to the front.

2. 8 measures in 2/4.

Jeté battu, ending sur le cou-de-pied back, assemblé croisé back. Repeat 8 times, in turn on the right and left leg. Each jump is done on 1 beat. Execute also in the reverse direction.

3. 16 measures in 2/4.

Rond de jambe en l'air sauté en dehors (right leg); at the end, assemblé to the side. Repeat on the left leg. Sissonne ouverte to the side at 45° (right leg), rond de jambe en l'air sauté en dehors (twice) and assemblé to the side. Repeat from the beginning on the other leg and execute en dedans. Each jump is done on 1 beat.

4. 8 measures in 2/4.

Two grandes sissonnes ouvertes in attitude croisée (right leg), ending with assemblé; 2 grands échappés in second position en tournant, changing feet, in half turns to the right side. Two grandes sissonnes ouvertes in croisée front, ending with assemblé. Two grands changements de pieds en tournant, in half turns to the left side and pas failli to the back. Each jump is done on 1 beat, pas failli on 2 beats.

5. 8 measures in 2/4.

Two sissonnes fondues to the side at 90°, right and left leg, 1 sissonne fondue at 90° in third arabesque, each on 2 beats; entrechat-quatre, royale, each on 1 beat. Repeat on the other leg. Execute also in the reverse direction.

6. 4 measures in 4/4 or 16 measures in 3/4 (Waltz).

Four temps liés sautés front at 90°, each on 4 beats or to 4 measures of a waltz. Execute temps liés to the back in the same way.

7. 8 measures in 4/4.

Fifth position, right foot front. On 2 beats, coupé (step) on the right foot and grand assemblé to the side; end in fifth position, left foot front; on 2 beats, turn on half toe to the right side (détourné). Repeat 3 times. Two grandes sissonnes tombées to the side (right leg), ending with pas de bourrée, each on 2 beats.

8. BRISÉ. Musical measure 4/4.

a) One measure: on the first beat, demi-plié; jump brisé front between the first and second beats; on the second beat, end the jump in demi-plié; on the third and fourth beats, stretch the knees. Repeat 8 times to the front and 8 times to the back.

b) Two brisés front, each on 1 beat; on 1 beat, stretch the knees; on 1 beat, demi-plié for the successive brisé. Repeat 4 times to the front and 4 times to the back.

c) Three brisés front, each on 1 beat; on 1 beat, royale. Repeat 4 times to the front and 4 times to the back.

9. 8 measures in 2/4.

Seven and again 7 petits changements de pieds en face, 7 en tournant to the left side, 7 en tournant to the right side, each on 1 beat.

10. TOURS EN L'AIR (for the men's lesson).

THIRD EXAMPLE OF EXERCISES ON POINTES

1. 64 measures in 3/4 (Waltz).

Temps liés with the bending of the body to the back and to the side, 4 front, 4 back, each in 8 measures.

2. 8 measures in 2/4.

Two échappés in second position, changing feet, each on 1 beat; 2 sissonnes simples, changing feet to the back, each on 1 beat. Repeat. Two échappés, each on 1 beat, and 3 sissonnes simples, each on half a beat. Repeat. Execute separately with sissonnes simples, changing feet to the front.

3. 16 measures in 2/4.

Sissonne ouverte at 45°, in a small pose effacée front (right leg), sissonne ouverte at 45°, in a small pose effacée back (left leg), each on 2 beats; a short coupé in plié on the left foot and 4 ballonnés effacés front (right leg) traveling forward, each on 2 beats; end the last ballonné in fifth position, right foot back. In a straight line to the right side, tour glissade en tournant en dehors (twice) each on 2 beats. Repeat from the beginning on the other leg. Execute separately in the reverse direction.

4. 32 measures in 3/4 (Waltz).

In 8 measures: 3 grandes sissonnes ouvertes in attitude effacée (right leg), the third sissonne with plié-relevé, end in fifth position, left foot front. In 8 measures: préparation from fifth position to fourth position for tour sur le cou-de-pied en dehors and tour en dehors to the left side; préparation from fifth position to fourth position and tour en dehors to the right side. Repeat from the beginning on the other leg.

5. PAS DE BOURRÉE SUIVI IN A LARGE CIRCLE. Musical measure 2/4, in a moderate tempo.

Stand near corner 8 in fifth position, right foot front, and in a straight line, dégagé the right foot and pas de bourrée suivi, traveling in a circle to the right side, facing the walls of the studio until the end, to corner 8. The right arm in third position, the left arm in second position. Repeat the same to the left side, starting from corner 2. The circle traveled on pointes must be large, if possible. The quantity of musical phrases is not limited to a definite plan, but depends solely on the size of the dance studio.

6. 16 measures in 2/4.

On 2 beats, préparation from fifth position to fifth position for tours sur le cou-de-pied en dehors; tour en dehors, 3 times in succession, each on 2 beats. The first and second tour ends in fifth position front, the third, in fifth position back. Execute 4 times, in turn to the right and left side. Execute also en dedans.

Second arabesque.

Fourth Lesson

EXERCISES AT THE BARRE

1. 16 measures in 4/4.

Two demi-pliés, each on 4 beats; on 4 beats, 1 grand plié; on 2 beats, 1 grand plié; on 2 beats, relevé on half-toe. Execute in first, second, fourth, and fifth positions.

2. BATTEMENTS TENDUS. 32 measures in 2/4.

Four battements tendus in demi-plié, 4 battements tendus (without plié) to the front, to the side, to the back and to the side, each on 4 beats.

Battements tendus jetés: 8 to the front, to the side, to the back, to the side, each on half a beat. Battements tendus jetés in first position: 4 times 7, each on half a beat; on the last battement tendu jeté, come up on half toe on the supporting leg, holding the working leg to the side at 45°.

3. RONDS DE JAMBE À TERRE AND GRANDS RONDS DE JAMBE JETÉS. 12 measures in 4/4.

On 2 introductory chords, préparation en dehors. Two ronds de jambe à terre, each on 1 beat; 3 ronds de jambe à terre, each on half a beat. Repeat. Four grands ronds de jambe jetés, each on 2 beats. Execute en dedans. In 2 measures: trace a half circle on the floor in plié en dehors, en dedans, soutenu in fifth position on half-toe, and bring the left foot sur le cou-de-pied back. In 2 measures: port de bras bending the body, on the supporting right leg, on half-toe.

4. BATTEMENTS FONDUS AT 45°. 12 measures in 4/4.

On 2 beats, fondu front; on 2 beats, plié-relevé with a half turn toward the barre; on 2 beats, transfer the working leg through a petit battement to the sur le cou-de-pied position front and repeat fondu to the front; on 2 beats, plié-relevé with a half turn away from the barre; on 2 beats, plié-relevé with a demi-rond to the side; on 2 beats, plié-relevé; on 2 beats, plié and from 45° tour sur le cou-de-pied en dedans; at the end open the working leg to the side at 45°. Repeat the whole combination in the reverse direction. Frappés: 5 to the side, each on half a beat, and on 3 half beats, flic-flac en tournant en dehors, end to the front at 45°; 6 frappés to the front and 1 to the side, each on half a beat. Repeat the frappés in the reverse direction with flic-flac en tournant en dedans.

5. RONDS DE JAMBE EN L'AIR. 8 measures in 4/4.

Three ronds de jambe en l'air en dehors, each on half a beat; end the third rond de jambe in a small pose effacée front, pointe tendue on the floor in plié. Repeat. Seven ronds de jambe en l'air en dehors, each on half a beat; end the seventh rond de jambe in a small pose écartée back, pointe tendue on the floor, in plié; on 4 beats, tour temps relevé en dehors; at the end, open the working leg to the side at 45° and follow with 7 ronds de jambe en l'air en dehors, each on half a beat. Repeat the whole combination en dedans.

6. BATTEMENTS BATTUS. 16 measures in 2/4.

Eight battements battus front, in épaulement effacé, each on 1 beat; 16 battements battus, each on half a beat. Repeat the battements battus back, in épaulement effacé.

7. BATTEMENTS DÉVELOPPÉS. 8 measures in 4/4.

First measure: développé ballotté front, passé through the knee at 90° and développé ballotté back, passé through the knee at 90°. Second measure: repeat again the preceding exercise, end the last ballotté back in fifth position. Third measure: développé on half-toe, to the side; on the third beat, plié; on the fourth beat, relevé on half-toe. Fourth measure: a short plié-relevé on half-toe, on the first, on the second and on the third beats (3 times); on the fourth beat, lower the working leg in fifth position. In 4 measures: repeat the whole combination in the reverse direction.

8. GRANDS BATTEMENTS JETÉS BALANCÉS (PREPARATORY STUDY). Musical measure 4/4.

a) Starting position: first position. On 2 preparatory chords, brush the working foot back, pointe tendue on the floor. First measure: on the first beat, throw the working leg through first position front at 90°, the body simultaneously bends back; on the second beat, hold the position; on the third beat, bring the working leg down in fifth position; simultaneously straighten the body; on the fourth beat, hold the position. Second measure: execute the same to the back. Repeat 8 times.

b) On the first beat, grand battement jeté balancé front; on the second beat, bring the working leg down in first position; on the third beat, grand battement jeté balancé back; on the fourth beat, bring the working leg down in first position, etc.

EXERCISES IN THE CENTER

1. SMALL ADAGIO. 16 measures in 4/4.

First measure: développé tombé in a big pose effacée front (right leg); at the end, the working foot is in sur le cou-de-pied position front. Second and third measures: repeat the preceding movement. Fourth measure: développé in écarté back (right leg) and demi-rond in fourth arabesque. Repeat on the other leg. Execute in a similar manner développés tombés in attitude effacé, ending with développé in écarté front and demi-rond in croisé front, in turn on the right and left leg.

2. BATTEMENTS TENDUS. 16 measures in 2/4.

Four battements tendus front (right foot), each on 1 beat; 3 battements tendus jetés, each on half a beat; 2 grands battements, each on 1 beat. Execute to the side, to the back and to the side. In 2 measures: on the left leg: tour sur le cou-de-pied en dehors, from fifth position, end in fifth position, left foot front. In 2 measures: 2 tours en dehors, end in fifth position, left foot back.

3. RONDS DE JAMBE À TERRE. 8 measures in 4/4.

On 2 introductory chords, préparation en dehors. Rond de jambe à terre en dehors en tournant in a half turn to side 5; 3 ronds de jambe à terre en face, facing side 5, each on 1 beat. Repeat ronds de jambe with a half turn to side 1 and follow with the execution en dedans, ending in fifth position, right foot front. In 2 measures: préparation and tour à la seconde en dehors from second position, to the right side. In 2 measures: préparation and tour à la seconde en dedans from second position, to the left side.

4. BATTEMENTS FONDUS AT 45°. 8 measures in 4/4.

Two fondus in a small pose effacée front, each on 2 beats; on 4 beats, a wide tombé and tour sur le cou-de-pied en dedans. From the sur le cou-de-pied position, repeat the fondus and tour on the other leg. From the sur le cou-de-pied position: 2 fondus in a small pose écartée front, each on 2 beats; on 4 beats, a wide tombé and tour sur le cou-de-pied en dedans. From the sur le cou-de-pied position, repeat fondu in écarté on the other leg and end with tour from fifth position. Execute in the reverse direction with tour en dehors.

5. GRAND FOUETTÉ EFFACÉ. 4 measures in 4/4.

Move on the diagonal from corner 6 to corner 2. Fifth position, left foot front. On the upbeat: a large step on the right foot, half-toe, to corner 2; on the first, second and third beats, grand fouetté effacé en dehors; on the fourth beat, pas de bourrée en dehors, changing feet. Execute 3 times; end the last pas de bourrée in fourth position, grande préparation for tour en dehors; on 4 beats, tour en dehors in attitude croisée. Execute grands fouettés effacés en dedans in a similar manner, ending with tour en dedans in croisée front.

6. PETITS BATTEMENTS SUR LE COU-DE-PIED. 8 measures in 2/4.

Six petits battements, each on half a beat; on 1 beat, demi-plié, open the working leg to the side at 45°; 4 tours fouettés at 45° en dehors en face, each on 1 beat. Repeat petits battements, with fouettés en tournant.

7. GRAND ADAGIO. 8 measures in 4/4.

First measure: grand plié in fifth position, right foot front; from deep plié, tour sur le cou-de-pied en dehors. Second measure: after the tour, remain on half toe and développé in effacé front (right leg), tombé-chassé to corner 2, end in fourth position effacée, grande préparation for tour en dedans. Third measure: tour en dedans in attitude effacée. Fourth measure: plié in attitude effacée allongée, and step back on the left foot, passé through first position back (right foot) and relevé in attitude croisée. Fifth measure: in the pose attitude, lean the body slightly downward and turn en dehors in pose croisée front. Sixth measure: passé at 90° to écarté front, moving the right shoulder to corner 8, then turn en dedans in first arabesque to corner 4. Seventh measure: tour lent en dedans in arabesque to side 7, passé through first position front to fourth position, grande préparation for tour en dehors. Eighth measure: tour en dehors, on the left leg, in pose effacée front.

ALLEGRO

1. 16 measures in 2/4.

Two assemblés to the side, changing feet to the front, each on 1 beat; 3 assemblés to the side, each on half a beat; 2 assemblés battus, each on 1 beat, and 2 sautés in fifth position (soubresaut) traveling forward. Repeat on the other leg and subsequently in the reverse direction.

2. 16 measures in 2/4.

Jeté battu, assemblé croisé back, on the right and left leg; 3 jetés battus on the right, left and right leg; end with assemblé. Repeat on the other leg and execute in the reverse direction. Each jump is done on 1 beat.

3. 8 measures in 2/4.

Four jetés fermés to the side without changing feet, each on 2 beats; 2 sissonnes tombées croisées back, 1 sissonne tombée croisée front, each on 2 beats; on 1 beat, grande sissonne ouverte in first arabesque; on 1 beat, pause in arabesque plié.

4. 16 measures in 2/4.

On 2 beats, rond de jambe en l'air sauté en dehors and assemblé to the side; on 2 beats, grande sissonne ouverte in third arabesque, assemblé; 2 sissonnes fondues in third arabesque, each on 2 beats. Repeat on the other leg and subsequently in the reverse direction. Execute grande sissonne ouverte and sissonnes fondues in poses croisées front.

5. 32 measures in 3/4 (Waltz).

In 4 measures: 2 grands échappés in second position, changing feet. In 2 measures: glissade to the side without changing feet and grand assemblé to the side. In 2 measures: relevé in fifth position, on half-toe and demi-plié for the successive jump. Repeat 4 times in turn on the right and left leg.

6. GRAND JETÉ IN ATTITUDE CROISÉE. Musical measure 4/4.

a) Move on the diagonal from corner 6 to corner 2. Préparation: right foot in croisé back, pointe tendue on the floor. On the first beat, step on the right foot, coupé effacé front and grand jeté in attitude croisée on the left leg;[1] on the second beat, end the jump in demi-plié; on the third beat, hold the pose in attitude; on the fourth beat, lower the right leg back in croisé back, pointe tendue on the floor. Repeat 4 times.

b) On the first beat, step coupé and grand jeté; on the second beat, end the jump in demi-plié; on the third beat, the following step coupé and grand jeté; on the fourth beat, end the jump in demi-plié, etc.

7. GRAND JETÉ IN FIRST ARABESQUE. Musical measure 4/4.

Préparation: left foot in croisé back, pointe tendue on the floor. On the upbeat, demi-plié on the right leg, the left foot sur le cou-de-pied back; on the first beat, coupé (left foot) and grand jeté on the right leg in first arabesque to corner 2; on the second beat, end the jump in demi-plié; on the third and fourth beats, passé through first position front (left foot) and step on the left foot, right foot back in croisé, pointe tendue on the floor. Repeat 4 times, in turn on the right and left leg.

8. 16 measures in 2/4.

Seven entrechats-quatre, 1 royale, traveling back, each on 1 beat. Repeat on the other leg and execute the exercise traveling forward.

9. 8 measures in 2/4.

Four grands changements de pieds, each on 1 beat; 7 petits changements de pieds, each on half a beat. Execute twice.

[1] Begin the step on the upbeat, and simultaneously execute the coupé and the jump on the first beat.

FOURTH EXAMPLE OF EXERCISES ON POINTES

1. 16 measures in 2/4.

Four échappés in second position, changing feet, each on 1 beat; 2 doubles échappés in second position, each on 2 beats. Repeat 4 échappés and follow with 2 échappés landing on one leg, the other sur le cou-de-pied back. Repeat from the beginning, ending the échappés on one leg with the other foot sur le cou-de-pied front.

2. 16 measures in 2/4.

Fifth position, left foot front. On 1 beat, jeté to the side on the right leg, the left foot sur le cou-de-pied front; plié-relevé (3 times), each on 1 beat; on 1 beat, jeté croisé front on the left leg, the right foot sur le cou-de-pied back; plié-relevé (3 times), each on 1 beat. Repeat jeté to the side and 3 pliés-relevés. Jeté croisé front, plié-relevé (3 times), each on 1 beat, and on 1 beat, pas de bourrée en tournant en dehors, changing feet. Repeat the whole combination on the other leg and subsequently in the reverse direction.

3. 16 measures in 2/4.

On 2 beats, jeté in third arabesque at 90° (right leg); on 2 beats, plié-relevé, end in fifth position. Repeat. On 2 beats, jeté in first arabesque at 90° to corner 2 (on the right leg); on 2 beats, plié-relevé, end in fifth position, left foot front; on 2 beats, préparation from fifth position to fourth position for tour sur le cou-de-pied en dedans, and on 2 beats, tour en dedans to the right side. Repeat the whole combination on the other leg.

4. 32 measures in 3/4 (Waltz).

Move on the diagonal from corner 6 to corner 2. In 8 measures: on the right leg: 4 grandes sissonnes ouvertes in first arabesque, end in fifth position, left foot back. In 8 measures: on the diagonal from corner 2 to corner 6, 4 tours glissades en tournant en dehors; at the beginning of the glissade, the left arm is in first position, the right in second position; at the end, the right arm is in first position and the left in second position. In 8 measures: on the diagonal from corner 6 to corner 2, pas de bourrée suivi starting on the right foot, the right arm in third position, the left in second position allongée; end in fifth position, left foot front. In 6 measures: in a straight line to the left side, starting on the left foot, pas de bourrée suivi, the left arm in third position, the right arm in second position. In 2 measures: step on the left foot to the side, in plié, jeté on the right leg in pose attitude croisée.

5. 4 measures in 4/4.

On 2 beats, préparation from fifth position to fourth position for tour sur le cou-de-pied en dehors; on 2 beats, tour en dehors. Repeat 4 times, in turn on the right and left leg. Execute also separately with 2 tours.[2]

6. 4 measures in 4/4.

On 2 introductory chords, demi-plié and come up in fifth position, on pointes. Four grands battements jetés in pose croisée front (right leg), 4 grands battements jetés in third arabesque (left leg), and 8 grands battements jetés to the side (right leg), each on 1 beat.

---

[2] It is desirable that the students execute 1 and 2 tours en dedans as well, depending on the ability of each.

Leg raised in front at 45°, in éffacé, on half-toe.

Second Semester Fifth Lesson

EXERCISES AT THE BARRE

1. 16 measures in 4/4.

One demi-plié, 2 grands pliés, each on 4 beats; 2 relevés on half-toe, each on 2 beats, in first, second, fourth, and fifth positions.

2. BATTEMENTS TENDUS. 32 measures in 2/4.

One battement tendu to the front, to the side, to the back and to the side, each on 1 beat; 4 battements tendus to the side, each on 1 beat;

on 2 beats, grand plié in second position; on 2 beats, stretch the foot, pointe tendue on the floor and close the working foot in fifth position back, then 2 doubles tendus, each on 2 beats. Repeat in the reverse direction, starting with the right foot to the back. Battements tendus jetés: 7 to the front, to the side, to the back and to the side, each on half a beat; on the seventh battement tendu jeté, end with demi-plié in each direction. Repeat battements tendus jetés.

3. RONDS DE JAMBE À TERRE AND GRANDS RONDS DE JAMBE JETÉS. 12 measures in 4/4.

On 2 introductory chords, préparation en dehors. Four ronds de jambe à terre, each on 1 beat; 7 ronds de jambe à terre, each on half a beat; 2 grands ronds de jambe jetés, each on 2 beats; 4 grands ronds de jambe jetés, each on 1 beat. Repeat en dedans. In 2 measures: trace a half circle on the floor, in plié, en dedans, en dehors, soutenu in fifth position on half-toe and bring the left foot sur le cou-de-pied front. In 2 measures: port de bras, bending the body, standing on the right leg, on half-toe.

4. BATTEMENTS SOUTENUS. 32 measures in 2/4.

With the right foot: 1 soutenu to the front, pointe tendue on the floor, 1 soutenu at 90°; with the left foot: 1 soutenu to the back, pointe tendue on the floor, 1 soutenu at 90°; with the right foot: 4 soutenus to the side at 90°, each on 2 beats. Repeat in the reverse direction, starting with the right foot to the back. Frappés: 7 to the side, each on half a beat; on 2 beats, tour sur le cou-de-pied en dehors from fifth position; on 2 beats, fondu to the side. Repeat the frappés, with tour en dedans. Doubles frappés: 16 to the side, each on 1 beat.

5. RONDS DE JAMBE EN L'AIR. 16 measures in 2/4.

Eight ronds de jambe en l'air en dehors, each on 1 beat; 15 ronds de jambe en l'air en dehors, each on half a beat. Repeat en dedans.

6. BATTEMENTS BATTUS AND PETITS BATTEMENTS SUR LE COU-DE-PIED. 16 measures in 2/4.

Fifteen battements battus to the front in épaulement effacé, each on half a beat; on the last battement battu, open the working leg in a small pose effacée front at 45°; 15 petits battements, each on half a beat; on the last petit battement, open the working leg to the side at 45°. Repeat in the reverse direction, ending the battements battus in a small pose effacée back at 45°.

7. BATTEMENTS DÉVELOPPÉS. 8 measures in 4/4.

First measure: développé front, on half-toe, 2 short balancés before the third and fourth beats, each on a quarter beat. Second measure: demi-rond to the side and 2 short balancés. Third measure: demi-rond to the back and 2 short balancés. Fourth measure: passé at 90° in pose écartée back, a short plié-relevé on half-toe, end in fifth position. Repeat en dedans.

8. GRANDS BATTEMENTS JETÉS BALANCÉS. 8 measures in 4/4.

First position. On 2 introductory chords, brush the working foot to the back, pointe tendue on the floor. On the first beat, battement balancé front; on the second beat, battement balancé back (brushing the foot quickly through first position, without delay); on the third beat, battement balancés front; on the fourth beat, keep the working leg off the floor at 90°. In the following measure, execute battements balancés to the back, to the front and to the back, keeping the working leg off the floor at 90° on the last battement balancé. Repeat from the beginning.[1] Eight grands battements jetés from first position to the side, each on 2 beats.

EXERCISES IN THE CENTER

1. SMALL ADAGIO AND BATTEMENTS TENDUS. 8 measures in 4/4.

First measure: grand plié in fifth position, right foot front; from deep plié, préparation for tour en dedans on the right foot in first arabesque. Second measure: come down from half-toe onto the flat foot and execute tour lent en dedans in arabesque. Third measure: from the arabesque pose, a quick passé through first position with the left foot front at 90° and with a half turn to corner 4 (raise the arms to third position) and turn en dedans in third arabesque. Fourth measure: from the arabesque pose, passé at 90° in pose effacée front on half-toe and come down in fourth position effacée to corner 8, grande préparation for tour en dedans. Fifth measure: tour en dedans in first arabesque. Sixth measure: passé through first position and step forward on the right foot in croisé back, left foot back, pointe tendue on the floor. Seventh measure: grand port de bras. Eighth measure: on the first beat, begin

---

[1] In the grands battements jetés balancés, the musical accent must occur when the leg is thrown upward. In this given combination, the simple grands battements jetés are also executed in the same way: on the first beat, throw the leg to 90°; on the second beat, end the battement in first position.

grand port de bras, in wide plié, the body leaning forward; on the second beat, transfer the body quickly onto the left leg in pose attitude effacée; on the third and fourth beats, relevé on half-toe. Battements tendus: 8 measures in 4/4. With the right foot: 4 battements tendus in a small pose effacée front, each on 1 beat; 5 battements tendus jetés, each on half a beat; on 3 half beats, flic-flac en dedans en face, end in a small pose effacée back; 4 battements tendus in effacée back; 5 battements tendus jetés and flic-flac en dehors en face, end with the working leg to the side at 45°; 4 battements tendus to the side, each on 1 beat; 7 tendus jetés, each on half a beat. Repeat battements tendus and battements tendus jetés to the side. In 2 measures: on the left foot: tour sur le cou-de-pied en dehors from second position. In 2 measures: 2 tours en dehors from second position.

2. BATTEMENTS SOUTENUS. 8 measures in 2/4.

Soutenu, pointe tendue on the floor in a small pose croisée front, en tournant en dedans; soutenu, pointe tendue on the floor, in a small pose croisée back en tournant en dehors; soutenu, pointe tendue on the floor to the side, en tournant en dehors, each on 2 beats; on 2 beats, 2 tours sur le cou-de-pied en dehors from fifth position. Repeat on the other leg. Execute separately in the reverse direction.

3. RONDS DE JAMBE EN L'AIR. 8 measures in 2/4.

Move on the diagonal from corner 6 to corner 2. Fifth position, right foot front. On 1 beat, jeté en tournant, traveling to the side in a half turn, on the right leg; on 1 beat, with the left leg, rond de jambe en l'air en dedans, end in plié; on 1 beat, on the left leg, jeté traveling to the side in a half turn; on 1 beat, with the right leg, rond de jambe en l'air en dehors, end in plié. Execute 6 times. On 2 beats, step onto the right foot and execute tour sur le cou-de-pied en dedans; end the tour in fourth position, préparation for tour sur le cou-de-pied en dehors; on 2 beats, 2 tours en dehors.

4. PETITS BATTEMENTS SUR LE COU-DE-PIED. 8 measures in 2/4.

With the right foot: 16 petits battements en face, 16 petits battements en tournant en dehors, each on half a beat. It is recommended to execute the petits battements sur le cou-de-pied en tournant in the following manner: 1 petit battement with a turn to corner 2, the other facing corner 2, 1 with a turn to side 3, the other facing side 3, and so on to corner 4, side 5, corner 6, side 7, corner 8, side 1.

5. GRAND ADAGIO. 12 measures in 4/4.

First measure: grand plié in fifth position, right foot front; from deep plié, tour sur le cou-de-pied en dehors on the left leg. Second measure: after the tour, plié on the left leg and step onto the right foot (half-toe) in first arabesque facing corner 2, the right arm raised to third position; end in fifth position, left foot front. Third measure: step onto the right foot, half-toe, to corner 2 and grand fouetté effacé en dehors, on 3 beats; end with pas de bourrée en dehors, changing feet. Fourth measure: from fifth position half-toe, turn to the right side (détourné) and pas failli front. Fifth and sixth measures: développé on half-toe (left leg) in pose effacée front, grand rond de jambe in écarté back and end in third arabesque; lower the leg in fourth position, grande préparation for tour en dedans. Seventh measure: tour à la seconde en dedans, end in fifth position, left foot front. Eighth measure: step on the left foot to corner 8 and grand fouetté effacé en dedans, on 3 beats; end with pas de bourrée en dedans, changing feet. Ninth and tenth measures: développé on half-toe in attitude effacée (right leg), grand rond de jambe to écarté front and croisé front; lower the leg in fourth position, grande préparation for tour en dedans. Eleventh measure: tour en dedans in second arabesque. Twelfth measure: on the first beat, hold the position in second arabesque on half-toe; on the second beat, come down in fifth position in demi-plié; on the third and fourth beats, pas failli back.

ALLEGRO

1. 8 measures in 4/4.

Two assemblés to the side, with the right and left leg, changing feet to the front, each on 1 beat; on 2 beats, échappé in second position and from second position, tour sur le cou-de-pied en dehors. Repeat 4 times and execute in the reverse direction with tours en dedans.

2. 8 measures in 2/4.

On 1 beat, with the right leg: ballonné battu, traveling to the side, end sur le cou-de-pied back; on 1 beat, assemblé croisé back; on 1 beat, entrechat-cinq back and on 2 half beats, pas de bourrée en tournant en dehors, changing feet. Repeat from the beginning. On 1 beat, with the left leg: ballonné battu, traveling to the side, end sur le cou-de-pied front; on 1 beat, assemblé croisé front; on 1 beat, entrechat-cinq front, and on 2 half beats, pas de bourrée en tournant en dedans, changing feet. Two pas de chat back, each on 1 beat; 3 pas de chat back, each on half a beat.

3. 16 measures in 3/4 (Waltz).

On the right leg: 2 sissonnes fondues in first arabesque to corner 2, 2 sissonnes fondues in pose effacée front from corner 2 to corner 6, (moving backwards) each in 2 measures. In 2 measures: on the right leg: sissonne tombée effacée front, end in fifth position, left foot front. In 4 measures: pas failli back, on the left and right leg. In 2 measures: 2 grands changements de pieds en tournant to the right side. Change the ending of this combination for the men: in the last 2 measures: execute relevé in fifth position half-toe and tour en l'air.

4. 8 measures in 2/4.

Grande sissonne ouverte in écarté back, assemblé, with the right and left leg, each on 2 beats; on 2 beats, with the right leg: sissonne tombée front in fourth position croisée, coupé with the left foot back and grand assemblé croisé to the front, the arms in third position; on 1 beat, stretch the knees; on 1 beat, demi-pilé for the following jump. Grande sissonne ouverte in écarté front, assemblé with the left and right leg, each on 2 beats; on 2 beats, with the right leg, développé in croisé front on half-toe, tombé, and on 2 beats, grand assemblé to the side.

5. 8 measures in 2/4.

Move on the diagonal from corner 6 to corner 2. Préparation: right foot back in croisé, pointe tendue on the floor. Step-coupé on the right foot in effacé front and grand jeté on the left leg in attitude croisée. Execute twice; and 2 times, grand jeté in third arabesque, each on 2 beats. In 4 measures: a big scenic sissonne on the right leg in first arabesque, a big scenic run to corner 4 and step into préparation for the execution of grands jetés on the other leg.

6. 8 measures in 4/4.

Sissonne ouverte to the side at 45°, rond de jambe en l'air sauté en dehors, assemblé, entrechat-quatre, 4 brisés forward. Repeat on the other leg and execute in the reverse direction. Each jump is done on 1 beat.

7. 16 measures in 2/4.

Move on the diagonal from corner 6 to corner 2. Fifth position, right foot front. Fifteen emboîtés to the front (4 small, 4 medium, and 7 grands emboîtés), each on 1 beat; raise the arms gradually, the left in second position, the right in third position; on 1 beat, assemblé. On the diagonal from corner 2 to corner 6 (backward): 16 petits changements de pieds, each on 1 beat; raise the arms gradually in third position, lower the arms through second position and close in the preparatory arm position.[2]

FIFTH EXAMPLE OF EXERCISES ON POINTES

1. 16 measures in 2/4.
Two sus-sous, traveling front, each on 1 beat; on 2 beats, échappé in second position, changing feet. Repeat on the other leg. Three sus-sous front, each on half a beat; 2 échappés in second position (the first, without changing feet, the second, changing feet), each on 1 beat. Repeat on the other leg. Execute also in the reverse direction.

2. 16 measures in 2/4.
Four ronds de jambe en l'air en dehors from fifth position, in turn with the right and left leg, each on 2 beats; with the right leg: 2 ballonnés effacés front, each on 2 beats; 4 ballonnés effacés front, each on 1 beat; gradually raise the arms, the left in third position, the right in second position; end in fifth position, right foot back. Repeat on the other leg. Execute also in the reverse direction.

3. 8 measures in 2/4.
On the diagonal from corner 6 to corner 2: 6 tours glissades en tournant, each on 2 beats; end the last tour glissade in fourth position, right foot back. On 2 beats, tour sur le cou-de-pied en dehors, end in fifth position. On 2 beats, grande sissonne ouverte in attitude croisée.

4. 4 measures in 4/4.
Grande sissonne ouverte in écarté back, with the right and left leg, each on 2 beats; on 4 beats, préparation from fifth position to fourth position for tour sur le cou-de-pied en dehors and 2 tours en dehors. Repeat on the other leg. Execute also in the reverse direction.

5. 16 measures in 3/4 (Waltz).
On 2 introductory chords, come up in first position on pointes. In 4 measures: pas couru to the back in a straight line from side 7, in the

---

[2] When several pas emboîtés, traveling forward or backward, are done in a fairly rapid tempo, it is required that the petits changements de pieds be executed on 1 beat each, instead of a half beat, which is the established tempo in the secondary level of instruction.

direction of side 3 (in profile to the mirror); in the fourth measure: a half turn to the right. In 4 measures: pas couru back from side 3 to side 7 and a half turn to the left. In 4 measures: pas couru back from side 7 in the direction of side 3. In 4 measures: jeté on the right leg, in croisé back, the left leg bent halfway to the back at 45°; 3 pliés-relevés, each in 1 measure (end the third plié-relevé in attitude croisée at 90°).

6. 32 measures in 3/4 (Waltz).

On 2 introductory chords, come up in fifth position on pointes, right foot front, the right arm in second position, the left arm in third position. In 8 measures: fourth port de bras (repeat twice). In 8 measures: lean the body forward, lower the left arm in first position and execute pas de bourrée suivi with a turn to the left side, on the spot; straighten the body, the arms in second position; end the turn in fifth position, on pointes, left foot front, the right arm in third position, the left arm in second position. Repeat on the other leg.

Pose écartée back.

Sixth Lesson

EXERCISES AT THE BARRE

1. 8 measures in 4/4.

Two grands pliés in first position, 2 grands pliés with port de bras in second position, 2 grands pliés in fourth position and 2 grands pliés with port de bras in fifth position, each on 4 beats.

2. BATTEMENTS TENDUS. 16 measures in 2/4.

Four battements tendus front, each on 1 beat; 5 battements tendus jetés, each on half a beat; on 3 half beats, flic-flac en tournant en dedans; at the end, the working leg is in the back at 45°; 4 battements tendus back, each on 1 beat; 5 battements tendus jetés, each on half a beat; on 3 half beats, flic-flac en tournant en dehors; at the end, the working leg is in front at 45°; 2 battements tendus front, side, back, and side, each on 1 beat; 16 battements tendus jetés in first position, each on half a beat; execute the last battement with a prolonged hold at 90° and relevé on half-toe on the supporting leg.

3. RONDS DE JAMBE À TERRE AND GRANDS RONDS DE JAMBE JETÉS. 12 measures in 4/4.

On 2 introductory chords, préparation en dehors. Eight ronds de jambe à terre, 8 grands ronds de jambe jetés, each on 1 beat. Repeat en dedans. In 2 measures: trace a half circle in plié en dedans, en dehors; end with a half turn away from the barre; at the end, the working leg is in front, pointe tendue on the floor, the supporting leg in plié. In 2 measures: port de bras, bending the body.

4. BATTEMENTS FONDUS AT 45° AND 90°. 16 measures in 2/4.

Two fondus front at 45°, each on 1 beat; on 2 beats, 1 fondu at 90°. Repeat to the side, to the back and to the side. Frappés: 7 to the side, each on half a beat; 4 doubles frappés, each on 1 beat. Repeat the frappés.

5. RONDS DE JAMBE EN L'AIR. 8 measures in 4/4.

On 4 beats, tour temps relevé en dehors; at the end, open the working leg to the side at 45°; 4 ronds de jambe en l'air en dehors, each on 1 beat; 7 ronds de jambe en l'air en dehors, each on half a beat; on 4 beats, plié and tour en dehors, sur le cou-de-pied from second position, leg raised at 45°. Repeat en dedans.

6. PETITS BATTEMENTS SUR LE COU-DE-PIED AND BATTEMENTS BATTUS. 16 measures in 4/4.

Fourteen battements battus front, in épaulement croisé, each on half a beat; on 1 beat, a small pose croisée front, pointe tendue on the floor, in plié; 14 battements battus front, in épaulement effacé, each on half a beat; on 1 beat, a small pose effacée front, pointe tendue on the floor, in plié; 24 petits battements, each on half a beat; on 4 beats, grand temps relevé en dehors. Repeat in the reverse direction.

7. BATTEMENTS DÉVELOPPÉS TOMBÉS. 32 measures in 3/4 (Waltz).

Three développés tombés in effacé front, 1 développé tombé in écarté back, 3 développés tombés in attitude effacée, 1 développé tombé in écarté front, ending each développé tombé sur le cou-de-pied, each in 4 measures.

8. GRANDS BATTEMENTS JETÉS POINTÉS. 8 measures in 2/4.

Two grands battements, each on 1 beat; 3 grands battements, each on half a beat, to the front, to the side, to the back and to the side.

EXERCISES IN THE CENTER

1. SMALL ADAGIO AND BATTEMENTS TENDUS. 8 measures in 4/4.

First measure: grand plié in first position; from deep plié, préparation on the left leg for tour en dehors in third arabesque. Second measure: plié in arabesque and relevé on half-toe in attitude croisée. Third measure: turn en dehors in pose croisée front. Fourth measure: plié in pose croisée and step forward onto the right foot on half-toe in third arabesque; come down in fourth position, grande préparation for tour en dehors. Fifth measure: tour en dehors in third arabesque; end in fifth position. Sixth and seventh measures: with the left leg: grand rond de jambe développé en dedans on half-toe; end in pose croisée front. Eighth measure: tombé on the left foot in pose fourth arabesque at 90°, in plié. Battements tendus and tours: 8 measures in 4/4. With the right foot: 8 battements tendus to the side en tournant en dedans, each on 1 beat; on the upbeat, open the arms from the preparatory (arm) position to the side and on the first tendu, raise the right arm in third position, turn the head to the right; on the last tendu, open the arms in second position. Battements tendus jetés: with the left foot, 7 in a small pose croisée front; with the right foot, 7 in a small pose croisée back; with the right foot in first position, 7 battements tendus jetés and 7 more, each on half a beat. End the last battement tendu jeté in fifth position, right foot front. On 4 beats, préparation from fifth position to fourth position for tour sur le cou-de-pied en dehors and tour en dehors; end in fourth position, right foot back. On 4 beats, bring the weight of the body onto the right leg in plié and execute 1½ tours en dedans on the right leg.

2. BATTEMENTS FONDUS AT 45°. 8 measures in 4/4.

On 2 beats, tour sur le cou-de-pied en dehors from fifth position, end on half-toe, the working foot sur le cou-de-pied; on 2 beats, double fondu croisé front. Repeat the tour and double fondu to the side. Frappés: 3 to the side, each on half a beat; 2 doubles frappés, each on 1 beat; on 4 beats, 2 tours sur le cou-de-pied en dehors from fifth position. Repeat from the beginning in the reverse direction with tours en dedans.

3. PETITS BATTEMENTS SUR LE COU-DE-PIED. 8 measures in 2/4.

Sixteen petits battements en tournant en dehors, each on half a beat (as described in the fifth lesson); 6 petits battements en face, each on half a beat; on 1 beat, demi-plié; open the working leg to the side at 45°, and 4 fouettés en dehors at 45°, each on 1 beat. Execute also en dedans.

4. GRAND ADAGIO. 48 measures in 3/4 (Waltz).

Préparation on the right leg, stretch the left foot in croisé back, pointe tendue on the floor. On the upbeat, plié and coupé on half-toe on the left leg. In 4 measures: with the right leg, grand fouetté en face en dehors (Italian).[1] In 4 measures: coupé, and with the left leg grand fouetté en face en dehors. In 4 measures: from the third arabesque pose en face, which ends the fouetté, passé at 90° with a turn toward corner 6; développé in pose effacée front on half-toe; a wide tombé and chassé to corner 6; end in fourth position effacée, grande préparation for tour en dedans. In 4 measures: a half turn in tour à la seconde en dedans to corner 2 (the arms in third position) and passé through first position in third arabesque pose in plié. In 8 measures: step backward on the right foot and with the left leg développé in pose croisée front; the left arm in third position, the right arm in second position; grand rond de jambe en dehors to fourth arabesque; plié and pas de bourrée en dehors en tournant; end in fourth position grande préparation for tour en dedans. In 4 measures: tour en dedans in pose croisée front; end in fourth position, grande préparation for tour en dehors. In 4 measures: tour en dehors in effacé front; end in fifth position, right foot front. In 8 measures: with the right foot, to corner 2: 3 tours glissades en tournant; end the third tour glissade en tournant in fifth position, right foot back, brush the left foot, pointe tendue on the floor to corner 8 and step in first arabesque in plié. In 4 measures: holding the arabesque pose, slowly stretch the knee of the supporting leg and come up on half-toe. In 4 measures: hold the arabesque position on half-toe.

---

[1] Carry the right leg, half-bent, at 90° front, rise on half-toe on the left leg, quickly do a grand rond de jambe to the back with the right leg and end in third arabesque en face, the left leg in demi-plié.

ALLEGRO

1. 16 measures in 2/4.

With the right leg: assemblé in a small pose croisée front; assemblé to the side, and assemblé in a small pose croisée back, each on 1 beat; 2 petits changements de pieds en tournant in half turns to the right side, each on half a beat; 4 assemblés battus, changing feet to the front, each on 1 beat. Repeat on the other leg and execute in the reverse direction.

2. 4 measures in 4/4.

Fifth position, left foot front. Jeté battu, traveling to the side, on the right leg; at the end, the left foot is sur le cou-de-pied front. Jeté, traveling in a small pose croisée front, on the left leg; assemblé back, royale. Ballonné effacé front and side with the right leg; at the end, the right foot is sur le cou-de-pied back; assemblé back, royale. Repeat from the beginning on the other leg. Each jump is done on 1 beat. Execute also in the reverse direction.

3. 4 measures in 4/4.

Grande sissonne ouverte to the side, assemblé with the right and left leg, each on 2 beats; sissonne fondue to the side, with the right and left leg, changing feet to the back, each on 2 beats; 2 grands temps liés sautés to the front, each on 4 beats. Execute also in the reverse direction.

4. 16 measures in 3/4 (Waltz).

In 4 measures: glissade to the side without changing feet; grand assemblé to the side; the arms in third position; 2 entrechats-quatre; gradually lower the arms in the preparatory position. In 4 measures: repeat the same on the other leg. In 4 measures: développé on half-toe in a big pose croisée front, tombé and grand assemblé to the side, the arms in third and second position allongée; entrechat-quatre; lower the arms in the preparatory position. In 4 measures: assemblé and développé on half-toe in a big pose croisée front, tombé grand assemblé to the side, entrechat-quatre (as in the preceding 4 measures, but on the other leg).

5. 16 measures in 3/4 (Waltz).

Fifth position, left foot front. In 12 measures: with the right foot: glissade to the side without changing feet; grand jeté in first arabesque; assemblé; end in fifth position, left foot front; entrechat-quatre. Execute 3 times. In 4 measures: with the right leg, failli front and turn in fifth position on half-toe (détourné) to the left side; at the end, the left foot is in front, the left arm in third position, the right arm in second position.

6. 16 measures in 2/4.

Seven brisés front, each on 1 beat; on 1 beat, royale. Repeat on the other leg and execute brisés to the back.

7. TOURS EN L'AIR (for the men's lesson).

8. 8 measures in 2/4.

Thirty-two petits changements de pieds, each on half a beat.

SIXTH EXAMPLE OF EXERCISES ON POINTES

1. 16 measures in 4/4.

Fifth position, right foot front. Four échappés in second position, changing feet, each on 2 beats, in the écarté front position (the right shoulder to corner 2, the left shoulder to corner 6, the arms in preparatory position, the head turned to the right). Keeping the same épaulement, execute 8 échappés, each on 1 beat; raise the arms gradually from the preparatory position to second and third positions and lower them again through second position back to the preparatory position. Two doubles échappés in fourth position croisée; 2 doubles échappés in fourth position effacée, each on 4 beats; end in fifth position, right foot back. Repeat from the beginning on the other leg.

2. 16 measures in 2/4.

Three sissonnes simples, changing feet to the back, each on 1 beat; on the third beat, hold the position on pointes longer, to the count of 3 half beats, and on the fourth half beat, come down in fifth position, demi-plié. Repeat 4 times and subsequently changing the feet to the front.

3. 16 measures in 2/4.

First and second measures: in a straight line to side 3, starting on the right foot; pas de bourrée suivi, the right arm in third position, the left arm in second position. Third and fourth measures: on the right leg, grande sissonne ouverte in first arabesque to side 3 and plié-relevé; end in fifth position, left foot front. In the following 4 measures: repeat the same on the left foot, starting in a straight line to side 7. Ninth and tenth measures: on the right foot, pas de bourrée suivi in croisé front, the arms in third position. Eleventh and twelfth measures: on the right leg, grande sissonne ouverte in third arabesque and plié-relevé; the arms come down from third position to first position and then stretch the hands through the tips of the fingers in arabesque position. Thirteenth and fourteenth measures: with the right foot, sissonne simple in tire-bouchon, changing the foot to the back; the right arm in third position, the left arm in second position; with the left foot, sissonne simple tire-bouchon, the left arm in third position, the right arm in second position. Fifteenth and sixteenth measures: 7 petits changements de pieds en tournant, on pointes, to the left side, each on half a beat.

4. 8 measures in 2/4.

Préparation from fifth position to fifth position for tour sur le cou-de-pied en dehors and 7 successive tours en dehors, each on 2 beats. Repeat on the other leg. End all tours in fifth position front, the last tour in fifth position back. Execute also en dedans.

5. Musical measure 2/4.

a) Fourth position en face. Tour en dehors sur le cou-de-pied; at the end, open the working leg to the side at 45°, and follow with 3 tours fouettés at 45° en dehors; end in fourth position in épaulement croisé. Tour and tours fouettés are done on 1 beat.

b) Tour en dehors and 5 tours fouettés to 45° en dehors, each on 1 beat; end in fourth position épaulement croisé; on 2 beats, hold the position. Repeat en dedans.

First arabesque.

Seventh Lesson

EXERCISES AT THE BARRE

1. 16 measures in 4/4.

Two demi-pliés, 2 grands pliés, each on 1 beat, in first, second, fourth, and fifth positions.

2. BATTEMENTS TENDUS. 32 measures in 2/4.

Three battements tendus front, on the third battement tendu, demi-plié, each on 1 beat; on 1 beat, a half turn on half-toe toward the barre; 3 battements tendus back, on the third battement tendu, demi-plié, each on 1 beat; on 1 beat, a half turn on half-toe toward the barre; 8 battements tendus to the side, each on 1 beat. Repeat in the reverse direction. Battements tendus jetés: 7 to the front, each on half a beat. After the seventh battement tendu jeté, hold the working leg off the floor at 45°. Seven jetés passés through first position to the back, front, back, front, etc., each on half a beat, on the last jeté-passé, hold the working leg off the floor in the back at 45°. Seven battements tendus jetés back and 7 jetés passés through first position, each on half a beat, on the last jeté passé, hold the working leg off the floor to the front at 45°. Thirty battements tendus jetés to the side, each on half a beat, end the last battement tendu jeté in plié, and on 1 beat, a half turn on half-toe away from the barre.

3. RONDS DE JAMBE À TERRE AND GRANDS RONDS DE JAMBE JETÉS. 12 measures in 4/4.

On 2 introductory chords, préparation en dehors. Six ronds de jambe à terre, 2 grands ronds de jambe jetés, each on 1 beat; 3 ronds de jambe à terre, repeat 3 times, each on half a beat, and 2 grands ronds de jambe jetés, each on 1 beat. Repeat en dedans. In 2 measures: trace a half circle in plié, en dedans, en dehors. In 2 measures: port de bras in a wide plié, bending the body.

4. BATTEMENTS SOUTENUS AT 45° AND 90°. 16 measures in 2/4.

One soutenu at 45°, 1 soutenu at 90° in a small and big pose effacée front, écartée back, effacée back, and écartée front, each on 2 beats. Frappés: 7 in écarté front, each on half a beat; 4 doubles frappés to the side, each on 1 beat; 7 frappés in écarté back, each on half a beat, and 4 doubles frappés to the side, each on 1 beat.

5. RONDS DE JAMBE EN L'AIR. 8 measures in 4/4.

On 4 beats, grand temps relevé en dehors; on the last beat, lower the working leg to the side at 45°; 4 ronds de jambe en l'air en dehors, each on 1 beat; 7 ronds de jambe en l'air en dehors, each on half a beat, and on 4 beats, tour sur le cou-de-pied with temps relevé en dehors; end in fifth position, the working leg back. Repeat en dedans.

6. PETITS BATTEMENTS SUR LE COU-DE-PIED AND BATTE-MENTS BATTUS. 16 measures in 2/4.

Seven battements battus front in épaulement effacé, each on half a beat, end the last battement battu in a small pose effacée front, pointe tendue in plié. Repeat. Twelve petits battements, each on half a beat and on 2 beats, a quick développé in pose écartée back. Repeat in the reverse direction.

7. BATTEMENTS DÉVELOPPÉS. 16 measures in 4/4.

First measure: grand rond de jambe développé en dehors on the flat foot and passé at 90°, in plié. Second measure: grand rond de jambe développé in plié and passé at 90° on half-toe. Third measure: repeat the exercise from the preceding second measure on half-toe and end in passé at 90°. Fourth measure: développé to the side and a half turn on the working leg toward the barre; at the end, open the left leg to the side at 90°. Repeat from the beginning with the left leg and execute en dedans with the right and left leg, with half turns on the working leg away from the barre.[1]

8. GRANDS BATTEMENTS JETÉS. 16 measures in 2/4.

Three grands battements, each on 1 beat; 2 battements tendus, each on half a beat; 2 grands battements, each on 1 beat; on half a beat, a smooth grand battement on half-toe (with a quick développé) and hold the leg at 90° for 2 half beats. Execute to the front, to the side, to the back and to the side.

EXERCISES IN THE CENTER

1. SMALL ADAGIO AND BATTEMENTS TENDUS. 4 measures in 4/4.

First measure: grand plié in second position with port de bras,[2] end with développé (left leg) in pose écartée back. Second measure: tour lent en dehors in pose écartée. Third measure: plié in écarté and a wide step on the left foot; a quick développé with the right leg in pose écartée front; passé through first position front; step on the right foot in a big pose croisée, left foot back, pointe tendue on the floor. Fourth measure: grand port de bras.

Battements tendus and tours: 8 measures in 4/4. With the left foot: 4

---

[1] This adagio is done on the right and left leg, without any pause. The développé in the beginning of each rond de jambe is done on the first beat of a measure.

[2] Before starting the grand plié, the arms, as always, open in second position. While going down, the right arm lowers to the preparatory position and reaches the position at the moment of the deep plié; the left arm remains in second position; the head turns to the left. Starting on the upward movement from plié, on the third beat, the right arm comes up through first position to third position; simultaneously, the left arm comes down in the preparatory position. On the fourth beat, ending the grand plié and développé with the left leg, the right arm opens in second position, the left arm comes up through first position to third position.

battements tendus croisés back, each on 1 beat; 7 tendus jetés, each on half a beat; the arms from pose croisée gradually open and close in the preparatory position. With the right foot: 4 battements tendus croisés front, each on 1 beat; 7 tendus jetés, each on half a beat; gradually the arms open in second position. With the right foot: 4 battements tendus to the side en tournant en dehors, each on 1 beat, in quarter turns; 7 battements tendus jetés en tournant en dehors, each on half a beat; end the turn facing side 1. On 4 beats, on the left leg: préparation from fifth position to fourth position for tour sur le cou-de-pied en dedans and tour en dedans, end in fourth position, left leg in the back; on 4 beats, 2 tours en dedans.

2. BATTEMENTS SOUTENUS AT 45°. 8 measures in 4/4.

With the right leg: soutenu at 45°, in a small pose effacée front; with the left leg: soutenu in a small pose effacée back, each on 2 beats; on 4 beats, with the right leg, dégagé effacé front at 45°, in plié; step on the right foot, half-toe and 2 tours sur le cou-de-pied en dedans, end in fifth position, demi-plié, left foot front. With the right leg: soutenu at 45°, in a small pose effacée back; with the left leg: soutenu in a small pose effacée front; with the right leg: dégagé effacé back at 45° in plié, step on the right foot, half-toe and 2 tours sur le cou-de-pied en dehors, end in fifth position, left foot back. Repeat from the beginning.

3. RONDS DE JAMBE EN L'AIR AND BATTEMENTS DIVISÉS EN QUARTS. 16 measures in 4/4.

On 4 beats, with the right leg: tour sur le cou-de-pied temps relevé en dehors; at the end, open the working leg to the side at 45°. Four ronds de jambe en l'air en dehors, each on 1 beat; 7 ronds de jambe en l'air en dehors, each on half a beat; end in a small pose effacée front, pointe tendue on the floor, in plié; 6 ronds de jambe en l'air, each on half a beat; end in fifth position left foot front. In 2 measures: with the left leg: 2 battements divisés en quarts front en dehors, end in fifth position, left foot back. In 2 measures: with the left leg: 2 battements divisés en quarts back en dehors, end in fifth position, left foot front. Repeat en dedans.

4. GRANDS BATTEMENTS JETÉS ON HALF-TOE. 8 measures in 2/4.

With the right leg: 4 grands battements in effacé front; with the left leg: 4 grands battements in effacé back; with the right leg: 6 grands battements in écarté back, each on 1 beat, end the sixth grand battement in fifth position, demi-plié, and on 4 beats, turn in fifth position on half-toe (détourné), the arms raised to third position; on 1 beat, hold the pose on half-toe.

5. GRAND ADAGIO. 48 measures in 3/4 (Waltz).

Fifth position, left foot front. On 2 introductory chords, a wide step on the left foot to the side, carry the right leg slightly off the floor, bring the right foot smoothly through the ankle of the supporting foot to the front, pointe tendue on the floor in préparation croisée. Raise the arms simultaneously: the left in third position, the right in second position; at the end of the préparation, the left arm opens in second position, the right arm lowers in the preparatory position and up to first (arm) position. At the beginning, the head is turned to the left, then at the end of the préparation, to the right. In 4 measures: assemblé croisé front and 2 tours sur le cou-de-pied en dehors from fifth position, end in pose third arabesque, the right foot, pointe tendue on the floor, in plié. In 4 measures: step on the right foot and with the left leg, développé in pose écartée front and demi-rond in attitude effacée. In 2 measures: coupé on half-toe on the left foot and with the right leg: grand fouetté effacé en dehors. In 2 measures: bring the right foot in fifth position, half-toe, come down in demi-plié and smoothly open the left leg (through cou-de-pied) in effacé front, pointe tendue on the floor; bend the body back, leave the arms in final pose fouetté. In 2 measures: coupé on half-toe on the left foot, bring the left foot to the right foot, and with the right leg, grand fouetté effacé en dedans. In 2 measures: bring the right foot into fifth position half-toe, come down in demi-plié and smoothly open the left leg in effacé back, pointe tendue on the floor; leave the arms in second and third positions, in allongé. In 4 measures: step back on the left foot in fifth position half-toe, the right foot back; turn on half-toe to the right side (détourné), lower the arms in the preparatory position; step forward on the right foot in a big pose croisée, left foot back, pointe tendue on the floor. In 4 measures: grand port de bras, end in fourth position, grande préparation for tour en dedans. In 4 measures: tour en dedans in second arabesque; at the end, passé through first position front in fourth position, grande préparation for tour en dehors. In 4 measures: tour en dehors in third arabesque, end in fifth position. In 4 measures: with the left leg: grand rond de jambe développé en dehors, end croisé back in plié; at the beginning, raise the arms in third position and at the end open them in second position. In 4 measures: pas de bourrée en tournant en dehors, changing feet, step onto the left foot to the side, bring the right foot in croisé front, pointe tendue on the floor. In 8 measures: with the right foot: 2 tours glissades en tournant to corner 2; end in fifth position, right foot back; 2 balancés in a small pose second arabesque with the right and left leg; step back on the right foot, left foot croisé front, pointe tendue on the floor, the right arm in third position, the left arm in second position allongée.

ALLEGRO

1. 16 measures in 2/4.

Two sissonnes fermées to the side with the right and left leg, 1 sissonne croisée front, 1 sissonne croisée back, each on 1 beat; 3 sissonnes fermées to the side with the right, left and right leg, each on half a beat; 2 entrechats-quatre, each on 1 beat. Repeat on the other leg and execute in the reverse direction.

2. 16 measures in 2/4.

With the right leg: sissonne ouverte to the side at 45° and pas de bourrée dessous en tournant; with the left leg: sissonne ouverte to the side at 45° and pas de bourrée dessus en tournant; with the right leg: sissonne ouverte to the side at 45°, rond de jambe en l'air sauté en dehors on 1 beat, and on the other beat, assemblé; with the left leg: rond de jambe en l'air sauté en dehors from fifth position, and, at the end, assemblé; with the right leg: rond de jambe en l'air sauté en dehors from fifth position and, without dropping the leg, jeté, traveling to the side; with the left leg: jeté croisé front, assemblé, 2 pas de chat back. Repeat on the other leg. Each jump and pas de bourrée is done on 1 beat. Execute also in the reverse direction.

3. 8 measures in 2/4.

With the right leg: grande sissonne ouverte in third arabesque, assemblé, grande sissonne ouverte in first arabesque, assemblé, end in fifth position, left foot front. With the left leg: grande sissonne ouverte in pose écartée back, assemblé and 2 grands changements de pieds. With the right leg: grande sissonne ouverte in pose croisée front, assemblé, grande sissonne in pose effacée front, assemblé, grande sissonne in pose écartée front, assemblé and 2 grands changements de pieds en tournant to the left side.[3] Each jump is done on 1 beat.

4. 4 measures in 4/4.

Grande sissonne ouverte in pose effacée front, temps levé, temps levé with demi-rond to the side, assemblé. Repeat 4 times, in turn on the right and left leg. Each jump is done on 1 beat.

5. 16 measures in 2/4. (Combination for the men).

Sissonne ouverte at 45° in pose effacée front, temps levé, cabriole at

---

[3] In the execution for the men, substitute changements de pieds with préparation in fifth position half-toe and execute tour en l'air.

45°, assemblé, end in fifth position back. Repeat 4 times, in turn on the right and left leg and execute in the reverse direction. Each jump is done on 1 beat.

6. 16 measures in 3/4 (Waltz).

Grand jeté from fifth position in attitude effacée, end with assemblé in fifth position front, 2 entrechats-quatre. Repeat 4 times, in turn on the right and left leg. Each jump is done in 1 measure.

7. 16 measures in 2/4.

Four brisés front, 4 brisés back, 6 brisés front, each on 1 beat; on 2 beats, pas de basque front. Repeat on the other leg. Execute also in the reverse direction.

8. 8 measures in 2/4.

Seven grands temps levés in first position (as if jumping from a spring-board), 7 grands temps levés in second position; end in fifth position and 16 petits changements de pieds, each on half a beat.

SEVENTH EXAMPLE OF EXERCISES ON POINTES

1. 8 measures in 4/4.

Right foot front: double échappés in fourth position croisée, right arm in third position, left arm in second position; double échappé in fourth position effacée, right arm opens in second position and the left arm is raised in third position, each on 4 beats. Four échappés in second position, changing feet, from which 2 are done en face (facing the mirror) and 2 en tournant in quarter turns to the left side, each on 2 beats. Repeat on the other leg facing side 5 (back to the mirror), execute the last 2 échappés with turns to the right side and end facing side 1 (mirror).

2. 16 measures in 2/4.

Two sissonnes simples, changing feet to the back, each on 2 beats; 4 sissonnes simples, in turn on the right and left leg, each on 1 beat. With the right leg: 2 ballonnés effacés front, each on 2 beats; 2 ballonnés effacés front, each on 1 beat and 1 ballonné effacé front, on 2 beats. Repeat on the other leg. Execute also in the reverse direction.

3. 8 measures in 4/4.

Two grandes sissonnes ouvertes in third arabesque, each on 2 beats; 4 ronds de jambe en l'air en dehors, in turn on the right and left leg, each on 2 beats; on 4 beats, sissonne ouverte at 45° in a small pose effacée front, tombé and 2 tours sur le cou-de-pied en dedans. Repeat on the other leg. Execute in the reverse direction with only 1 tour en dehors following the tombé.

4. 16 measures in 3/4.

In 2 measures: on the right leg: 6 temps glissés forward in demi-plié (with a sliding movement, brushing the feet on the floor) and a slight turn to the right side in pose first arabesque. In 2 measures: from pose arabesque: soutenu en tournant en dedans, plié on the right foot and pas de bourrée en dehors, changing feet. In 4 measures: repeat the same on the left leg. In 4 measures: on the right leg: 6 temps glissés forward on the diagonal to corner 2 in demi-plié in pose first arabesque, relevé on pointes in arabesque, end in fifth position, left foot front; grande sissonne ouverte in pose croisée front, the left leg half bent at 90° front. In 4 measures: on the left foot: pas de bourrée suivi in a straight line to side 7; at the end, grande sissonne ouverte in first arabesque to corner 8 on the left leg.

5. 8 measures in 4/4.

In 4 measures: on the diagonal from corner 6 to corner 2: 8 tours glissades en tournant, each on 2 beats, end the last tour glissade in fifth position, right foot back. In 2 measures: in a straight line to corner 8; 4 jetés on the left leg, traveling to the side, each on 2 beats; on the first and third jeté, the right foot is sur le cou-de-pied front, the left arm in first position, the right arm in second position; on the second and fourth jeté, the right foot is sur le cou-de-pied back, the right arm in first position, the left in second position. In 2 measures: right foot front; pas de bourrée suivi croisé back, the right arm in third position, the left arm in second allongé.

6. Musical measures 4/4.

Tours sur le cou-de-pied from fourth position en dehors and en dedans.

Pose écartée back.

Eighth Lesson

EXERCISES AT THE BARRE

1. 16 measures in 4/4.

Two demi-pliés, 2 grands pliés, each on 4 beats, in first, second, fourth, and fifth positions; 2 grands pliés in fifth position, each on 4 beats, and 2 ports de bras, bending the body, each on 4 beats.

2. BATTEMENTS TENDUS. 24 measures in 2/4.

Four battements tendus front, each on 1 beat; 5 battements tendus piqués, each on a quarter beat; a short pause, and again 5 battements tendus piqués, each on a quarter beat; bring the working leg to the side, pointe tendue on the floor. Repeat the same to the side, to the back and to the side; at the end, the working leg is in front, pointe tendue on the floor. Tendus jetés: 8 to the front, to the side, to the back and to the side, each on half a beat.

3. RONDS DE JAMBE À TERRE AND GRANDS RONDS DE JAMBE JETÉS. 12 measures in 4/4.

On 2 introductory chords, préparation en dehors. Six ronds de jambe à terre, each on 1 beat; on 2 beats, préparation en dehors; 4 ronds de jambe à terre and 4 grands ronds de jambe jetés, each on 1 beat. Repeat en dedans. In 4 measures: trace a half circle in plié on the floor, en dedans, en dehors, port de bras in wide plié, bending the body.[1]

4. BATTEMENTS FONDUS AT 45°. 12 measures in 4/4.

On 2 beats, fondu front; on 2 beats, a half turn toward the barre; meanwhile, bring the working foot sur le cou-de-pied front and back, and execute fondu back; on 2 beats, a half turn toward the barre; bring the working foot sur le cou-de-pied back and front and execute fondu front; on 2 beats, plié-relevé with demi-rond to the side; 2 doubles fondus to the side, each on 2 beats; on 4 beats, 1 tour sur le cou-de-pied en dehors from fifth position. Repeat from the beginning in the reverse direction. Frappés: 7 to the side, each on half a beat; 4 doubles frappés to the side, pointe tendue on the floor (at the end of each frappé, come down from half-toe on the flat foot, lowering the heel, each time), each on 1 beat. Repeat frappés.

5. RONDS DE JAMBE EN L'AIR AND BATTEMENTS BATTUS. 16 measures in 4/4.

Seven ronds de jambe en l'air en dehors, each on half a beat; 6 battements battus front in épaulement effacé, each on half a beat; on 1 beat, a small pose effacée front, pointe tendue on the floor, in plié; 7 ronds de jambe en l'air en dehors, each on half a beat; on 4 beats, 2 tours sur le cou-de-pied en dehors from fifth position, end to the side at 45°. Repeat from the beginning and execute the combination twice en dedans.

6. BATTEMENTS DÉVELOPPÉS. 8 measures in 4/4.

First measure: développé front; before the third and fourth beats, short balancés. Second measure: plié-relevé on half-toe with a half turn toward the barre; before the third and fourth beats, short balancés. Third and fourth measures: plié-relevé on half-toe with a half turn toward the barre and grand rond de jambe développé en dehors; end in attitude croisée. Repeat in the reverse direction.

---

[1] Take the left arm off the barre while bending the body, and bring it to the front in first position.

7. GRANDS BATTEMENTS JETÉS. 16 measures in 2/4.

Six grands battements front, each on 1 beat; on the seventh battement, hold the leg off the floor at 90° to the count of 3 half beats. Execute also to the side, to the back and to the side.

EXERCISES IN THE CENTER

1. SMALL ADAGIO AND BATTEMENTS TENDUS. 8 measures in 4/4.

First measure: grand plié in fifth position, right foot front; from deep plié, préparation on the left leg for tour en dehors in pose effacée front. Second measure: come down from half-toe onto the flat foot and execute tour lent en dehors in pose effacée. Third measure: from pose effacée, demi-rond to the side and passé at 90°, on half-toe. Fourth measure: grand fouetté effacé en dehors and step to the back in fifth position half-toe, left foot back, the right arm in third position, the left arm in second position. Fifth and sixth measures: with the left leg: grand fouetté effacé en dedans, grand rond to the side in attitude effacée and relevé on half-toe; end in fifth position, left foot front. Seventh and eighth measures: with the left leg: préparation and tour à la seconde en dehors from second position.

Battements tendus: 8 measures in 4/4. With the right foot: 8 battements tendus in a big pose écartée back; with the left foot: 8 battements tendus in a big pose écartée front, each on 1 beat. Battements tendus jetés: 7 to the side, with the right foot, each on half a beat; repeat 4 times. In 2 measures: with the left leg, tour sur le cou-de-pied en dedans from second position. In 2 measures: 2 tours en dedans from second position.

2. BATTEMENTS FONDUS AT 45°. 8 measures in 2/4.

On 2 beats, with the right leg: fondu in a small pose effacée front; on 2 beats, hold the position, plié-relevé in effacée front with a turn to corner 4. On 2 beats, fondu in pose effacée front to corner 4; on 2 beats, plié-relevé in effacé front with a turn to corner 6. On 2 beats, with the left leg: fondu in a small pose effacée back to corner 6; on 2 beats, hold the position; plié-relevé with a turn to corner 8. On 2 beats, with the right leg: fondu in pose effacée back to corner 8; on 2 beats, plié-relevé with a turn to corner 2.

3. RONDS DE JAMBE EN L'AIR. 8 measures in 4/4.

On 4 beats, 2 tours sur le cou-de-pied en dehors from fifth position; at the end, open the working leg to the side at 45°; 2 ronds de jambe en l'air en dehors, each on 1 beat; 3 and 3 more ronds de jambe en l'air en dehors, each on half a beat; on 2 beats, passé through first position front in fourth position, grande préparation for tour en dehors; on 4 beats, tour en dehors in pose effacée front; at the end, bring the working leg in fifth position back. Repeat on the other leg. Execute also en dedans, ending with tour in pose attitude effacée.

4. GRANDS BATTEMENTS JETÉS. 8 measures in 4/4.

In 4 measures: with the right leg: 4 grands battements croisés front; with the left leg: 4 grands battements in third arabesque and 4 grands battements in fourth arabesque; with the right leg: 4 grands battements to the side, each on 1 beat. In 2 measures: with the left leg, préparation

Battement fondu.

and tour à la seconde en dedans from second position. In 2 measures: with the right leg, préparation from fifth position to fourth position for tours sur le cou-de-pied en dehors, 1 tour and 2 tours en dehors.

5. GRAND ADAGIO. 8 measures in 4/4.

First measure: grand plié in fifth position, right foot front; from deep plié, tour sur le cou-de-pied en dedans. Second measure: with the left leg: développé on half-toe to the side; on the last beat, come down from half-toe onto the flat foot. Third measure: tour lent à la seconde en dedans. Fourth measure: from à la seconde position, come up on half-toe and turn to first arabesque in plié; step back and with the right leg, relevé at 90° in fourth arabesque. Fifth measure: from pose arabesque, turn en dehors in pose croisée front. Sixth measure: relevé on half-toe in croisé, tombé, chassé front, end in fifth position; step on the left foot back in préparation croisée, right foot front, pointe tendue on the floor. Seventh measure: plié on the right leg, then rise on half-toe and simultaneously throw the left leg in grand battement to the side at 90°, the arms raised in third position; turn to first arabesque in plié;[2] on the fourth beat of the measure, execute pas de bourrée en dehors, changing feet. Eighth measure: on the first beat of the measure, failli back with the left leg, stop on the right leg, the left foot stretched to the back in croisé, pointe tendue on the floor (pose fourth arabesque); on the second, third, and fourth beats, hold the pose fourth arabesque, pointe tendue on the floor.

ALLEGRO

1. 8 measures in 2/4.

Fifth position, left foot front. With the right leg: 2 assemblés to the side, the first changing the foot front, the second changing the foot back, each on 1 beat; 3 assemblés to the side, changing feet to the front, to the back, and to the front, each on half a beat; on 2 beats, with the left leg: glissade to the side, changing foot to the front; on 2

---

[2] This movement is a preparation for the training toward the grand fouetté à la seconde in first arabesque, executed with a step-coupé. In the given example, it is executed slowly on the first three beats of the seventh measure and bears the characteristics of a slow turn from à la seconde to first arabesque.

beats, with the right leg: glissade to the side, without changing feet and assemblé battu, changing foot to the front. Repeat the same on the other leg and execute in the reverse direction.

2. 16 measures in 2/4.

Fifth position, right foot front. On 2 beats, échappé battu, landing on one leg, the right foot sur le cou-de-pied back; on 2 beats, temps levé, assemblé croisé back; on 2 beats, with the right foot: glissade to the side, without changing feet, jeté battu to the side; at the end, the left foot is sur le cou-de-pied back; on 2 beats, temps levé and pas de bourrée en tournant en dehors, changing feet. Repeat on the other leg and execute in the reverse direction.

3. Musical measure 2/4.

Pas emboîté en tournant to the front and to the back, without traveling to the side; at the beginning of the study, each pas emboîté is done in a quarter turn; thereafter in a half turn.

4. 16 measures in 3/4 (Waltz).

In 4 measures: with the right leg, a small sissonne tombée in fourth position croisée; with the left leg: grand assemblé to the side, the left arm in third position, the right arm in second position, allongé; relevé in fifth position half-toe. In 4 measures: repeat the same with the left leg. In 8 measures: on the diagonal to corner 2, a sliding failli on the floor in second arabesque on the right leg and, again with the right leg, a grand assemblé in écarté front, the right arm in third position, the left arm in second position, allongé; relevé in fifth position, half-toe. Repeat failli, assemblé and relevé on half-toe.

5. 16 measures in 3/4 (Waltz).

Préparation on the right leg, the left foot in croisé back, pointe tendue on the floor. In 8 measures: with the right leg: glissade to the side without changing feet, grand jeté on the right leg in first arabesque, assemblé, end in fifth position, left foot front; entrechat-quatre. Repeat once more. In 4 measures: with the left leg, a small sissonne tombée in fourth position croisée; a short coupé with the right foot back; with the left leg, grand assemblé croisé front, the arms in third position; 2 entrechats-quatre, lower the arms gradually in the preparatory position. In 4 measures: with the left leg, a small sissonne tombée to the side; pas de bourrée en dehors, changing feet; step back on the left foot and take a préparation (the right foot croisé front, pointe tendue on the floor).[3]

---

[3] Substitute préparation in pose croisée front with tour en l'air for the men.

6. 4 measures in 3/4.

Fifth position, right foot front. Grand échappé in second position; from second position, grande sissonne ouverte in attitude effacée on the right leg; assemblé, end in fifth position, the left foot front. Execute 4 times in turn on the right and left leg. Each jump is done on 1 beat. Execute also with grandes sissonnes ouvertes in pose effacée front.

7. 4 measures in 2/4.

Sixteen petits changements de pieds, each on half a beat.

EIGHTH EXAMPLE OF EXERCISES ON POINTES

1. 16 measures in 2/4.

Four doubles échappés in second position, changing feet, each on 2 beats; 8 échappés in second position, traveling to the back, each on 1 beat. Repeat doubles échappés and execute 8 échappés, traveling forward.

2. 16 measures in 2/4.

Two sissonnes simples with the right and left leg, changing feet to the back, each on 1 beat; 3 sissonnes simples with the right leg, changing the foot to the back, to the front, to the back, each on half a beat. Execute 3 times, in turn with the right and left leg. On 2 beats, with the left leg, préparation from fifth position to fifth position and tour sur le cou-de-pied en dehors; on 2 beats, turn in fifth position to the left side (détourné). Repeat the whole combination on the other leg, and subsequently in the reverse direction.

3. 8 measures in 4/4.

With the right leg: grande sissonne ouverte in pose croisée front and in pose effacée front, each on 2 beats, end in fifth position, right foot back. Four sissonnes simples, traveling forward on the diagonal to corner 2, in turn with the right and left leg, changing feet to the front, each on 1 beat. On 4 beats, with the left leg, préparation from fifth position to fourth position for tour sur le cou-de-pied en dehors and tour en dehors. On 4 beats, with the right leg: préparation from fifth position to fourth position and tour sur le cou-de-pied en dehors. Repeat on the other leg.

4. 16 measures in 3/4 (Waltz).

In 8 measures: on the right leg, grande sissonne ouverte in pose écartée back and bring the body front with a slight turn to fifth position on pointes. Repeat once more. In 8 measures: on the right leg, grande sissonne ouverte in first arabesque to corner 2; plié in pose arabesque and pas de bourrée en dehors, changing feet, end in fourth position, préparation for tours sur le cou-de-pied en dehors; 2 tours en dehors. Execute also in the reverse direction.

5. 32 measures in 3/4 (Waltz).

In 4 measures: with the right foot, in a straight line, pas de bourrée suivi, the right arm in third position, the second in second position; end pas de bourrée in fifth position, left foot front, lower the arms in the preparatory position. In 4 measures: pas de chat back, pas de bourrée en dehors, changing feet, on the right and left leg. In 16 measures: repeat from the beginning with the left leg and once more with the right leg. In 4 measures: entrechat-quatre and sissonne simple, changing the foot to the back, in turn with the left and the right leg. In 4 measures: on the diagonal to corner 2, pas couru in first position forward, end with pas de chat forward, the arms in third position. Execute the combination in a quick tempo.

Sixth Year

In this year, the study of jumps in various ways and the development of the ballon quality in big jumps (bounce, springiness, elasticity of feet) will be stressed. Complicated combinations with beating steps performed in a quick tempo will be given as well. The exercises of previous years in combination with 2 tours from fifth position, with temps levé, and with préparations from second position at 45° are reiterated.

Sissonne passeé on pointes.

First Lesson

EXERCISES AT THE BARRE

1. 16 measures in 4/4.
Two demi-pliés, 2 grands pliés, each on 4 beats, in first, second, fourth, and fifth positions.

2. BATTEMENTS TENDUS. 32 measures in 2/4.
With the right foot, 4 battements tendus front; with the left foot, 4 battements tendus back; with the right foot, 8 battements tendus to the side, each on 1 beat. Repeat in the reverse direction, starting with the right foot back. Battements tendus jetés: 5 battements tendus jetés front, each on half a beat; on 3 half beats, flic-flac en tournant en dedans,

end in pose second arabesque at 45°; 5 battements tendus jetés back, each on half a beat, and on 3 half beats, flic-flac en tournant en dehors, end in a small pose effacée front; 7 and 7 more battements tendus jetés to the side, each on half a beat. Repeat battements tendus jetés in the reverse direction, starting with the right foot back.

3. RONDS DE JAMBE À TERRE AND GRANDS RONDS DE JAMBE JETÉS. 12 measures in 4/4.

On 2 introductory chords, préparation en dehors. Two ronds de jambe à terre, each on 1 beat; 3 ronds de jambe à terre, each on half a beat. Repeat. Two ronds de jambe à terre, 6 grands ronds de jambe jetés, each on 1 beat. Repeat en dedans. In 2 measures: trace a half circle on the floor, in plié en dehors, en dedans and relevé front at 90°, rising onto half-toe. In 2 measures: port de bras, bending the body, holding the leg front at 90°.

4. BATTEMENTS FONDUS AT 45°. 24 measures in 2/4.

On 2 beats, battement fondu front; on 2 beats, plié-relevé with a half turn away from the barre (the working leg remains in the front at 45°); on 2 beats, plié-relevé with a half turn away from the barre (the working leg is in the back at 45° at the end of the turn); on 2 beats, plié-relevé with demi-rond to the side; 2 fondus to the side, each on 2 beats. Frappés: 3 frappés to the side, each on half a beat; 5 frappés to the side, each on a quarter beat. Repeat fondus and frappés in the reverse direction, starting with the right leg back; execute the first plié-relevé with a half turn toward the barre. Doubles frappés: 12 to the side, each on 1 beat and in 2 measures: développé on half-toe in pose écartée back; a wide tombé on the working leg with a half turn away from the barre in pose first arabesque at 90° in plié.

5. RONDS DE JAMBE EN L'AIR. 8 measures in 4/4.

Three ronds de jambe en l'air en dehors, each on half a beat. Repeat once more. In the following measure, execute double rond de jambe en l'air (4 times consecutively) on a grace note before each beat. Three ronds de jambe en l'air, each on half a beat; on the third rond de jambe, plié, and on 2 beats, 2 tours temps relevé en dehors, end to the side at 45°; on 4 beats, double ronds de jambe en l'air (4 times consecutively) on a grace note before each beat. Repeat the whole combination en dedans.

6. PETITS BATTEMENTS SUR LE COU-DE-PIED AND BATTEMENTS BATTUS. 8 measures in 4/4.

Eight petits battements, each on half a beat, gradually raise the arm in third position; 12 battements battus in épaulement effacé, each on a quarter beat; on 1 beat, a small pose effacée front, pointe tendue on the floor in plié; 6 petits battements, each on half a beat; on 1 beat, plié, open the working leg to the side, pointe tendue on the floor; on 2 beats, soutenu en tournant en dedans, end in a small pose effacée back, pointe tendue on the floor, in plié; on 2 beats, a quick relevé on half-toe, in attitude effacée. Repeat the whole combination in the reverse direction.

7. BATTEMENTS DÉVELOPPÉS BALANCÉS. 4 measures in 4/4.

First measure: développé front, a quick balancé demi-rond to the side; before the third beat and without any hold of the leg; again demi-rond to the front (d'ici-de là),[1] end in fifth position. Second measure: développé to the side, a quick balancé demi-rond to the front and side; before the third beat, end in fifth position. Third measure: développé back, balancé demi-rond to the side and back. Fourth measure: développé to the side, balancé demi-rond to the back and to the side. Execute the exercise on the flat foot or on half-toe, depending on the proficiency in the step.

8. GRANDS BATTEMENTS JETÉS POINTÉS. 8 measures in 4/4.

Two grands battements pointés front, with the right leg, each on 1 beat; 3 grands battements pointés front, each on half a beat; 2 grands battements pointés back, with the left leg, each on 1 beat; 3 grands battements pointés back, each on half a beat; 2 grands battements pointés to the side, with the right leg, each on 1 beat; 3 grands battements pointés to the side, each on half a beat; on 4 beats, a quick développé on half-toe in pose écartée back, turn in attitude effacée. End in fifth position and repeat from the beginning in the reverse direction.

EXERCISES IN THE CENTER

1. SMALL ADAGIO. 8 measures in 4/4.

First measure: grand plié in first position, and from deep plié, tour sur le cou-de-pied en dehors, on the left leg; at the end (on the last beat), développé front, on half-toe, with the right leg. Second measure:

---

[1] French term used in the Soviet ballet terminology meaning "between here and there." It implies a sharp demi-rond of the leg without any break.

from the preceding pose (on the upbeat), bring the right leg down in first position and repeat grand plié with tour sur le cou-de-pied en dehors on the left leg; end with développé front on half-toe and demi-rond to the side.[2] Third measure: come down from half-toe, lowering the heel, onto the flat foot and execute tour lent à la seconde en dehors. Fourth measure: plié, holding the position à la seconde; a wide step on the right foot to the side, on half-toe, raising the left leg to the side at 90° in the manner of a grand battement; on the last beat, bring the working leg down in first position. Repeat the same with tour en dedans, starting with the first développé back, the second to the back with demi-rond to the side, etc.

2. BATTEMENTS TENDUS. 12 measures in 4/4.

Six battements tendus in a small pose croisée front; on the sixth battement tendu, demi-plié, each on 1 beat; on 2 beats, tour sur le cou-de-pied en dehors from fifth position. Six battements tendus in a small pose croisée back, demi-plié and tour sur le cou-de-pied en dedans from fifth position. Five battements tendus to the side, demi-plié, and 2 tours sur le cou-de-pied en dehors. Repeat 5 battements tendus and execute tours en dedans. Battements tendus jetés: 4 to the front, 4 to the side, 4 to the back and 4 to the side, each on half a beat, and in 2 measures: préparation and tour à la seconde en dedans from second position.

3. BATTEMENTS FONDUS. 8 measures in 4/4.

With the right leg, 1 fondu at 45° in a small pose effacée front, 1 fondu at 90°, in a big pose effacée front; with the left leg, 1 fondu at 45° in a small pose effacée back, 1 fondu at 90° in a big pose effacée back (the arms in allongé), each on 2 beats. With the right leg, 2 fondus at 90° in pose écartée back, each on 2 beats; on 2 beats, plié in pose écartée and pas de bourrée en tournant en dehors, changing feet; on 2 beats, with the right leg: soutenu en tournant en dehors, at the end open the working leg to the side at 45°. Frappés: 7 to the side, each on half a beat; on 2 beats, coupé right foot, and with the left leg grand fouetté effacée en dehors; on 2 beats, turn en dehors with passé at 90°; on 2 beats, a second fouetté effacé en dehors; on 2 beats, pas de bourrée en dehors, changing feet, end in fourth position, grande préparation for tour en dehors; on 4 beats, 2 tours tire-bouchon en dehors, raise the arms in third position. Execute also in the reverse direction.

[2] At the end of the year of instruction, this combination can be done in a more complicated way, by repeating the tour from demi-plié in first position a third time, and executing, on the last beat, grand rond de jambe développé on half-toe.

4. RONDS DE JAMBE EN L'AIR EN TOURNANT. 4 measures in 4/4.

On 4 beats, assemblé croisé front and 2 tours sur le cou-de-pied en dehors from fifth position; at the end open the working leg to the side at 45°. Two ronds de jambe en l'air en dehors, each on 1 beat; 3 ronds de jambe en l'air en dehors, each on half a beat and 8 ronds de jambe en l'air en tournant en dehors, each on 1 beat.[3] Execute also en dedans.

5. TOURS IN BIG POSES WITH COUPÉ-STEP ON A STRETCHED LEG. 4 measures in 2/4.

Move on the diagonal from corner 6 to corner 2. On the upbeat, demi-plié on the left leg, dégagé with the right leg in effacé front at 45°, the arms in first position slightly open. On the first beat, a wide step on half-toe on the right foot to corner 2 and tour en dedans in attitude effacée; simultaneously open the right arm in second position, raise the left arm through second position in third position, using the left arm in full force for the tour; on the first beat, come down on the left leg in plié (coupé), bend the right leg, and bring the right foot sur le cou-de-pied front; lower the arms in the preparatory position. Repeat the tour 4 times. Execute the tours in first arabesque and on the diagonal from corner 2 to corner 6 in effacé front at 90° in a similar manner.

6. GRAND ADAGIO. 12 measures in 4/4.

Fourth position croisée, right foot front. First measure: grand plié; from deep plié, half tour en dedans on the left leg in attitude, end in pose attitude croisée, facing side 1 (when rising on the upward movement from the deep plié, lift the left arm quickly in third position and then open in second position; simultaneously, lift the right arm quickly from second to third position). Second measure: hold the pose in attitude, come down in demi-plié, bring the left arm in third position, the right arm in first position, lean the body to the right, and execute tour lent en dehors. Third measure: from pose attitude, change to pose fourth arabesque, step to the back in fifth position, on half-toe; dégagé left foot front in croisé and come down in fourth position, grande préparation for tour en dedans. Fourth measure: a half tour en dedans in attitude, plié-relevé and then the second half tour en dedans, end in fifth position, right foot front. Fifth measure: with the left leg: développé to the side, passé at 90° with a turn en dehors to corner 6, plié and step front on the left foot to corner 6 in attitude effacée. Sixth measure: hold the pose, come down in plié, stretch the right leg in the back, right foot pointe tendue on the floor, bend the body to the

[3] Depending on the ability, ronds de jambe en l'air en tournant are done also, each on half a beat.

back, then lower the right arm into first position and quickly spring onto the right foot, half-toe, in first arabesque at 90°, facing corner 2; passé with the left foot through first position to the front in fourth position, grande préparation for tour en dedans. Seventh measure: tour in first arabesque, end with passé on the floor in first position to the front into fourth position, grande préparation for tour en dehors. Eighth measure: tour in pose effacée front on the left leg, end in fifth position, left foot front. Ninth and tenth measures: with the left leg, on half-toe, grand rond de jambe développé en dehors, end in pose third arabesque, plié and pas de bourrée en tournant en dehors, changing feet. Eleventh measure: with the left leg: pas de basque en tournant front in a half turn and pas de basque en tournant back in a half turn. Twelfth measure: with the left leg: failli in fourth position in préparation for tours sur le cou-de-pied en dehors and 2 tours en dehors. At the end of the tours, remain on half-toe on the supporting right leg; the left foot, from position sur le cou-de-pied front, opens halfway to the side and quickly returns sur le cou-de-pied back. Staying in first position, open the hands slightly from the wrist.

ALLEGRO

1. 8 measures in 2/4.

Two assemblés battus with the right and left leg, changing feet to the front, each on 1 beat; 3 assemblés croisés front, each on half a beat; 2 sissonnes fermées to the side with the left and right leg, changing feet, each on 1 beat; on 2 beats, entrechat trois back and assemblé croisé back. Repeat on the other leg, and execute in the reverse direction.

2. 8 measures in 2/4.

Sissonne ouverte to 45° in a small pose effacée front, 2 cabrioles at 45°, assemblé. Repeat 4 times, in turn with the right and left leg. Execute also in the reverse direction. Each jump is done on 1 beat.

3. GARGOUILLADE (ROND DE JAMBE DOUBLE) EN DEHORS AND EN DEDANS. Musical measure 2/4.

a) Gargouillade, ending in fifth position, each on 4 beats, and on 4 beats, gargouillade, this time ending with a sliding jump on the floor, similar to the concluding jump in a pas de basque.

b) First and second way of executing the gargouillade, each on 2 beats.

4. 16 measures in 3/4 (Slow Waltz).

Grande sissonne ouverte in attitude croisée, assemblé; grande sissonne ouverte in attitude effacée, assemblé; execute with the right and left leg. Grande sissonne ouverte croisée front, assemblé; grande sissonne ouverte effacée front, assemblé; execute with the right and left leg.

5. 8 measures in 2/4.

Execute the preceding combination (4) of grandes sissonnes ouvertes in a quick tempo.[4]

6. 8 measures in 2/4.

With the right leg: sissonne tombée in a wide fourth position effacée, stretch the left foot to the back, pointe tendue on the floor; a short coupé with the left foot back of the right foot and grand jeté on the right leg in attitude effacée; without dropping the left leg, end with pas failli in fifth position, left foot front. Repeat 4 times, in turn with the right and left leg.[5]

7. 4 measures in 4/4.

Move in a straight line from side 7 to side 3. Fifth position, right foot front. First measure: step to the side on the right foot and grand assemblé to the side with a half turn, the arms in third position, at the end, stop in fifth position with the back to side 1 (back to the mirror), the left foot in front, then turn to the right side facing side 1 on both flat feet. At the end of the half turn, the right foot is in front. Second measure: repeat once more. Third measure: step to the side, and grand assemblé en tournant, end in fifth position. Left foot front, stretch the knees, then demi-plié, and in the fourth measure, follow with 4 grands changements de pieds.

8. 16 measures in 2/4.

Two entrechats-quatre, each on 1 beat; 3 entrechats-quatre, each on half a beat. Repeat. Three échappés battus, changing feet, each on 2 beats; 2 royales, each on 1 beat. Repeat from the beginning on the other leg.

---

[4] In the sixth year, it is recommended that some uncomplicated combinations be performed changing tempi. For example: the first time, execute the combination slowly with a smooth, deep demi-plié, the second time, quickly, with a short, springboardlike takeoff from the floor.

[5] Following some lessons to acquire proficiency in the steps, this combination is performed in the reverse direction.

9. 16 measures in 2/4.

Tours chaînés: on the diagonal to corner 2, starting on the right foot: 3 chaînés, each on 2 beats; on 2 beats, demi-plié in fifth position, right foot front. Execute 4 times, end the last chaîné in fifth position, right foot back. Repeat again the same, but with 1 beat for each chaîné.

10. ENTRECHAT-SIX (for the men). Musical measure 2/4.

On the upbeat, demi-plié and relevé on half-toe in fifth position; on the first beat, demi-plié; on the second beat, entrechat-six. In the early stage of learning entrechat-six, execute the step facing the barre, then, depending on the proficiency in the step, in the center of the studio. In the second semester, execute from 4 to 8 entrechats-six consecutively.

11. 4 measures in 2/4.

Sixteen petits changements de pieds, each on half a beat.[6]

FIRST EXAMPLE OF EXERCISES ON POINTES

1. 16 measures in 2/4.

Two échappés battus, each on 2 beats; 2 échappés in second position, changing feet (on pointes), each on 1 beat; on 2 beats, sissonne simple, changing the foot to the back. Execute 4 times, in turn with the right and left leg.

2. 16 measures in 2/4.

Double rond de jambe en l'air en dehors from fifth position, with the right, the left and the right leg, each on 2 beats; on 2 beats, grande sissonne ouverte in third arabesque. Repeat on the other leg and subsequently en dedans.

3. 16 measures in 3/4 (Waltz).

Préparation on the left leg, right foot croisé front, pointe tendue on the floor. Step-coupé on the right foot in plié, spring onto pointes on the right foot, throw the left leg to the side as in a grand battement at 90°, raise the arms in third position, and turn to first arabesque in plié, executing grand fouetté à la seconde in first arabesque. Passé through first position with the left foot to croisé front, step-coupé in

---

[6] Each lesson, as usual, ends with port de bras and the bending of the body.

plié on the left leg and execute the second grand fouetté à la seconde in first arabesque. Execute this fouetté 5 times, each in 2 measures. In 2 measures: step back, on the left foot in fifth position, right foot back, demi-plié; and in 4 measures: pas de bourrée suivi croisé front, left foot front, the left arm in third position, the right arm in second position. In the last measure: execute 1 grande sissonne ouverte in attitude croisée, the left arm open in second position, the right arm raised in third position allongée.

4. 8 measures in 4/4.

Move on the diagonal from corner 6 to corner 2. Step onto pointes on the right foot in first arabesque and execute plié-relevé, traveling front, 3 times consecutively; end the third relevé in fifth position, right foot front. Repeat 2 times, from the beginning, executing all the plié-relevé, each on 2 beats. On 2 beats, préparation from fifth position to fourth position, left foot front; on 2 beats, tour sur le cou-de-pied en dehors, end in fourth position. On 4 beats, 2 tours sur le cou-de-pied en dehors, end in fifth position, right foot back and come up on pointes, the arms raised in third position.

5. 8 measures in 2/4.

Eight tours en dehors with dégagé on the diagonal, each on 2 beats.

6. Musical measure 2/4.

Tours chaînés on the diagonal (4 to 8 tours chaînés), each on 1 beat.

7. Musical measure 2/4.

Eight tours fouettés at 45°, or more, depending on the individual ability of each student.

8. Musical measure 3/4 (Waltz).

Fifth port de bras on pointes.

Pose écartée back at the barre.

Second Lesson

EXERCISES AT THE BARRE

1. 16 measures in 4/4.

Two demi-pliés, 2 grands pliés, each on 4 beats, in first, second, fourth, and fifth position.

2. BATTEMENTS TENDUS. 32 measures in 2/4.

Three battements tendus front, each on 1 beat; 2 battements tendus front, each on half a beat. Repeat. Six battements tendus to the side, each on 1 beat; on 2 beats, a half turn toward the barre on the substituted right leg and, at the end, open the left foot to the side, pointe tendue on the floor, and again a half turn toward the barre on the substituted left leg, and open the right foot to the side, pointe tendue on the floor; on the last half beat, demi-rond à terre to the back and repeat the whole combination from the beginning in the reverse direction. Battements tendus jetés: 7 to the front, to the side, to the back and to the side, each on half a beat; battements tendus jetés in first position: 3, 3, and 3 more, each on half a beat; 5 battements tendus jetés, each on a quarter beat. Repeat battements tendus jetés in first position.

3. RONDS DE JAMBE À TERRE AND GRANDS BATTEMENTS JETÉS PASSÉS. 12 measures in 4/4.

On 2 introductory chords, préparation en dehors. Eight ronds de jambe à terre, each on 1 beat; 4 grands battements jetés passés en dehors (to the front–to the back), each on 2 beats. Execute also en dedans. In 2 measures: trace a half circle on the floor, in plié, en dedans and demi-rond en dehors to second position, relevé to the side at 90°, rising on half-toe. In 2 measures: port de bras, bending the body to the left toward the barre, and raising the right arm in third position.

4. BATTEMENTS FONDUS AT 45°. 24 measures in 2/4.

On 2 beats, fondu front; on 2 beats, plié-relevé with demi-rond to the side; on 2 beats, plié on the supporting leg with the working leg extended at 45° and tour sur le cou-de-pied en dehors; on 2 beats, fondu to the side. Repeat fondus and from the position with the working leg at 45°, execute 2 tours sur le cou-de-pied en dehors; at the end, open the working leg to the side at 45°. Repeat from the beginning en dedans. Frappés: 3 to the side, each on half a beat; on 2 beats, a half turn toward the barre on the substituted right leg on half-toe; at the end, open the left leg to the side at 45° and again a half turn toward the barre on the substituted left leg on half-toe and open the right leg to the side at 45°. Repeat frappés; the half turns on the substituted leg are done away from the barre. Doubles frappés: 6 to the side, each on 1 beat; 3 to the side, each on half a beat.

5. RONDS DE JAMBE EN L'AIR. 8 measures in 4/4.

On 2 beats, tour sur le cou-de-pied temps relevé en dehors; at the end, open the working leg to the side at 45°; 3 ronds de jambe en l'air en dehors, each on half a beat. Repeat from the beginning. Five and 5 more ronds de jambe en dehors, each on a quarter beat; on 4 beats, 2 tours sur le cou-de-pied temps relevé en dehors. Execute also en dedans.

6. PETITS BATTEMENTS SUR LE COU-DE-PIED. 8 measures in 4/4.

Twenty-four petits battements, each on half a beat; on 4 beats, tour sur le cou-de-pied en dehors from fifth position, end à la seconde. Repeat petits battements; tour from fifth position is done en dedans and ends in pose attitude effacée.

7. BATTEMENTS DÉVELOPPÉS. 16 measures in 4/4.

First measure: demi-plié, stretch the working foot to the front, pointe tendue on the floor, relevé at 90° on half-toe, simultaneously stretch the knee of the supporting leg. Second measure: 3 short balancés, end in fifth position. Third and fourth measures: développé front on half-toe, grand rond de jambe en dehors and passé at 90°. Fifth, sixth, seventh, and eighth measures: hold the pose on half-toe, then développé front, grand rond de jambe en dehors, and, again without dropping the leg, grand rond de jambe en dedans, once again en dehors and end in fifth position. Repeat from the beginning in the reverse direction.

8. GRANDS BATTEMENTS JETÉS BALANCÉS. 8 measures in 2/4.

First position, the working leg stretched in the back, pointe tendue on the floor. Two grands battements balancés to the front–to the back, each on 1 beat; 3 grands battements balancés to the front–to the back–to the front, each on half a beat. On half a beat, hold the working leg front at 90°, and thereafter follow with the combination battements to the back–to the front, etc.

EXERCISES IN THE CENTER

1. SMALL ADAGIO AND BATTEMENTS TENDUS. 8 measures in 4/4.

First measure: grand plié in fifth position, right foot front; from deep plié, tour en dedans on the right leg in attitude effacée. Second measure: a half tour lent en dedans to pose attitude croisée. Starting the turn, bend the body slightly to the back and open the left arm in second position; at the end of the turn, lower the right arm in the preparatory position and through first position, raise the right arm to third position. The position of the body in attitude croisée is in the same position as in the pose fourth arabesque; the left shoulder is pulled back, the right arm in third position is turned to the left, elbow forward, the head is turned to the right and overlaps the arm in front. Third measure: from the preceding pose, bend to the right side, and stretch the knee of the working leg, execute a half turn en dehors in à la seconde position, facing side 5; plié and step on the left foot in first arabesque to side

3. Fourth measure: turn to side 1 (en dedans) and simultaneously execute grand rond de jambe en dedans in pose croisée front. Fifth measure: relevé on half-toe in pose croisée, a wide tombé and grand port de bras ending in fourth position, grande préparation for tour en dehors. Sixth measure: tour en dehors in attitude, end in fifth position. Seventh measure: with the right foot, trace a half circle on the floor in plié en dehors (rond de jambe à terre), end in fifth position on half-toe. Eighth measure: plié on the right leg, dégagé the left leg at 45° in effacé front to corner 8, come up on half-toe on the left foot and execute tour en dedans in first arabesque. Battements tendus and tours: 8 measures in 4/4. Four battements tendus with the right foot in a small pose effacée front, each on 1 beat; 5 battements tendus jetés, each on half a beat, and on 3 half beats, flic-flac en tournant en dedans, end in a small pose effacée back; 4 battements tendus in pose effacée back, 5 battements tendus jetés and flic-flac en tournant en dehors, end to the side at 45°; 4 battements tendus to the side, 5 battements tendus jetés and flic-flac en tournant en dehors, end in fourth position effacée to corner 2, in préparation for tour sur le cou-de-pied en dedans. In 1 measure: tour en dedans on the right leg, end in fourth position croisée (left foot front); in 1 measure: on the first and second beats, tour sur le cou-de-pied en dehors, on the third and fourth beats, 2 tours en dehors.

2. BATTEMENTS FONDUS AT 45°. 4 measures in 4/4.

On 2 beats, with the right leg, fondu in a small pose effacée front; on 2 beats, plié-relevé with a half turn en dedans to corner 6; at the end of the turn, the working leg is in effacé back; on 2 beats, bring the right foot by the way of a petit battement into the sur le cou-de-pied position front, and execute 1 fondu in a small pose effacée front to corner 6; on 2 beats, plié-relevé with a half turn en dedans to side 1; at the end of the turn, the working leg is in croisé back. Two doubles fondus to the side, each on 2 beats; on 4 beats, a wide tombé to the side in plié, on the right foot and tour à la seconde en dedans to the right side.

3. PETITS BATTEMENTS SUR LE COU-DE-PIED. 8 measures in 4/4.

Fifth position, épaulement effacé, right foot front. In 2 measures: with the right foot, 12 petits battements, each on half a beat; raise the arms gradually from the preparatory position, the left arm in third position, the right arm in second position. End the last petit battement in plié, on the supporting leg; lower the arms in the preparatory position, and on 1 beat, brushing the foot, pointe tendue on the floor, execute a jump jeté on the right leg front to corner 2. Raise the arms in first position, bend the body forward, stretch the left leg back in effacé at 45°. On 1 beat, hold the pose. In 2 measures: from the preceding pose, execute with the left foot 12 petits battements in épaulement croisé, gradually raising the arms, the right arm in third position, the left arm in second position; demi-plié on the supporting leg, lower the arms in the preparatory position, and jump jeté to corner 2. Raise the arms in first position, bend the body forward, the right leg stretched in the back, in croisé at 45°. In 2 measures: from the preceding pose, repeat petits battements with the right foot in épaulement effacé, a jump jeté, and in 2 measures: come up from demi-plié, turn in pose écartée back at 90°, relevé on half-toe, a wide tombé on the left foot and tour en dedans in pose second arabesque at 90°.

4. GRANDS BATTEMENTS JETÉS BALANCÉS TO THE SIDE IN SECOND POSITION.[1] Musical measure 2/4.

a) Fifth position, right foot front. On the first beat, with the right leg: grand battement to the side, bend the body to the left; on the second beat, bring the leg down in fifth position back, straighten the body. Repeat the same with the left leg, with the right leg, etc. At least 8 battements to the side. Execute also in the reverse direction, changing the foot to fifth position front.

b) On the first beat, battement with the right leg, and a hold to the side at 90°; on the second beat, with no delay in fifth position, execute 1 battement with the left leg, with a slight hold to the side at 90°, etc.

5. GRAND ADAGIO. 8 measures in 4/4.

First measure: with the right leg: sissonne tombée in fourth position croisée, grande préparation for tour en dedans; tour en dedans in attitude effacée, end in fifth position. Second measure: with the left leg: sissonne tombée in fourth position croisée, grande préparation for tour en dedans and tour in first arabesque, end in fifth position, right foot front. Third measure: grand échappé in second position and from second position, tour à la seconde en dehors to the right side. Fourth measure: from the à la seconde position, carry the working leg to écarté back, come down in fifth position, right foot back, and on the last 2 beats of the measure, execute gargouillade en dehors with the left leg. In 4 measures: repeat the adagio once more with the right leg.

[1] Unlike grands battements jetés balancés, which are executed by brushing the foot through first position during the exercises at the barre; those same battements, in the center of the studio, are performed in fifth position, alternating legs.

ALLEGRO

1. 16 measures in 2/4.

Four assemblés battus, in turn with the right and left leg, changing feet to the front, each on 1 beat; on 2 beats, échappé in fourth position croisée; on 2 beats, échappé in second position, and from second position, tour sur le cou-de-pied en dehors. Repeat on the other leg and subsequently in the reverse direction.

2. 8 measures in 2/4.

Sissonne ouverte at 45° en tournant en dehors in a small pose croisée front, assemblé croisé front. Execute 3 times, each on 2 beats. On 2 beats, sissonne ouverte at 45° en tournant en dehors, end to the side, assemblé to the side. Two pas de basque front en tournant in a half turn, each on 2 beats. Two entrechats-cinq back, end with assemblé back, each on 2 beats. Execute also in the reverse direction.

3. 8 measures in 2/4 or 16 measures in 3/4 (Waltz).

With the right leg: grande sissonne ouverte in attitude croisée, traveling forward and with a half turn en dedans to side 5, end with assemblé; grande sissonne ouverte in attitude croisée, traveling and with a half turn en dedans to side 1, end with assemblé, each on 2 beats. On 2 beats, with the left leg: on the upbeat, pas couru forward (4 steps—the fifth, step-coupé) and with the right leg, grand assemblé croisé front, the right arm in first position, the left arm in third position; on 2 beats, 2 entrechats-quatre; gradually lower the arms. Two grands échappés in second position, changing feet, each on 2 beats.[2] With the right leg: grande sissonne ouverte in pose croisée front, traveling to the back and with a half turn en dehors to side 5, end with assemblé; grande sissonne ouverte in pose croisée front, traveling to the back and with a half turn en dehors to side 1, end with assemblé, each on 2 beats.

4. 16 measures in 3/4 (Waltz).

Three sissonnes fondues to the side at 90°, with the right, the left, and the right leg, changing feet to the back; 1 sissonne fondue in pose third arabesque; 3 sissonnes fondues to the side, with the right, the

---

[2] Substitute the grands échappés for the men with relevé on half-toe in fifth position and entrechat-six (twice).

left and the right leg, changing feet to the front and 1 sissonne fondue in pose croisée front, each in 2 measures.

5. 8 measures in 4/4.

Fifth position, left foot front. Four brisés dessus-dessous (starting with the right leg), each on 2 beats; with the right leg: a small jeté, traveling to the side; with the left leg: a small jeté croisé front, each on 1 beat; repeat the jetés once more. On 4 beats, with the right leg: step-coupé front in effacé, grand jeté in attitude croisé on the left leg, assemblé. On the fourth beat, hold the position. Repeat from the beginning.

6. SOUBRESAUT. Musical measure 2/4.

a) Each soubresaut is executed in 2 measures.

b) Each soubresaut is executed in 1 measure.

7. 16 measures in 3/4 (Waltz).

In 4 measures: with the right leg, sissonne tombée in effacé front and 2 cabrioles at 45° in a small pose second arabesque, pas de bourrée en dehors, changing feet. In 4 measures: with the left leg: sissonne tombée in croisé front and 2 cabrioles at 45° in a small pose third arabesque, end with assemblé. In 4 measures: with the right leg, sissonne tombée in effacé front and 2 cabrioles at 45° in a small pose first arabesque, pas de bourrée en dehors, changing feet. In 2 measures: with the left leg: in a straight line, step to the side and grand assemblé en tournant, the arms in third position; end in fifth position, right foot front. In 2 measures: hold the position.

8. 16 measures in 2/4.

Move in a straight line from side 7 to side 3. Fifth position, right foot front. On 2 beats, 1 emboîté en tournant forward, traveling to the side in a half turn and assemblé front; on 2 beats, the second emboîté en tournant and assemblé front. Eight emboîtés en tournant forward consecutively, without assemblé, each on 1 beat; on 1 beat, assemblé to the side, end in fifth position, right foot back, and 3 entrechats-quatre, each on 1 beat. Repeat on the other leg. Execute also with emboîtés en tournant backward.

9. 4 measures in 2/4.

Starting on the right foot, on the diagonal to corner 2: 7 tours chaînés, each on 1 beat; on 1 beat, end the tours chaînés in fifth position, right foot back.

10. 8 measures in 2/4.

Thirty-two petits changements de pieds, each on half a beat.

SECOND EXAMPLE OF EXERCISES ON POINTES

1. 8 measures in 2/4.
Fifth position, left foot front. On 2 beats, starting on the right foot: glissade to the side, without changing feet, and assemblé battu, end in fifth position, right foot front; 2 sus-sous forward in a small pose croisée, each on 1 beat. Repeat on the other leg and subsequently in the reverse direction.[3]

2. 8 measures in 4/4.
Double rond de jambe en l'air en dehors from fifth position, with the right and left leg, each on 2 beats; with the right leg: grande sissonne ouverte in third arabesque, grande sissonne ouverte in first arabesque to corner 2 (on the right leg), each on 2 beats. Repeat on the other leg and subsequently in the reverse direction.

3. 32 measures in 3/4 (Waltz).
In 16 measures: with the right leg: grande sissonne ouverte in attitude croisée, plié (without dropping the working leg) and relevé in third arabesque; end in fifth position. Execute 3 times. With the right leg: grande sissonne ouverte à la seconde (without dropping the working leg), plié-relevé in first arabesque; end in fifth position, right foot front. In 8 measures: with the right leg to corner 2: 4 tours glissades en tournant, end in fifth position, right foot back. In 4 measures: with the left foot in a straight line to the left: pas de bourrée suivi, the left arm in third position, the right arm in second position; in the last measure: plié on the left leg, dégagé with the right leg to the side at 45°, open the arms in second position and turn toward corner 8. In 4 measures: tour en dehors with dégagé (to the left side), repeat twice, and end in fourth position croisée, left foot back, the right arm in third position, the left arm in second position, the head turned to the right.

4. 16 measures in 3/4 (Slow Waltz).
Move on the diagonal from corner 6 to corner 2. Fifth position, left foot front. In 4 measures: step on the right foot on pointes to the side, going toward corner 2; plié, and with the left leg: grand fouetté effacé en dehors, pas de bourrée en dehors, changing feet, end in fourth posi-

[3] It is recommended that simple allegro steps sometimes be combined with simple steps on pointes.

tion croisée and tour sur le cou-de-pied en dehors to the right side. In the following 8 measures: repeat the preceding combination twice; the last time, execute 2 tours sur le cou-de-pied en dehors. In 4 measures: on the upbeat, with the left foot: glissade croisée front (jumping), jeté on pointes on the left foot in attitude croisée, then, holding the pose, come down in plié; with the right foot: glissade croisée back (jumping), moving with a step on the right foot on pointes to side 5, execute 1½ tours en dedans, end in fifth position, left foot front.

5. 16 measures in 3/4 (Slow Waltz).

Move on the diagonal from corner 6 to corner 2. Fifth position, right foot front. In 4 measures: step to the side, on the right foot, on pointes, moving toward corner 2, and with the left leg: grand fouetté effacé en dedans, pas de bourrée en dedans, changing feet, end in fourth position croisée and tour sur le cou-de-pied en dedans to the right side; end in fifth position, left foot back. In the following 8 measures: repeat the preceding combination twice; the last time, execute 2 tours sur le cou-de-pied en dedans and end the tours in fifth position, left foot front. In 4 measures: step to the side on the right foot, on pointes, going toward corner 2 and come down in plié in a small pose effacée front, left foot, pointe tendue on the floor; rise on pointes while executing 2 battements battus front with the left foot, then come down in plié in pose effacée, pointe tendue on the floor; repeat the battements battus and follow with a wide tombé front on the left foot to corner 8 and execute 2 tours sur le cou-de-pied en dedans.

6. 8 measures in 2/4.

From corner 6 to corner 2: 7 tours chaînés, each on 1 beat, end in fifth position, right foot back; dégagé with the right leg to corner 2 and pas de bourrée suivi on the diagonal upstage to corner 6.

7. 8 measures in 2/4.

a) Eight tours en dehors with dégagé on the diagonal, each on 2 beats.

b) Eight tours en dedans with coupé (tours-piqué) on the diagonal, each on 2 beats.

8. Musical measure 2/4.

Tours fouettés at 45° en dehors and en dedans.

Third arabesque.

Third Lesson

EXERCISES AT THE BARRE

1. 16 measures in 4/4.
Two grands pliés in first position and 2 ports de bras bending the body;
2 grands pliés in second position and 2 relevés on half-toe; 2 grands
pliés in fourth position and 2 ports de bras, the first, bending the body
to the side toward the barre, the second, bending the body to the side
away from the barre; 2 grands pliés in fifth position and 2 ports de
bras, bending the body.

2. BATTEMENTS TENDUS. 32 measures in 2/4.

Seven battements tendus front, each on 1 beat (on the seventh battement: demi-plié); on 1 beat, a full turn in fifth position on half-toe toward the barre, end in plié; 7 battements tendus back (on the seventh battement: demi-plié), a full turn in fifth position on half-toe away from the barre, end in plié. Two battements tendus to the front, to the side, to the back and to the side, each on 1 beat; repeat and on the last battement, lower the arm in the preparatory position. Battements tendus jetés: 7 to the front, each on half a beat, gradually raise the arms in third position; 7 battements tendus jetés to the side, open the arms in second position and lower them in the preparatory position; 7 battements tendus jetés to the back, raise the arms in third position, and 7 battements tendus jetés to the side, open the arms in second position. Battements tendus jetés in first position: 7 and again 7, each on half a beat, 5 battements tendus jetés (repeat 4 times), each on a quarter beat.

3. RONDS DE JAMBE À TERRE, GRANDS RONDS DE JAMBE JETÉS AND GRANDS BATTEMENTS JETÉS PASSÉS. 20 measures in 4/4.

On 2 introductory chords, préparation en dehors. Four ronds de jambe à terre, each on 1 beat, 7 ronds de jambe à terre, each on half a beat; 4 grands ronds de jambe jetés, each on 1 beat (end the last rond de jambe jeté in front at 90°), and on 4 beats, execute port de bras, bending the body. From the preceding position, when the working leg is in front at 90°, repeat from the beginning en dedans (execute port de bras with the leg in the back at 90°). Four ronds de jambe à terre en dehors, each on 1 beat; 7 ronds de jambe à terre en dehors, each on half a beat; 4 grands battements jetés passés (to the front–to the back), each on 2 beats. Repeat the same en dedans. In 2 measures: trace a half circle on the floor, in plié, en dedans, en dehors; in 2 measures: port de bras in a wide plié and bending of the body.

4. BATTEMENTS FONDUS AT 45°. 24 measures in 2/4.

On 2 beats, tour sur le cou-de-pied en dehors from fifth position; on 2 beats, with the right leg: fondu to the front; on 2 beats, tour sur le cou-de-pied en dedans from fifth position on the right leg to the right side, and on 2 beats, with the left leg (transferring the left foot to the back with a petit battement): fondu to the back. With the right leg: double fondu to the front and to the side, each on 2 beats; on 2 beats, 2 tours sur le cou-de-pied en dehors from second position at 45°, and on 2 beats, 2 quick fondus to the side. Repeat from the beginning in the reverse direction. Frappés: 7 and again 7 to the side, each on half a beat; double frappés: 2, each on 1 beat; 3, each on half a beat; 2, each on 1 beat; 2, each on half a beat, and on 1 beat, a quick half turn toward the barre, on the substituted right leg on half-toe; at the end, open the left leg to the side at 45°.

5. RONDS DE JAMBE EN L'AIR AND PETITS BATTEMENTS SUR LE COU-DE-PIED. 16 measures in 3/4.

Five ronds de jambe en l'air en dehors, each on half a beat, and on 3 half beats, flic-flac en tournant en dehors, end to the side at 45°; 3 ronds de jambe en l'air en dehors, each on half a beat; on 2 beats, double rond de jambe en l'air (repeat twice, on the grace note, before each beat). Twelve battements battus front in épaulement croisé, each on a quarter beat; on 1 beat, tombé in plié on the right foot, stretch the left leg in the back in croisé, pointe tendue on the floor (in a small arabesque pose on the floor, on the diagonal away from the barre). On the upbeat, coupé on the left foot, half-toe, open the right leg to the side at 45°, and 6 petits battements, each on half a beat; at the end, open the working leg to the side at 45°. Repeat from the beginning in the reverse direction and end with petits battements and a quick développé in second arabesque at 90°.

6. BATTEMENTS DÉVELOPPÉS. 8 measures in 4/4.

First measure: on the first and second beats, développé front on half-toe and demi-rond to the side; before the third beat, a quick balancé-demi-rond (d'ici-de là) to the front and to the side; on the fourth beat, hold the position. Second measure: passé at 90° in attitude effacée, end in fifth position. Third measure: développé to the back on half-toe, demi-rond to the side and a quick balancé-demi-rond (d'ici-de là) to the back and to the side. Fourth measure: passé at 90° in pose effacée front, end in fifth position. Fifth measure: développé on half-toe to the side, demi-rond to the front and a quick balancé-demi-rond (d'ici-de là) to the side and to the front. Sixth measure: passé at 90° in pose écartée back, end in fifth position. Seventh measure: développé on half-toe, to the side, demi-rond to the back and a quick-balancé-demi-rond (d'ici-de là) to the side and to the back. Eighth measure: passé at 90° in pose écartée front, and on the last 2 beats, a wide tombé in plié on the working foot with a half turn toward the barre; at the end, développé with the left leg to the front at 90°, the supporting leg in plié.

7. GRANDS BATTEMENTS JETÉS. 8 measures in 2/4.

Two grands battements front, each on 1 beat; on 1 beat, 1 grand battement front with a quick demi-rond to the side; on 1 beat, 1 battement tendu to the side. Two grands battements to the side, each on 1 beat; on 1 beat, 1 grand battement to the side with a quick demi-rond to the back; on 1 beat, 1 battement tendu to the back. Execute also in the reverse direction.

EXERCISES IN THE CENTER

1. SMALL ADAGIO AND BATTEMENTS TENDUS. 4 measures in 4/4.

First measure: grand plié in first position; from deep plié, tour sur le cou-de-pied en dehors on the left leg, end in pose écartée back at 90°. Second measure: tour lent en dehors (half a turn) in pose écartée and tombé in plié on the right foot in pose third arabesque at 90° toward corner 8. Third measure: on the upbeat, on half a beat, relevé on half-toe, in attitude croisée and grand port de bras, ending in fourth position, grande préparation for tour en dehors. Fourth measure: tour à la seconde en dehors.

Battements tendus and tours: 8 measures in 4/4. With the right leg: 8 battements tendus doubles (lowering the heel in second position), each on 2 beats; battements tendus jetés: 16 en tournant en dedans, each on half a beat; in 2 measures: with the left leg, from second position, tour sur le cou-de-pied en dehors, 1 tour and 2 tours.[1]

2. BATTEMENTS DÉVELOPPÉS BALLOTTÉS AND GRAND FOU-ETTÉ EFFACÉ. 8 measures in 4/4.

On 4 beats, développé ballotté in effacé, with the right leg, to the front, with the left leg, to the back; on 2 beats, immediately from fifth position half-toe, execute grand fouetté effacé en dehors with the right leg, and on 2 beats, carry the working leg to the side at 90°, simultaneously come up on half-toe on the supporting leg. End in fifth position, right foot front. On 4 beats, développé ballotté in effacé with the left leg to the back and with the right leg to the front; on 2 beats, from fifth position half-toe, execute grand fouetté effacé en dedans with the left leg; on 2 beats, carry the working leg to the side at 90°; simultaneously come up on half-toe on the supporting leg. On the last beat, coupé on the left foot on half-toe, open the right leg to the side at 45°. Frappés: 7

---

[1] In senior lessons, the préparation and tours from second position can be broken down in the following manner: first measure: on the upbeat, demi-plié and relevé in fifth position on half-toe, the arms in first position. On the first beat, the working leg opens to the side at 45°, the arms open in second position, on the second beat, demi-plié in second position, the arms in first and second positions; on the third and fourth beats, execute tour with stop sur le cou-de-pied. Second measure: on the first beat, from the sur le cou-de-pied position, open the working leg to the side at 45°, open the arms in second position; on the second beat, demi-plié in second position, the arms in first and second positions; on the third beat, execute 2 tours; on the fourth beat, end in fifth position, demi-plié.

to the side en tournant en dehors, each on half a beat; turn to side 5 (1½ turns); 4 doubles frappés, each on 1 beat, ending the second half of the turn en dehors; on 4 beats, 2 doubles fondus to the side at 45°; on 4 beats, tombé on the right foot and 2 tours sur le cou-de-pied en dedans, ending in pose croisée front at 90°.

3. RONDS DE JAMBE EN L'AIR AND BATTEMENTS BATTUS. 8 measures in 4/4.

Préparation on the right leg, left leg stretched back, in croisé, pointe tendue on the floor. On the upbeat, dégagé with the left leg to the side at 45° and plié on the right leg; on 2 beats, pas de bourrée dessus-dessous en tournant, end in fifth position; on 2 beats, 2 tours sur le cou-de-pied en dehors on the left leg; at the end, open the right leg to the side at 45°. Four ronds de jambe en l'air en tournant en dehors, each on 1 beat (a half turn to side 5); 3 and again 3 ronds de jambe en l'air, each on half a beat (the second half of the turn to side 1); 5 ronds de jambe en l'air en dehors en face, each on half a beat, end the fifth rond de jambe in plié, in pose effacée front at 45°; on 1 beat, pas couru front to corner 2 (4 steps), end in a small pose effacée front in plié, right foot, pointe tendue on the floor. With the right foot: 12 battements battus front in épaulement effacé, each on a quarter beat; on 1 beat, come down in plié in pose effacée front, pointe tendue on the floor. Repeat battements tendus in pose effacée. Eight battements battus front in épaulement effacé, each on a quarter beat; on 2 beats, bring the working leg in a small pose effacée back at 45°, come down in plié on the supporting leg, and execute pas de bourrée en dehors, changing feet; end the pas de bourrée in fourth position, grande préparation for tour en dehors; on 4 beats, tour en dehors in pose attitude croisée, raise the arms in third position. Execute also en dedans with tour in pose croisée front; at the end, raise the arm corresponding to the supporting leg in third position, the other arm in first position.

4. GRANDS BATTEMENTS JETÉS. 4 measures in 4/4.

Starting position: fifth position, right foot front. On the first beat, with the right leg: grand battement croisée front. Lean the body back, the left arm in first position, the right arm in second position, turn the head to the right. On the second beat, bring the working leg down in first position, holding the épaulement croisé and leaving the arms in the preceding position. On the third beat, grand battement in first arabesque. On the fourth beat, bring the working leg down in first position, épaulement croisé. Execute in a similar manner 6 grands battements; end the last battement (in first arabesque) in fifth position épaulement croisé, right foot back. On 2 beats, with the left leg: préparation from fifth position to fourth position for tours sur le cou-de-pied en dehors; on 2 beats, 2 tours en dehors.

5. GRAND ADAGIO. 12 measures in 4/4 or 48 measures in 3/4 (Waltz).

First measure: grand plié in fifth position, right foot front; from deep plié, tour en dedans sur le cou-de-pied, end in first arabesque to side 3. Second measure: tour lent en dedans in pose arabesque. Third and fourth measures: an even tilt downward (penché), holding the upper body in the arabesque pose. Fifth measure: relevé in arabesque on half-toe; on the last beat of the measure, passé through first position to the front in fourth position, grande préparation for tour en dedans. Sixth measure: tour en dedans in first arabesque on the left leg. Seventh measure: passé at 90° with a half turn en dehors to corner 4 in pose effacée front, on half-toe, and tombé, then pas chassé front, end in pose second arabesque at 90°, in plié on the right leg. Eighth measure: passé at 90° with a half turn en dehors to corner 8 in pose effacée front, on half-toe, tombé and pas chassé front, end in fourth position effacée to corner 8, grande préparation for tours en dedans. Ninth measure: 2 tours tire-bouchon en dedans, raise the arms in third position. Tenth measure: from the tire-bouchon position, tombé on the right foot in plié, raise the left leg to the back in croisé at 90°, lean the body downward (penché), lower the arms in first position and, while stretching the knee on the supporting leg, execute a turn en dehors in pose écartée front; at the end of the turn, the left shoulder is directed toward corner 2, the right shoulder toward corner 6. Eleventh measure: tombé to corner 2 on the left foot in plié in fourth arabesque, stretch the supporting knee and execute demi-rond to the side, while coming up on half-toe, and end in fifth position, right foot front. Twelfth measure: with the right leg front, pas de basque front, ending in fourth position, préparation for tours sur le cou-de-pied en dehors and 2 tours en dehors with a stop in attitude croisée, the arms raised in third position.

ALLEGRO

1. 16 measures in 2/4.

Two sissonnes fermées to the side with the right and left leg, changing feet to the back, each on 1 beat; on 2 beats, with the right leg: gargouillade en dehors; on 2 beats, with the left leg: double rond de jambe en l'air sauté en dehors, end with assemblé; on 2 beats, a similar rond de jambe and assemblé with the right leg. Repeat the combination on the other leg and execute in the reverse direction.

2. 8 measures in 4/4.

Fifth position, left foot front. On the right leg: jeté to the side; at the end, the left foot is sur le cou-de-pied back; temps levé, temps levé en tournant en dehors (during the jump, transfer the left foot sur le cou-de-pied front), assemblé croisé front. Repeat the whole combination 2 more times. With the right foot: glissade to the side without changing feet, jeté to the side; at the end, the left foot is sur le cou-de-pied back; assemblé croisé back, entrechat-quatre. Repeat from the beginning on the other leg. Each jump is done on 1 beat.

3. 4 measures in 4/4.

In a straight line from side 7 to side 3 (starting on the right leg): 4 jetés en tournant, traveling to the side in half turns, each on 1 beat; 4 emboîtés en tournant forward, traveling to the side in half turns, each on 1 beat; on 4 beats, sissonne tombée front to corner 2 on the right foot, 2 cabrioles at 45° in a small pose second arabesque, end with assemblé in fifth position, left foot front; on 4 beats, sissonne tombée croisée back on the left foot (transferring the left foot to the back during the sissonne), 2 cabrioles at 45° in a small pose croisée front, assemblé. Execute also in the reverse direction. Execute the first jetés en tournant with a turn en dehors, the second jetés en tournant, en dedans, etc., and emboîtés en tournant backward.

4. 8 measures in 2/4.

On 2 beats, grand échappé in second position, changing feet; on 2 beats, soubresaut, bending the body. Execute 4 times, in turn with the right and left leg.

5. 16 measures in 3/4 (Waltz).

Move on the diagonal from corner 6 to corner 2. Fifth position, right foot front. Passing springboardlike pas failli in second arabesque and grand assemblé in écarté back; the right arm in third position, the left arm in second allongé. Execute 4 times. On the diagonal from corner 2 to corner 6 (upstage) with the left foot: glissade backward in position écartée without changing feet and grande sissonne ouverte in first arabesque; turn the body to corner 2. Execute 3 times; the last sissonne ends with assemblé in fifth position, the left foot front, and grand changement de pieds, the arms raised in third position.[2]

---

[2] Substitute grands changements de pieds with entrechat-six for the men.

6. 16 measures in 3/4 (Waltz).

Move on the diagonal from corner 2 to corner 6 (upstage). Fifth position, left foot front. Step-coupé on the left foot toward corner 6 and grand assemblé en tournant; raise the arms in third position; end in fifth position, right foot front. Step to corner 2 on the right foot in pose second arabesque, left foot back, pointe tendue on the floor. From second arabesque position, step-coupé on the left foot toward corner 6 and grand assemblé en tournant; step to corner 2 on the right foot in second arabesque pose and repeat grand assemblé en tournant. Two grands changements de pieds, lower the arms from third position in the preparatory position.[3] With the right leg to corner 2: sissonne tombée in a wide fourth position effacée, coupé with the left foot back, grand jeté on the right leg in attitude effacée, a passing, springboardlike pas failli in pose second arabesque and grand assemblé battu to the side; raise the left arm in third position, the right arm in first position.

7. 16 measures in 3/4 (Waltz).

Préparation on the left leg, the right leg stretched in croisé front, pointe tendue on the floor. In 4 measures: step effacé back in plié on the right foot and jeté passé front at 90°,[4] raise the left arm in third position, the right arm in second position; pas couru back (starting on the right foot, 4 steps back) toward corner 4, step effacé back in plié and jeté passé front at 90°, the right arm in third position, the left arm in second position. In 4 measures: run off to the back (still facing the mirror) to corner 6 and step in fifth position, right foot front. In 8 measures: a small sissonne tombée with the right leg in front to corner 2 in fourth position effacée and jeté passé back at 90°; the right arm in third position, the left arm in second position allongée; pas couru forward (4 steps) toward corner 2 and jeté passé back at 90°. Repeat pas couru and jeté passé. With the right foot: glissade forward to corner 2 and grand pas de chat front, the left arm in third position, the right arm in first position. Hold the final pose on the left leg, the right leg in croisé back, pointe tendue on the floor.[5]

8. 16 measures in 2/4.

Fifth position, left foot front. Starting with the right foot, execute brisé-dessus-dessous, 4 times, each on 2 beats; with the right foot: 2 brisés front, each on 1 beat; 3 brisés, each on half a beat; with the left foot:

[3] For the men's lesson, substitute with 2 entrechats-six.
[4] Jeté passé front is performed without moving forward, but upward with the jump, by throwing the leg front; jeté passé back, again, is done by throwing the leg back and taking flight during the jump.
[5] All pas courus are done on the upbeat.

2 brisés back, each on 1 beat; 2 brisés back, each on half a beat, and on half a beat, royale. Repeat the whole combination on the other leg.

9. TOURS-SISSONNE TOMBÉE. Musical measure 2/4.

Execute 4 to 8 tours in a straight line to side 1 and on the diagonal. Study each tour on 2 beats, then, depending on the knowledge of the step, execute each tour on 1 beat.

10. 4 measures in 2/4.

Sixteen petits changements de pieds, each on half a beat.

THIRD EXAMPLE OF EXERCISES ON POINTES

1. 8 measures in 4/4.

Four échappés in second position, starting with the right foot front, changing feet, each on 1 beat; on 4 beats, échappé in second position, right foot front, landing on the left foot, the other foot sur le cou-de-pied back, and 2 pliés-relevés, end in fifth position. On 4 beats, échappé in second position, landing on the right foot, the other sur le cou-de-pied back and 2 pliés-relevés, end in fifth position. Three sautés in fifth position on pointes, each on half a beat; on the third sauté, come down in demi-plié; on 2 beats, turn in fifth position on pointes to the left side (détourné); end in fifth position demi-plié. Repeat from the beginning on the other leg.

2. 8 measures in 4/4.

Four sissonnes simples, changing feet to the back, in turn with the right and left leg, each on 1 beat; on 4 beats, préparation from fifth position to fifth position and tour sur le cou-de-pied en dehors, in turn with the right and left leg. Repeat from the beginning and execute also in the reverse direction.

3. 16 measures in 3/4 (Waltz).

Préparation on the right leg, the left leg stretched in croisé front, pointe tendue on the floor. In 1 measure: grande sissonne ouverte on the right leg in first arabesque in a straight line to side 3, and brush the left foot on the floor, beyond the right foot front, with a great move forward. In 1 measure: step on the left foot in fifth position front, sissonne simple on the right foot (the left foot sur le cou-de-pied front) in épaulement effacé, the arms in crossed position front, move to low first position.

Starting from the preceding position, execute another grande sissonne ouverte in first arabesque on the left leg in a straight line to side 7 and sissonne simple on the left foot in épaulement effacé. Execute the combination 6 times; the sixth time, substitute sissonne simple by standing in fifth position, on pointes, right foot front, and on the last beat, step forward on the right foot in plié to corner 2, dégagé with the left leg to the side at 45°. Execute tour en dehors with dégagé, on the left leg (3 times), each tour in 1 measure, end in fifth position, right foot back; in 1 measure: grande sissonne ouverte on the right leg, the left leg half bent in croisé front, the right arm in third position, the left arm in second position.

4. 16 measures in 2/4 (pizzicato).

Préparation on the left leg, the right leg stretched in croisé front, pointe tendue on the floor. On the upbeat, demi-plié; on 2 beats, execute grand fouetté en face, step on the right foot on pointes (step-coupé), end in pose attitude effacée; on 2 beats, coupé in plié on the left foot and bring the left foot back of the right foot, bring the right foot sur le cou-de-pied front (keeping épaulement effacé) and 1 emboîté forward on the right leg, traveling forward on the diagonal. On 2 beats, step onto the left foot, and execute the second grand fouetté en face in attitude effacée; on 2 beats, coupé and 1 emboîté. Execute in the same way, grand fouetté in first arabesque pose (twice), then 3 jetés fondus front on the diagonal to corner 8, each on 2 beats (on the right, left and right foot); step onto the left foot on pointes in first arabesque at 90°; come down in demi-plié, and, holding the pose, execute 3 pliés-relevés, each on 2 beats, moving on the diagonal backward, toward corner 4; on the fourth relevé, stay in pose arabesque on pointes for a long time.

5. 8 measures in 2/4.

Préparation from fifth position to fifth position and 7 tours sur le cou-de-pied en dehors from fifth position moving forward on the diagonal, each tour on 2 beats.

6. PRACTICE OF TOURS CHAÎNÉS AND TOURS FOUETTÉS.

Attitude croisée, on pointes.

Fourth Lesson

EXERCISES AT THE BARRE

1. 16 measures in 4/4.

Two demi-pliés, 2 grands pliés in first position, each on 4 beats; 2 grands pliés in second position, each on 4 beats; on 4 beats, bend the body to the side toward the barre; on 4 beats, bend the body to the side away from the barre. Two demi-pliés, 2 grands pliés in fourth position, each on 4 beats; 2 grands pliés in fifth position and 2 ports de bras, bending the body back, each on 4 beats.

2. BATTEMENTS TENDUS. 32 measures in 2/4.

Eight battements tendus front, each on 1 beat; 5 battements tendus to the side, each on 1 beat; on the fifth battement, demi-plié, and on 1 beat, a full turn in fifth position on half-toe toward the barre; on 2 beats, 1 battement tendu to the side in demi-plié and a full turn on half-toe toward the barre. Repeat in the reverse direction, starting with the right foot back. Battements tendus jetés: 7 to the front, each on half a beat; 5 to the side, each on half a beat; on 3 half beats, flic-flac en tournant en dehors, end in a small pose écartée back. Seven and again 7 battements tendus jetés in a small pose écartée back, each on half a beat. Repeat battements tendus jetés in the reverse direction.

3. RONDS DE JAMBE A TERRE AND GRANDS RONDS DE JAMBE JETÉS. 12 measures in 4/4.

On 2 introductory chords, préparation en dehors. Three ronds de jambe à terre and 1 grand rond de jambe jeté, each on 1 beat; repeat 3 times. Seven ronds de jambe à terre en dehors, each on half a beat. Repeat from the beginning en dedans. In 2 measures: trace a half circle in plié on the floor en dedans, en dehors and relevé back at 90° on half-toe. In 2 measures: plié-relevé with a half turn away from the barre and port de bras, bending the body, the leg in front at 90°.

4. BATTEMENTS FONDUS AT 45°. 16 measures in 2/4.

On 2 beats, double fondu front; on 2 beats, plié-relevé with a full rond en dehors to the back; on 2 beats, tour sur le cou-de-pied en dedans (from the position with the working leg in the back at 45°), and on 2 beats, fondu to the side. One fondu front, 1 fondu to the side, 1 fondu to the back and 1 fondu to the side, each on 1 beat. Frappés: 3 frappés to the side, 3 doubles frappés to the side, each on half a beat. Repeat from the beginning in the reverse direction; execute tour en dehors, from the position with the working leg in front at 45°.

5. RONDS DE JAMBE EN L'AIR. 8 measures in 4/4.

Two ronds de jambe en l'air en dehors, each on 1 beat; 3 ronds de jambe en l'air en dehors, each on half a beat. On 2 beats, a half turn on half-toe toward the barre on the substituted right foot, and at the end, open the left leg to the side at 45°, and again a half turn on the substituted left foot toward the barre; at the end, open the right leg to the side at 45° and execute 3 ronds de jambe en l'air en dehors, each on a quarter beat; on 2 beats, développé to the side on half-toe, and on 2 beats, flic-flac en tournant en dehors, end with the leg to the side at 90°. On the last half beat, lower the working leg at 45°; thereafter, repeat the whole combination en dedans.

6. PETITS BATTEMENTS SUR LE COU-DE-PIED. 16 measures in 2/4.

Fourteen petits battements, each on half a beat; on 1 beat, come down from half-toe onto the flat foot, open the working leg to the side, pointe tendue on the floor. Repeat once more. Twenty-four petits battements, each on a quarter beat; on 2 beats, come down from half-toe onto the flat foot, open the working leg to the side, pointe tendue on the floor. Repeat 24 petits battements.

7. BATTEMENTS DÉVELOPPÉS. 8 measures in 4/4.

First and second measures: développé front on half-toe, plié-relevé with a half turn toward the barre, plié-relevé with a half turn again toward the barre, end in fifth position. Third measure: développé tombé in pose effacée front, end the développé effacé front on the last beat of the measure. Fourth measure: from the pose effacée, demi-rond in pose écartée back, flic-flac en tournant en dehors, end in écarté back at 90° and bring the working leg down in fifth position. In the following 4 measures: repeat the whole combination in the reverse direction.

8. GRANDS BATTEMENTS JETÉS. 16 measures in 2/4.

Two grands battements front, side, back, and side, each on 1 beat; 4 grands battements jetés passés en dehors (to the front–to the back), each on 2 beats. Repeat the same in the reverse direction.

EXERCISES IN THE CENTER

1. SMALL ADAGIO AND BATTEMENTS TENDUS. 4 measures in 4/4.

First measure: grand plié in first position; from deep plié, tour à la seconde en dehors on the left leg. Second measure: grand plié in second position; from deep plié, tour en dehors in pose attitude croisée on the left leg. Third measure: from pose attitude, turn en dehors with passé at 90°; at the end, développé to the side. Fourth measure: plié on the supporting leg, step onto half-toe, on the right foot, and execute tour à la seconde en dedans; end in fifth position, left foot front. Battements tendus: 8 measures in 4/4. With the left foot: 6 battements tendus in a big pose croisée front, each on 1 beat; 3 battements tendus jetés, each on half a beat; with the right foot: 6 battements tendus to the side, each on 1 beat; 3 battements tendus jetés, each on half a beat.

With the left foot: 6 battements tendus in a big pose croisée back, each on 1 beat; 3 battements tendus jetés, each on half a beat; with the right foot: 4 battements tendus to the side, each on 1 beat; 5 battements tendus jetés, each on half a beat; on 3 half beats, flic-flac en tournant en dehors, end in fourth position croisée, in préparation for tours sur le cou-de-pied en dedans. In 1 measure: tour en dedans, end in fourth position, left foot back; in 1 measure: 2 tours en dedans, end in fourth position, left foot front and 2 tours sur le cou-de-pied en dehors.

2. BATTEMENTS FONDUS AT 45°. 8 measures in 4/4.

On 2 beats, 2 tours sur le cou-de-pied en dehors from fifth position on the left leg; on 2 beats, fondu with the right leg in a small pose croisée front; on 2 beats, 2 tours sur le cou-de-pied en dedans from fifth position on the right leg; on 2 beats, bring the left foot to the back, by way of a petit battement back and execute fondu in a small pose croisée back; with the right leg: 2 fondus to the side, each on 2 beats; on 4 beats, plié, and from 45°, 2 tours sur le cou-de-pied en dehors; at the end, open the working leg to the side at 45°. Frappés: 7 frappés to the side, each on half a beat; 4 doubles frappés, each on half a beat. On 2 beats, with the right leg: fondu front; on 2 beats,

Attitude effacée.

with the left leg: fondu back; on 4 beats, with the right leg: fondu to the side at 90°, plié and relevé with demi-rond in pose attitude croisée. Repeat the whole combination in the reverse direction.

3. PETITS BATTEMENTS SUR LE COU-DE-PIED. 8 measures in 2/4.

Fourteen petits battements en tournant en dehors, each on half a beat; gradually raise the arms from second position, the left arm in third position and the right arm in first position. End the turn toward corner 2 and on 1 beat, tombé front in plié on the right foot, dégagé with the left leg to the side at 45°; tour en dehors with dégagé in the direction of corner 2 (twice), each on 2 beats; end the second tour in plié on the supporting left leg and, stepping forward on the right foot, execute 1 and 2 tours, en dedans with coupé, each on 2 beats. When executing 2 tours, raise the left arm in third position and the right arm in first position.

4. GRANDS BATTEMENTS JETÉS BALANCÉS. 8 measures in 4/4.

Three grands battements jetés balancés in second position, with the right, left and right leg, each on 1 beat; hold the third battement at 90° to the count of 1 beat. Execute 3 grands battements, changing feet to the back (4 times) and 3 grands battements, changing feet to the front (4 times).

5. GRAND ADAGIO. 12 measures in 4/4.

First measure: grand plié in fifth position, right foot front; from deep plié, 2 tours sur le cou-de-pied en dehors on the left leg. Second measure: with the right leg: développé à la seconde and passé on the floor through first position into third arabesque, demi-plié. Third measure: tour lent en dehors in pose arabesque. Fourth measure: from pose arabesque, passé at 90° on half-toe in pose effacée front, a wide tombé on the right foot in plié in pose effacée back at 90° allongé; on the last beat of the measure, pas de bourrée en dehors, changing feet, end in fourth position, grande préparation for tour en dedans. Fifth measure: tour en dedans in attitude. Sixth measure: from pose attitude, grand rond de jambe en dedans on half-toe in pose croisée front. Seventh measure: a wide tombé on the right foot in plié and on the first 2 beats of the measure, execute the first half of a grand port de bras (in wide plié); on the second 2 beats of the measure, a quick transfer back onto the left leg in first arabesque at 90°. Eighth measure: step-coupé front on the right foot and grand fouetté à la seconde to first arabesque, step-coupé front on the left foot and execute the second grand fouetté à la seconde in first arabesque. Ninth measure: from pose arabesque, passé at 90° in croisé front in plié (the arms in first position) and step on the right foot in fourth arabesque at 90°. Tenth measure: tour lent en dehors in pose fourth arabesque. Eleventh measure: plié in arabesque, step back on the left foot and a half turn in fifth position on half-toe, to the left side, stopping with the back to the mirror in fifth position, left foot front, the left arm in third position, the right arm in second position, the head turned to the left; plié and pas failli with a turn toward the mirror. Twelfth measure: step on the right foot on half-toe to corner 2, then 2 tours sur le cou-de-pied en dedans, end in fifth position, left foot front, and soubresaut.

ALLEGRO

1. 16 measures in 2/4.
Three sissonnes fermées to the side, with the right, left, and right leg, changing feet to the back, each on half a beat; 2 entrechats-quatre, each on 1 beat; 2 gargouillades en dehors, each on 2 beats. Repeat on the other leg and subsequently in the reverse direction.

2. 8 measures in 4/4.
With the right leg: 2 ballonnés in pose effacée front, each on 1 beat; 2 ballonnés in pose effacée front, each on half a beat; on 1 beat, assemblé to the side; on 1 beat, with the left leg: sissonne ouverte at 45° in a small pose croisée front; 2 cabrioles at 45°, each on 1 beat; on 1 beat, assemblé. Repeat on the other leg and subsequently in the reverse direction.

3. 16 measures in 3/4 (Waltz). Tempo moderate.
In 8 measures: ballotté front, assemblé, ballotté back, assemblé. Repeat. In 8 measures: 4 ballottés front, back, front, back (without assemblé), pas failli (from the position of the last ballotté), and 2 soubresauts.

4. 8 measures in 2/4.
With the right leg front: grand échappé in second position without changing feet, grand échappé en tournant without changing feet (a full turn), each on 2 beats. Two grands changements de pieds, each on 1 beat; on 2 beats, relevé in fifth position on half-toe and entrechat-six.[1] On 2 beats, with the left leg: sissonne ouverte to the side at 45° and pas

[1] Substitute 2 grands changements de pieds with 2 entrechats-six in the men's lesson; later, relevé in fifth position half-toe and 2 tours en l'air.

couru in fifth position, left foot back (5 steps) moving in a straight line to the right side; end in fifth position, demi-plié; on 2 beats, with the right leg: sissonne ouverte to the side at 45° and pas couru in fifth position, right foot back, moving in a straight line to the left; on 2 beats, repeat sissonne ouverte and pas couru with the left leg; on 2 beats, with the right foot: glissade to the side without changing feet (right foot front) and grand assemblé to the side, brush the right foot back and raise the arms in third position.

5. 16 measures in 3/4 (Waltz).

On the diagonal from corner 6 to corner 2: pas couru (2 steps, the third step-coupé) and grand jeté in attitude croisée; execute 3 times.[2] End the third grand jeté with assemblé, royale. A big scenic sissonne in first arabesque on the right leg with a turn to the right, a big scenic run to corner 4; step into préparation for the execution of grands jetés in the other direction (corner 4 to corner 8).

6. 16 measures in 3/4 (Waltz).

On the diagonal from corner 6 to corner 2: glissade forward, without changing feet (left foot front), grand jeté in first arabesque on the right leg, assemblé, end in fifth position, left foot front; entrechat-quatre. Execute 3 times. In a straight line to the left side: with the left leg, a big sissonne tombée to the side, pas de bourrée, changing feet, glissade to the side without changing feet and grand jeté in attitude effacée. Hold the pose in attitude plié.

7. 4 measures in 4/4.

On the diagonal from corner 6 to corner 2. Préparation on the right leg, the left leg stretched in front in croisé, pointe tendue on the floor. On 2 beats, step-coupé on the left foot and grande cabriole in pose effacée front; on 2 beats, assemblé in fifth position, right foot back and entrechat-quatre; on 2 beats, glissade forward to corner 2, grande cabriole in effacé front; on 2 beats, assemblé, entrechat-quatre. Repeat glissade-cabriole. On 4 beats, sissonne tombée front to corner 2 on the right foot, 2 cabrioles in pose first arabesque, assemblé.[3]

8. 16 measures in 3/4 (Waltz).

Préparation on the left leg, the right leg stretched in front, in croisé, pointe tendue on the floor. In 8 measures: step-coupé on the right foot and grand fouetté sauté à la seconde in first arabesque. Repeat the same with step-coupé on the left and right foot, ending with pas

---

[2] All pas courus are done on the upbeat.
[3] When this is to be executed by girls, substitute the grandes cabrioles with the training step toward the grande cabriole, namely, temps levé in big poses.

failli. In 8 measures: with the right foot: pas couru forward (4 steps, the fifth step-coupé), grand assemblé croisé front, the arms in third position. Step toward corner 2 on the right foot in pose second arabesque, pointe tendue on the floor; step-coupé on the left foot on the diagonal toward corner 6 (upstage) and grand assemblé en tournant, end in fifth position, right foot front; jump onto the right foot, half-toe, in first arabesque at 90° and, holding the pose, come down in demi-plié.

9. 8 measures in 2/4.

In a straight line from side 7 to side 3: 4 emboîtés front, moving to the side in half turns, each on 1 beat; 6 emboîtés front, moving to the side in half turns, each on half a beat, and on 1 beat, assemblé front. Four emboîtés back, moving to the side (from side 3 to side 7) in half turns, each on 1 beat; 6 emboîtés back, each on half a beat; on 1 beat, assemblé back.

10. 8 measures in 2/4.

Fifth position, left foot front. Start on the right leg and execute brisé dessus-dessous (3 times), each on 2 beats; on 2 beats, pas de bourrée en tournant en dehors, changing feet and entrechat-quatre. With the right leg: on the diagonal front to corner 2: 2 tours sissonnes tombées, each tour on 2 beats; 3 tours sissonnes tombées, each tour on half a beat, and on 1 beat, step on the right foot in a big pose effacée back, left foot back, pointe tendue on the floor.

11. 8 measures in 2/4.

Thirty-two petits changements de pieds, each on half a beat.

FOURTH EXAMPLE OF EXERCISES ON POINTES

1. 8 measures in 2/4.

Sixteen échappés in second position, changing feet, each on 1 beat.

2. 16 measures in 2/4.

Four sissonnes simples, in turn with the right and left leg, changing feet to the back, each on 1 beat; double ronds de jambe en l'air en dehors with the right and left leg, each on 2 beats. Repeat from the beginning and subsequently in the reverse direction.

3. 16 measures in 2/4 (Polka).

Three gargouillades en dehors, each in 1 measure; in 1 measure: 2 pas de chat back. Two gargouillades en dehors, each in 1 measure; in 2 measures: preparation from fifth position to fifth position and tour sur le cou-de-pied en dehors. Repeat the same from the beginning and, at the end, execute 2 tours en dehors from fifth position. Execute also in the reverse direction.

4. 8 measures in 4/4.

Move on the diagonal from corner 6 to corner 2. On 1 beat, on the right leg: jeté, traveling to the side in a half turn (stop with the left shoulder toward corner 2); on 1 beat, from 45°: tour sur le cou-de-pied en dedans on the right leg, end with the left shoulder toward corner 2; open the left leg to the side at 45°. On 1 beat, jeté, traveling to the side in a half turn, on the left leg and tour sur le cou-de-pied en dehors on the left leg. Repeat jetés and tours 2 more times. On 4 beats, pas de bourrée suivi on the diagonal upstage to corner 6 (right foot front), dégagé with the left leg in the direction of corner 8, and on 4 beats, pas de bourrée suivi on the diagonal upstage to corner 4, end in demi-plié in fifth position and repeat the whole combination on the other leg.

5. 16 measures in 3/4 (Waltz).

Fifth position, right foot front. In 4 measures: with the right leg: préparation from fifth position to fourth position for tours sur le cou-de-pied en dehors and 2 tours en dehors. In 4 measures: with the left leg: préparation from fifth position to fourth position (bring the left leg to the back) for tours sur le cou-de-pied en dedans and 2 tours en dedans; end in fifth position, left foot front. In 4 measures: on the left leg, grande sissonne ouverte in third arabesque and, from 90°, bring the right leg down and brush through with the right foot to fourth position effacée, the left arm in front, the right arm in second position, préparation, and 2 tours sur le cou-de-pied en dehors on the right leg, end in fifth position, left foot front.[4] In 4 measures: on the left leg: grande sissonne ouverte in third arabesque; hold the pose, come down in demi-plié; glissade with the right foot front on the diagonal and grand pas de chat front, raise the arms in third position.

6. 16 measures in 2/4.

On 2 beats, préparation from fifth position to fifth position and 11 tours

---

[4] Such a stop after the tours en dehors is an exception to the rule, though it is fairly accepted in the senior lessons.

sur le cou-de-pied en dehors from fifth position, moving forward on the diagonal to corner 2, each on 2 beats; end in fifth position, right foot front; execute tours glissade en tournant 4 times on the diagonal front to corner 2, each on 2 beats, end in fourth position croisée, right foot back, the left arm in third position, the right arm in second position.

7. 8 measures in 2/4.

Seven tours en dehors with dégagé on the diagonal, each on 2 beats; end the seventh tour with tombé forward in pose arabesque at 45°, and on 2 beats, execute 2 tours sur le cou-de-pied en dedans.

8. PRACTICE OF TOURS CHAÎNÉS AND TOURS FOUETTÉS.

Seventh Year

At this level, the execution of all fundamental movements is carried through with finishing touches to reach the perfection of classical dance. The accompanying tempo picks up speed, in comparison with the preceding lessons.

Temps levé in attitude croisée.

First Lesson

EXERCISES AT THE BARRE

1. 16 measures in 4/4.

Two demi-pliés, each on 4 beats; on 4 beats, 1 grand plié; on 2 beats, 1 grand plié, and on 2 beats, relevé on half-toe in first, second, fourth, and fifth positions.

2. BATTEMENTS TENDUS. 24 measures in 2/4.

Four battements tendus front, each on 1 beat; 3 battements tendus jetés, each on half a beat; on 2 half beats, flic-flac en dehors, with a half

344

turn; 4 battements tendus front, 4 battements tendus to the side, each on 1 beat. Repeat the whole combination in the reverse direction; subsequently execute 6 battements tendus jetés to the side, each on half a beat; on 2 half beats, flic-flac en tournant en dedans; repeat 6 battements tendus jetés and flic-flac en tournant en dehors. Sixteen battements tendus jetés in first position, each on half a beat.

3. RONDS DE JAMBE À TERRE AND GRANDS RONDS DE JAMBE JETÉS. 12 measures in 4/4.

En dehors: 4 ronds de jambe à terre, each on 1 beat; 2 grands ronds de jambe jetés, each on 1 beat; 3 grands ronds de jambe jetés, each on half a beat; 3 ronds de jambe à terre, each on half a beat; 5 ronds de jambe à terre, each on a quarter beat; on 2 beats, trace a half circle on the floor in plié en dehors, and on 2 beats, a quick half circle on the floor en dedans. Repeat en dedans from the beginning, and in 4 measures: execute 2 port de bras in deep plié, bending the body.

4. BATTEMENTS FONDUS AT 45°. 16 measures in 2/4.

Two doubles fondus front, each on 2 beats; on 2 beats, 1 double fondu to the side, and 2 doubles fondus, each on 1 beat. Frappés to the side: 5 frappés and 2 doubles frappés, each on half a beat; 5 frappés, each on a quarter beat; on 2 beats, tombé on the working foot in fifth position back, plié, bring the left foot sur le cou-de-pied front, a full turn on half-toe away from the barre, transferring the left foot sur le cou-de-pied back, coupé on the left foot half-toe, and end with the working leg opened to the side at 45°. Repeat the whole combination in the reverse direction.

5. RONDS DE JAMBE EN L'AIR. 8 measures in 4/4.

On 2 beats, tour temps relevé en dehors; on 2 beats, 2 tours temps relevé en dehors; at the end, open the working leg to the side at 45°. Two ronds de jambe en l'air en dehors, each on 1 beat; on 2 beats, 2 doubles ronds de jambe en l'air (on the grace note before each beat); 5 doubles ronds de jambe en l'air and again 5 doubles ronds de jambe en l'air, each on a quarter beat. On 2 beats, développé to the side at 90°, and on 2 beats, 2 ronds de jambe en l'air at 90°. Repeat from the beginning en dedans.

6. PETITS BATTEMENTS SUR LE COU-DE-PIED AND BATTEMENTS BATTUS. 8 measures in 4/4.

Twelve battements battus front in épaulement effacé, each on a quarter beat; on 1 beat, a small pose effacée front, pointe tendue on the floor in plié; on 2 beats, passé at 45° on half-toe in a small pose effacée back, in plié (the working leg remains at 45°), and on 2 beats, 2 tours sur le cou-de-pied en dedans; at the end, open the working leg to the side at 45°. Twelve petits battements, each on a quarter beat; on 1 beat, développé in écarté back at 90°; on 2 beats, a turn fouetté en dehors, again in pose écartée back, and on 2 beats, demi-rond in attitude effacée allongée. Repeat from the beginning in the reverse direction.

7. BATTEMENTS DÉVELOPPÉS. 8 measures in 4/4 or 32 measures in 3/4 (Waltz).

First measure: grand rond de jambe développé en dehors, on half-toe. Second measure: a quick passé through first position demi-plié, raising the working leg front at 90°, then relevé on half-toe, on the first beat; on the second beat, a half turn toward the barre, come down in plié; on the third beat, passé through first position in demi-plié, raise the working leg to the front at 90° and relevé on half-toe; on the fourth beat, a half turn away from the barre, come down in plié. Third measure: passé at 90° in effacé front on half-toe, développé tombé, step back in pose effacée front at 90°. Fourth measure: a turn fouetté en dehors in pose effacée front and demi-rond in pose écartée back. Repeat the whole combination en dedans.

8. GRANDS BATTEMENTS JETÉS. 16 measures in 2/4.

Two grands battements front, 2 grands battements (smooth, with a quick développé), rising on half-toe. Execute the same with the left leg to the back, with the right leg to the side and 4 grands battements in écarté back, each on 1 beat. Repeat the whole combination in the reverse direction.[1]

EXERCISES IN THE CENTER

1. SMALL ADAGIO AND BATTEMENTS TENDUS. 8 measures in 4/4.

First measure: grand plié in fifth position, right foot front; from deep plié, 1½ tours sur le cou-de-pied en dedans, end in first arabesque to side 7. Second measure: lean the body slightly downward (penché) and

[1] In the senior grades, the seventh and eighth years, the exercises at the barre are reduced to only one example, described herewith. It is certainly up to the experienced teacher conducting the lesson to choose the construction of each exercise at the barre, which will in turn reflect the construction of the exercises in the center of the studio. The construction of each lesson proposes 4 set examples of exercises in the center of the studio.

turn en dedans in first arabesque to corner 2; raise the right arm to the height of the third (arm) position and straighten the body. Third measure: lean the body slightly downward (penché) and bring the left leg in pose écartée back. Fourth measure: a wide tombé on the left foot and with the right leg, fondu at 90° in pose écartée front, tombé on the right foot and 2 tours sur le cou-de-pied en dedans; end in pose attitude effacée. Fifth measure: from pose attitude, carry the left leg to the side and to croisé front, come up on half-toe, and bring the working leg down in fourth position croisée, grande préparation for tours en dedans. Sixth measure: 1½ tours à la seconde en dedans, end in fourth arabesque in plié. Seventh measure: step back on the right foot, and, with the left leg, développé to the side and demi-rond in pose attitude croisée. Eighth measure: on 3 beats, renversé en dehors (without changing feet in the pas de bourrée) and, on the fourth beat, stay in fifth position, demi-plié, left foot back. Battements tendus and tours: 8 measures in 4/4. With the left foot: 4 battements tendus in pose fourth arabesque; with the right foot: 2 battements tendus in a small pose effacée front and 2 battements tendus again in the same pose but with a turn to corner 4; 4 battements tendus with the left foot in pose fourth arabesque (facing corner 4), 2 battements tendus with the right foot in a small pose effacée front to corner 6 and 2 battements tendus to corner 8. Face side 1, and, with the right foot to the side, 14 battements tendus jetés, each on half a beat; on 2 beats, flic-flac en tournant en dedans, ending in fourth position, préparation for tours sur le cou-de-pied en dehors; in 1 measure: execute 1 and again 1 tour; in 1 measure: 2 and again 2 tours en dehors, to the right side.

2. BATTEMENTS FONDUS. 4 measures in 4/4.

With the right leg: 2 battements fondus at 45° in a small pose effacée front, each on 1 beat; on 2 beats, 1 battement fondu at 90° in effacé front, coupé; on 2 beats, with the left leg: grand fouetté effacé en dedans; on 2 beats, carry the working leg to the side at 90°; on 4 beats, plié and tour en dehors in attitude croisée, coupé, and with the right foot: 7 frappés to the side, each on half a beat. Repeat from the beginning in the reverse direction, with tour in pose croisée front and substitute frappés with petits battements sur le cou-de-pied.

3. GRANDS BATTEMENTS JETÉS. 4 measures in 4/4.

Four grands battements in pose croisée front, to the side and in pose third arabesque, each on 1 beat. On 4 beats, with the left leg: grand échappé in second position and 2 tours à la seconde en dehors.

4. GRAND ADAGIO. 8 measures in 4/4.

First measure: on the diagonal to corner 2, on the right foot: tours chaînés, end in first arabesque at 90° on the right leg, in plié. Second measure: tour lent en dedans in arabesque, plié. Third measure: passé at 90°, with a turn en dedans to corner 6 in pose croisée front, come up on half-toe, chassé, come down in plié on the left leg in pose third arabesque, passé at 90°, with a turn en dehors to corner 2 in pose effacée front, come up on half-toe, chassé, end in fourth position effacée, grande préparation for tours en dedans. Fourth measure: 2 tours in pose attitude effacée. Fifth measure: a preparatory relevé on half-toe in attitude effacée and on the first 2 beats of the measure, grand fouetté en tournant en dedans in pose third arabesque; on the third and fourth beats, carry the left leg to the side and come up on half-toe. Sixth measure: grand fouetté en tournant en dedans in first arabesque facing corner 2 and step back in fifth position, half-toe, left foot front. Seventh measure: balancé in a small pose second arabesque on the left and on the right foot, step on half-toe on the left foot and 2 tours sur le cou-de-pied en dedans, end the tours in a big pose croisée front. Eighth measure: from pose croisée, tombé, grand assemblé in écarté front, relevé in fifth position, half-toe and entrechat-six.

ALLEGRO[2]

1. 16 measures in 2/4.

Two échappés battus, sissonne ouverte battue to the side at 45°, assemblé, 2 brisés to the front. Repeat 4 times, in turn with the right and left leg. Execute also in the reverse direction.

2. 8 measures in 2/4.

With the right leg: sissonne ouverte en tournant en dehors at 45° in a small pose croisée front, assemblé; with the left leg: sissonne ouverte en tournant en dedans in a small pose croisée back, assemblé,[3] 3 ballonnés battus to the side, with the right leg, moving forward, assemblé. Repeat the whole combination on the other leg.

3. 16 measures in 3/4 (Waltz).

With the right leg: grande sissonne ouverte in attitude croisée, assemblé, sissonne renversée en dehors, glissade to the side without changing

---

[2] All new steps are studied separately and thereafter added to a combination.

[3] For the men, it is recommended that the sissonnes ouvertes be executed with a double turn.

feet and grand jeté to the side on the right leg, passé left foot through first position, ending in attitude croisée (right leg), assemblé, entrechat-six. Repeat the whole combination on the other leg and subsequently in the reverse direction.

4. 8 measures in 2/4.

With the right leg: sissonne simple, end in effacé front and grand fouetté sauté effacé en dehors, failli-coupé and grand jeté in third arabesque, glissade to the side without changing feet, a small cabriole fermée to the side with the left and right leg. With the left leg: sissonne simple, end in effacé back and grand fouetté sauté effacé en dedans, failli (traveling backward); on the right leg: sissonne tombée effacée front, 2 cabrioles at 45° in pose seconde arabesque, assemblé.

5. 16 measures in 3/4 (Waltz).

On the diagonal from corner 6 to corner 2, starting on the right foot: pas couru (4 steps, the fifth, step-coupé), grand jeté in attitude croisée, assemblé, entrechat-six (the arms in third position). Repeat on the left foot on the diagonal to corner 8 and on the right foot again to corner 2. At the end, execute tours chaînés to corner 2 and end the chaînés in fifth position, right foot back.

6. 4 measures in 4/4.

In a straight line from side 7 to side 3, with the right leg: 2 sauts de basque starting with step-coupé, each on 4 beats (execute the saut de basque on 2 beats, and on 2 beats remain in demi-plié, in the concluding position of the jump). Two sauts de basque in succession, each on 2 beats, sissonne ouverte to the side, pas de bourrée en tournant en dehors, changing feet and turn in fifth position on half-toe (détourné).

7. 4 measures in 4/4.

On the diagonal upstage from corner 2 to corner 6: 2 jetés entrelacés with a wide step, each on 4 beats (on 2 beats, 2 jetés, and on 2 beats, hold the concluding pose in first arabesque, demi-plié). Three jetés entrelacés in succession, each on 2 beats; end with assemblé.

8. 8 measures in 2/4.

On the diagonal from corner 6 to corner 2, starting on the right leg: 12 emboîtés en tournant in half turns, traveling front, each on half a beat; step-coupé on the right foot to corner 2 and grand assemblé en tournant to the right side.[4] Execute starting on the left leg on the diagonal to corner 8.

---

[4] For the men, execute grand assemblé battu en tournant.

9. Musical measure 2/4.

Tours sissonnes tombées on the diagonal in effacé and in croisé, each tour on 1 beat or on half a beat.

10. 8 measures in 2/4.

Seven entrechats-quatre and 1 royale, in turn on the right and left foot and 16 petits changements de pieds, each on half a beat.[5]

FIRST EXAMPLE OF EXERCISES ON POINTES[6]

1. 16 measures in 2/4.

Two échappés in second position, changing feet, 2 échappés en tournant in half turns, each on 1 beat; 3 sus-sous, traveling forward, each on half a beat, and on 2 beats, double échappé in second position, changing feet. Repeat on the other leg and execute 2 more times with sus-sous to the back.

2. 8 measures in 2/4 (pizzicatto).

Préparation: left foot back in croisé, pointe tendue on the floor. On the upbeat, demi-plié, coupé on pointes on the left foot; with the right leg: double rond de jambe en l'air en dehors, end on the first beat in demi-plié on the left leg. On the second, third, and fourth beats, repeat the double rond de jambe en l'air en dehors 3 times, without coming down in fifth position; 2 jetés en tournant in a straight line, moving to the side in half turns, each on 1 beat; on 1 beat, double rond de jambe en l'air en dehors; on 1 beat, pas de bourrée dessous en tournant, end in demi-plié on the right foot, the left foot sur le cou-de-pied back, coupé, and repeat the combination once more. Execute also in the reverse direction.

3. 16 measures in 3/4 (Waltz).

Préparation: left foot front in croisé, pointe tendue on the floor. In 4 measures: step-coupé on the left foot and grand pas de chat front; grande sissonne ouverte with the right leg in effacé front, and without coming

---

[5] Each lesson ends with a port de bras and bending of the body.

[6] One should not be limited to the construction of set examples. It is indispensable to cover the study of the ballet repertoire by learning parts or full variations and codas from the old classical works and from contemporary ballets, with due regard for the individuality and possibilities of each participant.

off pointes, grand rond in effacé back, end with pas de bourrée en dehors, changing feet. In 4 measures: grande sissonne ouverte in fourth arabesque, on the right leg, plié-relevé, end in fifth position. In 4 measures: with the right leg, grande sissonne ouverte in écarté back; with the left leg, préparation from fifth position to fifth position and 2 tours sur le cou-de-pied en dehors. In 4 measures: starting on the right foot to corner 2, 6 tours chaînés, step on the right foot in pose croisée, the left foot back, pointe tendue on the floor, the right arm in third position, the left arm in second position.

4. 8 measures in 2/4.

In 6 measures: on the diagonal from corner 6 to corner 2: pas de bourrée suivi, the right arm in third position, the left arm in second position allongée. In 2 measures: pas failli in fourth position, préparation for tours sur le cou-de-pied en dehors and 2 tours to the right side, end in fourth position, the arms in the position of third arabesque.

5. 8 measures in 2/4.

Préparation: left foot back, in croisé, pointe tendue on the floor. On the upbeat, dégagé with the left foot to the side and pas de bourrée dessus en tournant, end on the first beat; on the second beat, with the right foot: pas de bourrée dessous en tournant; on the third and fourth beats, tour en dehors with dégagé on the left leg (twice). Repeat the combination 4 times, moving on the diagonal from corner 6 to corner 2.

6. 16 measures in 2/4.

Entrechat-quatre, sissonne simple, changing the foot to the back, each on 1 beat. Repeat on the other leg. Four sissonnes simples, changing the foot to the back, each on 1 beat. Repeat from the beginning and execute once more with sissonnes simples, changing the foot to the front.

Pose arabesque éffacée on pointes.

Second Lesson

EXERCISES IN THE CENTER

1. SMALL ADAGIO AND BATTEMENTS TENDUS. 8 measures in 4/4.

First measure: grand plié in second position with port de bras; from deep plié, tour en dehors in pose écartée back, on the right leg. Second measure: from pose écartée, turn into pose first arabesque, facing corner 2. Third measure: lean the body all the way down (penché) and straighten the body back into the initial position of arabesque. Fourth measure: coupé, on the left foot half-toe; with the right leg: grand fouetté effacé en dehors, a quick turn en dehors on half-toe with the passé at 90° (on half a beat), and a second fouetté effacé en dehors. Fifth measure: step back on the right foot half-toe; with the left leg: développé in pose effacée front and grand rond de jambe to the side and to the back. Sixth measure: coming up on half-toe, a half turn on the supporting leg en dehors (on the first beat of the measure) with the back to side 1 (mirror); at the end of the turn, the left leg is in front at 90°, and execute a grand rond de jambe to the side and to the back. Seventh measure: coming up on half-toe, make a half turn en dehors facing side 1 (mirror); at the end of the turn, the left leg is in front at 90°; a demi-rond to the side and plié on the supporting leg. Eighth measure: come up on half-toe on the left foot and execute a tour à la seconde en dedans, raising the arms in third position, end the tour in pose seconde arabesque at 90°, in plié.

Battements tendus and tours: 8 measures in 4/4. With the right foot: 4 battements tendus in a small pose croisée front, each on 1 beat; 6 battements tendus jetés, each on half a beat, and on 2 half beats, flic-flac en tournant en dedans, ending in a small pose croisée back. Repeat battements tendus and battements tendus jetés in croisé back, with flic-flac en dehors, ending to the side at 45°. Four battements tendus to the side, each on 1 beat; 7 battements tendus jetés, each on half a beat, and in 2 measures: from second position, 1 tour, 2 tours and 2 tours sur le cou-de-pied en dehors.

2. BATTEMENTS FONDUS AT 45°. 8 measures in 4/4.

Three doubles fondus to the side, each on 2 beats; on 2 beats, from the preceding position, when the working leg is extended to the side at 45°, 2 tours sur le cou-de-pied en dehors, end to the side at 45°; 7 frappés to the side, each on half a beat; on 2 beats, développé in pose effacée front at 90°; on 1 beat, a quick turn fouetté en dehors in pose effacée front; on 1 beat, bring the working leg down in fifth position back, and subsequently repeat the whole combination in the opposite direction.

3. RONDS DE JAMBE EN L'AIR AND RENVERSÉ. 4 measures in 4/4.

On 4 beats, développé front, demi-rond de jambe to the side and a quick passé through first position in attitude croisée; on 4 beats, renversé en dehors, ending that step on the third beat of the measure; on the fourth beat, come up on half-toe, while opening the working leg to the side at 45°. Seven ronds de jambe en l'air en dehors, each on half a beat; on 2 beats, développé in attitude croisée, and on 2 beats, renversé en dehors. Repeat from the beginning en dedans.

4. GRAND ADAGIO. 8 measures in 4/4.

First measure: grand plié in fifth position, right foot front; from deep plié, 2 tours sur le cou-de-pied en dehors on the left leg, end à la seconde. Second measure: tour lent en dehors à la seconde. Third measure: plié on the supporting leg, and with a wide step transfer the weight of the body onto the right foot, half-toe, lift the left leg to the side at 90° and execute grand fouetté en tournant en dehors in pose croisée front. Fourth measure: come down in fourth position croisée, grande préparation for tours en dedans and execute 2 tours in first arabesque. Fifth measure: on the first 2 beats of the measure, passé through first position with the right foot front in pose croisée back, the left foot pointe tendue on the floor; on the second 2 beats, grand port de bras, ending in fourth position, grande préparation for tours en dedans. Sixth measure: 2 tours in pose croisée front. Seventh measure: from pose croisée, grand rond in écarté front and in attitude effacée; end in fifth position, left foot front. Eighth measure: on the left leg: 6 jumps à terre en tournant en dedans in first arabesque (execute 2 full turns on the spot), and immediately 2 tours tire-bouchon en dedans, raising the left arm in third position and the right arm in first position.

ALLEGRO

1. 16 measures in 2/4.

Four assemblés battus, in turn with the right and left leg; gargouillade en dehors, 2 entrechats-quatre; repeat on the other leg and subsequently in the reverse direction.

2. 4 measures in 4/4.

With the right leg: double rond de jambe en l'air sauté en dehors and pas de bourrée dessous en tournant; with the left leg: double rond de jambe en l'air sauté en dedans and pas de bourrée dessus en tournant; on the right leg: 2 sissonnes fermées battues in a small pose croisée back, grande sissonne soubresaut in attitude croisée, a short coupé on the left foot, and, with the right leg, grand assemblé to the side, end in fifth position, right foot back. Repeat from the beginning on the other leg, and subsequently in the reverse direction.

3. 16 measures in 3/4 (Waltz).

With the right leg: grande sissonne ouverte en tournant en dehors in pose croisée front, assemblé and grande sissonne ouverte en tournant en dehors à la seconde, assemblé; on the left leg: sissonne tombée effacée front and grand assemblé en tournant to corner 8, end in fifth position, right foot front; grande sissonne ouverte in third arabesque on the left leg, the right leg moves back during the jump, assemblé; grande sissonne en tournant en dedans (to the left side) in attitude croisée, assemblé and grande sissonne ouverte en tournant en dedans à la seconde, assemblé. With the right leg: sissonne tombée to the side (small passing jump), pas de bourrée, and 2 entrechats-six.[1]

4. 8 measures in 2/4.

In a straight line from side 7 to side 3, starting on the right leg: 2 sauts de basque with step coupé, 1 saut de basque with chassé, end with assemblé to the side and royale; in a straight line from side 3 to side 7, starting on the left leg: 3 sauts de basque with step-coupé with opposite turns of the body in the air (to the left side), end with assemblé back, entrechat-quatre. Each saut de basque is done on 2 beats.

5. 32 measures in 3/4 (Waltz).

Move on the straight line from corner 8 to corner 2. Fifth position, left foot front. Brisé forward, left arm in second position, right arm in first position, a small pas de chat front, transfer the right arm in second position, the left arm in first position. Repeat. Glissade to the side, without changing feet, grand jeté to the side on the right leg, passé with the left foot front and step in attitude croisée, the right arm in third position, the left arm in second position, sissonne tombée en tournant en dehors and cabriole fermée at 45° on the left leg in fourth arabesque. Repeat from the beginning. From corner 2, turn to the right and moving in a straight line to corner 4, through side 3, execute glissade, grand jeté in pose second arabesque, in turn on the right and left leg (4 times in succession), reaching corner 4, turn the body on the diagonal facing corner 8 and again execute glissade, grand jeté in second arabesque (3 times in succession); sissonne tombée in effacé front, on the left leg, coupé and grand jeté in attitude effacée.

6. 16 measures in 3/4 (Waltz).

Préparation: left foot front, in croisée, pointe tendue on the floor. In 4 measures: step-coupé on the left foot and with the right leg: grande cabriole in pose effacée front, assemblé, end in fifth position, right foot

---

[1] For the men, substitute with relevé in fifth position on half-toe and 2 tours en l'air to the left side.

back, entrechat-quatre. In 4 measures: glissade forward to corner 2, without changing feet; with the right leg, grande cabriole in pose effacée front, assemblé, entrechat-quatre. In 4 measures: repeat glissade, grande cabriole, temps levé in pose effacée, tombé, and a quick pas de bourrée en dehors, changing feet. In 4 measures: step on the right foot in first arabesque, left foot, pointe tendue on the floor, facing corner 2 and moving upstage on the diagonal to corner 6, execute chassé and grand assemblé en tournant.

7. 16 measures in 3/4 (Waltz).

On the diagonal upstage from corner 2 to corner 6: 3 jetés entrelacés, starting with a wide step in pose first arabesque, each in 2 measures; in 2 measures: from pose arabesque, fall back on the left leg in plié and 1 tour en dehors on the right leg with dégagé in first arabesque at 90°. In 4 measures: a big scenic sissonne on the left leg in second arabesque, a big scenic run to side 1, step on the right foot in pose third arabesque, left foot pointe tendue on the floor. In 4 measures: starting with a wide step upstage, 2 jetés entrelacés to side 5 with épaulement croisé, the arms in third position.

8. 16 measures in 2/4.

Fifth position, right foot front. With the left foot, entrechat-cinq back, assemblé; with the right foot, entrechat-trois back, assemblé; with the right foot, entrechat-cinq back, assemblé; with the left foot, entrechat-trois back, pas de bourrée en tournant en dehors, changing feet. Repeat from the beginning on the other foot and subsequently in the reverse direction. The combination is performed to a quick tempo.

9. 4 measures in 2/4.

Sixteen petits changements de pieds, each on half a beat.

SECOND EXAMPLE OF EXERCISES ON POINTES

1. 16 measures in 2/4.

Two échappés in second position, changing feet, each on 1 beat, starting on the right and left leg, in turn; with the right foot: 3 sissonnes simples en tournant, changing feet to the right side, each on half a beat. Repeat from the beginning on the other leg. Four double ronds de jambe en l'air en dehors, each on 2 beats, in turn with the right and left leg. Repeat again with ronds de jambe en l'air en dedans.

2. 32 measures in 3/4 (Waltz).

In 8 measures: jeté on the right leg in attitude croisée, the right arm in third position, the left arm in second position; plié-relevé in attitude; plié-relevé in pose fourth arabesque, plié and pas de bourrée en tournant en dehors, end in demi-plié on the left leg; dégagé with the right foot in effacé front, pointe tendue on the floor. In 8 measures: with the right leg, double rond de jambe en l'air en dehors in épaulement effacé (2 times in succession) each time rising on pointes and ending the ronds de jambe in effacé front, pointe tendue on the floor; double rond de jambe en l'air again in effacé; a wide tombé on the right foot and 2 tours sur le cou-de-pied en dedans. In 8 measures: jeté back on the right leg in pose croisée front at 90°; 2 pliés-relevés in pose croisée; plié and pas de bourrée en tournant en dedans, changing feet. In 8 measures, starting on the left foot: glissade to the side (jumping) without changing feet; grand assemblé to the side; grande sissonne ouverte in attitude croisée, on the left leg; on the right leg: sissonne ouverte in effacé back at 45°; a wide tombé and 2 tours sur le cou-de-pied en dehors.

3. 16 measures in 2/4.

In 2 measures: on the diagonal from corner 6 to corner 2, starting on the right foot: pas de bourrée suivi, end in fifth position, demi-plié, right foot front. In 2 measures: 5 jumps à terre en tournant to the right side in first arabesque on the right leg, and tour tire-bouchon en dedans; raise the arms in third position; end in plié on the right leg, the left foot in a small pose croisée front, pointe tendue on the floor. In the following 12 measures: repeat the combination, starting on the left foot facing corner 8; thereafter on the right and left foot, facing corners 2 and 8.

4. 8 measures in 6/8.

On the first beat of the first measure, step on the right foot on pointes in a small pose in second arabesque and execute 4 jumps on pointes, each on 1 beat; on the sixth beat, come down in demi-plié and simultaneously bend and bring forward the left leg in effacé front. In the following measure: execute similar jumps on the left leg. Subsequently, in 1 measure: execute jumps en tournant en dedans on the right leg, as well as in pose second arabesque, and in 1 measure: step on the left foot to the side, on pointes, 2 jumps in a small pose croisée front with the right leg half bent to the front at 45°, demi-plié in fifth position and turn on pointes (détourné on pointes) end in fifth position, demi-plié. Repeat from the beginning on the other leg.

5. 8 measures in 4/4.

In 2 measures: on the diagonal from corner 6 to corner 2, starting on the right leg, 6 emboîtés front on pointes, en tournant in half turns, each on 1 beat; on 2 beats, come down in fifth position, demi-plié. In 2 measures: pas de bourrée suivi to corner 2, right foot front, then, standing on pointes, bring the left foot into fifth position front on the last half beat of the second measure, and repeat from the beginning on the other leg, toward corner 8. The combination is performed to a quick tempo.

6. 16 measures in 2/4.

On the diagonal from corner 6 to corner 2, execute 1 tour en dedans with coupé (3 times in succession), each tour on 2 beats, and on 2 beats, 2 tours en dedans with coupé. Repeat 4 times.

7. PRACTICE OF TOURS CHAÎNÉS AND TOURS FOUETTÉS.

Instructor Lydia Michaelovna Tiuntina teaching the seventh year class.

Third Lesson

EXERCISES IN THE CENTER

1. SMALL ADAGIO AND BATTEMENTS TENDUS. 8 measures in 4/4.

First measure: grand plié in first position; from deep plié, tour à la seconde en dehors, on the left leg. Second measure: plié with the leg extended à la seconde and tour en dehors in attitude. Third measure: from pose attitude, turn en dehors to corner 6, in the pose effacée front; end the turn facing side 1, carrying the working leg from pose effacée to the side. Fourth measure: plié on the supporting leg and tour en dedans in pose croisée front. Fifth measure: a wide tombé on the right foot and grand port de bras, ending in fourth position, grande préparation for tour en dehors. Sixth measure: tour in third arabesque. Seventh measure: on the upbeat, come up on half-toe on the supporting leg, in attitude croisée, and start a grand port de bras from deep plié, on the first beat of the measure; on the second beat, after the full circular bend of the body to the left side, transfer the body onto the left leg in fourth arabesque at 90°; on the third and fourth beats, demi-rond to the side. Eighth measure: grand fouetté en tournant en dedans in pose attitude croisée allongée and step back in fifth position on half-toe. Battements tendus and tours: 8 measures in 4/4. With the right foot: 4 battements tendus doubles (lowering the heel in second position at each battement), each on 2 beats; 4 battements tendus to the side, each on 1 beat, and 7 battements tendus jetés en tournant en dedans, each on half a beat. In 2 measures: on the right leg, 1 and 2 tours sur le cou-de-pied en dedans from second position; end in fourth position, préparation for tours en dehors, left foot front. In 2 measures: 2 tours sur le cou-de-pied en dehors, end in fourth position; plié, with the right leg to the back in fourth position and, transferring the weight of the body onto the right leg, execute 2½ tours en dedans.

2. BATTEMENTS FONDUS AT 45°. 4 measures in 4/4.

Two doubles fondus in a small pose croisée front, 2 doubles fondus to the side, each on 2 beats; 3 ronds de jambe en l'air en dehors, each on half a beat; 2 doubles ronds de jambe en l'air en dehors, ending in demi-plié, each on 1 beat; on 2 beats, développé in third arabesque, and on 2 beats, renversé en dehors. Execute in the opposite direction.

3. GRANDS BATTEMENTS JETÉS. 8 measures in 2/4.

With the right leg: 2 grands battements in effacée front; 2 grands battements (smooth, through a quick développé), in effacé front, each on 1 beat. With the left leg, repeat the same in effacé back, and with the right leg to the side, end in fifth position, left foot front. Sissonne tombée on the left leg in fourth position croisée, préparation for tours sur le cou-de-pied en dedans; 2 tours en dedans, end in first arabesque at 90°.

4. GRAND ADAGIO. 8 measures in 4/4.

Préparation on the right leg, left foot back in croisé, pointe tendue on the floor. On the upbeat, demi-plié and dégagé with the left foot to the side. First measure: pas de bourrée dessus-dessous en tournant, end in fifth position, préparation for tours sur le cou-de-pied en dedans, 2 tours en dedans on the right leg, end à la seconde. Second measure: grand fouetté en tournant en dedans in pose attitude effacée and grand fouetté en tournant en dedans in first arabesque, facing side 3. Third measure: step back on the left foot; with the right leg, développé in pose écartée back, plié, and pas de bourrée en tournant en dehors; end in fourth position, grande préparation for tours en dehors. Fourth measure: 2 tours in third arabesque; on the last half beat of the measure, a short plié on the left leg, come up on half-toe, and throw the right leg to the side, in the manner of a grand battement. Fifth measure: grand fouetté en tournant en dehors in pose croisée front, relevé on half-toe in croisé and bring the leg down in fourth position, grande préparation for tours en dedans. Sixth measure: 2 tours in second arabesque, end in fifth position, left foot front; on the last half beat of the measure, execute a quick développé with the left leg in croisé front, on half-toe. Seventh measure: a wide tombé, chassé front, end in fourth position, grande préparation for tours en dehors; 2 tours tire-bouchon en dehors, with the arms in third position, end in fifth position, right foot back. Eighth measure: with the left leg, sissonne tombée front in a wide fourth position effacée, coupé with the right foot, and grand jeté in attitude effacée; at the end, rise slowly on half-toe, in pose attitude effacée.

ALLEGRO

1. 16 measures in 2/4.

Two assemblés to the side, with the right and left leg, changing feet to the front, 2 jetés battus to the side with the right and left leg, end in sur le cou-de-pied back position, each on 1 beat. Repeat 4 times, then a short coupé and repeat from the beginning in the reverse direction.

2. 16 measures in 2/4.

Fifth position, right foot front. A small sissonne tombée croisée front en tournant en dehors, to the right side and a small cabriole fermée on the right leg in third arabesque, 2 entrechats-quatres. Execute 3 times. With the left foot: glissade to the side, without changing feet and grand assemblé battu; with the right foot: entrechat-cinq back, assemblé. Repeat from the beginning on the other leg. Each jump is done on 1 beat.

3. 16 measures in 3/4 (Waltz).

On the diagonal from corner 6 to corner 2, with the right leg: a small sissonne tombée effacée front and a small cabriole fermée in second arabesque, end in fifth position, left foot front. With the left leg: repeat the same sissonne tombée and cabriole fermée. With the right leg: sissonne tombée effacée front, 2 cabrioles at 45° in second arabesque and pas de bourrée en dehors, changing feet. On the right leg: 2 jetés renversés en dehors; with the left leg: sissonne tombée front in fourth position croisée, coupé with the right foot and grand jeté on the left leg in attitude croisée (en tournant, to the left side), coupé and a second grand jeté in attitude croisée; end with assemblé.

4. 16 measures in 3/4 (Waltz).

Fifth position, left foot front. On the diagonal from corner 6 to corner 2, with the right foot: glissade forward, without changing feet, grand jeté in first arabesque, assemblé, end in fifth position, left foot back, entrechat-six. Execute 3 times, but end the last assemblé in fifth position with the left foot front and entrechat-six. In a straight line, to the left side: glissade, without changing feet, grand jeté in first arabesque on the left leg, then, without dropping the working leg, grand jeté in first arabesque on the right leg and again on the left leg; both times, turn the body during the jump, in a straight line to the right and to the left side.

5. 4 measures in 4/4.

On the diagonal upstage from corner 2 to corner 6: 2 jetés entrelacés, starting with a wide step back; 2 jetés entrelacés with chassé, in first arabesque; failli-coupé, step, grand assemblé croisé front, turn in fifth position half-toe to the right side (détourné) and 6 tours chaînés to corner 2, end in first arabesque demi-plié, at 90°.

6. 8 measures in 4/4.

In 2 measures: on the diagonal from corner 6 to corner 2, with the right leg: 2 sauts de basque with step-coupé, 2 sauts de basque with chassé, raise the arms in third position during the jumps. In 2 measures: a big scenic sissonne in first arabesque, with a turn to the right, a big scenic run to corner 4, step in fifth position, left foot front. In 4 measures: on the diagonal from corner 4 to corner 8: tour sissonne tombée, repeat 4 times, each tour sissonne on 2 beats; 6 tours sissonne tombée, each on 1 beat; 2 tours sissonne tombée, each on half a beat and step on the left foot in pose effacée back, right foot back, pointe tendue on the floor.

7. 8 measures in 2/4.

In a straight line from side 7 to side 3: 4 jetés battus en tournant, traveling to the side in half turns, each on 1 beat; 6 emboîtés front en tournant in half turns, traveling to the side, each on half a beat; assemblé to the side; 2 brisés front, each on 1 beat; 3 brisés front, each on half a beat; 2 brisés back, each on 1 beat; 3 brisés back, each on half a beat.

8. 8 measures in 2/4.

Seven temps levés in first position, 7 in second position and 16 petits changements de pieds, each on half a beat.

THIRD EXAMPLE OF EXERCISES ON POINTES

1. 16 measures in 2/4.

Two échappés in second position, changing feet, each on 1 beat; 3 échappés, each on half a beat; 2 sus-sous, moving forward, each on 1 beat; 3 sus-sous, each on half a beat. Repeat on the other leg and subsequently in the reverse direction.

2. 32 measures in 3/4 (Waltz).

In 8 measures: on the right leg to corner 2: grande sissonne ouverte in first arabesque, plié-relevé; grande sissonne ouverte in first arabesque, plié-relevé with passé at 90° and a turn of the left shoulder to corner 2 in pose écartée front; end pas de bourrée en tournant en dedans, changing feet. In 4 measures: with the right foot: pas de bourrée suivi in croisé front. In 4 measures: with the left leg to the side: grande sissonne ouverte à la seconde, plié on the supporting right leg and tour tire-bouchon en dedans, raise the right arm in third position, the left arm in first position. Repeat from the beginning on the other leg.

3. 16 measures in 3/4 (Waltz).

Fifth position, right foot front. In 2 measures: with the left leg: grande sissonne ouverte in pose écartée front, passé through first position with the left foot front and turning en dedans to corner 4, lift the left leg; simultaneously come up on pointes and turn in pose attitude croisée, the left arm in third position, the right arm in first position (elementary grand fouetté en dedans). In 2 measures: from attitude, throw the left leg with passé at 90° swiftly in pose écartée front, come down in fifth position, demi-plié, left foot front and turn in fifth position on pointes (détourné), raising the arms in third position. In 4 measures: repeat from the beginning. In 4 measures: starting on the right foot back, pas de bourrée suivi in a straight line to the right, end in fourth position croisée, left foot front. In 4 measures: 2 tours sur le cou-de-pied en dehors, end in fourth position; 2 tours en dehors, end in fourth position.

4. 16 measures in 2/4.

On the diagonal from corner 6 to corner 2, execute tour en dehors with dégagé, 3 times in succession, each tour on 2 beats, and on 2 beats, 2 tours en dehors with dégagé. Repeat 4 times.

5. 8 measures in 2/4.

Préparation from fifth position in fifth position and 15 tours in succession sur le cou-de-pied en dehors from fifth position, traveling forward on the diagonal, each tour on 1 beat.

6. PRACTICE OF TOURS CHAÎNÉS AND TOURS FOUETTÉS.

Attitude, on half-toe, at the barre.

Fourth Lesson

EXERCISES IN THE CENTER

1. SMALL ADAGIO AND BATTEMENTS TENDUS. 8 measures in 4/4.

First measure: grand plié in fifth position with port de bras, right foot front; from deep plié, 2 tours sur le cou-de-pied en dehors on the left leg, end in pose écartée front at 90°, the left arm in third position, the right arm in first position. Second measure: tour lent en dehors in pose écartée. Third measure: passé with the right leg at 90°, rising on half-toe to pose in third arabesque, in plié; passé at 90°, rising on half-toe to pose in effacé front, in plié. Fourth measure: passé at 90°, rising on half-toe to pose in third arabesque, in plié and tour en dehors in attitude. Fifth measure: renversé en dehors and développé with the left leg to the side. Sixth measure: relevé on half-toe and demi-rond in pose effacée front, in plié; relevé on half-toe and grand rond en dehors in pose effacée back, in plié. Seventh measure: pas de bourrée ballotté in effacé, starting to corner 2, to the front, to the back, to the front, to the back. Eighth measure: step on the left foot, half-toe and execute tour en dehors in pose effacée front.

Battements tendus: 4 measures in 4/4. With the right foot: 4 battements tendus in a big pose effacée front; with the left foot: 4 battements tendus in a big pose effacée back; with the right foot: 4 battements tendus in a big pose écartée back, each on 1 beat, and 8 battements tendus jetés in écarté back, each on half a beat. In 2 measures: with the left leg (on the right leg): sissonne ouverte at 45°, on half-toe, in croisée front, come down in fourth position, préparation for tour sur le cou-de-pied en dedans; 1 tour en dedans to the left side, end in fourth position, right foot front, then 2 tours en dedans to the right side, end in fourth position, left foot front and 2 tours en dehors to the right side.

2. BATTEMENTS FONDUS AT 90°. 4 measures in 4/4.

With the right leg: 2 battements fondus in a big pose effacée front; with the left leg: 2 battements fondus in first arabesque, each on 2 beats; 2 battements fondus to the side at 90°, each on 2 beats; on 4 beats, plié and tour en dehors in fourth arabesque. Repeat from the beginning on the other leg and subsequently in the reverse direction with tour in croisé front.

3. GRANDS BATTEMENTS JETÉS BALANCÉS IN SECOND POSITION. 8 measures in 2/4.

Three grands battements to the side, changing feet back, each on half a beat, on the third battement, hold the working leg at 90°. Repeat 4 times and execute 4 times changing feet to the front.

4. GRAND ADAGIO. 12 measures in 4/4.

First measure: grand plié in fifth position, right foot front; from deep plié, 2 tours sur le cou-de-pied en dedans, end in attitude effacée. Second measure: from pose attitude, grand rond de jambe to the side, in pose effacée front; relevé on half-toe and come down in fourth position effacée, grande préparation for tours en dedans. Third measure: 2 tours in attitude effacée. Fourth measure: from pose attitude, a wide tombé and chassé back, end in fifth position, right foot front; développé on half-toe in croisé front, with the right leg; a wide tombé and chassé front, end in fourth position, grande préparation for tours en dedans.

Fifth measure: 2 tours à la seconde en dedans. Sixth measure: from the position à la seconde, grand fouetté en tournant en dedans in pose fourth arabesque and renversé en dehors in attitude, bringing the right arm up in third position. Seventh measure: with the left leg: développé in croisé front and renversé en dedans through écarté front. Eighth measure: to corner 8: pas couru front, end in a small pose effacée front in plié, the left foot, pointe tendue on the floor; 4 battements battus (each on a quarter beat) in effacé front and come down in effacé front, pointe tendue on the floor, in plié. Repeat the battements battus in effacé front, then follow through with 1 petit battement, bringing the left foot to the back and développé in attitude effacée. Ninth measure: tour lent en dedans in attitude. Tenth measure: coupé with the left foot on half-toe and with the right leg, grand fouetté effacé en dehors, a wide step back on the right foot half-toe, and, with the left leg, grand fouetté effacé en dedans. Eleventh measure: step on the left foot, half-toe and execute 1 tour en dedans in first arabesque, plié on the supporting leg and again 1 tour in attitude effacée, end in fifth position, right foot front. Twelfth measure: failli in fourth position, préparation for tours sur le cou-de-pied en dehors, 2 tours, end in a big pose écartée back, the arms in third position, bring the right leg down in fifth position back and soubresaut.

ALLEGRO

1. 16 measures in 2/4.

With the right leg: 3 assemblés croisés front; with the left leg: 3 assemblés croisés back, each on half a beat; with the right leg: sissonne ouverte battue to the side at 45°, assemblé, on 2 beats; with the left leg: 2 sissonnes fermées battues in a small pose croisée back, each on 1 beat. Repeat on the other leg and subsequently in the reverse direction.

2. 8 measures in 2/4.

With the right leg: sissonne ouverte at 45° en tournant en dehors in a small pose effacée front, 2 cabrioles at 45° in effacé, assemblé, end in fifth position, right foot back; sissonne ouverte at 45° en tournant en dedans in a small pose effacée back, 2 cabrioles at 45° in effacé, assemblé, end in fifth position, right foot front. Starting with the left foot: 2 brisés dessus-dessous; with the left foot, glissade to the side without changing feet, a small cabriole fermée to the side; with the right foot, glissade to the side without changing feet and a small cabriole fermée to the side.

3. 8 measures in 3/4.

On the right leg to corner 2: grand jeté from fifth position in first arabesque and without dropping the left leg, grand jeté back; at the end of the jeté, the right leg opens with a développé effacé front at 90°, assemblé, end in fifth position, right foot back; 3 entrechats-quatre, 2 grands pas de basque front. Repeat grand jetés on the left leg to corner 8, 3 entrechats-quatre and 2 grands pas de basque back.

4. 16 measures in 3/4 (Waltz).

Préparation: left foot front, in croisé, pointe tendue on the floor. With the right foot: glissade forward to corner 2, without changing feet and grande cabriole effacée front; with a temps levé on the supporting leg, carry the right leg in effacé back in first arabesque, end with pas de bourrée en dehors, changing feet. Repeat the same with the left and the right foot. With the left foot: glissade to the side, without changing feet, grand fouetté sauté à la seconde in first arabesque, failli and entrechat-six de volée in pose écartée front.

5. 8 measures in 3/4 (Waltz).

On the diagonal from corner 6 to corner 2, starting on the right foot: glissade forward, without changing feet; 6 grands jetés, pas de chat and step on the right foot half-toe, in first arabesque.

6. 8 measures in 4/4.

Fifth position, right foot front. With the right leg: grande sissonne ouverte to the side; with a temps levé on the supporting leg, demi-rond in third arabesque; temps levé with a half turn en dehors, simultaneously passé at 90° with the right leg and développé in pose croisée front at 90°, assemblé. Facing side 5, grande sissonne ouverte to the side with the left leg, with a temps levé on the supporting leg, execute a demi-rond in pose croisée front, temps levé with a half turn en dedans, facing side 1, simultaneously passé at 90° with the left leg in third arabesque, assemblé. Sissonne tombée in effacé front on the right foot, 2 grandes cabrioles in first arabesque, assemblé and 4 entrechats-six. Repeat from the beginning on the other leg.

7. GRANDES PIROUETTES WITH RELEVÉ FOR THE MEN.

8. 16 measures in 2/4.

Seven brisés front with the right foot, royale; 7 brisés front with the left foot, royale. Execute also in the reverse direction. The combination is performed to a quick tempo.

9. Sixteen petits changements de pieds, each on half a beat.

FOURTH EXAMPLE OF EXERCISES ON POINTES

1. 16 measures in 2/4.

Right foot front: 3 échappés in fourth position croisée, each on 1 beat; on 1 beat, turn in fifth position to the left side (détourné). Repeat on the other side. Right foot front: préparation from fifth position to fifth position and tour sur le cou-de-pied en dehors, 3 times in succession. Repeat préparation and tours to the left side. Repeat the combination with tours en dedans.

2. 16 measures in 2/4.

With the right leg: on 1 beat, a double rond de jambe en l'air en dehors; on 1 beat, passé with the right foot through first position in demi-plié back at 45°; on 2 beats, pas de chat, pas de bourrée en dehors, changing feet. Repeat once more. A double rond de jambe en l'air en dedans with the left leg and with the right leg, each on 2 beats; with the right leg: 5 sissonnes simples en tournant, to the right side, the first 2 sissonnes each on 1 beat, and the last 3 sissonnes, each on half a beat. Repeat with the other leg.

3. 32 measures in 3/4 (Waltz).

Fifth position, left foot front. In 4 measures: step on the right foot to corner 2, and with the left leg, grand fouetté effacé en dehors, plié-relevé in attitude allongée. In 4 measures: repeat grand fouetté and relevé in attitude. In 4 measures: starting on the left foot, pas de bourrée suivi, in croisé front, end in plié on the left foot, and dégagé with the right foot to the side at 45°. In 4 measures: tour fouetté en dedans (twice), pas de bourrée dessus en tournant and step in fifth position, on pointes. In 4 measures: step on the left foot to corner 8, with the right leg; grand fouetté effacé en dedans, plié-relevé in pose effacée front. In 4 measures: repeat the grand fouetté and relevé in pose effacée. In 4 measures: with the left foot: pas de bourrée suivi to the side, end in fourth position croisée, transferring the left foot back. In 4 measures: tour sur le cou-de-pied en dehors, end to the side at 45°; tour fouetté en dehors (twice) and pas de bourrée dessous en tournant.

4. 16 measures in 2/4.

Move on the diagonal from corner 6 to corner 2. Préparation on the right leg, the left foot in croisé back, pointe tendue on the floor. On

Fourth position croisée on pointes.

the upbeat, dégagé with the left leg to the side, in plié, and turn to corner 2. On 2 beats, pas de bourrée dessus-dessous en tournant; on 2 beats, tour and tour en dehors on the left leg with dégagé; tour en dedans on the right leg, with coupé, (4 times in succession), each on 1 beat; step on the right foot, on pointes, in first arabesque at 90°; 5 pliés-relevés in arabesque, traveling on the diagonal to the back, each on 1 beat; after the fifth relevé, coupé on the left foot in plié, on 1 beat, and on 2 beats, 2 tours sur le cou-de-pied en dedans on the right leg, end in fifth position, left foot front. Six sissonnes simples, in turn with the right and left foot, changing feet to the front moving slightly on the diagonal to corner 2, each on 1 beat; end the sixth sissonne in fourth position croisée, left foot front; on 2 beats, 2 tours sur le cou-de-pied en dehors, end in fifth position, right foot back. On the diagonal, moving upstage: 7 jetés fondus to the back (with a smooth step) in turn with the right and left leg, each on 1 beat; after the seventh jeté fondu, come up on pointes on the right foot in first arabesque at 90°, on 1 beat.

5. 8 measures in 2/4.

Sixteen tours fouettés, each on 1 beat.

6. 8 measures in 2/4.

Come up in fifth position, on pointes. Eight grands battements jetés to the side, in turn with the right and left leg, changing feet to the back and 8 grands battements jetés to the side, changing feet to the front, each on 1 beat.

Eighth Year

Stressing the physical development of virtuosity and artistry.

Développé à la seconde (120°). Graduate class.

First Lesson

EXERCISES AT THE BARRE

1. 16 measures in 4/4.
Two demi-pliés and 2 grands pliés in first and second positions; 2 grands pliés in fourth and fifth positions, each on 4 beats; 2 ports de bras, bending the body backward; 1 port de bras bending the body to the side toward the barre and 1 port de bras bending the body away from the barre, each on 4 beats.

2. BATTEMENTS TENDUS. 32 measures in 2/4.

Two battements tendus in demi-plié, to the front, to the side, to the back, and to the side, each on 1 beat; 4 battements tendus to the side, without plié, each on 1 beat; 3 and again 3 battements tendus to the side, each on half a beat. Repeat in the reverse direction. Battements tendus jetés: 7 to the front, 7 to the side, each on half a beat; 5 battements tendus jetés in first position (repeat 4 times), each on a quarter beat, with a hold at 45° on each fifth battement tendu jeté. Repeat battements tendus jetés in the opposite direction.

3. RONDS DE JAMBE À TERRE. 24 measures in 2/4.

En dehors: 4 ronds de jambe à terre, each on 1 beat; 3 ronds de jambe à terre, each on half a beat; 5 ronds de jambe à terre, each on a quarter beat, end pointe tendue on the floor front; a quick passé to the back, to the front at 45°, each on half a beat; 3 grands ronds de jambe jetés en dehors, each on 1 beat, and 2 grands ronds de jambe jetés, each on half a beat. Repeat from the beginning en dedans and in 8 measures: trace a half circle on the floor in plié en dedans, en dehors, relevé to the back at 90°, rising on half-toe and port de bras, bending the body.

4. BATTEMENTS FONDUS AT 45°. 24 measures in 2/4.

On 2 beats, fondu to the front; on 2 beats, plié and relevé with a half turn away from the barre (the working leg is extended to the front); on 2 beats, passé through first position in demi-plié to the back and a half turn on half-toe toward the barre; at the end, the working leg is in front at 45°; on 2 beats, plié-relevé with demi-rond to the side; on 2 beats, 2 pliés-relevés; on 2 beats, plié and 2 tours sur le cou-de-pied en dehors; 2 doubles fondus to the side, each on 2 beats. Repeat in the reverse direction. Frappés: 6 to the side, each on half a beat, and on 2 beats, flic-flac en tournant en dedans with a hold to the side at 45°. Repeat frappés, flic-flac en tournant en dehors; 3 doubles frappés, each on half a beat. Repeat 2 more times and on 2 beats, execute flic-flac en tournant en dedans with a hold in pose écartée front at 90°.

5. RONDS DE JAMBE EN L'AIR. 8 measures in 4/4.

Four ronds de jambe en l'air en dehors, each on 1 beat; 5 and again 5 ronds de jambe en l'air en dehors, each on a quarter beat; on 4 beats, développé in pose écartée back and 2 ronds de jambe en l'air en dehors at 90°; on 4 beats, demi-rond in attitude effacée, flic-flac en tournant en dehors, ending in a big pose effacée front, carry the working leg to the side and lower at 45° in second position. Repeat from the beginning en dedans.

6. PETITS BATTEMENTS SUR LE COU-DE-PIED. 16 measures in 2/4.

Eight doubles frappés to the side, pointe tendue on the floor in second position, with a double stroke of the working foot sur le cou-de-pied, rising on the supporting leg on half-toe and lowering the heel, each on 1 beat; 28 petits battements, each on a quarter beat, and on 1 beat, come down in demi-plié, open the working leg to the side, pointe tendue on the floor. Repeat from the beginning.

7. BATTEMENTS DÉVELOPPÉS. 32 measures in 3/4 (Waltz).

In 4 measures: développé front, on half-toe, demi-rond to the side, passé at 90°, in attitude effacée. In 4 measures: tour fouetté en dedans, ending in pose attitude effacée, 2 times in succession; carry the working leg in pose écartée front, end in fifth position. In 4 measures: développé back, on half-toe, demi-rond to the side, passé at 90°, in pose effacée front. In 4 measures: tour fouetté en dehors, ending in pose effacée front, 2 times in succession; carry the working leg in pose écartée back, end in fifth position. In 4 measures: développé to the side, on half-toe, demi-rond to the front, passé at 90° in pose écartée back. In 4 measures: 2 short balancés, tombé in fifth position on the right foot, in plié and développé to the front with the left leg, bending the body back; end in fifth position. In 4 measures: développé to the side, on half-toe, demi-rond to the back, passé at 90° in pose écartée front. In 4 measures: 2 short balancés, tombé in fifth position, on the right foot, in plié, pose arabesque at 90°, with the left leg and a half turn on half-toe toward the barre. At the end, the left leg is in front at 90°, the left arm in third position.

8. GRANDS BATTEMENTS JETÉS. 8 measures in 2/4.

Grand battement front with demi-rond to the side, ending pointe tendue on the floor, in second position. From this position, execute the following grand battement to the side with demi-rond to the back, ending pointe tendue on the floor to the back. Thereafter, execute the same grand battement back, to the side and from side to the front, each grand battement on 1 beat. Two grands battements front in fifth position and 2 grands battements to the side, each on 1 beat. Repeat the whole combination in the reverse direction.

EXERCISES IN THE CENTER

1. SMALL ADAGIO AND BATTEMENTS TENDUS. 4 measures in 4/4.

First measure: grand plié in fifth position, right foot front; from deep plié, 1½ tours en dedans on the right leg in a big pose croisée front, ending in fourth arabesque (right leg). Second measure: lean the body downward (penché) and straighten back in arabesque. Third measure: from pose arabesque, a half turn en dehors in position à la seconde and half a tour lent en dehors to side 1. Fourth measure: passé through first position in third arabesque in demi-plié and a quick turn en dehors on half-toe with passé at 90°, in pose effacée front; end in fifth position, left foot back. Battements tendus and tours: 8 measures in 4/4. With the right foot: 4 battements tendus in a small pose croisée front; with the left foot: 4 battements tendus in a small pose croisée back, each on 1 beat; with the right foot: 3 battements tendus to the side, each on 1 beat, and on 1 beat, tour sur le cou-de-pied en dehors from fifth position. Repeat the battements tendus to the side and tour from fifth position en dedans. Battements tendus jetés: 7 to the side, each on half a beat, and on 4 beats, préparation and 2 tours sur le cou-de-pied en dehors from second position. Repeat battements tendus jetés and 3 tours en dehors from second position.

2. BATTEMENTS FONDUS AT 90°. 8 measures in 4/4.

First measure: with the right leg: 2 battements fondus at 90° in effacé front. Second measure: bring the right leg down in fourth position effacée and execute 2 tours en dedans in attitude effacée on the right leg. Third measure: tombé back on the left foot and tour en dehors in third arabesque, plié and 2 tours tire-bouchon en dehors. Fourth measure: from the tire-bouchon position, lower the right leg, bent halfway in front, to 45°, and renversé en dehors with grand rond de jambe en dehors. Ending renversé pas de bourrée, come down on the right leg in plié and execute 2 tours sur le cou-de-pied en dedans on the right leg, end with coupé on half-toe on the left foot, open the right leg to the side at 45°. Fifth and sixth measures: with the right leg: 7 and again 7 frappés to the side, each on half a beat. Seventh measure: with the right leg: 2 fondus at 90° in pose effacée back. Eighth measure: tombé back on the right foot and 2 tours en dehors in pose effacée front, the left arm in third position, the right arm in first position, the hands stretched out front in position arabesque allongée.

3. GRAND ADAGIO. 8 measures in 4/4.

First measure: grand plié in fifth position, right foot front; from deep plié, grande sissonne ouverte on the right leg in third arabesque. Second measure: tour lent en dehors in arabesque, plié. Third measure: come up on half-toe in attitude croisée and on the first 2 beats of the measure, execute a grand port de bras, ending in fourth position, grande préparation for tours en dedans; 2 tours in pose croisée front. Fourth measure: from pose croisée, renversé en dedans, a quick développé with the left leg on half-toe in attitude croisée, tombé and chassé back. Fifth measure: with the right leg, préparation in second position and 2 tours à la seconde en dehors. Sixth measure: from the à la seconde position, execute renversé (attitude) en dehors, step on the left foot to the side and step forward on the right foot in fourth arabesque at 90°. Seventh measure: from fourth arabesque, renversé in écarté, plié in pose écartée back and step onto the left foot in first arabesque at 90° to corner 6. Eighth measure: plié in pose arabesque and grand jeté on the right leg in pose first arabesque to corner 2, pas de bourrée en dehors, changing feet, end in fourth position, préparation for tours sur le cou-de-pied en dehors and 3 tours en dehors to the right side, ending in pose third arabesque, pointe tendue on the floor.

ALLEGRO

1. 16 measures in 2/4.

Four assemblés battus, in turn on the right and left leg, changing feet to the front, each on 1 beat; 2 échappés battus in second position, changing feet, each on 2 beats. Repeat from the beginning and subsequently in the reverse direction.

2. 16 measures in 2/4.

Starting right foot front: sissonne ouverte en tournant en dehors at 45° in a small pose croisée front, assemblé; sissonne ouverte en tournant en dehors, in a small pose écartée back, assemblé. Three brisés front en tournant en dedans (to the left side) in a full turn, dégagé the right foot in effacé back and pas de bourrée, changing feet. Double rond de jambe en l'air sauté en dehors, assemblé, with the right, the left, and the right leg; entrechat-cinq back with the right foot, a sharp coupé and with the left leg: assemblé front in a small pose croisée. Repeat from the beginning on the other leg. Execute also in the reverse direction.

3. 16 measures in 3/4 (Waltz).

Starting right foot front: grande sissonne ouverte en tournant en dehors in pose écartée back with the right leg, assemblé; grande sissonne ouverte in fourth arabesque on the right leg, with a full turn of the body to the right side, assemblé. Two grands pas de basque front, with the right and left leg. Sissonne tombée on the right foot front to corner 4 and grande cabriole in first arabesque, a second cabriole in first arabesque to corner 6, a third cabriole turning to corner 8. With a half turn to the left, starting with the left foot (back to side 1, mirror), glissade to the side, grand jeté in third arabesque to corner 2, on the left leg and with the right foot, glissade forward to corner 2 and pas de ciseaux.

4. 16 measures in 3/4 (Waltz).

On the diagonal from corner 6 to corner 2, with the right foot: pas couru and grand jeté in attitude croisée. Repeat. Glissade forward with the right foot, grande cabriole in pose effacée front and 2 small jetés; on the diagonal upstage to corner 6: jeté entrelacé in croisé with chassé, the arms in third position; execute 3 times; step on the right foot, half-toe, turning quickly to corner 6 and 2 tours sur le cou-de-pied en dedans, end in pose effacée back at 90°, the arms in position allongée to the front.

5. 32 measures in 3/4 (Waltz).

In 16 measures: préparation: right foot front, in croisé, pointe tendue on the floor. Glissade to the left side, without changing feet, grande cabriole fouetté à la seconde in first arabesque, pas de bourrée en dehors, changing feet; at the end, sissonne simple in a small pose croisée on the left leg, the right foot sur le cou-de-pied back. Repeat the same combination to the right and left side. Glissade to the right side, on the right foot, without changing feet, grande cabriole fouettée à la seconde in first arabesque and grand fouetté sauté en tournant en dedans in third arabesque. In 16 measures: on the diagonal to corner 2, with the right foot: chassé forward in effacé front and 2 tours en l'air to the right side; with the left foot: chassé croisé front and 2 tours en l'air to the left side; with the right foot: chassé effacé front and 2 tours en l'air to the right side; on the left leg: grande sissonne tombée to the side pas de bourrée en dehors, changing feet; with the left leg: a small assemblé to the side, end in fifth position left foot front, lean the body to the left; sissonne soubresaut on the left leg in pose effacée back allongée. The last 16 measures of this combination are executed by the men only and not the women.

6. 4 measures in 4/4.

On the diagonal from corner 6 to corner 2, with the right leg: 2 jetés à terre, each on 2 beats; 4 jetés à terre, each on 1 beat; on 2 beats, step on the right foot half-toe in first arabesque facing corner 2, and come down in fifth position, demi-plié, left foot front; on 2 beats, sissonne tombée en tournant en dehors, on the right leg in croisé front, turn to the right side (détourné) and on 4 beats, tours chaînés, starting on the right foot, in direction croisé to corner 8; at the end, step on the right foot in pose croisée, the left foot back, pointe tendue on the floor.

7. 8 measures in 2/4.
Four entrechats-six, each on 1 beat; 7 petits changements de pieds, each on half a beat. Repeat.[1]

FIRST EXAMPLE OF EXERCISES ON POINTES[2]

1. 8 measures in 4/4.
Three sissonnes simples, changing the foot to the back, on the right, the left and the right leg, each on 1 beat; on 1 beat, grande sissonne ouverte in attitude croisée, the right arm in third position, the left arm in first position. Repeat on the other side. On 4 beats, with the right leg: préparation from fifth position to fifth position and tour sur le cou-de-pied en dehors, 3 times in succession. On 4 beats, with the left leg: préparation from fifth position to fifth position and tour sur le cou-de-pied en dehors, 3 times in succession. Repeat the whole combination from the beginning.

2. 16 measures in 3/4 (Waltz).
Préparation: right foot back, in croisé, pointe tendue on the floor. In 4 measures: step on the right foot, on pointes to corner 2 and grand fouetté effacé en dehors, failli, grand assemblé in pose écartée front. In 4 measures: with the right leg (on the left leg): 4 sissonnes simples en tournant to the right side. In 4 measures: step on the right foot, on pointes, to corner 2 and tour en dedans sur le cou-de-pied, the right arm in third position, the left arm in first position; step on the

---

[1] Each lesson, as usual, ends with port de bras and bending the body.
[2] In accordance with the complete study of the program, one teaches excerpts from the ballet repertoire at the end of the lesson.

left foot, on pointes and tour en dehors, raising the left arm in third position and lowering the right arm in first position; plié on the left foot and 2 tours en dedans on the right leg; end in fifth position, plié, left foot front; a quick turn in fifth position, on pointes, to the right side (détourné), raising the arms in third position. In 4 measures: préparation from fifth position to fourth position and 2 tours sur le cou-de-pied en dehors.

3. 32 measures in 3/4 (Waltz).

In 4 measures: on the right leg: grande sissonne ouverte in attitude croisée, plié on the supporting leg (without coming down in fifth position) and renversé en dehors. In 4 measures: on the left leg, grande sissonne ouverte in third arabesque, plié on the supporting leg and 2 tours tire-bouchon en dehors, end in fifth position. In 4 measures: dégagé the right foot to the side, pointe tendue on the floor and pas de bourrée suivi in a straight line to the left side, right foot front. In 4 measures: on the right leg: grande sissonne ouverte in croisé front, plié on the supporting leg and renversé en dedans. In 4 measures: on the left leg: grande sissonne ouverte in attitude croisée and renversé en dehors. In 4 measures: on the right leg: grande sissonne ouverte in third arabesque, plié and 2 tours tire-bouchon en dehors. In 4 measures: on the diagonal to corner 2, starting on the right foot: 4 tours glissades en tournant. In 4 measures: tours chaînés, end on the last beat of the measure, in first arabesque at 90°.

4. 4 measures in 4/4.

Préparation: right foot front, in croisé, pointe tendue on the floor. First measure: plié on the right leg and a half tour en dedans in attitude effacée, plié in attitude, again half tour en dedans in attitude effacée, plié and 1 tour in attitude effacée en dedans, end with passé through first position on the left foot to the front in plié in pose fourth arabesque, right foot back, pointe tendue on the floor. Second measure: coupé with the right foot and repeat all tours on the left leg. Third measure: coupé with the left foot and starting on the right foot, pas de bourrée suivi in the direction croisé front to corner 8. Fourth measure: with the right leg: préparation from fifth position to fourth position, 2 tours sur le cou-de-pied en dedans, end in fifth position, right foot front, and spring on the right foot onto pointes in attitude croisée allongée.

5. 8 measures in 2/4.

Eight tours fouettés at 45°, with the right leg en dehors; with the left leg, en dedans, in succession: 8 tours fouettés at 45° with the right leg en dehors.

Grande jeté. Graduate class.

Second Lesson

EXERCISES IN THE CENTER

1. SMALL ADAGIO AND BATTEMENTS TENDUS. 8 measures in 4/4.

First measure: demi-plié in fifth position, right foot front, open the arms to the side in a lower second position; 2 tours sur le cou-de-pied en dehors on the left leg, raising the arms in third position, end in demi-plié on the left leg; extend the right leg in effacé front at 45°, and lower the arms in second position. Second measure: step on the right foot in attitude effacée and follow through with tour lent en dedans to corner 6, passé through first position with the left foot in pose croisée front at 90°, on half-toe. Third measure: a wide tombé in plié, on the left foot; raise the right leg back at 90°, lean the body downward (penché) while stretching the supporting leg and turn en dehors in pose écartée front. Fourth measure: plié in pose écartée, step on the right foot, half-toe and follow through with 1½ tours en dedans in attitude effacée, raising the left arm in third position, the right arm in first position; end in pose attitude croisée. Turn the hands in and stretch forward in position arabesque allongée, looking at the left hand. Fifth measure: from pose attitude, take fourth position croisée, move the right arm to the side into second position and the left arm into first position; grand plié; from deep plié, tour en dehors in fourth arabesque, on the right leg. Sixth measure: plié-relevé in pose arabesque with a turn en dehors to corner 4, shifting the left leg to pose croisée front; raise the arms in third position, turn en dehors, on half-toe, executing a grand rond de jambe en dehors with the left leg and ending in first arabesque, facing corner 2. Seventh measure: tombé back on the left foot and 2 tours en dehors in third arabesque. Eighth measure: from pose arabesque, renversé en dehors, end in fifth position and follow through with glissade en tournant en dehors, on the left foot, to the left side.

Battements tendus: 4 measures. With the right foot: 8 battements tendus to the side, each on 1 beat; 16 battements tendus jetés, each on half a beat. In 2 measures: with the left leg, préparation from fifth position back to fourth position and tour sur le cou-de-pied en dedans on the right leg; end in fourth position, left foot front; 2 tours en dedans to the left side, end in fourth position, right foot front and 3 tours en dedans to the right side.

2. BATTEMENTS FONDUS AT 45°. 8 measures in 4/4.

With the right leg: 3 fondus in a small pose effacée front, each on 1 beat; on 1 beat, remaining on half-toe, carry the working leg into a small pose effacée back. Three fondus in a small pose effacée back, each on 1 beat; on 1 beat, carry the working leg into a small pose effacée front; on 1 beat, tombé front on the right foot and tour sur le cou-de-pied en dedans; on 1 beat, tombé in fifth position on the left foot and tour sur le cou-de-pied en dehors; on 2 beats, 2 tours temps relevé en dehors on the left leg, end in développé front, on half-toe; on 2 beats, grand rond de jambe in attitude croisée; on 2 beats, renversé en dehors and open the left leg to the side at 45°. With the left leg: 14 petits battements en tournant en dedans, each on half a beat; on 1 beat, come down on the left foot in plié and stretch the right leg in croisé back, pointe tendue on the floor. On 2 beats, tombé on the right foot in plié to side 5 and 1½ tours sur le cou-de-pied en dedans, end in pose croisée front at 90°; on 2 beats, renversé en dedans; on 4 beats, step forward on the right foot in pose fourth arabesque at 90° and renversé in écarté.

3. GRAND ADAGIO. 16 measures in 3/4 (Waltz).

Fifth position, right foot front. In 4 measures: grand échappé in second position and 2 tours à la seconde en dehors on the left leg; plié on the left leg, holding the right leg à la seconde and 2 tours tire-bouchon en dehors, end in fifth position, right foot back. In 4 measures: grand échappé in fourth position croisée and 2 tours en dedans in first arabesque, on the left leg. In 4 measures: from pose arabesque, grand fouetté en tournant en dedans in third arabesque and also in first arabesque. In 4 measures: from pose arabesque, step-coupé front on the right foot and pas de ciseaux, failli and entrechat-six de volée in pose écartée front.

ALLEGRO

1. 16 measures in 2/4.

Two assemblés battus with the right and left leg, changing the feet to the front, each on 1 beat; 3 assemblés without beats, each on half a beat; on 1 beat, sissonne ouverte battue to the side at 45°; on 1 beat, pas de bourrée dessous en tournant; 3 brisés front, each on half a beat. Repeat on the other leg and subsequently in the reverse direction.

2. 8 measures in 3/4.

First measure: with the right leg, sissonne soubresaut in attitude croisée, assemblé, entrechat-quatre. Second measure: with the right leg, sissonne soubresaut in attitude effacée, assemblé, entrechat-quatre, end in fifth position, left foot front. Third measure: with the left leg, sissonne renversée en dehors, entrechat-quatre. Fourth measure: with the left foot front: glissade to the left side, grand assemblé battu back, entrechat-quatre. Fifth measure: with the left leg, grande sissonne ouverte in pose croisée front, passé at 90° in first arabesque with temps levé on the right leg, assemblé. Sixth measure: with the left leg, sissonne renversée en dedans, entrechat-quatre. Seventh measure: starting on the left foot, glissade to the side, entrechat-six de volée to the side, relevé in fifth position, on half-toe. Eighth measure: 3 entrechats-six.

3. 16 measures in 3/4 (Waltz).

Fifth position, right foot front. In 4 measures: in a straight line from side 7 to side 3, starting on the right foot: chassé and saut de basque, chassé and grande cabriole in first arabesque to side 3. In 4 measures: from side 3 to side 7, starting on the left foot, chassé and saut de basque, chassé and grande cabriole in first arabesque to side 7. In 4 measures: starting on the right foot to side 3, chassé, saut de basque and sissonne renversée en dehors with grand rond de jambe en dehors, end in fifth position, right foot front. In 4 measures: on the diagonal to corner 2: 3 jetés à terre and the fourth jeté ends in pose first arabesque, in plié.

4. 16 measures in 3/4 (Waltz).

In 8 measures: on the diagonal from corner 2 to corner 6: 3 jetés entrelacés in first arabesque with chassé, step back on the left foot and again on the right foot, ending in préparation, left foot front in croisé, pointe tendue on the floor. In 8 measures: starting with the right foot on the diagonal to corner 2: glissade forward and 7 grands jetés (successively) and pas de chat.

5. 8 measures in 2/4.

Step on the left foot to corner 8, in pose first arabesque, the right foot back, pointe tendue on the floor and moving in a circle through spots 1, 2, 3, 4, and 5, execute 5 jetés entrelacés with chassé, reaching corner 6 on the fifth jeté. On the sixth chassé, turn on the diagonal from corner 6 to corner 2 and execute the sixth jeté entrelacé down on the diagonal, ending facing corner 6. A quick turn of the body to corner 2 and stepping on the right foot, continue with tours chaînés.[1]

6. 16 measures in 2/4.

Fifth position, left foot front. Seven brisés front en tournant en dedans (turn to the left side), a quick dégagé with the right foot in effacé back at 45° and pas de bourrée en dehors, changing feet. Starting on the left foot: 3 brisés dessus-dessous, pas de bourrée en tournant en dehors and royale. Repeat from the beginning on the other leg.

7. 16 measures in 3/4 (Waltz).

Twelve entrechats-six (starting right foot front); with the right leg, préparation from fifth position to fifth position on half-toe and 2 tours sur le cou-de-pied en dehors; left foot front, relevé in fifth position on half-toe and 2 tours sur le cou-de-pied en dehors.[2]

---

[1] According to the ability of the students, jetés entrelacés in a circle can be executed to the tempo of a waltz.

[2] For the men, tours sur le cou-de-pied are replaced by relevés in fifth position, half-toe, and 2 tours en l'air to the right and to the left side.

8. 8 measures in 2/4.

Three petits changements de pieds, again 3 changements de pieds and 7 changements de pieds, each on half a beat. Repeat.

SECOND EXAMPLE OF EXERCISES ON POINTES

1. 16 measures in 2/4.

Fifth position, right foot front. Four échappés in second position, changing feet, each on 1 beat; 3 sissonnes simples, changing feet to the back, each on 1 beat, end the third sissonne in fourth position and tour sur le cou-de-pied en dehors. Repeat the whole combination on the other leg and subsequently in the reverse direction. Tours sur le cou-de-pied en dedans must end in fifth position front.

2. 16 measures in 3/4 (Waltz).

In 4 measures: double rond de jambe en l'air en dehors with the right and left leg. In 4 measures: jeté on the right foot in third arabesque at 90°, plié-relevé in attitude croisée. In 4 measures: jeté to the side on the left foot, the right foot sur le cou-de-pied back, and without closing the feet in fifth position, plié on the left leg and sissonne ouverte en tournant en dehors in a small pose croisée front, end in fifth position. In 4 measures: double rond de jambe en l'air en dedans with the left leg and pas de bourrée suivi, in the direction croisé front (to corner 2). Repeat the whole combination on the other leg.

3. 8 measures in 4/4.

Step on the right foot in a big pose croisée back, pointe tendue on the floor. First measure: grand port de bras, ending in fourth position, grande préparation for tours en dedans. Second measure: tour à la seconde en dedans on the right leg, plié, pas de bourrée dessus en tournant, step back on the left foot and spring slightly on the right foot, on pointes in the à la seconde position. Third measure: grand fouetté en tournant en dedans in third arabesque and again in first arabesque. Fourth measure: step back on the left foot front in fifth position, on pointes and turn to the right side (détourné), step to the side on the left foot in plié and renversé en dehors in attitude, passé in first position with the right foot front in plié in pose fourth arabesque, left foot back, pointe tendue on the floor. Fifth and sixth measures: coupé on the left foot in plié and on the diagonal to corner 2 execute tour en dedans in attitude effacée with coupé on the right leg, 4 times in succession. Seventh and eighth measures: step on the right foot and turning the body facing side 5, continue with pas de bourrée suivi in a straight line to side 7 (back to the mirror); on the last 2 beats of the eighth measure, come down on the right foot in plié, with a turn of the body toward the mirror, then dégagé with the left leg to the side at 45° and 2 tours sur le cou-de-pied en dehors on the left leg, ending in fourth position, raise the left arm in third position and the right arm in second position.[3]

4. 4 measures in 2/4.

On the upbeat, demi-plié on the right leg, the left foot sur le cou-de-pied back and coupé on the left foot on pointes. Fourteen ronds de jambe en l'air, hopping on pointes, traveling on the diagonal to corner 2, each on half a beat; on 1 beat, come down in fifth position demi-plié and relevé on pointes, in fifth position.

5. 32 TOURS FOUETTÉS AT 45° (taking into account the capabilities of each student).

[3] Repeat the combination with 2 tours à la seconde en dedans.

Attitude croisée, on pointes, left arm in third position.

Third Lesson

EXERCISES IN THE CENTER

1. SMALL ADAGIO AND BATTEMENTS TENDUS. 4 measures in 4/4.

First measure: grand plié in fifth position, right foot front; from deep plié, 2 tours tire-bouchon en dehors, end in pose écartée back. Second measure: tour lent en dehors in pose écartée and when ending the turn, carry the right leg in first arabesque. Third measure: plié in pose arabesque, step on the right foot on half-toe and tours en dehors in attitude croisée, the right arm in third position, the left arm in first position; end the tours in pose fourth arabesque. Fourth measure: plié in arabesque, tour en dedans in pose croisée front and renversé en dedans. Battements tendus: 4 measures: with the right foot: 2 battements tendus in pose écartée back, each on 1 beat; 5 battements tendus jetés, each on a quarter beat; with the left foot, 2 battements tendus in pose croisée back, each on 1 beat; 5 battements tendus jetés, each on a quarter beat; with the right foot: 2 battements tendus and 5 battements tendus jetés in pose croisée front; with the left foot, 2 battements tendus and 5 battements tendus jetés in pose écartée front. In 2 measures: starting with the right leg, pas de basque front, ending in fourth position, préparation for tours, 1 tour, 2 tours, and 3 tours sur le cou-de-pied en dehors.

2. BATTEMENTS FONDUS. 4 measures in 4/4.

With the right leg, 2 fondus to the side at 45°, each on 1 beat; on 2 beats, 1 fondu at 90°. Execute 3 times, then tombé from 90° onto the right foot and on 4 beats, 2 tours à la seconde en dedans, plié and 2 tours tire-bouchon en dedans.

3. RONDS DE JAMBE EN L'AIR. 8 measures in 4/4.

With the right leg, 5 ronds de jambe en l'air en dehors, each on a quarter beat; on 2 beats, tombé in fifth position on the right foot, in plié, the left foot sur le cou-de-pied back, and coupé on the left foot, on half-toe, while opening the right leg to the side at 45°. Five ronds de jambe en l'air en tournant en dehors to side 5, each on a quarter beat; on 2 beats, plié in fifth position, right foot back, a half turn on half-toe to side 1 (détourné); at the end, the right foot is in front. On 2 beats, with a step to corner 2, on the right foot: 2 tours sur le cou-de-pied en dedans, coupé, and on 2 beats, repeat 2 tours en dedans, ending in a big pose croisée front. Tombé front on the left foot and on 2 beats, pas de ciseaux, step-coupé front, and on 2 beats, repeat pas de ciseaux. Coupé on half-toe on the left foot, open the right leg to the side at 45°; 5 ronds de jambe en l'air en dedans and again 5 ronds de jambe en l'air en dedans, each on a quarter beat; on the last rond de jambe, plié on the supporting leg. On 2 beats, a wide step on the right foot to the side and 2 tours sur le cou-de-pied en dehors, ending in attitude croisée. Tombé back on the left foot and on 2 beats, pas de ciseaux back, step-coupé back and on 2 beats, repeat pas de ciseaux. On 2 beats, from the preceding final pose in effacé front in plié, passé through first position in third arabesque, on half-toe, and on 2 beats, renversé en dehors. On 2 beats, with the right leg, gargouillade en dedans.

4. GRAND ADAGIO. 32 measures in 3/4 (Waltz).

A big pose croisée back on the right leg, the left foot stretched in the back, pointe tendue on the floor. In 4 measures: grand port de bras, ending in fourth position, grande préparation for tours en dedans. In 4 measures: 2 tours in first arabesque. In 4 measures: from pose arabesque, lean the body downward (penché) and straighten back into the starting position. In 4 measures: grand fouetté en tournant en dedans in third arabesque, relevé in attitude croisée on half-toe; a wide tombé to the back, chassé, end in fifth position, and a quick développé with the right leg in écarté back. In 4 measures: a wide tombé, chassé in écarté back, end in fifth position, left foot front and step forward on the left foot in fourth arabesque at 90°. In 4 measures: renversé in écarté, then a second renversé in écarté immediately from pose écartée back, end in fifth position, right foot back. In 4 measures: step on the left foot to corner 8 in plié, and 10 jumps (hops) à terre[1] en tournant en dedans in attitude effacée (execute in a circle, 2½ circles), end in attitude croisée. In 4 measures: coupé on the right foot, step on the left foot to corner 8, and 9 tours chaînés, ending in a pose on the left knee, the right arm in third position, the left arm in first position, the body leaning to the left side.

ALLEGRO

1. 16 measures in 2/4.

Two échappés battus with the right and left leg, each on 2 beats; on 1 beat, with the left leg, entrechat-cinq back, a short coupé, and with the right leg, 2 ballonnés effacé front, each on 1 beat; 1 ballonné, on half a beat; on half a beat, assemblé to the side. Repeat the whole combination on the other leg and subsequently in the reverse direction.

2. 16 measures in 3/4 (Waltz).

In 4 measures: double rond de jambe en l'air sauté en dehors at 90°, assemblé with the right and left leg. In 4 measures: with the right leg, grande sissonne ouverte en tournant en dehors à la seconde, assemblé; on the left leg: 2 sissonnes fermées in fourth arabesque. In 4 measures: with the left leg, double rond de jambe en l'air sauté en dehors at

---

[1] Jumps à terre like hops are steps in which the pointed feet hardly leave the floor as opposed to jumps of elevation.

90°, in the écarté back position. Concluding the jump, follow through with passé at 90° and step forward on the left foot half-toe, in attitude effacée; come down in fifth position in épaulement croisé, right foot back; repeat double rond de jambe en l'air sauté en dehors at 90° and step on the left foot in first arabesque; end in fifth position, right foot front. In 4 measures: 3 brisés front en tournant en dedans (turn to the right side), raising the left arm in third position, the right arm in second position, dégagé with the left foot in effacé back at 45° and pas de bourrée en dehors, changing feet. Execute also in the opposite direction.

3. 4 measures in 4/4.

First measure: in a straight line from side 7 to side 3 starting with the right leg: 4 sauts de basque with a short step-coupé, each on 1 beat. End the fourth saut de basque in attitude croisée, raising the left arm in third position, the right arm in first position. Second measure: from pose attitude, 4 jumps (hops) jetés à terre en dehors in a circle, each on 1 beat; come up on half-toe and pas de bourrée en tournant en dehors, changing feet. Third measure: with the right leg: chassé in direction croisé front and 2 tours sur le cou-de-pied en dehors from fifth position, ending in first arabesque.[2] Fourth measure: failli, coupé, grand jeté on the right leg in third arabesque; from pose arabesque, sissonne fermée back with the left leg in effacé front, close left foot front, a short coupé with the right foot back and grand jeté en tournant in attitude croisée on the left leg.

4. 16 measures in 3/4 (Waltz).

Fifth position, left foot front. In 4 measures: step-coupé front on the left foot; with the right leg, grande cabriole fermée in écarté front and turn in fifth position, half-toe, to the left side (détourné). In 8 measures: repeat grande cabriole fermée twice and turn in fifth position half-toe, to the left side (détourné). In 4 measures: turn in fifth position, half-toe to the right side (détourné) and 3 jumps (hops) à terre on the right leg to corner 8, step on the right foot, half-toe, in attitude croisée, the right arm in third position, the left arm in second position.

5. 8 measures in 2/4 or 16 measures in 3/4 (Waltz).

Move on the diagonal from corner 6 to corner 2. Préparation on the right leg, the left foot in croisé back, pointe tendue on the floor. On the upbeat, dégagé with the left foot to the side, turn facing corner 2, and pas de bourrée dessus en tournant. In 4 measures: end pas de bourrée dessus en tournant on the first beat of the first measure and

[2] For the men, replace by 2 tours en l'air, ending in first arabesque.

grand jeté in attitude effacée, ending on the second beat; repeat pas de bourrée dessus en tournant and grand jeté 3 more times. In 4 measures: on the diagonal from corner 2 to corner 6, with the left leg, chassé and grande cabriole fouettée in fourth arabesque, chassé with the right leg and grande cabriole fouettée in first arabesque, chassé with the left leg and jeté entrelacé in first arabesque; step-coupé front on the left foot and pas de ciseaux.

6. 16 measures in 2/4.

Move in a circle from corner 2, through side 3, corner 4 and side 5, to corner 6. Fifth position, right foot front. Eight emboîtés front en tournant in half turns, moving to the side, each on half a beat; 7 jumps (hops) jetés à terre en tournant en dedans in first arabesque, moving in 2 circles, each on half a beat; on half a beat, coupé on the left foot in plié, the right foot sur le cou-de-pied front. Repeat emboîtés and jumps jetés à terre 2 more times, the last time execute 6 jumps à terre, and on 1 beat, from pose arabesque, tour en dedans sur le cou-de-pied on the right leg, end in fifth position, left foot front, facing corner 2. Three small pas de chat back, each on 1 beat; on 1 beat, pas de bourrée en tournant en dehors, changing feet and starting with the right foot front to corner 2: 2 tours sissonnes tombées, each on 1 beat, 2 tours sissonnes tombées, each on half a beat, and on 1 beat, step on the right foot in pose first arabesque, left foot back, pointe tendue on the floor.

7. 8 measures in 2/4.

Thirty-two petits changements de pieds, each on half a beat.

THIRD EXAMPLE OF EXERCISES ON POINTES

1. 4 measures in 4/4.

Fifth position, right foot front. On 2 beats, pas de bourrée dessus-dessous en tournant, starting the first pas de bourrée on the upbeat; on 2 beats, starting from fifth position: tour sur le cou-de-pied en dehors to the right side, repeat twice and end the second tour in plié, open the right leg to the side at 45°; on 4 beats, 4 jetés en tournant in half turns, traveling to the side, with petits battements sur le cou-de-pied; on 2 beats, pas de bourrée dessous-dessus en tournant; starting from fifth position, right foot front; tour sur le cou-de-pied en dedans to the right side, end in fifth position, left foot front; on 4 beats, 5 steps moving back, on pointes, starting with the right foot, end the fifth step in fourth position and tours sur le cou-de-pied en dehors to the right side.

2. 32 measures in 3/4 (Waltz).

In 8 measures: with the right leg, grande sissonne ouverte in pose écartée back, plié-relevé in attitude effacée. Repeat. In 8 measures: with the left leg, grande sissonne ouverte à la seconde, plié-relevé in first arabesque; plié in arabesque, step on the left foot on pointes and follow through with 2 tours sur le cou-de-pied en dehors, end in fourth position, right leg back, and 2 tours sur le cou-de-pied en dedans. Repeat from the beginning.

3. 16 measures in 6/8.

On 2 beats, on the diagonal from corner 6 to corner 2, starting on the right foot: pas de bourrée suivi. In 2 measures: failli in fourth position, 2 tours sur le cou-de-pied en dehors, ending in plié on the left leg, step forward on the right foot and tours chaînés, stop in fifth position, right foot back. In the following 12 measures, repeat the same, starting on the left leg in the direction toward corner 8, then starting on the right leg in the direction toward corner 2 and again on the left leg toward corner 8.

4. Musical measure 2/4.

Pas ballonné, traveling on the diagonal, with jumps (hops) on pointes on the supporting leg, in poses effacées and écartées front. Execute 8 to 16 ballonnés.

5. TOURS PIQUÉS IN A CIRCLE.

Fourth Lesson

EXERCISES IN THE CENTER

1. SMALL ADAGIO AND BATTEMENTS TENDUS. 8 measures in 4/4.

First measure: grand plié in fifth position, right foot front; from deep plié, 2 tours sur le cou-de-pied en dehors on the right leg, the left foot sur le cou-de-pied back, the left arm in third position, the right arm in second position allongée. Second measure: coupé with the left foot on half-toe, plié, and with the right leg, tour à la seconde with grand temps relevé en dehors, plié and tour en dehors in attitude. Third measure: coupé with the right foot and with the left leg, grand fouetté effacé en dehors; then quickly, on half a beat, come down in plié on the left leg, extend the right leg in effacé front, pointe tendue on the floor, lean the body to the back; coupé with the right foot on half-toe, and with the left leg, grand fouetté effacé en dedans. Fourth measure: from the concluding pose in effacé, grand rond de jambe on half-toe in pose écartée back and attitude croisée; end in plié on the right leg, the arms in position allongée. Fifth measure: from pose attitude, a quick turn en dehors on half-toe with passé at 90° in pose croisée front, a wide tombé in plié and step back on the right foot, half-toe in pose croisée front (développé tombé). Sixth measure: coupé with the left foot on half-toe, plié, and with the right leg, tour à la seconde with grand temps relevé en dedans; plié on the supporting leg and tour en dedans in pose croisée front. Seventh measure: from pose croisée, grand rond de jambe in attitude effacée, tour fouetté in attitude effacée, passé with the right foot through first position to the front and step on it in a big pose croisée back, the left foot back in croisé, pointe tendue on the floor. Eighth measure: grand port de bras in deep plié, bending the body and on the last beat of the measure, step quickly forward on the right foot, transferring the body forward in pose third arabesque at 90°.

Battements tendus: 4 measures; with the right foot, 4 battements tendus croisé front, open the arms gradually, the left in third position, the right in second position; with the left foot, 4 battements tendus croisé

Graduation performance at the Kirov Theatre 1975.
Divertissement from the ballet Paquita.

back, changing the position of arms to fourth arabesque; with the right foot, 4 battements tendus to the side, each on 1 beat; 6 battements tendus jetés en tournant en dedans with the right foot, each on half a beat, and on 2 half beats, flic-flac en tournant en dedans, end in fourth position, préparation for tours en dehors, right foot back. In 2 measures: 1 tour sur le cou-de-pied en dehors; at the end, open the right leg to the side at 45°; 2 tours en dehors from second position (45°) and 3 tours en dehors from second position (45°).

2. BATTEMENTS FONDUS AT 45°. 8 measures in 4/4.

With the right leg: on 2 beats, fondu in a small pose croisée front; on 2 beats, tombé on the right foot and 2 tours sur le cou-de-pied en dedans; without closing the foot in fifth position, continue with the left leg; on 2 beats, fondu in a small pose croisée front; on 2 beats, tombé on the left foot and 2 tours sur le cou-de-pied en dehors; with the right leg: 2 fondus to the side, each on 2 beats; 5 frappés, each on half a beat, and 2 doubles frappés, each on half a beat. Repeat from the beginning on the other leg and subsequently in the reverse direction.

3. GRANDS BATTEMENTS JETÉS. 8 measures in 4/4.

With the right leg: 4 grands battements in pose croisée front, 4 grands battements with the left leg, in third arabesque; 3 grands battements pointés with the right leg in pose écartée back, each on 1 beat, end in fifth position, demi-plié, right foot back; on 1 beat, turn in fifth position half-toe to the right side (détourné). With the right foot: step-coupé front, and on 2 beats, pas de ciseaux; on 2 beats, from pose arabesque, rise on half-toe, passé at 90° in pose écartée back, end in fifth position, right foot back, and repeat from the beginning on the other leg.

4. GRAND ADAGIO. 32 measures in 3/4 (Waltz).

Fifth position, right foot front. On the upbeat, demi-plié, 2 tours sur le cou-de-pied en dehors, end in plié on the left leg and with the right foot, dégagé at 45°, in croisé front. In 4 measures: step on the right foot in attitude croisée (in the first measure); raise the right arm in third position, the left in second position, thereafter move in position fourth arabesque. In 4 measures: lean the body downward in position arabesque (penché) and from the penché, turn quickly en dehors, facing corner 4 in a big pose effacée front on half-toe. In 4 measures: a wide tombé on the left foot, chassé to corner 4, end in fourth position effacée, grande préparation for tours en dedans and 1½ tours en dedans in attitude, the arms in third position. In 4 measures: from pose attitude, grand rond de jambe en dedans in pose effacée front, come up on half-toe, a wide tombé on the right foot and 2 tours en dedans in second arabesque. In 4 measures: from pose arabesque, grand fouetté en tournant en dedans in attitude effacée allongée and jeté back (jumping) in fourth position croisée, grande préparation for tours en dehors. In 4 measures: 2 tours en dehors in attitude, plié on the supporting leg and 2 tours in third arabesque. In 4 measures: coupé on the right foot, throw the left leg à la seconde, by way of a grand battement and grand fouetté en tournant en dehors in pose croisée front, renversé en dedans, through the position écartée front, end in fifth position, préparation for tours en dedans, right foot front. In 4 measures: 2 tours sur le cou-de-pied en dedans on the right leg, end in plié on the right leg, dégagé with the left leg in croisé front at 45°, step on the left foot, half-toe, in attitude croisée, the left arm in third position, the right arm in second position, and move into pose fourth arabesque at 90°, in plié.

ALLEGRO

1. 16 measures in 2/4.

Two sissonnes fermées battues to the side, with the right and left leg, changing feet to the back, each on 1 beat; on 2 beats, pas de basque front en tournant (with a full turn); 2 gargouillades en dehors with the left and the right leg, each on 2 beats. Repeat from the beginning on the other leg and subsequently in the reverse direction.

2. 8 measures in 2/4.

Grande sissonne ouverte in pose écartée back and assemblé, with the right and the left leg, each on 2 beats;[1] on 2 beats, with the left leg: jeté renversé en dehors to the left side; 3 sissonnes fermées on the right leg in pose fourth arabesque, each on half a beat. Grande sissonne ouverte in pose écartée front, assemblé with the left and the right leg, each on 2 beats; on 2 beats, with the right leg: jeté renversé en dedans; on 2 beats, step-coupé on the right foot to corner 2 and grand assemblé en tournant to the left side.[2]

3. 32 measures in 3/4 (Waltz).

Fifth position, right foot front. On the upbeat, with the left leg, a small chassé back, hardly traveling back. In 4 measures: a small jump sissonne ouverte on the left leg in croisé, then a smooth développé through

---

[1] For the men, replace by grandes sissonnes ouvertes battues.
[2] For the men, replace by grand assemblé en tournant battu.

cou-de-pied extending the right leg in croisé front at 45°, tombé, glissade with the left foot to the left side and entrechat-six de volée. In 4 measures: repeat the same on the other leg. In 8 measures: step on the right foot, half-toe in first arabesque, facing corner 2; come down in plié and, moving on the diagonal upstage to corner 6; jeté entrelacé in first arabesque with chassé (repeat 3 times). Hold the pose in arabesque briefly. In 8 measures: on the diagonal to corner 2: pas failli (3 times), entrechat-six de volée in pose écartée front and turn in fifth position on half-toe to the left side (détourné). In 8 measures: in a straight line to the left side, with the left leg: sissonne tombée to the side, a quick passing pas de bourrée, without changing feet, sissonne tombée and grande cabriole fermée in first arabesque, end in fifth position, right foot front; with the right leg: préparation in second position (by way of a battement à la seconde at 45°) and tours sur le cou-de-pied en dehors.[3]

4. 16 measures in 3/4 (Waltz).

Move on the diagonal from corner 4 to corner 8. Fifth position, right foot front. In 4 measures: starting on the right foot front, sissonne tombée front in fourth position croisée and grande sissonne à la seconde de volée en tournant en dedans, plié on the supporting leg and, holding the left leg to the side at 90°, pas de bourrée dessus en tournant, entrechat-quatre. In 4 measures: repeat the combination once more. In 4 measures: with the right leg: sissonne tombée in fourth position croisée front, step-coupé and grand jeté en tournant in attitude croisée (turn to the left side, with the back to the mirror); step-coupé, grand jeté en tournant in attitude croisée (turn to the right side with the back to the mirror), and coupé, grand jeté in attitude croisée (without a turn, toward the direction of corner 8). In 4 measures: with the left foot: glissade to the left side, grande cabriole fermée in pose écartée front (left leg) and failli with the right leg to corner 8, ending on the right leg in a big pose croisée back, the left foot back in croisé, pointe tendue on the floor.

5. 16 measures in 3/4 (Waltz).

Saut de basque and chassé, starting on the right foot, in a circle; start from corner 8, travel through side 1, corner 2, side 3, corner 4, side 5, and to corner 6, execute 5 sauts de basque en tournant. On the chassé before the sixth saut de basque, turn the body from the direction to corner 6 on the diagonal facing corner 2 and follow through with 3 sauts de basque en tournant in succession, ending with chassé forward,

[3] The number of tours depends on the individual capabilities of each student.

facing corner 2. Starting on the left foot, sauts de basque are performed in the opposite direction, starting from corner 2.

6. 8 measures in 3/4.

Grand échappé in second position with temps levé in second position, without changing feet; sissonne soubresaut in attitude effacée, assemblé, entrechat-quatre. Execute 4 times in succession, in turn on the right and left leg.

7. 16 measures in 2/4.

With the right foot: 3 brisés front, each on 1 beat; on 1 beat, royale. Repeat on the left foot. On the upbeat, coupé on the left foot in plié, bring the right foot sur le cou-de-pied front and follow through with 6 emboîtés en tournant in half turns to the front in a straight line, sideways (from side 7 to side 3), each on half a beat; on 1 beat, assemblé front. Six emboîtés en tournant in half turns to the back (right foot front moves back and in succession for each emboîté, the working foot is placed in the back). Travel in a straight line to the left side from side 3 to side 7, each emboîté on half a beat; on 1 beat, assemblé back. Repeat from the beginning on the other leg.

8. 4 measures in 2/4.

Sixteen petits changements de pieds, each on half a beat.

FOURTH EXAMPLE OF EXERCISES ON POINTES

1. 16 measures in 2/4.

Fifth position, right foot front. Four échappés in second position, changing feet, each on 1 beat. Two sissonnes simples, changing feet to the back with the right and left leg; 2 sissonnes simples en tournant in half turns with the right leg, changing the foot to the back and to the front, each on 1 beat. Repeat from the beginning. Three sissonnes ouvertes at 45° in second arabesque on the right, left and right leg, traveling forward, each on 1 beat; on 1 beat, pas de chat forward. Repeat the whole combination on the other leg.

2. 48 measures in 3/4 (Waltz).

In 8 measures: jeté on the right leg in first arabesque at 90°, plié and 2 pliés-relevés in arabesque traveling forward on the diagonal, plié and tour sur le cou-de-pied en dedans. In 8 measures: repeat the same on the left leg. In 8 measures: jeté on the right leg in first arabesque at 90°, plié and 3 pliés-relevés, traveling forward on the diagonal; end in fifth position, left foot front, and follow through with dégagé with the right foot, pointe tendue on the floor to corner 2. In 8 measures: pas de bourrée suivi upstage on the diagonal to corner 6, right foot front; step on the left foot; in the last measure: right foot front in croisé, pointe tendue on the floor, préparation. In 16 measures: tours chaînés on the diagonal to corner 2; in the last measure: come up on pointes on the right leg in first arabesque at 90°.

3. 32 measures in 3/4 (Waltz).

Préparation on the right leg, the left foot croisé back, pointe tendue on the floor. On the upbeat, dégagé with the left leg to the side at 45° and pas de bourrée dessus en tournant; end in plié on the left leg, on the first beat of the first measure, right foot sur le cou-de-pied front. In 4 measures: renversé en dehors with grand rond de jambe en dehors; ending the pas de bourrée, a tombé on the right foot and 2 tours sur le cou-de-pied en dedans. In 4 measures: on the left leg, grande sissonne ouverte in third arabesque and renversé en dehors. In 8 measures: step on the right foot, on pointes to side 3 and follow with tours en dedans in first arabesque; without lowering the working leg, plié on the supporting leg and follow through with the second tour in arabesque, plié on the supporting leg, then again the third tour in arabesque, plié and 2 tours sur le cou-de-pied en dedans, end in fifth position, left foot front. Repeat the whole combination on the other leg, starting with pas de bourrée dessus en tournant and dégagé from fifth position.

4. Musical measure 2/4.

Tours en dehors with dégagé, ending each tour in a big pose écartée front. Execute 8 tours on the diagonal and subsequently with dégagé, ending in a big pose in effacé front and croisé front.

5. Musical measure 2/4.

Tours chaînés in a circle to the right side and also to the left side. The number of tours chaînés depends on the individual capabilities of each student.

100 Lessons in Classical Ballet